FLUID RUSSIA

A VOLUME IN THE NIU SERIES IN

Slavic, East European, and Eurasian Studies
Edited by Christine D. Worobec

For a list of books in the series, visit our website at cornellpress.cornell.edu.

FLUID RUSSIA

BETWEEN THE GLOBAL AND THE NATIONAL IN THE POST-SOVIET ERA

VERA MICHLIN-SHAPIR

NORTHERN ILLINOIS UNIVERSITY PRESS
AN IMPRINT OF CORNELL UNIVERSITY PRESS
Ithaca and London

Copyright © 2021 by Cornell University

All rights reserved. Except for brief quotations in a review, this book, or parts thereof, must not be reproduced in any form without permission in writing from the publisher. For information, address Cornell University Press, Sage House, 512 East State Street, Ithaca, New York 14850. Visit our website at cornellpress.cornell.edu.

First published 2021 by Cornell University Press

Library of Congress Cataloging-in-Publication Data

Names: Michlin-Shapir, Vera, author.
Title: Fluid Russia : between the global and the national in the post-Soviet era / Vera Michlin-Shapir.
Description: Ithaca [New York] : Northern Illinois University Press, an imprint of Cornell University Press, 2021. | Series: NIU series in Slavic, East European, and Eurasian studies | Includes bibliographical references and index.
Identifiers: LCCN 2021021951 (print) | LCCN 2021021952 (ebook) | ISBN 9781501760549 (hardcover) | ISBN 9781501760556 (epub) | ISBN 9781501760563 (pdf)
Subjects: LCSH: Culture and globalization—Russia (Federation) | Nationalism—Russia (Federation)—History—20th century. | Nationalism—Russia (Federation)—History—21st century. | National characteristics, Russian—History—20th century. | National characteristics, Russian—History—21st century.
Classification: LCC DK510.762 .M54 2021 (print) | LCC DK510.762 (ebook) | DDC 947.086—dc23
LC record available at https://lccn.loc.gov/2021021951
LC ebook record available at https://lccn.loc.gov/2021021952

To my beloved Saar, Ari, and Moriah

We live in a globalising world. That means that all of us, consciously or not, depend on each other.
—Zygmunt Bauman

Contents

Acknowledgments ix

Note on Transliteration xi

Introduction: Russia Thrusts into the Global World   1

Part One: Fluid Citizenship: Citizenship Policy in Post-Soviet Russia   13

1. The Unmaking of the Soviet Project   15
2. Seeking Stability in a Fluid Russia: Russian Citizenship under Putin   41

Part Two: Fluid Words: Discourse on National Identification   65

3. Media Discourse in the 1990s   67
4. Media Discourse under Putin: Fluid Words and Fluid Screens   87

Part Three: Fluid Times: Practices of the Russian National Calendar   125

5. From the Soviet Calendar to Russian Calendars   127
6. Putin's National Calendar: A Solid Experience or Floating Ice?   154

Epilogue: Fluid Russia: Lessons,
Implications, and Prospects
for the Future   177

Notes   189
Bibliography   221
Index   241

Acknowledgments

This book is a product of real and virtual dialogues I held over the years with friends, colleagues, and family members. I would like to thank them for helping me to formulate my thoughts and arguments.

I am deeply indebted to my supervisors at Tel Aviv University, Iris Rachamimov and Vera Kaplan, for their guidance, motivation, and invaluable experience. I wish to thank the former heads of the School of Historical Studies at the university Aviad Kleinberg and Leo Corry for lending the school's much-needed institutional support during the research for this book. I also thank Eilat Shalev-Arato.

I am grateful to my editor Amy Farranto for her interest in this project and for her support and help in publishing this book. I am thankful to the reviewers of the manuscript, Vera Tolz, Marlene Laruelle, and Ivan Kurilla, who reviewed it in an earlier version, as well as to the two anonymous reviewers from Cornell University Press. I thank researchers from the Levada-Centre for providing me with polling materials that were used in part three of this book. I also thank Diana Rubenenko, Meira Ben-Gad, and Daniela Tsirulnik for their help with the manuscript.

Over the years, I have benefited from the attention and interest with which my family followed my research. I am thankful to them for our long conversations on the meaning of identity and the place of Russianness in our own family. I am forever indebted to them for their love and for never letting me down: my mother Rita, Evgenii, Julia, Vadim, Misha, and Luda.

Note on Transliteration

Throughout the text, notes, and bibliography I have followed the US Board on Geographic Names system of transliteration from Russian. In a limited number of cases in the text, specifically regarding names, I have altered the transliteration system to reflect common English usage. For instance, the famous Russian TV presenter is mentioned in the text as Vladimir Solovyov, not Vladimir Solov'yëv, and the Russian writer is transliterated in the text as Alexander Prokhanov, not Alexandr Prokhanov.

FLUID RUSSIA

Introduction
Russia Thrusts into the Global World

"When Tatarsky was out walking one day, he stopped at a shoe shop." So begins Victor Pelevin's novel *Babylon*. Pelevin's protagonist, Tatarsky, sees "in the midst of a chaos of multicolored Turkish handicrafts" some "unmistakably Soviet-made shoes." Tatarsky then has a "piercing recognition" and realizes that "the new era obviously had no use for them," and he "knew that the new era had no use for him either."[1] Pelevin refers to Tatarsky as part of Generation P—the generation that was introduced to Pepsi-Cola as the first, and for many years the only, foreign product sold in the Soviet Union.[2] This generation grew up in the late-Soviet period, a time of political and economic stability (although not prosperity), and reached maturity around the time the system unraveled. In the first decade of Russian independence, Generation P experienced the dissolution of a reality where having access to only one type of soft drink represented not only a deprived existence but a secure and stable one.

In the aftermath of the collapse of the Soviet Union, while Boris Yeltsin struggled for a democratic revolution, surviving an attempted coup in 1993 and an electoral near defeat by the communists in 1996, Generation P felt that its personal and collective identity was dissolving. Yeltsin's democracy offered no national idea to replace the Soviet sense of self and society.[3] Vladimir Putin described these upheavals as "a genuine drama" for the Russian nation.[4] When Putin was installed as president, his proclaimed goal was to reinstate a unified Russian identity. In his words: "For such a complex, federatively composed, ethnically and religiously diverse country as Russia, one of the most important unifying factors should be general Russian patriotism."[5]

The annexation of Crimea in March 2014 marks, to date, the pinnacle of these efforts. In addition to serving as a geopolitical asset for Russia, Crimea is a location of great significance for Russia's national identity. Crimea, where the Old Rus was Christianized, was until 1954 part of the Russian Soviet Federative Socialist Republic (RSFSR), and in the post-Soviet period many Russians continued to view it as part of their homeland.[6] In the aftermath of the annexation, Putin stated that "the events in Crimea and Sevastopol shook society. It turns out that patriotism is still out there, somewhere, only we are not always aware of it. Yet, it is an integral part of our people, part of our identity."[7] Apart from an outburst of patriotism after the annexation of Crimea, however, Russian society under Putin continued to manifest a sense of dislocation regarding its national identity.

What are the origins of this sense of dislocation? What fuels it? How can it be reversed, if it can be at all?

A large body of literature has attempted to answer these questions. Some scholars have claimed that this sense of confused, crisis-ridden, and disoriented national identity is rooted in Russia's history as a multiethnic empire lacking clear geographical borders and with historical, cultural, social, and psychological links to both the West and the East.[8] As the historian Anne Applebaum put it: "Russia's ill-defined boundaries, open spaces and indeterminate, midcontinental geography are the source of much confusion.... When the Soviet Union fell apart, the Russians found themselves ... once again wondering 'who we are'."[9] Vera Tolz and Valery Fyodorov (the former, an academic scholar of Russian studies; the latter, director general of the Russian polling institute VTSIOM) each separately pointed out that this ambiguity in the post-Soviet period led to multiple competing visions of the national group: Russia as a civic state, as a union of eastern Slavs, as an empire, and as an ethnic Russian nation.[10]

Other scholars have underlined the novelty of Russia's post-Soviet experience. In their edited volume *After Empire: Multiethnic Societies and Nation-Building*, Karen Barkey and Mark Von Haggen examined four modern imperial collapses—the Soviet, Russian, Habsburg, and Ottoman—and argued that scholars should treat postimperialist states and societies as unique.[11] Research on Russian nationalism by such scholars as Itzhak Brudny and Marlene Laruelle focused on its increasing appeal to the post-Soviet public.[12] While they showed a historical continuity of nationalist ideas from Soviet times, they underlined that a central theme of this later nationalism was the Russian people's post-Soviet victimhood.¹³ This sense of victimhood and humiliation is linked to what some scholars term the Weimar Russia scenario. Researchers like Rogers Brubaker, Niall Ferguson, Andreas Umland, and Anatol Lieven claimed that the post-Soviet disorientation, however novel to Russia, echoes features of the Weimar Republic—loss of status, economic decline, compatriots left outside the country's borders, and fragile democratic institutions.¹⁴ This scenario, which proposed that a violent fascist backlash would reinstate a clear identity, attracted further interest in the 2010s, and particularly during the period around the annexation of Crimea.¹⁵ An edited volume by Pal Kolsto and Helge Blakkisrud suggested that such a backlash may now be underway, in the form of a dangerous shift, during Putin's third and fourth terms in office, toward an exclusivist ethnic version of Russian national ideology.¹⁶

These analyses, while insightful, are lacking in several respects. First, they fail to provide sufficient explanation as to why, after almost three decades of independence, the dislocation of national identity has persisted in Russia. Second, the academic debate implies a binary classification of Russian identity, as either perennially divided and dysfunctional or as based on postimperial reactionism and belligerence. Last, it regards identity as a finite construct rather than an open-ended dynamic and does not consider the global context, within which identities are increasingly flexible.

A few researchers have offered different perspectives and examined the impact of temporal and global changes on Russian identity. Most recently, political scientist Gulnaz Sharafutdinova used social identity theory to explain the pivotal place of identity politics in post-Soviet Russia and their contribution to Putin's popularity.¹⁷ Sharafutdinova convincingly analyzed post-Soviet insecurities about national identity by using Western sociological tools. The anthropologist Serguei Oushakine drew attention to the new circumstances that shaped post-Soviet life in the Siberian city of Barnaul.¹⁸ While he underlined how feelings of loss shaped Russians' post-Soviet identity, he also focused on the impact on society of neoliberal economic reforms. Kirill Kobrin, editor of the Russian journal *Neprikosnovennyi zapas*, also acknowledged the profound impact of neoliberal thinking on Russian identity.¹⁹

The present research, as well, suggests an alternative outlook that diverges from traditional considerations of Russian identity. It argues that the debate on Russian national identity fails to consider the impact of globalization and late modernity on Russian society and national identity. The fall of the Soviet Union set in motion a chain of events that caused disruptions above and beyond the direct consequences of the Soviet imperial collapse. It opened Russia to the temporal context of globalization—to cross-border flows of capital, goods, and labor, as well as increased access to travel, communication technologies, and information outlets. These were implemented within the framework of rapidly adopted neoliberal economic reforms and ideologies. This late modern and global context affected the formation of post-Soviet national identity in Russia far more than has been previously acknowledged.

This book underlines that although Russians experienced acute shocks to their identity following the collapse of the Soviet Union, large numbers of people around the world had similar experiences—even in ostensibly stable contexts. In the late modern globalized world, institutions and identities have become fragmented and flexible, a state for which the sociologist Zygmunt Bauman used the metaphor "liquid." Identity becomes, as Bauman noted, "a bunch of problems rather than a single-issue campaign."[20] In this temporal context, the Russian experience of loss is far from unique, though naturally it has its distinctive Russian features. This book looks at ways in which Russian identity is expressed as a late modern experience, referred to here as *fluid Russianness*.

Historical Dislocations of Russian Identity

Post-Soviet Russia inherited categorical and spatial dislocations from both Russian and Soviet history, which informed the Russian identity search. First, tsarist Russia and the Soviet Union were empires that never managed to construct a homogenous categorical identification.[21] The tsar's subjects developed a sense of cross-estate national identity later than their European counterparts and in fact never fully unified across ethnicities, despite periodic attempts at Russification. The tsars preferred vertical loyalty to Russian categorical national identification—all were "the Tsar's subjects."[22] Hence, only in the late nineteenth century did the Russian nobility, and later the intelligentsia, promote a national identification independent of the tsar.[23] In the Soviet era, the regime's policies toward minorities encouraged ethnic and cultural diversity and granted minority groups territorial autonomy, as long as they showed an overarching commitment to Soviet identification. Russianness was an exception.[24] At first the Bolsheviks vigorously opposed any notion of Russian particularity. From the 1930s, however, they resolved the problem by accepting Russianness as an integral part of Soviet identification.[25]

Second, beyond the multiethnic character of the tsarist and Soviet empires, for both, their spatial links with the West and the East led to a sense of ambiguity. From the time of Peter the Great, the West was for Russia an object of imitation, comparison, and imagination. This view is strongly apparent in the works of nineteenth-century Westernizers like Alexander Herzen. It was also evident in the policies of 1990s neoliberal reformers in Yeltsin's cabinet, who opened Russia to globalization, such as Yegor Gaidar, Anatoly Chubais, and Andrei Kozyrev. While the West is embodied in specific countries—France, Germany, the United States, and Israel—it can also be seen as fictional: a figment of the imagination, representing a wide range of ideas.[26]

Russia's association with the East is channeled through the ideological tenets of Eurasianism and Slavophilism. Eurasianism, which originated among Russian exiles in Europe in the 1920s and 1930s, holds that Russian national identity is neither Western nor Asiatic but a third "supranationality . . . [that] is a new expression of Russianness."[27] Slavophilism originated in the nineteenth century and opposed the imitation of Western ideas.[28] Its adherents claimed that Russians were held together by a moral bond, not by a social contract as in the West, and they regarded the Russian Orthodox Church as the only true church.[29] Neo-Eurasianism became one of the most popular ideologies within the post-Soviet Russian right wing, led by Alexander Dugin.[30] In government policy, these ideas were expressed in the establishment of the Eurasian Union, a free-trade zone for Russia, Kazakhstan, Armenia, Kyrgyzstan and Belorussia. Slavophile ideas are often expressed by figures in the Russian Orthodox Church and by right-wing nationalists like the writer Alexander Prokhanov.[31] These historical sources of ambiguity of identity contributed to the post-Soviet sense that Russian national identity was lost.

In the post-Soviet period, Russianness was in flux in new and more extreme ways—a situation that was largely seen as the result of the Soviet Union's collapse. After the collapse, repatriation, labor migration, and immigration blurred the boundaries of the national category, as friends, family, and countrymen turned into foreigners. In 1991, 25 million ethnic Russians and 11 million Russian speakers, who were viewed as an integral part of the Russian national collective, found themselves outside the borders of Russia.[32] These communities were cut off from what they perceived as their homeland while not being fully accepted in the newly formed states where they resided. Some encountered hostile attitudes, and many in the Baltic states were left stateless. The status and treatment of these people became an important issue in Russia. Moreover, between 1989 and 2002, Russia experienced migration on a grand scale, with vast flows in both directions: 10.9 million people migrated in, and 4.1 million migrated out.[33] Emigrants of Jewish, German, and Greek origin formed Russian-speaking communities in their new countries. At the same time, labor migrants from Central Asia and internal migrants from the Caucasus within Russia changed the demographics of Russian cities.

Furthermore, the dissolution of the Soviet Union created borders that were different from what most Russians perceived as their national homeland. The

RSFSR, which became Russia, was not a Russian territory in the Soviet Union but simply a territory, which was not designated as belonging to other Soviet nationalities.[34] Its population included smaller non-Russian ethnic groups that were not considered nations by the Bolsheviks, such as the Tatars and the Bashkirs, and it lacked any form of Russian self-government or cultural institutions.[35] From the 1930s, the Soviet Union as a whole was considered pervasively Russian. Although the regime maintained a considered ambiguity over whether the union was a Russian nation state or a multinational federation, Russians perceived its entire territory as their home.[36] Moreover, in the 1990s Russia chose not to claim territories from the Soviet republics that had historically been Russian lands, like Crimea, or that were heavily populated by ethnic Russians and Russian speakers, like North Kazakhstan.[37] Hence, Russia's borders, as Rogers Brubaker notes, seemed to "lack historical sanction," and there were several versions of the Russian homeland—the Russian Federation, the entire territory of the former USSR, the eastern Slav republics (the Russian Federation, Belorussia, and Ukraine), or lands with a Russian majority.[38] Over the last thirty years, these post-Soviet conditions, together with the historical ambiguities, created a consensus both broad and deep that in Russian society and its political establishment that Russia is experiencing an unprecedented crisis in its national identity.

Putin embraced the feeling that Russian identity was lost after the collapse of the Soviet Union. He focused his first presidency on restoring to Russia a stable and unified sense of identity.[39] This rhetoric had already gained traction in society through such political leaders as Vladimir Zhirinovsky and Gennady Zyuganov, who used it in their electoral campaigns in the 1990s.[40] But Putin was the president, and he had the gravitas to turn rhetoric into policy. In December 2000 Putin reinstated the Soviet anthem, which had been abolished by Yeltsin, with new lyrics by Sergey Mikhalkov, who had written the original Soviet lyrics. In 2002 Putin introduced a new citizenship law to stabilize the citizenry. In 2005, Russian Unity Day was established on November 4, which corresponded with a tsarist holiday.[41] Russia's relations with the former Soviet republics were characterized by strong language and, sometimes, the use of force, which peaked in 2014 in Crimea.

Yet even after the annexation of Crimea, the liberal director of the Levada Centre polling institute, Lev Gudkov, and President Putin agreed on one thing—Russia was still in search of itself. Gudkov noted: "Against the background of . . . nationalism in the [former Soviet] republics, in countries in Eastern and Central Europe, where nationalism was . . . a modernizing movement [of] national consolidation . . . , the Russian movement was purely reactive."[42] In the same vein, in 2018 Putin noted that Russians "must strengthen [their] identity"—explicitly recognizing that policy efforts, even after two decades, had not yet borne sufficient fruit.[43] Why, despite so much effort, does the feeling of dislocation remain unresolved?

The answer put forward by this book is closely tied to the temporal context of Russia's post-Soviet search for identity. In the three decades of Russian independence, meanings and expressions of national identity have been shifting around the world. In the twentieth century, the analysis of nationalism and national identity was characterized by a debate between four main approaches: primordialists, perennialists, modernists, and ethnosymbolists. Primordialists viewed the nation as an existing entity and a social structure natural to human existence. Perennialists, such as Azar Gat, did not consider the nation as a natural entity but viewed it as a recurrent phenomenon in history.[44]

Modernists such as Ernest Gellner, Benedict Anderson, and Eric Hobsbawm argued that the nation is a product of modernization, typified by such characteristics as mass education, the industrial revolution, and urbanization. Anderson defined the nation as "an imagined political community," while Gellner described it as a construct created by the mutual recognition of belonging and shared culture in a modernist urbanized and industrialized society.[45] Hobsbawm, in a Marxist analysis, claimed that the nation was constructed deliberately by the elites in the nineteenth century "as devices to ensure . . . social cohesion."[46] Ethnosymbolists, such as Anthony Smith, criticized the modernists. They claimed that "what gave nationalism its power" to unify people were "myths, memories, traditions, and symbols of ethnic heritage," which preexisted modernity.[47] Despite the socially contingent, mythicized, and seemingly abstract nature of national identities, these scholars agreed that national identities created powerful political realities that "made it possible," as Anderson put it, "for so many millions of people, not so much to kill, as willing to die for."[48] From all the different types of identities that modern men and women feel attached to, national identity was different because it required the highest and most exclusivist commitment and was regulated by the institutions of the nation-state.[49]

During the second half of the twentieth century, and increasingly toward its end, the place of national identities started to shift. Globalization changed the relationship between nation-states, citizens, and national identities. The global era was termed *late modernity*. Bauman also called it "liquid modernity," and Anthony Giddens referred to it as "high modernity."[50] Both Bauman and Giddens deliberately avoided the term *postmodernity*, arguing that the end of the twentieth century still retained plenty of continuity with classical modernity.[51] They agreed with the modernists about the origins of national identity and the focal place it occupied in modern political life. From their point of view, in the current age modernity itself began to change due to globalization and neoliberal economics, with far-reaching consequences for national identity. Globalization caused the fragmentation of modernist social institutions, among them national identity, which lost its preeminence in people's lives. Bauman used the metaphor of liquids to describe this process of fragmentation: Liquids "cannot hold their shape.... [They] neither fix space nor bind time."[52]

Globalization and neoliberal economics, the two pillars of late modernity, liberated social and economic forces that require institutions to stay flexible. In neoliberalism, political judgments shift toward economic evaluations, and the needs of markets represent the common good.[53] For neoliberalism, the production of national ideology by the nation-state seems pointless, as markets require the exact opposite of solid national institutions; they require flexibility and adaptability. Hence, in globalized late modernity, as Giddens noted, "change" becomes "not just [a] continuous and profound [process]; rather, change does not consistently conform either to human expectation or to human control."[54]

To facilitate globalization, nation-states willingly relinquished their monopoly over the production of ideology as well as some of their other powers. This was done in favor of allowing greater freedom and for the facilitation of an ever more interconnected international system of trade.[55] For instance, the European Union (EU) challenges the primacy of national identities of member states with European supranationality, and the International Monetary Fund (IMF) sets a global financial policy and can limit decision making by states seeking its assistance. Transnational corporations, especially in the tech industry, operate under complex corporate and tax structures that keep them removed from the jurisdiction of national governments. These political-economic realities are accompanied by ever more flexible labor markets, fueled by increased migration, and the rapid development of information technologies, which allow the emergence of a truly globalized world.

The state's retraction from the production of national ideology, the pervasiveness of neoliberal economic logic, and the emergence of a global world had massive consequences for the construction of identities, specifically for the concept of national identity. Bauman and Giddens observed that with the state's withdrawal from creating national content, the responsibility for structuring identities shifted toward individual agency.[56] Individuals are now expected to construct their identities themselves, choosing continuously from different options, while bearing in mind the system's requirement for flexibility.[57] Or as Bauman put it, "identities were given a free run: and it is now up to individual men and women to catch them in flight, using their own wits and tools."[58] This placed national identities, which are "unequivocal allegiances" based on "exclusive fidelity," in particular jeopardy.[59]

The jeopardy in which national identity finds itself in late modernity as a weaker and more fragmented institution does not mean that it has disappeared from the world. The sociologist Michael Billig, speaking of Western countries, suggests that in these circumstances, banal and everyday practices and gestures represent identification with the nation. He notes: "In the established nations there is a continual 'flagging,' or reminding, of nationhood. . . . In so many little ways the citizenry is daily reminded of its national place in the world of nations."[60] So while the institutions of classical modernity, including national identity, have become fragmented and flexible, national identity has continued to be part of our lives, albeit in weaker forms. Late modern identification is elastic and often centered on civic conceptions and a rhetoric of inclusion. These are expressed on the individual rather than state level, in keeping with the late modern liberation of the individual. Yet the individualization and banalization of national belonging and its new tacit forms of signaling do not preclude aggression and violence.

The disruptions created by late modernity regularly give rise to calls for exclusivist revision and to violent outbursts. Constructing one's own identity is a complicated and not necessarily pleasant task.[61] Giddens noted that nationalism serves the psychological function of providing ontological security, which is produced through the repetition of routines that ensure continuity of identity.[62] The removal of certainties that stemmed from the stable institutions of classical modernity, such as national identity, disrupts this ontological security. These precarious conditions are often followed by a "longing for identity [that] comes from the desire for security."[63] In late modernity people become freer but also feel less secure, and in an attempt to reinstate their sense of security, they often seek to reinforce their national identities.

This theoretical background is of acute importance for the study of post-Soviet Russia, as late modernity was the social system it embraced in 1991 and, as this book shows, has not diverged from to this day. When the Soviet Union collapsed, reformers in Yeltsin's government, like Yegor Gaidar and Anatoly Chubais, were guided by neoliberal ideology, which is inevitably tied to globalization and late modernity. Putin's rise to power and his project to reaffirm a stronger Russian identity should be construed as a campaign to address a deficit of ontological security that was lost in the post-Soviet quest to integrate into the neoliberal global world. Putin never isolated Russia from the global world, however. In this temporal context, Russia's inability to create a unified national identity is not unique.

Without denying the impact of Russian historical dislocations and the collapse of the Soviet Union, this book focuses on how late modernity shaped the experience of Russian national identification in the post-Soviet era. It considers a situation where, in the globalized modern era, which is the relevant context in the aftermath of the collapse of the Soviet Union, the state of Russian national identification is not abnormal or in crisis. Both the sense of disorientation and Putin's continuous attempts to rearticulate a unified national identity can be explained within the theoretical frame of late modernity.

Within that theoretical framework, this book tests the hypothesis that Russian national identification is a late modern experience and that the global context has altered the internal balance of Russian identification. More precisely, this book argues that in line with late modern trends, Russian national identification is predominantly an inclusive project, one reflecting chiefly Russia's multiethnic composition (in Russian, *Rossiyane*), and only supplemented by ethnic Russian features (in Russian, *Russkiy*), such as language, culture, and religion. That identification, referred to in this work as fluid Russianness, is a banal experience that is expressed in implicit ways and performed through individualized practices. This hypothesis is tested in the realms of citizenship legislation, the media, and holiday practices in post-Soviet Russia.

In the global context, our terminology needs to be adapted. The relevance of the term *identity* diminishes. Instead, the term *identification*, defined as "a state of being or feeling oneself to be closely associated with a group," is more appropriate and sensitive to the weak qualities of national identity in late modernity, as multiple, unstable, in flux, and fragmented.[64] For similar reasons, the national group or collective with which the association is formed is not referred to here as a *nation*.[65] Instead, this book prefers the term *national in-group*. This choice of language avoids the theoretical baggage carried by the concept of nationhood and suggests an intuitive, phenomenological interpretation of belonging based on individuals' subjective experience of being "in" or "out."

This book examines the experience of Russian national identification from three different vantage points: the state, the media, and the wider public. Part one studies identification through the evolution and implementation of citizenship legislation in Russia. Chapter 1 focuses on the attempts of the Russian state in the 1990s to determine who belonged to the Russian national in-group. It shows that Russia's citizenship legislation and its implementation were affected by global trends, as well as uniquely Russian features. Chapter 2 outlines how from Putin's ascent to power, his regime sought to stabilize the citizenry and to control migration. These policies had limited success due to the deep penetration of late modern trends and neoliberal economics in Russia. The findings of both chapters show that citizenship in Russia became fragmented, or fluid, making national identification a more flexible and elastic concept too.

Part two focuses on the Russian media's discourse on national identification. Chapter 3 observes the evolution of different discourses on national identification in the printed media in the 1990s and explores how these discourses corresponded with the global discourse of flexibility. Chapter 4 looks at the media discourse from 2000 in print media and in televised broadcasts, when the Russian media fell under government pressure and later control. This chapter looks at the success and limits of the government's discourse of stability, which aimed to curtail the penetration of the global discourse of flexibility.

Part three moves beyond the dimension of speech to the dimension of practice, and specifically, the national calendar. It investigates which holidays individuals in Russia preferred to celebrate and how they celebrated them. Chapter 5 deals with the fragmentation of the Soviet national calendar in the 1990s and the rise of competing calendars and contested Russian holidays. This chapter shows that, as in other late modern societies, contested holidays in Russia reflected increased freedom in society but were also accompanied by a certain unease, as holidays no longer bound the national collective together, and the competing visions disrupted the continuity of identity. The last empirical chapter, chapter 6, describes how Putin's administration altered the calendar in the 2000s and 2010s around religious and military themes. This chapter finds that these efforts had a profound impact on Russian society, but as Russia remained part of the global world, they could not erode the experience of fluid Russianness.

This book helps explain how social life in Russia was transformed along the lines of late modern neoliberal globalization and how these trends affected Russian national identification. As borders opened, censorship lifted, and Marxist-Leninist ideology was cast aside, individuals were ever freer to travel, to live where they wanted, to express what was on their minds, and to perform whatever practices they saw fit. As a result, citizenship no longer held the same institutional control over people's identification. In discourse, flexibility prevailed, and the debate focused on proposing inclusive means of identification. In terms of the national calendar, the public reproduced practices that denoted a devolved sense of national belonging.

This book also sheds light on further impacts of late modernity on the Russian experience. In the 1990s Russia joined the globalizing world, but alongside freedom, the disruptions and challenges of late modernity were revealed. The requirement for flexibility fragmented social institutions and disrupted routines that in the late-Soviet era had given meaning to citizens' identities and created a sense of security. This gave rise to a longing for a firmer identity and to nostalgic yearnings for Soviet ways of life that were (like all nostalgic memories) remembered as having been safe, pleasant, and secure. These processes revealed the dialectic that sits at the core of late modernity—the struggle between freedom and security.

Such findings articulate the complexities of identity formation in the late modern world and challenge the assumption that freedom on a global scale is always a welcome experience. Putin's rise to power and his project to reaffirm a stronger identity should be understood not as uniquely Russian diversions from liberal democracy but as parts of a broader phenomenon of challenges to neoliberal globalization. At the same time, the limitations of Putin's efforts are also instructive. This book shows that what developed in Putin's Russia, more than a unified and solid national identity, was a hybridization between elements that were open and inclusive and others that reflected a more superficial adherence to a strong national identity. Fluid Russianness continued developing as a durable, flexible, and evolving experience of national identification, in line with global trends.

Russia's experience teaches us that a complete rollback of the impacts of globalization is impossible, but the subversion of liberal tools and global trends for illiberal ends is far easier than has been commonly presumed. As neoliberal globalization faces growing challenges from left-wing and right-wing political movements, which call for firmer national identities and more sovereignty, Russia's experience can be an instructive example of how these processes unfold.

PART ONE

Fluid Citizenship

Citizenship Policy
in Post-Soviet Russia

CHAPTER 1

The Unmaking of the Soviet Project

Svetlana Alexievich, the 2015 Nobel Prize laureate for literature, explained the Soviet national experience as the result of a "Marxist-Leninist laboratory" that "gave rise to a new man: Homo Sovieticus." The *Homo sovieticus* "isn't just Russian, he's Belorussian, Turkmen, Ukrainian, Kazakh." She confesses that "although we now live in different countries and speak different languages, you couldn't mistake us for anyone else."[1]

The Union of Soviet Socialist Republics (USSR) was an amalgamation of peoples and identities brought together under an overarching Soviet identification, in which the Russian language and culture played a central role. As it disintegrated, the unravelling of the Soviet state challenged the identification and rights of *Homo sovieticus* on its territories. Nowhere was this more pronounced than in Russia, the center and successor of the Soviet Union. The breakdown of the Soviet political structure raised questions that went to the very core of the new Russian identity. Russia's legislators had to determine who the Russian people were: who belonged to the national in-group and shared a sense of belonging and identification with the new Russian state and who should be awarded the political, social, and economic rights that citizenship conferred. This difficult task was similar to experiences of other post-imperial states—the conundrum of addressing mixed ethnic and national populations after years of coexistence and their inevitable mismatch with the newly formed geographical entities.[2]

For Russia, at the heart of the heterogenous reality stood two major outcomes of the Soviet imperial project. After 1991, 36 million people—25 million ethnic Russians and 11 million Russian speakers, who identified with Russia linguistically and culturally—remained outside the territory of Russia. These groups included large concentrations of ethnic Russians and Russian speakers, like in North Kazakhstan, East Ukraine, and Crimea. Many in Russia considered these people as kin, part of an imagined national in-group. At the same time, newly established Russia included numerous ethnic minority groups, forming approximately 20 percent of its population.

The main legislation in this period was the Federal Law on Citizenship of the RSFSR from 1991, whose aim was to resolve the problems of a mixed Soviet population and accommodate certain former Soviet citizens in the citizenry. Scholars, such as the social scientist Oxana Shevel, described this citizenship legislation as very inclusive to former Soviet citizens, ideological and permissive.[3] Its consequences—or, rather, perceived consequences—were, however, a migration surge of millions into Russia and a sense that the citizenry was becoming uncertain and insecure. Other scholars, such as the professor of law George Ginsburgs, noted the importance of *implementation* in understanding Russian citizenship legislation.[4] Ginsburgs explained that chaotic and often corrupt implementation practices were the source of Russia's perceived difficulties in creating a stable citizenry.

The temporal context of the collapse of the Soviet Union was no less important than the direct consequences of imperial Soviet disintegration. This was largely overlooked by Russian policy makers and scholars alike. While the government focused on the place of Russians and Russian speakers in the citizenry, the new migration space, created by late modern trends of freedom of movement and deregulated economic systems, became a determining factor in the inability to produce a stable sense of citizenship. This chapter focuses on the abrupt change from Soviet socialism to a global free-market economy and how this affected migration, citizenship, and their perception in society. The sense of dissatisfaction with citizenship laws and sense of insecurity in the public was a result of the fragmentation of the institution of citizenship that is characteristic of the late modern period. In this sense Russia's situation was much closer to the late modern concept of citizenship in Western countries, which were also struggling with these dynamics of citizenship fragmentation.

Citizenship in the Disintegrating Soviet Union, 1989–1991

Attempts to counter the Soviet mixing of populations through citizenship legislation started in the late 1980s on the periphery of the Soviet Union—in the Baltic republics. When Soviet power loosened in 1987–1988, the Baltic states strove to increase their autonomy within the union and set their eyes on full independence. As part of this effort, they launched campaigns that aimed to delineate their citizenries. Central to those campaigns was a debate on ways to prioritize citizens over migrants—mostly Russians and Russian speakers who had moved to the republics after 1940.[5] These were the first signs of the looming postimperial syndrome, grappling with the mixed populations and essentially trying to unentangle them. This brought the issue of Russianness to the fore.

The core of the problem in the Baltic states was their claim that they had been illegally incorporated into the Soviet Union in 1940 and that the Soviet regime purposefully undermined their demographics.[6] Indeed, after 1945 the Soviets established numerous military and military-industrial facilities in the Baltic states, which were staffed primarily by Russians and Slavic persons, who were Russified and were later labeled Russian speakers, and who moved to these republics in large numbers.[7] In the late 1980s, during glasnost, the scale of migration was revealed.[8] In Latvia, the percentage of ethnic Latvians decreased from 77 percent in 1939 to 52 percent in 1989. In Estonia, the percentage of Estonians dropped from 90 percent in 1939 to 61 percent in 1989.[9] These figures caused outrage and led many in those republics to consider legal options that would reinstate their prewar citizenries, based on the logic of "restoration of independence."[10] In 1987–1991 political groups circulated versions of possible citizenship laws that excluded residents who had arrived after 1940.[11] Although not yet adopted, the laws threatened the future status of Russians in these republics.

Meanwhile, in Moscow, two centers of political power were forming—Soviet power under Gorbachev and a new Russian leadership around Yeltsin. The first legal response to the Baltic republics' moves came from the Soviet center. In 1990, in a bid to gain control over the institution of citizenship, Gorbachev signed the new Soviet citizenship law, which tried to restrain the Baltic republics from excluding Russians and Russian speakers from their citizenries. The Law on Citizenship of the USSR from 1990 stated that Soviet citizens were simultaneously citizens of their republics and of the union and that union citizenship was equal to all.[12] However, by 1991 the Soviet Union was unraveling, and Soviet attempts to regain control became futile.

After the failed coup of August 1991, Gorbachev had no political capital, and the initiative lay with the republics' leaders, including Yeltsin, who positioned himself against Gorbachev in his own bid for Russian independence.[13] From this point, the status of Russians and Russian speakers outside Russia had become Yeltsin's problem too. This was not easy for him. Politically, he was on the side of the national elites in the republics who wanted independence, some of whom were accused of discriminating against Russians and Russian speakers. As a result, in the early 1990s Yeltsin was expected to defend Russians and Russian speakers in the republics, while he was also perceived to be working contrary to their interests. In the Baltic republics, local Russians called him Judas.[14]

Russia's First Citizenship Law, 1991

The Russian citizenship law was adopted in November 1991 against the backdrop of these events and after most republics (except the Baltic states) had adopted citizenship laws.[15] It is unclear whether in November Yeltsin had already set his mind on full independence outside the union, but as the law suggests, it was a strong possibility.[16] The first Russian citizenship law expressed two sets of ideas.

The first was Russia's interest in transforming into a democratic liberal state that embraced Western principles of globalization, human rights values, and trends of late modernity. These elements articulated an inclusive and civic vision of identification in the law. Most enlightening in this regard was article 13, stipulating that citizenship could be acquired through recognition of citizenship (*priznanie grazhdanstva*).[17] As of February 6, 1992, Russia recognized all permanent residents of the RSFSR as Russian citizens. This type of policy favored by international norms is called *zero option*. By choosing it, Russia accepted inclusive liberal norms.[18] Further, article 13-2 stipulated that recognition of citizenship also applied to those who were born in the RSFSR, or if at least one of their parents was a Soviet citizen and permanently resided on the territory of the RSFSR (as a birthright).[19] Russian citizenship could also be acquired by birth (*po rozhdeniyu*).[20] Hence, the law combined the two principles of determining citizenship: the first, by origin (jus sanguinis) which gives preference to the origins of the parents (birthright), and the second, jus soli, which accords importance to the place of birth.[21] This was (and is) the practice of most Western countries and demonstrated an inclusive agenda.[22] Moreover, the law also expressed an obligation to reduce statelessness according to international legal norms. This meant that Russia was opening itself to the influences of globalization and late modern trends of inclusivity and the flexibility of identities. As we will see later, this had far-reaching effects on the concept of citizenship and perceptions of identity.

Despite the law's inclusiveness and compliance with international legal practices, it also bore a second set of ideas—namely, characteristics of Russia's primacy among the republics. The person who led this policy was Valery Tishkov, Yeltsin's nationalities minister and Russia's leading ethnographer. His assessment was as follows: "A man born in Alma-Ata, who studied in Leningrad, and worked in Kharkov, had the full right to acquire citizenship not only of Kazakhstan, Russia, and Ukraine, but also of any other state formed on the territory of the former USSR."[23] Tishkov, who held liberal views, chose to see the inclusive qualities of the Soviet imperial laboratory and its product—the *Homo sovieticus*. However, this typical Soviet citizen was based on Russian linguistic and cultural characteristics, and so although the law never specifically referred to ethnic Russians, the emblematic Soviet citizen who it tried to cater for was in many cases either an ethnic Russian or a Russified individual (a Russian speaker). This was reinforced by the evolving reality, for as the union was coming to its end, it became increasingly clear that ethnic Russians and Russian speakers were the predominant group that did not fit the new nationalizing realities of the newly formed post-Soviet states. This meant that the law positioned Russia as the material and spiritual caretaker of the rights of ethnic Russians and Russian speakers in the post-Soviet space.[24]

Hence, the law demonstrated the need to address the challenges of the ensuing imperial Soviet collapse. A situation where millions of ethnic Russians or Russified people—who culturally and linguistically identified with Russia and might soon find themselves outside the Russian state—dictated policy. This resulted in the most exceptional method of acquiring Russian citizenship—citizenship registration (*grazhdanstva v porjadke registratsii*).[25] The law recognized the special kinship between Russia and the citizens of the former Soviet Union.[26] This was specifically expressed in articles 18-3 and 18-4, which stated that former Soviet citizens residing on the territories of former Soviet republics who had not acquired citizenship of their republic within three years since the law came into force and declared their desire for a Russian citizenship were eligible for citizenship.[27] The same applied to former Soviet citizens who became stateless persons, although they had to make the declaration within a year (again, as an expression of concern for the reduction of statelessness). Article 18-5 stated that foreign citizens or stateless persons who were born in the RSFSR, or at least one of their parents was born in the RSFSR, could register as citizens within a year of the law's coming into force.[28]

The naturalization method, legally called "admission into citizenship" (*priem v grazhdanstvo*), expressed similar views. Here the required residency

Table 1 Main Methods for Acquisition of Citizenship under the 1991 Citizenship Law

	RECOGNITION	REGISTRATION	NATURALIZATION	BIRTH
Eligibility	Zero option—RSFSR residents on December 6, 1992, or born in the RSFSR, or one parent permanently resided in the RSFSR	Former Soviet citizens who resided in the former Soviet republics and did not acquire citizenship within three years and declare interest in Russian citizenship (for stateless persons, one-year deadline)	Five years residency (could be waived for former Soviet citizens)	Children of Russian citizens

period of five years in order to naturalize could be reduced or waived for former Soviet citizens.[29] Other principles stipulated an obligation to protect the rights of Russians abroad, while dual citizenship was accepted only when it was endorsed by international treaties between Russia and a specific state.[30] These articles, presented in table 1, allowed multiple paths to citizenship. Although worded inclusively and without ethnic reference, they were intended for people alienated by their new republics—those who were least likely to acquire citizenship, those denied citizenship, or those who chose to waive it. Most likely these were ethnic Russians and those strongly identifying with Russia or those who had nowhere else to go. This expressed the particular Russianness of the law, which tried to address the post-Soviet unmixing of populations but did so in an inclusive manner without inserting an ethnic Russian or cultural clause and by referring to all former Soviet citizens.

Less than two months after passage of the 1991 citizenship law, Yeltsin signed the Belavezha Accords, which dissolved the Soviet Union. From this point, the 1991 citizenship law had to regulate a new and complex reality. The new Russian state apparatus was weak, and events were moving fast—the shock therapy of neoliberal economic reforms, the movement of people across newly formed national borders, and erupting ethnic conflicts on the Soviet periphery. The ability of the 1991 Russian citizenship law to effectively regulate this situation would shortly be tested.

Implementation of the 1991 Citizenship Law

In 1992–1993 almost two million people moved to Russia from former Soviet republics.[31] This might suggest that the inclusiveness of the 1991 law resulted in, or at least facilitated, an immigration surge to Russia. However, a closer look shows that in the new conditions of hastened independence, the ability of the 1991 citizenship law to effectively regulate citizenship and migration was limited. Specifically, the law's execution by the bureaucracy and the early attitudes of Yeltsin's administration complicated the acquisition of Russian citizenship by former Soviet citizens, despite the inclusiveness of the law. Two main obstacles prohibited many Russians and Russian speakers, as well as other former Soviet citizens, from acquiring Russian citizenship under the 1991 law.

The first obstacle was the ban on dual citizenship for applicants. The 1991 citizenship law included provisions in articles 18-3 and 18-4 that required the applicant to waive or renounce the citizenship of his or her republic of residence.[32] In bureaucratic terms, in the 1990s (and even in the early 2000s), having Russian citizenship or citizenship of any other former Soviet republic meant that a person had in their Soviet passport either a Soviet residency registration (*propiska*), which stated their permanent place of residence, or a stamped citizenship liner (*vkladysh*).[33] Russian authorities (consulates for those applying abroad and the Ministry of the Interior for those applying in Russia), prior to stamping the applicant's Soviet passport with Russian citizenship, expected applicants to obtain a document stating that they relinquished or waived their citizenship in their former republic of residence.[34] Such documents were hard to obtain, especially if the applicant had left their republic of residence and applied through the Ministry of the Interior in Russia, since their ability to access the bureaucracy in their republic was limited.[35] Those who failed to provide the necessary documents were directed to the naturalization path, which required five years of residency in Russia.

The ban on dual citizenship was not an accidental policy outcome, and it complicated the lives of Russians and Russian speakers. It was in line with Yeltsin's administration's early ambivalent approach toward Russians and Russian speakers, who were perceived as pro-union.[36] After independence, Russia's foreign minister Andrei Kozyrev adhered to the same hesitant course of policy.[37] He was adamantly opposed to dual citizenship, as it could have resulted in mass acquisitions of Russian passports and would have been perceived as intervention in the internal affairs of the newly independent republics. He preferred to address the issue of dual citizenship via international agreements with former Soviet republics.[38] However, the republics refused to sign dual citizenship agreements, and the provisions in the Russian law became a de facto ban on dual citizenship. This ban posed a serious dilemma for Russians and Russian speakers in former Soviet republics. Events surrounding the collapse of the Soviet Union moved rapidly, and people were considering their options in an environment of uncertainty. If obtaining Russian citizenship meant waiving their rights in their places of residence for many years, or even generations, the choice was not so clear. Even in Estonia and Latvia, where most Russians and Russian speakers were in danger of becoming stateless, Russians sought for ways to safeguard their rights.

The second obstacle that prohibited former Soviet citizens from acquiring Russian citizenship was the Soviet practice of propiska, which was used as a condition for eligibility. In the Soviet Union, every citizen was required to live according to their propiska—that is, they had to register in their place of residence and to reside in their place of registration. The 1991 law required former Soviet citizens who wished to move to Russia and acquire citizenship to "relocate with the intention to take up permanent residency."[39] The post-Soviet form of propiska was named "registration" (*registratsiya*), which was meant to be a simple statement of where one resided. Accounting for the changing circumstances of freedom of movement, the government created two categories of registration: permanent registration or temporary registration.[40] However, the local Ministries of the Interior in Russia's regions conditioned the acquisition of citizenship on a Soviet-style propiska in the form of a stamp in one's passport that indicated a place of residence and required the person to live at the indicated address (hence, permanent registration).

This practice created a serious hurdle for those who wished to acquire citizenship. If one had decided to move to Russia and applied for citizenship through the Ministry of the Interior, one would often be refused due to the lack of registration, which was difficult to obtain in the absence of citizenship.[41] Some local authorities introduced a fee for registration. In Moscow, the fee was astronomical. In August 1994, for example, the fee was 10 million rubles for Russian citizens (about 5,000 USD, five hundred times the minimum wage) and 20 million rubles for Commonwealth of Independent States (CIS) citizens.[42] Registering was almost impossible for someone applying from their republic of residence outside Russia who did not have family in Russia to register with. As one migrant quoted by the migration scholar Moya Flynn noted: "It was difficult to get a job at the factory because I didn't have a *propiska*. It was impossible to get one. In Novosibirsk, they were very expensive, a permanent *propiska*. And without a *propiska*, . . . you can't do anything."[43]

This bureaucratic practice was deemed illegal by the federal center, yet it was unable to enforce its will. In 1992 the Russian Constitutional Court ruled that the place of residence should be considered when applying for citizenship rather than the possession of a permanent registration (propiska). In June 1993, the Presidential Administration passed the Law on the Rights of Citizens to Freedom of Movement, the Choice of a Place of Stay and Residence within the Russian Federation (O prave grazhdan Rossiyskoy Federatsii na svobodu peredvizheniya, vybor mesta prebyvaniya i zhitel'stva v predelakh Rossiyskoy Federatsii), which banned the use of the Soviet-style propiska.⁴⁴ The law also clearly stated that registration should be free of charge.⁴⁵ The federal center in Moscow, however, was embroiled in internal political struggles, and regional authorities were emboldened to continue the practice of propiska, which limited access to citizenship for former Soviet citizens.⁴⁶ Hence, the flow of people into Russia cannot be solely attributed to the inclusiveness of the 1991 law, as its application was limited by ingrained bureaucratic practices.

A New Migration Space

Something quite different from the consequences of the 1991 law, and no less important, was happening in post-Soviet Russia. The collapse of the Soviet Union created a new migration space with patterns that were unknown during the Soviet era. Internal borders became open international borders. The Bishkek Treaty of 1992 introduced a free visa zone within the CIS. The movement of people from third countries was still regulated by a visa system, but the borders were largely open for travel. The labor and housing markets were liberalized, and people could gain employment freely and let, rent, and buy housing according to their financial means and free will. These characteristics of post-Soviet migration were not only a result of the collapse of the Soviet Union but also tied to the temporal context in which these events were taking place—the globalized late modern era, when travel was increasingly free and transportation, communication, and finance transfers were becoming increasingly accessible, accompanied by deregulation in the economy.

In Soviet times, internal migration was also widespread. In fact, it had been noted that Soviet migration was even higher than post-Soviet flows.⁴⁷ The Soviet migration space was closed off, however, from the outside world; large Soviet population flows were directed by the state, and population movement was controlled by the authorities and regulated by propiska. The biggest state-directed migration flows were eastward. In the 1940s and 1950s, during the Second World War and in the Virgin Lands Campaign (1954), the Soviet state directed a large influx of Russians and Slavs to Central Asia.⁴⁸ By the 1970s, the Soviet trend of migration started to reverse back to the RSFSR as Brezhnev initiated the construction of the Baikal-Amur Mainline (BAM), a railway line that stretched across the union and attracted a large number of Soviet workers. He also led a policy of indigenization, encouraging members of titular nations to assume key posts in the republics.⁴⁹ In the 1970s, this resulted in the migration of half a million Russians and Russian speakers from Kazakhstan and 100,000 Russians from Kyrgyzstan, a trend that continued in the

1980s.⁵⁰ Hence, by the 1980s Russians and Russians speakers were already returning in large numbers to the western republics of the union (including the RSFSR, Ukraine, Moldova, Belorussia, and the Baltic republics), but they were moving within state-controlled flows of population and within the state-controlled system of propiska.

Within that state-controlled system of migration, Soviet citizens were provided employment, housing that could be registered with propiska, education for their children, and social services. Any deviations from residency or work at the place of registry were deemed criminal and punishable.⁵¹ Theoretically though, once a sentence had been served, a person would once again be provided with employment and housing; they would then thus have a propiska and be able to resume a normative legal life.⁵² The Soviet system did not work as smoothly as outlined above. In many cases, people could obtain employment an housing through personal, family, and professional networks and not via the state. Nonetheless, the basic premises of the system were set forth with a functioning internal logic, which allowed people to reasonably easily lead a legal way of life.

The post-Soviet migration space was not only a new postimperial migration space but also deregulated, in line with globalized trends of late modernity and neoliberal economic thinking. The direction of migration flows was no longer directed by the state in accordance with central plans and was unaccompanied by state-provided employment and housing. After the collapse, people were free to move wherever they saw fit. In this environment, migration became much more Russia centered, as Russia seemed like the most appropriate destination politically and economically.⁵³ Neither was it a neat stream of migrants consisting only of ethnic Russians who were looking to reunite with their countrymen and countrywomen. It was a disordered movement of heterogeneous people across new international borders in the visa-free regime that was established in 1992. These new migrants arrived in a deregulated socioeconomic situation. The government had no tools to address this migration, and people were expected to fend for themselves. These were the characteristics of the globalized late modern condition—people were freer to move and were expected to make their own choices and consequently look after themselves.

In the post-Soviet context, propiska was no longer workable as a system of control, and in this migratory environment, as Alexander Osipov notes, its continued use gave rise to a legal gray zone in Russia.⁵⁴ The institution of Russian citizenship began to fragment in this gray zone, which worked as follows. If a Soviet citizen arrived in Russia after February 1992 but did not acquire a certificate that they had waived their former citizenship or could not provide registration in Russia, they would not receive Russian citizenship; however, neither would they be deported. This person could remain in Russia carrying a Soviet passport. If a public official stopped this person, the only way in which they were breaking the law was their lack of a propiska, which at that point was in itself a vague legal instrument. If this person spoke the language, they could (albeit with some difficulties) find employment in the free-market economy and feel quite at home. They could live for years in this legal limbo—neither a citizen nor a fully illegal migrant, as the 1991 law was devised specifically for people like them and the federal authorities deemed this denial of citizenship as illegal.

This legal gray zone was a type of fragmentation of citizenship specific to Russia's circumstances yet was closely related to the consequences of global trends in other places. As in any other country in a globalized late modern society, the experience of life was shaped in the interaction between local circumstances and international trends. Hence, while the overall trend was that institutions became more flexible and their position in the society was disintegrating, a multiplicity of factors contributed to how this trend was generated in each case. In the case of Russian citizenship, this fragmentation was shaped in the interaction between the 1991 citizenship law, post-Soviet migration flows, global deregulated travel, and the neoliberal economic and bureaucratic practices of regional authorities. In this interaction, a specifically Russian fragmentation of the institute of citizenship was taking place, manifested in the creation of a gray zone of citizenship, where citizenship was losing its primacy as something that dictated belonging and granted rights and, in fact, was becoming more fluid.

"Go Back to Russia": Russians and Russian Speakers Abroad

The process of late modern fragmentation created a growing sense in Russia that its citizenship policy was underperforming. This was not far from the truth, as the situation was uncontrolled in ways that Russians had never experienced. Yet most political attention was drawn to the difficult conditions that Russians and Russian speakers faced in the former Soviet states. A short overview of these conditions shows why this issue gained political potency in Russia.

In 1992–1994, Estonia and Latvia rejected the practice of zero option and opted for laws that excluded large parts of the Russian and Russian-speaking population from its citizenry.[55] As a result, in 1992 in Estonia roughly 500,000

Russians and Russian speakers remained stateless.[56] In 1994, the Latvian citizenship law left about 700,000 people stateless.[57] Naturalization in these countries, which required a language exam, was a long and difficult path for most Russians and Russian speakers, who did not speak Estonian and Latvian. Moreover, psychologically, the loss of legal and social status was particularly hard for these communities that did not perceive Estonia and Latvia as a foreign country.[58] In both countries, statelessness impinged on political and property rights (investments by foreigners were regulated) and barred those individuals from work in the public sector, including in the state education system.[59]

In other former republics, Russians found themselves at odds with the new regimes. In Ukraine, Russians constituted about 20 percent of the population and were in a problematic political position. Ethnic Russians and Russified Ukrainians lived in the heavy industrial urban centers in the east and would have gained from closer relations with Russia, where their products had compatible markets and trusted customers. Ethnic Ukrainian communities were concentrated in the west and saw greater opportunities in integrating with Europe. This created two competing visions for the future of Ukraine.[60] Another newly independent state with a large Russian minority was Kazakhstan. With a community of 6.2 million people, constituting 37 percent of the population and 70–80 percent in the northern regions, ethnic Russians in Kazakhstan expected to have a privileged position but soon found themselves at odds with the regime.[61] Since 1989 President Nursultan Nazarbayev had pursued a policy of linguistic and ethnic Kazakhization.[62] The main Russian party, Lad, and the cultural association Russkaya Obshchina found that their relations with the authorities were quickly worsening, and by 1994 Kazakhs dominated politics.[63]

Ethnic conflicts and civil war tore the post-Soviet space, often endangering minorities—Russians and Russia speakers among them. In 1989 in Uzbekistan, where there were 1.6 million Russians (8 percent of the population), a pogrom against Meskhetian Turks in the Fergana Valley, a region between Uzbekistan, Kyrgyzstan, and Tajikistan, spread fears among Russians of further interethnic confrontations.[64] The journalist and author Jonathan Steele, who traveled in Fergana after the pogrom, recalled that period.[65] His host in Fergana town, a Russian who had moved there twenty years earlier from central Russia, told him that 20,000 of 130,000 Russian residents, together with other minorities (Tatars and Jews), had already left. His wife described the hostile attitudes: "When I go to the bazaar, they say 'Go back to Russia.' When they don't give me my change and I ask for it, they say 'Go back to Russia.'"[66] By 1992 civil wars were raging in Tajikistan, Nagorno-Karabakh, Ossetia, and Abkhazia, while in Moldova tensions between ethnic Russians and Moldovans resulted in open conflict and the de facto secession of the Russian-populated Transdniestria region.

The new nationalist opposition in Russia rallied around the cause of ethnic Russians and Russian speakers, placing Russianness firmly on the political agenda of citizenship legislation. In reality, the difficulties of Russians and Russian speakers in the former Soviet republics were only scantly related to the complications of acquiring citizenship in Russia, while other factors contributed to the decision of whether to emigrate. For instance, the flow of migrants from the Baltic states was always small, despite legal hardship and due to positive economic prospects there. The opposition, however, made a political point of the difficulties experienced by ethnic Russians and Russia speakers and tied it to difficulties in accessing citizenship. It accused the Russian government of not doing enough to ensure that Russians' and Russian speakers' rights and safety were being upheld. In 1993, Dmitry Rogozin, the Russian deputy prime minister between 2011 and 2018, together with General Alexander Lebed, a prominent politician in the 1990s, established the Congress of Russian Communities (Kongress russkikh obshchin), which campaigned for the rights of Russians and Russian speakers.[67] Rogozin repeatedly called for the Russian government to intervene to protect Russians and Russian speakers abroad: "Only an immediate intervention by the Russian Foreign Ministry to protect the interests of Russian citizens and those who have expressed a desire to be so, can stop a possible disaster."[68]

Against this backdrop, by 1993 Yeltsin's and Kozyrev's hesitant approaches and the difficulties associated with acquiring citizenship in Russia seemed inappropriate. Yeltsin's administration found that they had to address the situation of Russians and Russian speakers even if initially they were not fully inclined to do so. Yet they were called to solve the shortcomings of citizenship in Russia by addressing only one factor: the postimperial unmixing of people, or the place of ethnic Russians and Russian speakers. Politically motivated, this ignored the evolving situation of migration, where there were more factors at play—bureaucratic practices in Russia and the consequences of globalization and late modernity. Thus, legislation revisions aimed at mending the problems associated with Russian citizenship had poor prospects.

A Proactive Government Approach, 1993–1995

Between 1993 and 1995, the Russian government took several legislative measures to better address this postimperial situation and ease access to citizenship for ethnic Russians and Russian speakers. In 1993 the government introduced de facto dual citizenship and dropped the requirement for registration (propiska). In 1994 it addressed the need to strengthen relations with Russians and Russian speakers abroad, who were referred to as compatriots (*sootechestvenniki*), and in 1995 it extended the date for former Soviet citizens to apply for a Russian citizenship.

By 1993 the ban on dual citizenship was the main grievance of ethnic Russians and Russian speakers abroad against the authorities of the newly independent states (Russia included). In Russia it became clear that Kozryev's attempt to conclude dual citizenship agreements with the republics was not materializing, as the only such treaty was signed with Turkmenistan.[69] Henceforth, the Russian government decided to address dual citizenship unilaterally. In June 1993 an amendment to the law removed the requirement for former Soviet citizens to renounce their other citizenship in order to acquire Russian citizenship.[70] It stated: "A person who is a citizen of the Russian Federation shall not be recognized as belonging to the citizenry of another state."[71] In the same year, the government adopted a law concerning forced migrants and another concerning refugees, which recognized the rights of former Soviet citizens and were meant to help them financially in their move to Russia.[72]

Practically, this meant that prospective applicants no longer had to provide a document proving that they did not possess another citizenship and allowed further access to former Soviet citizens.[73] De facto, this was dual citizenship. Furthermore, it legally dropped the requirement of propiska and allowed former Soviet citizens to freely apply for the citizenship stamp in their Soviet passports at Russian consulates in their places of residence.[74] Indeed, from this point, according to Ginsburgs, the flow of applicants in the former Soviet republics increased, with long queues forming outside Russian consulates.[75] Ginsburgs found that by 1996 about 900,000 people had acquired Russian citizenship through consulates abroad.[76] In theory, these people were eligible for financial assistance.

In August 1994 a new government resolution on measures to support compatriots abroad was published. It stated that "the resolution of questions of financial, economic, social and military-political cooperation between Russia and certain states will be made contingent on the concrete position the leadership of these states take in recognizing the rights and interests of Russians on their territory."[77] This decree was a strong political shift away from early visions of cordial relations with former Soviet states and the idea that Russia's primacy meant caring for all former Soviet citizens equally. It was a victory for figures like Rogozin, who kept accusing the government of not doing enough to protect the rights of Russians everywhere who were suffering "destruction, humiliation and plight."[78] In this spirit, the government established a Governmental Commission on the Affairs of Compatriots and deferred the 1991 law deadline for application for citizenship from 1995 to December 2000.[79]

These legislative changes were meant to fix the problematic situation of citizenship in Russia by addressing the problems of ethnic Russians and Russian speakers in the former Soviet states and to allow parts of the Russian in-group to join the citizenry. If the problems that Russia was facing were primarily postimperial, these changes could have worked. Yet, as noted earlier, the institution of citizenship in Russia was fragmenting and devolving not only because of postimperial conditions.

The Erosion of the Institution of Citizenship

It very quickly became apparent that the legislative measures introduced by the government were unable to correct the problems associated with citizenship in Russia and to regulate migration effectively. By making provisions for Russians and Russian speakers without considering the consequences of globalization and local bureaucratic practices, the government unintentionally contributed to the proliferation of practices that eroded the central place of citizenship as a social institution that denotes belonging and grants rights. After the aforementioned legislations came into force, a growing number of people within Russia were living in a legal gray zone and had different rights granted to them by multiple authorities (Russia being only one of them).

The implementation of dual citizenship contributed to this in the following way. Since the Russian law scrapped the need to waive former citizenship, former Soviet citizens who applied for Russian citizenship at consulates abroad were stamped with a Russian citizenship liner even if they had a valid propiska stamp from their republic. Carrying such a passport in Russia was legal, yet most republics had banned dual citizenship, and there such a passport was considered illegal. In this system, the ability to exercise the right to dual citizenship with Russia depended on the lack of enforcement of the ban in the republic of residence.[80] The number of Russian people who acquired citizenship outside Russia (about 900,000 by 1996) indicated that many had taken this path and carried a passport that was illegal in their country of origin.[81] In some republics, notably in Ukraine and Uzbekistan, people engaged in the practice of "losing" passports.[82] A person would declare that they had lost the Soviet passport and would get a new national passport from the republic of residence; meanwhile, they would stamp the Soviet passport, which was declared lost, with a liner attesting to Russian citizenship.[83]

As a result of the de facto recognition of dual citizenship, by the mid-1990s a growing number of people in the former Soviet republics and in Russia had links to several political authorities, not all of which were legally sound. Hence, in the postimperial, late modern context of early Russian independence, people found themselves in what the Austrian social scientist Rainer Bauböck described as citizenship constellations—that is, "a structure in which individuals are simultaneously linked to several political entities."[84] Unlike in Western Europe, which was the focus of Bauböck's research, in former Soviet states linking oneself to multiple authorities was seen as a matter of survival. For many, additional Russian citizenship was an insurance policy against the deteriorating political and economic conditions in the former Soviet states.[85] These people wanted two citizenships because they hoped to safeguard their rights. They did not want to miss the deadline for applying for Russian citizenship and then find themselves stuck in a country where their rights were being impinged on and their future was uncertain. It was a more complex situation than simply choosing a citizenship due to national belonging.

If the consequences of dual citizenship were not complex enough, the official dropping of the requirement for propiska in 1993, without the ability to force the executive organs in the regions to follow suit, made the institution of citizenship even more ambiguous. Regional branches of the Ministry of the Interior ignored the legal changes on the federal level and continued to require a registration (propiska) when applying for citizenship within Russia.[86] Hence, throughout the 1990s, despite abolishing the institution of propiska in numerous legislations, its successor—registration—remained the "deciding insignia of a citizen of Russia."[87] This was particularly true in Moscow, where registration regulations were strictest; it increased the sense of uncertainty, since the federal center was seen as unable to enforce its will on the executive branches in the regions. This feeling was also exacerbated by the federal government's failure to provide the financial assistance that it had promised in the laws concerning forced migrants and refugees.[88]

In this context, the 1993 legislation that allowed citizenship without a registration requirement but could not enforce it only furthered the emergence of a large legal gray zone. It allowed more people access to citizenship, while local law enforcement organs did not act lawfully and did not allow them full citizenship. The lack of clear objectives for law enforcement organs and lax control by the center created widespread predatory behavior. The police often used the precarious situation of migrants in Russia for harassing them, in particular those migrants from the Caucasus and Central Asia. For example, registration in a certain flat could initiate numerous checks of the property by the police.[89] As a result, some tenants avoided registration out of fear of further harassment. Landlords were also generally wary of registration, due to past conceptions of propiska as indicating ownership and due also to a general distrust of the police.[90] People who could not or chose not to register were pushed into the growing gray zone, where rights might have accrued to them via federal legislation, but in practice they were denied access to these rights.

Finally, the category of compatriots, which aimed to remedy problems faced by Russians and Russian speakers and strengthen Russianness in citizenship legislation, contributed in its own way to the erosion of the institution of citizenship. Instead of solidifying people's positions as either citizens or noncitizens, it signaled that Russia was willing to take a more aggressive line regarding the place of ethnic Russians and Russian speakers abroad and that they continued to have a special status in Russia. This encouraged legal choices that reinforced complex citizenship constellations, besides dual citizenship.

An incident in Crimea and citizenship choices in Estonia and Latvia provide good examples. In the aftermath of the government resolution that conditioned Russian relations with states on the rights and interests of Russians on their territory, for at least a little while Russia seemed to put its passports where its mouth was. In 1995, in response to the Ukrainian parliament abolishing the Crimean Constitution, Russian authorities set up a consulate in Sevastopol and started to issue Russian passports on-site.[91] Ukraine, which banned dual citizenship, called Russia to close the unauthorized consulate. Russia denied the episode and claimed that it was a planned visit by the consular officer from Kiev.[92] This was an outstanding episode, yet the practice of Ukrainians, particularly in Crimea, acquiring Russian citizenship without forfeiting their Ukrainian passport continued throughout the 1990s. It is unclear, even to Ukrainian authorities, how many people acquired Russian passports in Crimea over the years. Taras Kuzio, a scholar of Ukraine, cites different sources presenting figures as low as 6,000 and as high as 100,000. (The highest figure was cited by the deputy secretary of the Ukrainian National and Security Council.)[93] This was a clear sign that Russia was willing to pursue bolder policies vis-à-vis Russians and Russian speakers abroad.

In Estonia and Latvia, involvement was more nuanced. Estonian and Latvian citizenship laws excluded hundreds of thousands of ethnic Russians and Russian speakers from their citizenry.[94] Due to the large numbers of stateless persons, and spurred by European and international pressure, Latvia and Estonia introduced a special status for Russians and Russian speakers who did not receive citizenship. Starting in the mid-1990s, in Latvia they received a status of noncitizens, and in Estonia they were issued so-called alien passports. These were literally gray passports that extended residency rights and afforded freedom of movement similar to Latvian and Estonian passports but failed to grant full citizenship status.[95] For many people, such a solution seemed more appropriate than the long and difficult naturalization process.

Russia's acknowledgment of former Soviet citizens in Latvia and Estonia as compatriots further emboldened them not to take up full citizenship. Furthermore, it allowed them visa-free travel, while if they acquired a local passport, they would have needed a visa to enter Russia. Together with better economic conditions in these countries and the prospects of EU integration, these gray statuses presented an attractive option.[96] Overall, Russia's new policy direction encouraged ethnic Russians and Russian speakers not to choose one specific citizenship but to opt for citizenship constellations, where they received rights granted by several authorities, Russia among them.

Hence, the new government course of policy in 1993–1995, which aimed to create order in the citizenship situation by addressing the needs of Russians and Russian speakers, unintentionally made the institution of citizenship in Russia more fragmented and fluid. De facto dual citizenship, dropping propiska, and legislation that identified Russians in the new states as compatriots resulted in a growing number of people who were living in the legal gray zone and increased the sense of vagueness of the contours of the Russian citizenry.

The Smirnov Case, 1996

If more proof was needed that the legislative measures of 1993–1995 were unable to address the evolving citizenship situation in Russia, it came in 1996. In the obscure legal state of affairs and illegal enforcement of the 1990s, it was only a matter of time until cases of a Soviet citizen who was wronged by the system would reach Constitutional Court appeals. This happened in May 1996, when the Russian Constitutional Court ruled in the case of Smirnov against the state. This case was an example of one person who was plunged into the legal gray zone, but it was also important as it had further political consequences.

A. V. Smirnov was a typical Soviet citizen. He was an ethnic Russian, who was born in 1959 in the RSFSR in the Moscow oblast and resided there until he was twenty years old. In 1979, he married and moved to the Latvian Soviet Socialist Republic (SSR) for permanent residency.[97] In 1992 Smirnov divorced, returned to Russia, and took up permanent residency in the Moscow oblast and received a propiska.[98] Alas, he returned to Russia after the February 6, 1992, date that was indicated in the 1991 law as the cut-off date for people to be considered under the citizenship *recognition* path. Hence, he was directed by the authorities to the citizenship *registration* path.[99] Smirnov refused to register for citizenship and demanded to be recognized as a citizen, as indicated in article 13-2 in the 1991 citizenship law, which stipulated that recognition of citizenship also applied to those who were born on the territory of the RSFSR. He appealed all the way to the Supreme Court and was overruled every time, until in May 1996 the Constitutional Court ruled in his favor to be recognized as a Russian citizen.[100]

The ruling underlined that since Russian citizenship is assigned as a birthright and cannot be revoked involuntarily, according to article 6 of the Russian Constitution (as well as the Universal Declaration of Human Rights) and regardless of the place of residence, Smirnov had to be recognized as a Russian citizen.[101] The court ruled section 3 of article 18 in the 1991 citizenship law—the section under which those who were born on the territory of the RSFSR were directed to the citizenship registration process rather than receiving recognition as Russian citizens—to be unconstitutional. This ruling could not be applied directly to the majority of the 25 million ethnic Russians who lived outside of Russia. However, it provided an opportunity for the opposition to fuel a political debate on whether Russian citizenship legislation appropriately addressed the rights of Russians and Russia speakers abroad and supported the formation of a desired Russian citizenry.

In the aftermath of the Smirnov decision, a parliamentary battle raged around the rights of Russians and Russian speakers for Russian citizenship. Once more, the debate mostly ignored the new complex migration situation that was evolving in Russia and focused solely on Russians and Russian speakers.

In June 1996 State Duma member Sergei Baburin took the initiative to promote his agenda through the crack opened by the Constitutional Court. Baburin was at the time a leading right-wing politician with a nationally infused agenda[102] He proposed a draft law whose wording was in line with the Constitutional Court's ruling in the Smirnov case. It stated that a person is recognized as a citizen of Russia if he or she fulfilled the following criteria: they were born on territory that at the time of their birth belonged to the RSFSR; they did not voluntarily renounce their Russian citizenship; they left the territory of the RSFSR but remained within the former Soviet Union; they did not receive citizenship of another state; and they returned for permanent residency in Russia.[103]

Baburin's real intention was, however, to recognize as Russian citizens all those who had not received citizenship in their republics of residence, without their intent and without setting a deadline for requests.[104] His arguments were grounded on Russia's primacy among the former Soviet republics as the legal successor of the Soviet Union. As such, he argued, Russia could not deny former Soviet citizens their right to be recognized as Russian citizens.[105] Such a law would apply mainly to ethnic Russians and Russian speakers, who were more likely not to receive citizenship in the newly independent states or did not voluntarily renounce their Russian citizenship. Baburin's proposal was passed in its first hearing in June 1996 but was sidelined by a competing proposal.

In May 1997, the Presidential Administration submitted a similar proposal. It concentrated on amending the sections deemed unconstitutional in the 1991 law but did not make the legal leap that would link Russia's succession of the Soviet Union with the automatic recognition of certain groups as Russian citizens. The version submitted by the Presidential Administration was passed in its first reading in September 1997. In the second reading in February 1998, Georgy Tikhonov, a member of the Committee on CIS Affairs and Relations with Compatriots, made an emotional appeal where he emphasized kinship with Russians abroad and described them as victims of the collapse of the Soviet Union. He stated: "The Belavezha Accords denied 25 million people of their motherland, and if we accept the law . . . as it is presented by the committee today, we will deny these 25 million people their citizenship."[106] The draft law was defeated in its second reading and finally removed from the agenda the next year, without resolving the constitutional inconsistency within the 1991 citizenship law.[107]

The Compatriots Law, 1999

The next legislation relating to citizenship took place in March 1999, on the initiative of the opposition, when the Russian Duma adopted the Law on Russian State Policy towards Compatriots Abroad (Zakon o gosudarstvennoy politike Rossiyskoy Federatsii v otnoshenii sootechestvennikov za rubezhom; hereafter, the 1999 Compatriots Law).[108] Once again this legislation focused on the rights of Russians and Russian speakers, and once more it had consequences that blurred the contours of the Russian citizenry. This law did two things: defined again who was a compatriot and created a legislative path for acquisition of citizenship by compatriots. According to article 1 in the 1999 Compatriots Law, compatriots were "persons who were born, resided or residing in the same state and have common traits of language, religion, cultural heritage, as well as their descendants."[109] The law referred to the "originality" (*samobytnost'*) of compatriots—namely, their language, religion and culture, which linked them to Russia.[110] Relating to originality indicated that compatriots were assumed to speak Russian and feel close to Russian culture and the Russian Orthodox Church. This basically revealed that compatriots were former Soviet ethnic Russians and Russian speakers, without openly saying so.[111]

However, the application of the law was quite odd and undermined the sense that citizenship was meant to grant rights to a specific group of people that were considered part of the national in-group. The acquisition of citizenship by compatriots, as set out in article 11 of the 1999 Compatriots Law was used for specific groups of former Soviet citizens who lived in the breakaway republics of Georgia and Moldova and were not necessarily ethnic Russians or Russian speakers by origin (at least not in Abkhazia, where most residents are members of Caucasian ethnic groups, which were not Russified).[112] This novel aspect of Russian citizenship policy illustrated Russia's growing appetite for the strategic use of citizenship to foster ties with groups of former Soviet citizens in order to promote its foreign policy objectives, as was seen in the short episode of issuing passports in Crimea in 1995. In the breakaway regions in Georgia (Abkhazia and South Ossetia) and Moldova (Transdniestria), the acquisition of Russian passports became common and a pretext for Russia's involvement in their affairs.[113] This practice of issuing Russian passports in breakaway republics further undermined the institution of citizenship as a stable category with well-defined rules on membership.

The Smirnov case, the ensuing parliamentary debate, and the 1999 Compatriots Law showed that even as the decade drew toward a close, the challenge of forming a stable and secure citizenry in Russia was unattainable. The changing global circumstances that were influencing migration were largely ignored, and the debate focused on Russians and Russian speakers. The opposition was pushing for further provisions to assist ethnic Russians and Russian speakers abroad to fix the Russian citizenry and further their nationally infused agenda. Progovernment forces resisted this as an unconstructive step that could result in legal complications and conflict with former Soviet states.[114] But they also failed to account for the broader picture of changing migration circumstances. Yeltsin was weak and did not control the Duma, where starting in 1995 the Communists and other opposition parties had almost 50 percent of the seats, and the legislative debate on citizenship was becoming radically politicized. The Russian government had no vision and no ability to drive a new policy that would stabilize the situation of citizenship. In this situation the legal gray zone was expanding and deepening as a Russian type of late modern citizenship fragmentation.

Migration and Citizenship in Russian Late Modernity

If the defining experience of citizenship in Russia was an increasing legal gray zone and a citizenry where citizenship was becoming fragmented and fluid, what were its characteristics by the end of the decade?

The opening of borders and new freedom of movement unleashed one of the largest international migration waves in history in the former Soviet space, with Russia being its prime recipient of migrants. About 6 million people moved to Russia during the first decade of independence, and it became the second biggest host of immigration after the United States.[115] Out of these, about 4 million immigrated to urban centers in Russia.[116] In terms of inclusion in the Russian citizenship, according to Ginsburgs, by 1996 about 1.5 million people had received Russian citizenship.[117] This means that if admission to citizenship remained on the same path as it had since 1996 (and as we know that it did), millions of people who arrived in Russia during the 1990s remained without Russian citizenship. This wave of migration was not expected to dwindle. The number of those who dreamed about moving to Russia was far larger.[118] A study of public opinion in 1998–1999 found that 60 percent of Russians in Central Asia wanted to leave.[119] This meant that in Central Asia alone close to 3.7 million people expressed interest in emigrating to Russia.[120]

Post-Soviet migration waves were not only large but also heterogeneous—people from different backgrounds were moving for different reasons. In the early 1990s, due to deteriorating security situations, Azerbaijan, Uzbekistan, Georgia, Moldova, and Tajikistan were the leading countries of origins of migrants to Russia. The North Caucasus was also a region subject to conflict, from which people migrated internally to other parts of Russia.[121] By 1994 economic motivations started to play a greater role.[122] That year the number of immigrants peaked, reaching over a million people, and at the same time the countries of departure shifted to Kazakhstan, Ukraine, and Uzbekistan, as well as the rest of Central Asia.[123] During the 1990s, internally displaced persons (IDPs) from the North Caucasus and laborers from the Russian federal autonomies in the Caucasus moved to Russian cities seeking safety and employment. Although they were Russian citizens and migrated internally within Russian borders, their lack of registration (propiska) branded them as illegal migrants.

In the free-market economy, immigration was also a personal endeavor. Testimonies of those who fled conflicts show that they were totally self-dependent, despite the stipulations in the laws concerning forced migrants. As one person who settled in Saratov said: "I do not hope for any kind of help, and to go [to the authorities for help, will be] a waste of time."[124] Since migration was an individual choice, migrants had one thing in common that stemmed from the free-market economy: the migrants were the best prospects for themselves and their families.

The Russian state was called on to address the intensifying migration flow, but as in other states that embraced globalization and neoliberalism, in the new reality their capabilities were limited. In Russia, the state authorities withdrew from their central position of ordering life. They no longer provided people with housing or employment, and people were expected to fend for themselves in the new economic conditions. Hence, the situation was not fully in the government's hands. These difficulties became associated with general insecurity and instability following the collapse of the Soviet Union; however, they were happening elsewhere in the globalized world, with similar consequences for the institution of citizenship. An overview of the political agendas in France, Germany, the United Kingdom, and the United States reveals that over the past twenty years, migration and access to rights and citizenship have become salient issues.[125] There too, as the social scientist Yasmin Soysal noted, increased migration led to transformations in the institution of citizenship as a prime signifier of national identity and belonging.[126] More Europeans had rights granted to them outside the social institute of citizenship, and, as Bauböck noted, many more had complex legal positions that linked them to several political authorities.[127] This made citizenship more flexible.

Yet each country, Russia included, had specific conditions that dictated the interaction between migration, the state, and the institution of citizenship in the new global circumstances. One of the most important characteristics in Russia (besides the Russians abroad) was the sharp shift between the omnipotent and omnipresent Soviet state and the deregulated neoliberal settings, in line with the shock-therapy economic policies therein. Almost overnight, migration went from being under near total control of the state to near total freedom of movement, as connected to and influenced by a free-market economy. Hence, the state had even less control over the situation than in other places that experienced a more gradual opening to globalization. The consequences of the sharp Russian transition to the globalized and deregulated context created a fragmentation in the institution of citizenship that went even further than in other parts of the world.

In these circumstances of devolved authority and a weak federal center, regional authorities were free to continue using the propiska, which in turn encouraged illegal behavior by the migrants. This system, which in post-Soviet Russia had no internal logic, criminalized Russians and Russian speakers who did not have a permanent place of residence, while driving labor migrants into a shadow economy. Some people bribed the police, while others found ways to circumvent the system altogether by avoiding public places and public transport in order to avoid the police.[128] In the field of labor migration, the situation was worse. While Russia became the largest receiving country for labor migrants from the CIS, employing irregular migrants outside the legal system became endemic in the Russian labor market.[129] In the shadow economy, all sorts of rights could be denied—for instance, in Moscow in 1996, Mayor Yuri Luzhkov passed a decree denying education to the children of unregistered parents.[130] The city court overruled that decree, but such restrictions reoccurred in different places.

Illegal behavior also became widespread among the police, who were charged with an illogical and meaningless task.[131] The propiska system was used for profiteering and ethnic discrimination. The citizenship registration track, which included the demand to present a propiska, was also a huge source of corruption.[132] Witnesses reported that in the 1990s in Moscow it was virtually impossible to gain Russian citizenship without bribing the officers concerned.[133] Moreover, local authorities used it as a means for ethnic discrimination.[134] For example, Meskhetian Turks who fled the 1989 pogroms in the Fergana Valley were denied propiska in the southern region of Russia, Krasnodar, while persons of Slavic descent were reportedly registered with no obstacles.[135] Similar behavior was noted in the Abkhaz case, where most people received Russian citizenship as a result of article 11 in the 1999 Compatriots Law but were denied access to the rights afforded by citizenship since the police refused to issue them internal passports and a propiska.[136]

This raises another Russia-specific condition of migration, where ethnicity and Russianness played an important role. In Russia, ethnic affiliation was a decisive factor in attitudes toward migrants: Slavic migrants were overall viewed positively, while Caucasian and Central Asian immigrants were viewed negatively.[137] The diversity of the vast movement of people further increased the sense that there was something wrong with Russian migration and citizenship. A false sense developed within the Russian public that Russia was being flooded with people from Central Asia and the Caucasus. In 1993 Zhirinovsky expressed this sentiment by saying: "In my apartment I am the master. And I myself will decide who to call to visit, and to whom I do not even have to open the door. . . . Southerners have already flooded all of Moscow, and even Vietnamese, Chinese, Kurds. . . . Moscow and other Russian cities should not be cheap hotels"[138] This was a false perception as two-thirds of the people who moved to Russia in 1990–2003 were ethnic Russians.[139] Nonetheless, illegal migration became a serious concern, and there was a sense that the wrong groups of migrants were entering Russia in large numbers and in an uncontrollable manner.[140]

This was not too dissimilar to what happened in the West, where the process of globalization also increased migration. From the 1980s there were calls to restrict migration, and this issue has been linked to matters of security and public order.[141] This reveals an integral feature of globalization, where openness and freedom have caused a sense of loss and disorder. This has resulted in the main dialectic of late modernity—freedom versus security. On the one hand, political and economic systems have encouraged openness, deregulation, and more freedom, which causes institutions to fragment. But on the other hand, deregulation and fragmentation have increased the sense of insecurity and almost immediately created public resonance that has called for more control and regulation. Freedom of movement and neoliberal economics have increased migration, but the sense that the movement of people has been too large and chaotic calls to control the flows. As this dialectic has not been resolved anywhere else, it raises the question whether it could have been resolved, or at least mitigated, in Russia.

Fluid Russian Citizenship

In the 1990s Russian citizenship was in flux. This was an expected result of the collapse of the Soviet state. It placed Russianness very high on the political agenda, with immediate bearing on citizenship legislation. The 1991 citizenship law and subsequent legislations tried to address the needs of millions of *Homos sovieticus*, most of whom were Russians and Russian speakers, who had strong links to Russia and were scattered around the former Soviet space. Russia was a favorable destination, and in their own eyes, they were not immigrants. As one migrant quoted by Flynn said: "If I had gone somewhere like Israel, or somewhere else, like America, then I would be an immigrant. But I have come home, it is my *rodina* (motherland)."[142] Legislation in the 1990s reflected attempts to deal with this vast legal, political, and moral postimperial challenge: the disentangling of imperial populations. As shown, there were numerous attempts to do so—the 1991 law with its amendments in 1993 and 1995, the 1994 laws on forced migrants and refugees, and the 1994 and 1999 legislation on assistance to compatriots. None however was able to bring order to the developing situation.

The situation of citizenship in Russia was also a result of late modern global trends—the opening of borders, labor migration, and a deregulated economic system. In the new deregulated circumstances, the Russian government was withdrawing from ordering society: it did not control population flows; nor did it take care of employment or housing for the new migrants. This was an abrupt change from the previous state-controlled system, and for many people it created a strong feeling of insecurity. Local bureaucracy engaged in the illegal enforcement of an old population-control method—the propiska. But it clashed with new migration trends. It pushed people into the shadow economy and a space of undetermined legal status—the legal gray zone. By doing so, it eroded the role played by citizenship as a sole institution that granted rights and denoted identification. The Russian gray zone became a manifestation of the fragmentation of the institution of citizenship, which ceased to be the prime insignia in society. It changed form and meaning from one individual to another. Some people may have had a Soviet passport with a propiska; others had dual citizenship in their passport that was declared as lost, or even noncitizenship from a Baltic state.

These two factors that shaped Russian citizenship in the 1990s—the postimperial place of Russians and Russianness in the citizenry and the late modern characteristics of the migration space—make fluid Russianness an appropriate analytical framework. The interaction between these factors has been largely overlooked when dealing with citizenship and migration in late modern post-Soviet Russia. The experience of Russian citizenship can be seen as being much closer to the Western experience, and not necessarily abnormal and in need of fixing. This also raises the question of whether in the globalized late modern context stable citizenship is achievable or even desirable. Yet with the approach of the deadline set by the 1995 amendment of the 1991 law (December 31, 2000), public and political displeasure with the sense of insecurity and demand for greater control of migration and citizenship made the situation ripe for a change of course in citizenship legislation.[143]

CHAPTER 2

Seeking Stability in a Fluid Russia
Russian Citizenship under Putin

By the end of 1999, the sense within the political elite and the public that Russian citizenship legislation was not performing its stated purpose made the situation ripe for policy change. The new Russian president Vladimir Putin, who positioned himself as the leader who would reinstate Russian citizens' sense of stability, security, and normality, was set to normalize citizenship policies too. In 2002, President Putin introduced a restrictive law aimed at making citizenship legislation more stable.[1] In 2006 he introduced the Compatriots' Resettlement Program, which aimed to attract the desirable type of migrants to Russia: young professionals from a Russian or Russian-speaking background.

These efforts fell short of satisfying concerns, which was reflected in continuous debates and critiques of the government's policies. As with policies in the 1990s, in the 2000s scholars explained policy failures through the prism of confused policies bureaucratic practices. While Shevel argued that Russia's citizenship policies were purposely ambiguous, due to a vague definition of the Russian nation, Osipov explained the perceived failure of the 2002 law by noting that when considering policy implementation, the evolution between the 1990s and 2000s was less striking. This chapter will argue that it was the government's disregard for the new late modern trends that shaped Russian citizenship that doomed its policies to fail.

When Putin came to power in December 1999, the deadline for acquisition of Russian citizenship by former Soviet citizens through citizenship registration was a year away. Even before December 31, 2000, arrived, the police were instructed to toughen the procedures of granting citizenship to most former Soviet citizens. An internal instruction of the Ministry of the Interior dated August 22, 2000, revealed that the police had updated its Order of Documentation of Residence Permits (Vid na zhitel'stvo) of former Soviet citizens permanently residing on the territory of the Russian Federation who did not document their belonging to the citizenship of a certain CIS state and/or citizens of CIS states.[2] This document contained an extremely elaborate set of regulations regarding the documentation of former Soviet citizens. It stipulated that a former Soviet citizen must have a new bureaucratic certificate, a residency permit, on top of permanent registration (the propiska).[3] This was a serious complication. For many who moved to Russia, even the requirement of permanent registration was too complex to comply with, as they could not provide certification of property ownership or a long-term lease and thus remained with temporary registration. Those who still had a Soviet passport were also asked to present proof that they did not hold citizenship of their former republic, restoring a procedure that had been abolished in 1993.[4] This effectively put into question the future status of millions of former Soviet citizens who throughout the 1990s lived in the legal gray zone. Indeed, with the regulation's entry into force in October 2000, the number of registered arrivals dropped precipitously by 84 percent in comparison to the previous month.[5] This meant that it had become virtually impossible to legally register for citizenship in Russia.

The 2002 Citizenship Law

In April 2001 Putin made his big move to formally toughen citizenship legislation. He proposed a new citizenship law that removed all favorable clauses for acquisition of Russian citizenship by former Soviet citizens. The draft law was discussed in the Duma in 2001–2002 and adopted in May 2002. This legislation presented a sharp break from the 1991 law and its amendments. The "General Procedure of Admission to the Citizenship of Russia," outlined in article 13 of the 2002 law, stated that eligibility for naturalization pertained to residency on "the territory of Russia for five uninterrupted years since being granted a residency permit and before applying for admission to citizenship."[6] The person had to have a source of income, renounce their previous citizenship (unless there was an international treaty that regulated dual citizenship), and demonstrate proficiency in the Russian language (pass a language test).[7] The only two provisions for former Soviet citizens were that the period of residence could be shortened if a person was born on the territory of Russia, if a person was unable to work and had an adult offspring who was a Russian citizen, or if they remained stateless in the former Soviet republics. The last clause could have been taken up by stateless Russian persons in Estonia and Latvia, but by 2002 they enjoyed most civic rights granted in the framework of noncitizenship status, and very few of them wanted to migrate. Procedures for acquiring a Russian citizenship set out in the Law on the Legal Status of Foreigners (Federal'nyy zakon o pravovom polozhenii inostrannykh grazhdan) were even more complex than those listed in the Interior Ministry's instruction from 2000.[8] To legally settle in Russia, the applicant had to acquire a temporary (three-year) residence permit within sixty days.[9] The issuance of permits was regulated by government quotas, which were set by the federal regions of Russia (republics, krais, and oblasts). After obtaining a temporary residence permit (*razresheniye na vremennoye prozhivaniye*), prospective citizens could apply for a residency permit (*vid na zhitel'stvo*), which could be acquired only one year following receipt of a temporary residence permit and had to be applied for no less than six months before its expiration.[10] The residency permit was issued for five years, with the option of renewal, after which an application for citizenship could be submitted (see table 2).[11]

This very strict legislation was part of Putin's broader agenda—ending the time of transition of the 1990s and starting normalization through a centrally managed state system.[12] The 2002 law was presented as a measure meant to overturn the chaotic citizenship and migration situation, relieve the economic burden on Russia, and create a stable and normal citizenship policy. In September 2002 Putin noted that "the flow [of immigrants] is swelling, while the social burden rests on the Russian budget, including the payment of pensions. . . . And those who live here permanently do not always have enough

Table 2 Acquisition of Citizenship under the 2002 Citizenship Law

PHASES OF ACQUISITION OF CITIZENSHIP	REQUIREMENTS
1. Temporary Residency Permit	Applied for within sixty days and subject to government quotas
2. Residency Permit	Applied for after one year and no less than six months before expiration of temporary residency permit; valid for five years and subject to renewal
3. Citizenship	Required: proof of five years of uninterrupted residency with residency permit, source of income; renounce previous citizenship and proficiency in Russian
4. Exemptions	Born in Russia Elderly parents High achievements

money to ensure a decent life for their own pensioners."[13] He added that the "Law on Citizenship and the Regulations on Foreign Citizens has been passed in order to create the basis for a normal policy in that field."[14]

As part of Putin's attempt to create a normal citizenship, the fields of citizenship and migration has undergone a process of conceptual securitization—when civilian spheres of life are seen as being under threat and need to be controlled and protected by the state.[15] This was linked with Putin's strengthening of the state apparatus that he called "vertical of power" (*vertikal' vlasti*). These themes were reflected in debates in the Duma and the Federation Council. A pro-Putin member of the Duma, Valerii Grebennikov, stated that "[the 1991 citizenship law] turned Russia into a passageway, into some sort of a cheap hotel where homeless and criminals can arrive absolutely freely and get a Russian Citizenship."[16] A Federation Council member said: "The complication of the procedure of obtaining a Russian citizenship is precisely the establishment of order in the country. Today [acquisition of citizenship] is a very easy procedure, from all ends [of the world] people enter the country. Even Wahhabis."[17] Illegal migrants, who were effectively everyone who could not register for a propiska, were portrayed as dangerous elements who could not be part of the in-group and posed a threat to Russia's national security.[18]

This law was severely criticized by professional authorities and scholars who were familiar with the complexities of citizenship and migration in Russia. First, it was pointed out that proponents of the law overlooked the difficult tasks that Russia faced in the 1990s and the complex situation with Russian and Russian speakers in the former Soviet states. In 2002, former minister Tishkov, who in his ministerial career addressed the unmixing of postimperial Soviet populations, warned that "the new Citizenship Law . . . , would not fix, but would aggravate some of the mistakes and problems that arose from the collapse of the Soviet Union."[19] The mistakes that Tishkov had in mind were Yeltsin's government's inability to stick to an agreed deadline for applications for citizenship and to solve the heinous problem of registration (propiska), which barred millions of people from accessing their rights.[20]

Second, the economic logic of the law, raised by Putin, was also questioned. A globalized neoliberal economy required the movement of people across borders and flexible labor conditions, specifically in states that experienced demographic decline, like Russia. Professional forecasts suggested that immigration was necessary for Russia's economic performance in the global market economy.[21] Russia's population was steadily aging and shrinking, with mortality rates particularly high among working-age males. Between 1993 and 2000, Russia's population decreased from 148.6 to 146.6 million people and by 2002 to 145.5 million people.[22] These figures would have been much worse if not for migration. Russian statistics consistently showed that migration compensated for high natural decline in working age population.[23] Hence, the full scale of natural decline was not showing in official figures due to compensation by migration.[24] Russia's labor shortages were indeed a core issue for a country that was intent on joining the globalized world. Even without demographic decline, stopping migration in the new and more flexible economic system by complicating citizenship registration seemed like a course of policy that was unlikely to work. But in the Russian case, the forecast seemed even bleaker.

Last, this law seemed preposterous in a system where for years bureaucratic practices had overridden federal legislation. This was an important point noted by Osipov. From a legal-enforcement point of view, it was unclear how the 2002 law would bring order into the legal gray zone of citizenship implementation. Already in the 1990s many people were unable to fulfill the complex set of requirements and satisfy corrupt authorities to legally register in Russia. From 2000 they faced an even more draconian set of requirements, which they were again unable to satisfy.[25] They continued to live in Russia unregistered but were now formally labeled illegal migrants.[26] Hence, it was unclear how the 2002 law would change this situation.

In his comments from 2002, Putin showed that he was aware of the economic need for migrants in neoliberal globalized countries. He noted that he did not want to halt migration: "In general, attracting migrants . . . is necessary and good for Russia, just like it is for other industrialized countries."[27] Putin and proponents underlined that their aim was to control migration in line with EU and UN standards.[28] In a way they were correct. The restrictions in the 2002 law were similar to Ayelet Shachar's findings in developed countries that restrict migration to protect their resources.[29] Yet, even with restrictions in place, migration posed a challenge for Western countries, and migration control would have been even harder for Russia, which had parts of the ingroup abroad and faced sharp population decline and a corrupt bureaucracy. Nonetheless, Putin's inclination for control and stability made the 2002 law his chosen course of action. With these apparent shortcomings in the 2002 law, the next years would reveal its ineffectiveness in normalizing and stabilizing the situation and its impact on Russia's citizenship.

Foreigners in Their Own Country: Implementation of the 2002 Law

In the aftermath of the 2002 law, acquiring Russian citizenship indeed became far more difficult, yet not necessarily more normal. Excluding millions of former Soviet citizens who did not possess a permanent registration (propiska) or had not been born on the territory of the RSFSR from the Russian citizenry did not make citizenship feel stable or secure. This revealed the harsh truth about the law—many of the people who were described as dangerous criminals and Wahhabis were in fact ethnic Russians and Russian speakers who had been residing in Russia for years and whose only crime was that they had temporary registration. Ignoring the consequences of the collapse of the Soviet Union, when people moved to Russia in large numbers as part of the postimperial unmixing of people, the complex bureaucratic practices that emerged in Russia and, very importantly, the consequences of late modernity did not help in consolidating a stable Russian citizenship.

Examples of such people, who were suddenly labeled illegal, began surfacing almost immediately after the passage of the 2002 law. Nearly every week, newspapers brought to the public's attention ridiculous and Kafkaesque situations in which normative people—who were not considered strangers—found themselves. Each story was even more ridiculous than the previous one. One such example came from the Republic of Udmurtia, of the Volga Federal District, in the Urals. There, one Russian person, ironically with the surname Russkikh, found himself a foreigner in his own country.

In April 2002, Fedor Russkikh, born and raised in Udmurtia, who held a Soviet passport (with a permanent registration stamp) and was a retired officer of the regional Ministry of the Interior, approached the authorities in his native region to exchange his Soviet passport for a Russian one.[30] Russkikh's request was denied. The reason for the denial was lack of a propiska on February 6, 1992.[31] Indeed, between 1990 and March 1992, he was on a waiting list for housing. In March 1992 he got a flat, together with a permanent registration, and hence his permanent registration (propiska) was stamped in March 1992—a month after the cutoff date. Now he was directed to the tiresome procedure of acquiring Russian citizenship, which would have taken a decade.

Shocked by this turn of events, Russkikh appealed to the court and went all the way up to the regional Supreme Court, where his appeal was denied. In the midst of his bureaucratic torment, Russkikh wrote a complaint letter to the Ministry of the Interior pointing to the travesty of his being denied a passport. He noted that over the years his passport had been reviewed by the authorities (for updates) without any complaint and that he worked in the past in the Ministry of the Interior and received a pension for his service. In response to the letter, his pension was also taken away (since he was not a citizen).[32] Finally, the prosecutor of the Udmurtia Republic came to Russkikh's assistance and helped to overrule the decision, issued him a passport, and reinstated his pension.[33] Russkikh's experience was an extreme case of legal and bureaucratic blindness, but there were many similar cases of Russians who fell victim to this law.

In 2003 Putin admitted that the 2002 law had failed. Similar to how legislative failures were framed in the 1990s, he focused on the fact that the 2002 law was unable to address the needs of Russians and Russian speakers and the consequences of the collapse of the Soviet Union. He stated, "Over a million people who came to Russia after the collapse of the Soviet Union and since the new law on citizenship was passed have found themselves in an extremely difficult situation."[34] He explained that "the laws passed last year were designed to bring order to migration flows and make them transparent. What we have ended up with . . . creates serious problems for a large number of people. I consider it our duty to fix this situation."[35]

Less than a year and a half after the 2002 law was passed, it was amended to create provisions for former Soviet citizens. It allowed former Soviet citizens who were permanently registered in Russia on July 1, 2002, to apply for citizenship in a fast procedure until January 2006.[36] It also included provisional criteria for a simplified procedure for former Soviet citizens who had graduated from higher education institutions in the Russia, Second World War veterans, and former Soviet citizens who had served in the Russian Armed Forces and security agencies.[37] In December 2005 the deadline for applications in the fast procedure was extended until January 1, 2008.

These amendments again did not acknowledge the changing ways of life in Russia, which were not only connected to the collapse of the Soviet Union and were not solely related to the place of Russians and Russian speakers. The 2003–2005 amendments ignored the most crucial factor of life in Russia—for over a decade, for good or for bad, Russians had been fending for themselves without assistance from the state. People were relocating, traveling, and working without state-planned interventions. It is true that for many this experience was not pleasant: extreme poverty, crime, and feelings of loss of identity were all part of post-Soviet life. But this created certain dynamics that could not be overturned with a stroke of a pen or a strict new citizenship law. The sort of order that Putin envisaged and promised the Russian public was unachievable in globalized free-market circumstances. It was especially unlikely in Russia, where bureaucratic practices created a particularly poignant and specifically Russian fragmentation of the institution of citizenship in the form of that burgeoning legal gray zone, in which the criminalization of innocents, denial of rights, bribery, and extortion were widespread. Ignoring these realities and fixing provisions only for Russians and Russian-speakers was unlikely to yield a better citizenship policy for Russia.

Hence, even after the amendments came into force, the situation was not normalized. In a 2006 interview, Russia's leading ethnographer and former minister, Tishkov, minced no words in attacking the government for the situation that emerged. He said:

> Not migrants, but mindless laws pose a threat to Russia's national security. Since 1991, probably about 10 million migrants arrived in our country, mainly from the former Soviet republics. Of these, 90% are illegal . . . not because they hide, but because they cannot register. I personally tried to help several scientists from Uzbekistan . . . to register in Moscow. It did not work out, there were too many artificial obstacles. Our laws make people illegal, driven underground. In 2002, the State Duma adopted a harmful law on citizenship. . . . If we do not attract migrants from the former Union now, then we will have to import Ethiopians. . . . All countries, which have achieved technical development . . . have not been [able to succeed] without migrants.[38]

In 2006 Tishkov described a grim situation—the 2002 law injured former Soviet citizens in Russia and adversely affected its future economic prospects. According to his account, the 2003 amendments did not assist former Soviet citizens, many of whom were Russians and Russian speakers, in legalizing their status in Russia, and countless people were being driven underground. Tishkov's own testimony was fantastical, as he, the architect of Russia's first citizenship law, had been unsuccessful in helping his colleagues to register. This was precisely what Osipov was indicating—in Russia, stricter legislation only reinforced people's inability to lead a legal way of life, and by doing so it aggravated and expanded the legal gray zone. But Tishkov also pointed to other factors that the 2003 amendments did not address at all—in the globalized world, Russia had a growing need for migrants, and migrants from former Soviet countries might be the best option for Russia's economy.

This turned the spotlight on a crucial economic factor that had been overlooked in the 1990s but by the mid-2000s was starting to be discussed. A *Novaya Gazeta* article from 2008 described the post-2002 law migration situation: "Migrants stay in Russia because of jobs. . . . Migrants from the CIS enter Russia legally, visa free, and then—boom, they find themselves in a trap. No [work permit] quotas, and an 'illegal [migrant]' is created. [To law enforcement:] Please, use [them]."[39] Migration is an integral part of a globalized free-market economy, and migrants would keep coming into Russia as long as the economic situation would allow them to. If Russia wanted to remain part of the globalized free-market economy, migration could not be stopped by strict controls and the strict legislation of the 2000s only increased illegal behavior, abuse, and profiteering.[40]

The Compatriots' Resettlement Program (2006)

Putin was well aware of the ideas that Tishkov had put forward and the need for more flexible citizenship legislation. As early as 2002 he noted that an "influx of compatriots from abroad [is needed], especially for tackling economic issues."[41] Eventually, his government had to seek a balance between several needs. One was the desire to uphold the image of controlled migration and stable citizenry. Another was the position of Russians and Russian speakers from former Soviet republics. Last, and even more challenging, Russia had to deal with the need for the free movement of population in the globalized market economy, where Russia wanted to compete as a global power with resurgent energy.

In 2006–2008 Putin chose to relieve some of the tensions arising from these conflicting needs by devising a program that would kill two birds with one stone.[42] The State Program for Assistance of Voluntary Resettlement to the Russian Federation of Compatriots Residing Abroad (O merakh po okazaniyu sodeystviya dobrovol'nomu pereseleniyu v Rossiyskuyu Federatsiyu sootechestvennikov, prozhivayushchikh za rubezhom, known as the Compatriots' Resettlement Program) was intended to create the controlled and managed immigration of Russians and Russian speakers, to assist Russia in its demographic and economic challenges. Or as it was officially put: the Compatriots' Resettlement Program's aim was "to unite the potential of compatriots residing abroad with the developmental needs of Russia's regions" and to "stabilize the size of the population, . . . firstly on territories which are of strategic importance to Russia."[43] The number of compatriots who were expected to resettle in Russia by 2015 was 300,000.[44] The program seemed like a commendable effort to make citizenship more accessible to Russians and Russian speakers. But it had provisions that ignored the late modern circumstances of migration and favored control over flexibility. These aspects complicated the execution of the program.

On the one hand, the program was welcoming, with very inclusive eligibility criteria. Prospective participants had to be eighteen or older, able to work, with professional qualifications, work experience, and knowledge of the Russian language to an extent that would allow them to assimilate into society; they had to meet the conditions set for acquiring a residency permit (*vid na zhitel'stvo*), in case it was required.⁴⁵ Although the program aimed to attract Russians and Russians speakers, an outright ethnic criterion was not included in the eligibility clauses. Alexander Zhuravsky and Olga Vykhovanets, both officials from the Federal Migration Service (FMS), noted that including an ethnic criterion in the eligibility clauses would have been deemed in Russia as unacceptable and would have generated political outrage.⁴⁶ Instead, the program took a more lenient approach and referred to the legal provisions laid out in the 1999 Compatriots Law and its definition of compatriots as persons of common originality. Moreover, the program's guidelines emphasized the requirement of knowledge of the Russian language and on attracting migrants who would be "easily integrated . . . with no xenophobic sentiment fueled in society."⁴⁷ It thus opened Russia's doors to people of Slavic origin and from Russified minorities.

Prospective applicants in the Compatriots' Resettlement Program were promised Russian citizenship under a simplified procedure that conferred far-reaching rights. In 2008, article 14 of the 2002 citizenship law was amended to allow participants in the program waivers from time of residency in Russia, proof of legal means of subsistence, and proof of knowledge of the Russian language. (They were expected to speak Russian.)⁴⁸ Compatriots and members of their families were not subject to restrictive government quotas for immigration, which should have made their access to citizenship almost automatic.⁴⁹ Compatriots' social rights were granted from the moment they arrived in Russia: they were allowed to work and acquire professional education; they were granted access to medical care and social services; their children had the right to an education.⁵⁰ They were exempt from customs taxes on their belongings, entitled to compensation for money spent on application for the program and for travel expenses, and given unemployment benefits for six months and a one-time allowance of 40,000 rubles for participants who would move to certain regions.⁵¹

At the same time, the Russian government placed strict conditions on prospective participants to increase control over the process and ignored the new late modern circumstances. It also did not account for the specifically Russian complications of illegal bureaucratic practices. The program divided the regions participating in the program into three categories—designated A, B, and C—according to the needs of each region. Regions most in need of immigration were designated as A, and those that needed immigration the least were designated as C.⁵² Areas A were mainly border regions, such as Kamchatski Krai and Kaliningradskaya Oblast, where the population was shrinking.⁵³ Areas B were regions with labor shortages, such as Novosibirskaya Oblast, and areas C were economically stable areas, such as Novgorodskaya Oblast.⁵⁴ Some regions were subdivided internally, and more attractive areas within them designated as C, while other areas were designated as B or A.[55] Some very attractive destinations, like Moscow, did not participate in the program. Assistance to prospective immigrants, such as unemployment benefits and the one-time allowance, was conditioned on relocation to strategic areas designated as A and B.[56] Moreover, at the initial stages of the program, resettlement was contingent on finding a job in the designated area prior to relocation.

The government did not consider the late modern circumstances where people relocate freely to destinations offering jobs and economic prospects. This meant that migrating via the program made no sense as migrants generally wished to move to more developed western parts of Russia. Most areas designated by the program were the remote, border, and eastern regions, which did not have well-paying jobs and infrastructure. In this situation, the only advantage for migrating with the Compatriots' Resettlement Program was the prospects of easier access to citizenship. But even that was not guaranteed.

The administrative procedures of application to the program ignored the bureaucratic practices that made acquisition of citizenship in Russia extremely complex. The procedures were so complex that even if they did not prevent prospective applicants from applying, applicants were unlikely to receive citizenship. Participants had to apply at the Russian consulate or to representatives of the FMS in their country of residence.[57] If the application was successful, the prospective participant was contacted and asked to apply for a certificate of participation in the program. If no complications arose, the certificate would be granted within sixty days and was valid for three years.[58] The participant was expected to relocate to Russia independently. Upon arriving in Russia, compatriots were expected to immediately apply for a temporary residency, and their certificate had to be stamped by the FMS in their place of residence.[59] Applications for citizenship under a simplified procedure had to be made afterward. Compensations and the one-time allowance were also applied for after arriving in Russia, and in accordance with the designation of the place of residence (A, B, or C).[60] These regulations were hard to follow and were likely to be complicated by illegal bureaucratic practices, such as bribes, and thus dimmed the prospects for fast-tracked citizenship. These procedures favored control over flexibility and complicated successful absorption.

Despite initial interest, the number of people that the program attracted was very small. In 2008–2010 only 28,086 people resettled in Russia through the Compatriots' Resettlement Program.[61] With concentrated efforts and some reforms, by the end of the seven years of the program, in 2014, the number of participants had reached 150,000 (half of the target number).[62] As noted by the Russian sociologist Olga Zevelva, of those who participated in the program, only 58 percent received Russian citizenship, while in similar programs in Kazakhstan and Germany, 76 percent and 100 percent of participants received citizenship, respectively.[63] In Russia, unlike in other countries, even for those who managed to fulfil the conditions, the bureaucracy blocked the way to citizenship. For instance, the Russian NGO Civil Assistance Committee revealed that many participants in the Compatriots' Resettlement Program were often denied citizenship due to lack of a permanent registration and were pushed to the legal gray zone.[64] They gave the example of Dmitry, a young ethnic Russian from Lithuania, who in 2006 participated in the Compatriots' Resettlement Program yet was unable to acquire citizenship because he could not arrange a permanent registration for himself.[65] These were negative, if unsurprising, results.

Lessons (Not) Learned from the Compatriots' Resettlement Program

The failure of the Compatriots' Resettlement Program caused public frustration in Russia. One of Russia's top television hosts, Vladimir Solovyov, whose shows will be discussed in later chapters, lashed out in 2011 on his television show: "Why did only 26,000 people come [to Russia] in the Compatriots' Resettlement Program? Why are the compatriots who are coming the badly Russian-speaking compatriots?"[66] Irina Ilina, a journalist, herself an immigrant from Uzbekistan, wrote that Russia's immigration policy was that of a small and overpopulated country, while in fact it was a large and underpopulated one.[67] This frustration was understandable. Why was a country with a readily available pool of appropriate candidates for immigration unable to take advantage of this much-needed human resource?

While the current study claims that the program's failure was due to the government's disregard of global and local circumstances, other analyses offered different explanations. Scholars like Zevelova and Shevel argued that the vague conceptual framework of the program—being neither a typical repatriation program nor a labor import scheme—impeded its success.[68] They claimed that the definition of compatriots was too vague and the program did not contain an ethnic clause, as was the case elsewhere, in Germany, Kazakhstan, and Israel. Nor was the program a labor import enterprise like in Western countries, including the United States, Canada, New Zealand, and lately Germany and France, which attracted highly qualified professionals.[69] The government officials Zhuravsky and Vykhovanets noted that Russia's situation was unique and it "could not borrow from the repatriation experience of mono-ethnic states such as Germany . . . or even Kazakhstan since Russia is a multi-ethnic state."[70] They pinned the failure of the program on insufficient funds allotted for successful absorption of the participants in the labor market.[71]

Yet the testimonies of those who took part in the Compatriots' Resettlement Program support the argument of this chapter, that the real shortcomings were in the government's inability to create a migratory framework appropriate for the globalized era in which it was operating. Roman Romanovsky, a young journalist from Kaliningradskaya Oblast, a Russian enclave on the Baltic shore, investigated the local Compatriots' Resettlement Program in his region. He found that one of the results of the division of regions into categories A, B, and C was that about a third of the participants chose to relocate to the Kaliningradskaya Oblast. Romanovsky pointed out that even in Kaliningrad, which was regarded as an attractive destination for resettlement, by 2011 only 4,000 people had arrived out of the 10,000 expected participants.[72]

Romanovsky found that lack of employment and housing in the regions designated for the resettlement of compatriots became the most obvious and dire reason impeding successful relocation. Several resettled participants from the Caucasus and Central Asia testified that they were unable to find suitable employment that would have allowed them to rent or buy an apartment, while affordable housing was not available.[73] In Kaliningrad, participants who were unable to afford housing could stay for two years at a resettlement center built by the regional authorities. The conditions in the facility were poor, with communal bathrooms and kitchens. A representative of the local authorities testified that it was the only such center in the entire country, meaning that in other regions there was absolutely no assistance with housing.[74] Hence, the government constructed a program that was meant to manage and control migration and make it a state-sanctioned endeavor but lacked the capacity to help the people involved.

Directing people to move to less developed, peripheral regions of the country might serve a purpose in an authoritarian centralized state like the Soviet Union, but in the globalized free market economy, such a program was not feasible. For example, in the Soviet Virgin Lands Campaign people were also encouraged to move to remote underpopulated regions in Central Asia, while the Soviet state guaranteed employment, housing, and social services for its participants. In the post-Soviet Compatriots' Resettlement Program, such arrangements could not be made, because the state had ceased to order life as it used to. Yet the restrictions, reminiscent of the Soviet approach, remained in place. A successful resettled family, who emigrated from Latvia, reaffirmed this problem, as they shared their feelings that the program allocated jobs to people in an arbitrary way, which reminded them of a Soviet approach to division of labor.[75] The program's rigid approach toward relocation and the strict administrative procedures not only prevented people from participating but also reduced the resettlement prospects of those who chose to resettle in Russia. In the free market context, the failure of the program was not conceptual vagueness or lack of funds but rather that it did not allow people to make relocation decisions according to their best prospects for a successful absorption.

The Compatriots' Resettlement Program fell victim to the same bureaucratic practices that ignored the consequences of late modernity and complicated legal immigration in the 1990s, and in the 2000s, such practices were backed by the federal center. In the 1990s, bureaucratic practices reflected the clash of interests between federal organs and local law enforcement elites, which acted in unlawful ways to continuously exercise population movement control through the enforcement of propiska. This complicated the ongoing processes of a society in flux, which was dealing with the consequences of the postimperial unmixing of people, as well as with the new nature of a free and globalized migration space. In the 2000s, as visible in the 2002 citizenship law and the Compatriots' Resettlement Program, the federal center realigned itself with the controlling nature of the bureaucratic practices of the 1990s.

In a way, in the 2000s the Russian state retreated to its traditional role expressed in the popular Russian saying that the strictness of Russian laws was mitigated by the nonmandatory nature of their implementation.[76] Osipov observed that the Russian state was "traditionally trying to manage all spheres of social life" and that "the system takes upon itself an impracticable volume of work and introduces regulations which are objectively unfeasible."[77] This led to nominal laws that had no real bearing on the consequent relations in society, while enforcement was selective and corrupt.[78] These controlling tendencies clashed with the changes in the migration space and economic liberalization and undermined the center's ability to govern effectively. As the government was moving away from the failed Compatriots' Resettlement Program, the lessons from its shortcomings were not learned, and the same controlling tendencies continued.

Carriers of Russian Language: Ukraine and Crimea

In March 2014, an amendment to the 2002 citizenship law gave hope that the government would finally insert some flexibility into citizenship legislation.

The proposed amendment offered a simplified procedure to citizenship for those who were acknowledged as native Russian speakers (*nositeli russkogo yazyka*). The timing of this amendment (just a week before the annexation of Crimea) and the changes it underwent during debate in the State Duma, however, revealed that it was never meant to make citizenship legislation more flexible. The amendment was put together hastily by the FMS by order of President Putin and presented to the Duma on March 11, 2014—a week before Russia annexed Crimea on March 18, 2014.[79] The eligibility proposed in the amendment pertained to people who resided in Russia or in territories that were part of the Russian Empire or the Soviet Union and could prove the use of the Russian language in their household and in their cultural life. Such proof should have been demonstrated in an interview with a representative of the FMS. Native Russian speakers were exempted from the residency requirement and the Russian language test, required in the 2002 law. They were still required to renounce their foreign citizenship.

The debate around this amendment revealed the fault lines along which thinking on migration and citizenship in Russia was formed. On the one hand, civil society activists, who wished to help people in the legal gray zone, welcomed the amendment. Members of the Civil Assistance Committee testified that in 2014, there were thousands of people who had resided in Russia since the 1990s who were denied citizenship due to the lack of a propiska.[80] On the other hand, right-wing politicians opposed the amendment due to fears of the uncontrolled migration of undesirable groups. The main resistance came from the Just Russia faction in the Duma. Mikhail Eme'lyanov, from this faction, warned that the amendment threatened Russian national security, as it would allow the legalization of illegal migrants who would be able to vote in elections while they remained loyal to their native countries.[81] Oleg Nilov, also from Just Russia, agreed with the need to give preference to Russians and Russian speakers abroad but warned of the risk that the "10–15 million migrants who today complicate the lives of our native people" would try to use these provisions to obtain citizenship.[82] Yet this amendment was never meant to help Russians and Russian speakers in the gray zone; nor could a minority faction in the Duma have challenged this presidential draft law.

The government had its own political designs for this legislation. During debate concerning the legislation in the Duma, the FMS added a territorial clause to the amendment, revealing the real intention behind it—to add populations in annexed territories to the citizenry. The territorial clause limited the application for the simplified procedure to those whose ancestors lived on the territory of the former union republics or the Russian Empire, within the current borders of the Russian Federation.[83] This meant that Russian native speakers had to live on historic Russian territories, which were recognized as part of the Russian Federation, to be eligible for a Russian passport. Indeed, the Russian media confirmed that this amendment was linked with the crisis in East Ukraine and the annexation of Crimea.[84] As if no lessons had been learned from the shortcomings of the Compatriots' Resettlement Program, Russian officials proposed that new immigrants from Ukraine would populate the Russian Far East and Siberia.[85] Hence, this amendment was not an attempt to ease citizenship legislation and allow easier legal routes to Russian citizenship but a political move to ease the quick incorporation of Crimea and the admission of Ukrainian citizens. But even in Crimea, where the Russian government tried to be as inclusive as possible and moved swiftly to issue citizenship, strict bureaucratic practices inhibited the smooth operation of issuing passports.

The Annexation of Crimea (2014)

The annexation of Crimea brought the issue of citizenship to the fore. As noted in the first part of this chapter, many residents of Crimea had illegally obtained Russian citizenship in the 1990s. In the aftermath of the referendum on joining Russia, Russia and the Republic of Crimea signed an agreement that accepted Crimea and the city of Sevastopol into the Russian Federation.[86] Article 5 in the agreement stated that Ukrainian citizens and stateless persons permanently residing on the territory of Crimea were recognized as citizens of Russia.[87] Those who did not wish to acquire a Russian passport were given one month to notify the authorities of their decision.[88]

The right of Crimean residents to a Russian passport seemed straightforward, and in December 2014, the head of the Crimean Federal Migration Services, Pyotr Yarosh, declared that the issuance of passports had been completed—1.56 million Crimeans had received Russian passports.[89] But things were more complicated. The agreement between Russia and Crimea made acquisition of Russian citizenship contingent on permanent residency in Crimea at the time it came into force. This created complications for prospective citizens. As a result, by May 2015 there were still about 100,000 people in Crimea who were unable to acquire Russian citizenship since they had failed to register permanently in Crimea prior to the coming into force of the agreement.[90]

The Russian authorities claimed that many of those who could not present a permanent residency were refugees from East Ukraine who had fled the atrocities. According to the Crimean ombudswoman, Crimea had received about 200,000 refugees from mainland Ukraine.[91] In the Crimean case, the

Russian authorities were more lenient than in mainland Russia. Illegal residents of Crimea could prove residency if they presented the court with proof that they lived in Crimea, such as lease agreements, bills, or doctor's notes. After a favorable decision by the court, the proof had to be presented to the FMS for confirmation and issuance of a passport.[92] But this path to citizenship was very costly, complicating the lives of refugees fleeing the war in East Ukraine. This complication pushed many into an undetermined legal status and introduced the Russian legal gray zone into Crimea. Hence, despite the public campaign to paint the annexation of Crimea as an act to reinforce normality and concern for the security of Russians and Russian speakers, the situation in Crimea in fact featured a much more complex reality with multiple obstacles to citizenship.

Dual Citizenship Control and the Isolation of Russia

A further attempt to control citizenship took place in August 2014, when the Duma approved a law that required Russians to declare the possession of additional citizenships. Until 2014 Putin's government only disallowed dual citizenship to those who acquired Russian citizenship through the naturalization process. But those who acquired citizenship in the 1990s or by birthright were free to live in one of the most common late modern citizenship constellations—dual citizenship—and to enjoy rights granted by two or more states. Since 2014 these Russians could no longer enjoy this situation away from the watchful eye of an increasingly isolationist Russian regime.

The legislation of the law was curious and sent an alarming message to those who held dual citizenship. Originally, it was put forward by the head of the Constitutional Committee in the Federation Council (Russia's upper house), Andrei Klishas.[93] Quickly the draft law was taken over by the controversial State Duma member Andrei Lugovoi, who, according to the British authorities, had assassinated the former Russian intelligence officer Alexander Litvinenko in London in 2006 with radioactive poison.[94] The man who showed the world that Russia's traitors would be found and killed was now the face of legislation that would reveal the alleged double allegiances of certain Russian citizens. Although the law did not ban dual citizenship and the punishment for concealing it was a fine and community work, the message was clear—in the aftermath of Crimea, multiple belongings were viewed with suspicion.[95]

This was a further retrenchment from late modern trends, but it could only go so far. Globalization was and still is a major force to be reckoned with, especially since Putin was not withdrawing Russia from the global trade system and was not closing its borders. In the late 2010s, amid Russia's economic slowdown, alarm bells were ringing about Russia's demography. In this period, the Russian population continued to decline, but Russia's restrictive policies and its economic downturn made it less attractive to labor migrants.[96] In 2020, some restrictions were retracted by the government, and dual citizenship was allowed for those who chose to naturalize in an attempt to encourage migration.[97] These steps, however, are unlikely to reverse Russia's downward population trends, especially due to the expected human and economic costs of the coronavirus pandemic. This may cause a full-scale demographic crisis in Russia in the coming years. While some of the factors contributing to this grim scenario were unforeseen, the Russian government's long record of denying the new flexible nature of citizenship and migration in late modernity placed Russia in a disadvantageous position to address its demographic challenges.

Economic Opportunities and Citizenship in Russia

One of the most profound ways in which citizenship remained less strictly defined and more amorphous as a social institution was in the intersection between economic opportunities, citizenship policy implementation, and belonging. In Russia, as in many other places in the late modern globalized world, money could buy citizenship as well as belonging. Despite Russia's growing isolation and preference for migration control in the 2010s, money could still circumvent many restrictions.

A satirical sketch of the connection between money, citizenship, and belonging was painted by the Russian pop singer Natali and actor-rapper MC Doni (Doni Islamov). Natali and MC Doni's duet depicted a post-Soviet immigrant Cinderella story of sorts. The camera showed laborers of Caucasian or Central Asian appearance at a construction site. One of them, played by MC Doni—a big, bold, bearded non-Slavic laborer—sang: "I worked at a construction site, went on the Metro / No registration, just lucky / I wanted to rise up." As MC Doni walked the streets of Moscow, he suddenly found a mysterious credit card with a black star, which belonged to a rich man, played by the famous Russian rapper Timati (Timur Yanusov).[98] MC Doni's fortunes instantly changed. He sang: "Once I changed the route / Good-bye Ravshan, farewell Dzhamshut[99] / Hello Moscow, Blackstar, I'm here / I have a beard and I am 'in.'" Natali—a blond, blue-eyed Slavic pop queen—sang back to him, "You're so handsome with a beard . . . I dream of a duet."[100] MC Doni changed his life for the better and was accepted immediately when he gained a fortune. In the globalized world, having a fortune blurred the traditional concepts of citizenship and belonging—if you have money, you are "in" (regardless of one's physical traits, which in other circumstances could play against one's inclusion).

In Russia, having or not having money could change your position vis-à-vis citizenship legislation in two ways. First, since corruption was rife and implementation of citizenship regulations was selective, bribing the relevant authorities could resolve many problems and allowed the purchase of citizenship altogether. A simple small bribe to a policeman on the street might give a one-time waiver to those who lacked registration. A more substantial sum could smooth out certain problems with applications. Bribing more senior authorities could also resolve situations in which prospective applicants simply had not complied with the eligibility criteria and basically allowed the purchase of citizenship. Bribes were often expected, even when the applicants for citizenship had complied with the legislation. Having money determined whether one could or could not reside legally in Russia and acquire citizenship.

Being poor would have condemned a person to the gray zone and almost surely prevented them from acquiring citizenship. The head of the Civil Assistance Committee gave the example of Nina and Alexandra Kuznetzov, a mother and daughter who moved to Russia from Tajikistan in 1992.[101] In the absence of funds or family to support them, they were unable to register in the early 1990s. Instead, they had to focus on their financial survival and could not deal with legalizing their status or naturalizing. Those sorts of people—who, according to the NGO's records, numbered in the tens of thousands—had no real chance of being accepted into the citizenry, especially once the stricter 2002 law was in place. They remain for decades in an illegal status.[102] The journalists who reported the story emphasized that Nina and Alexandra were "from the former Soviet Union and [spoke] Russian freely," underlining that people like them were considered part of the Russian national in-group, and their exclusion due to financial hardship was unjust.[103]

Second, having money or powerful connections in Russia allowed prospective applicants to completely avoid the Kafkaesque Russian citizenship legislation and implementation policies. The most famous and celebrated example was that of the French actor Gerard Depardieu, who in 2013 found economic refuge in Russia. In late 2012 Depardieu got into a publicized conflict with the French authorities and with the former president Francoise Holland over a planned increase in taxes for the very rich. He requested to relinquish his French citizenship and applied for a Belgian passport. In the absence of a reply from the Belgian authorities, Depardieu was unable to renounce his French passport, as the French legal code did not allow the termination of French citizenship if a person did not hold another citizenship.[104]

On January 3, 2013, Putin signed a decree granting Depardieu Russian citizenship.[105] The Kremlin's spokesman, Dmitri Peskov, cited Depardieu's contribution to the Russian culture when he played Rasputin in a film in 2011 as a pretext for Putin's decision. Depardieu's choice of a new country was not due to his identification with Russia, although he did say, "I love your country, Russia—its people, its history, its writers."[106] It was Russia's flat 13 percent income tax that attracted Depardieu to acquiring Russian citizenship. The Russian authorities used Depardieu's immigration to Russia for publicity purposes to show Russia as an attractive immigration destination for the rich and famous.

Depardieu's case demonstrated that while the government favored strict citizenship policy as a means to create a managed and secured citizenry, economic means could overpower any such policy. In Russia, as in other parts of the globalized world, immigration and citizenship legislation did not apply in the same way to those with fame and fortune. In this context, money was a factor that fragmented the institution of citizenship—it could quickly overturn someone's legal status, allowing them political and economic rights, without denoting deeper identification with the state. The ethnic factor, which played an important part in the branding of Central Asian laborers as illegal and unwanted, was unlikely to apply to wealthy and better-connected businessmen from the same countries.

Russia's rich also acquired dual citizenships from European countries. While Lugovoi was promoting the murky law that required Russians to report their dual citizenship, the US State Department revealed that Gennady Timchenko, a close associate of Putin, held several passports. In addition to having Russian citizenship, he held Finnish and Armenian (his place of birth) passports, while his family resided in Switzerland.[107] MC Doni was right to fantasize that fortune would rid one of any legal problems or difficulties with acceptance and belonging. In reality, the imaginary Uzbek-laborer-turned-oligarch from the pop music clip was likely to acquire acceptance not only in Russia but in other attractive destinations of the globalized late modern world.

A book by the US-based journalist Atossa Araxia Abrahamian, *The Cosmopolites: The Coming of the Global Citizen*, sketched some features of the evolving relationship between money, globalization, and citizenship. She noted that in the globalized late modern world, "like ships flying flags of convenience, more people carry nationalities of convenience, and a growing number of countries have stepped up to accommodate them."[108] Essentially, she showed that an increasing number of people, specifically a segment of the financial elites, were engaging in the purchase of citizenships. In this context, the definition of citizenship as a social institution that grants social, economic, and political rights by a certain state and denotes belonging seems less relevant. This is not to say that having money erases all administrative boundaries. Even the very rich would have to put much time and effort into obtaining the citizenship of a well-respected Western country. Yet, in the globalized world, in Russia, as elsewhere, economic status allowed much flexibility regarding travel, relocation, and acceptance. In August 2013 Depardieu received an honorary Belgian citizenship. When asked whether he feels French, Russian, or Belgian, he replied, "I am a free man."[109]

Russian Citizenship in the Global World

In the 2000s Putin tried to normalize the devolved situation around citizenship by introducing a new strict regulation, in line with stern migration controls that had been enacted in other globalized counties that were trying to manage increased migration. The 2002 citizenship law removed almost all favorable causes for former Soviet citizens and branded all those living in the legal gray zone as illegal migrants. But Putin could not remove Russia from the two concurrent trends that shaped its realities—the consequences of the collapse of the Soviet empire and the globalized late modern context. Both clashed with his legislation and inhibited its ability to stabilize citizenship.

The strict criteria of the 2002 law clashed with the postimperial post-Soviet reality where Russians and Russians speakers moved to Russia in the 1990s in large numbers, and many were still interested in joining them. It revealed that the eligibility criteria in the 1991 law were not ideological but were responding to the real needs of Russians and Russian speakers abroad. These criteria were meant to allow these people, commonly regarded as part of the Russian national in-group, to join the new citizenry. In the aftermath of the 2002 law's entry into force, it was revealed that labeling these people as illegal migrants did not improve the migration situation in Russia. The newspapers were filled with stories of normative Russians and Russian-speaking people who were denied access to citizenship. It became clear that the rights of Russians and Russian speakers who had already moved to Russia and even those who remained abroad could not be disregarded.

Russians also discovered the economic need for migration. Even extreme critics of migration accepted that migration was necessary and that not only ethnic Russians were welcome in Russia but also Russified individuals (Russian speakers). For instance, in 2013 Zhirinovsky made the following comments: "I walked along the boulevard. There was a young couple of, probably, Uzbeks. A female, male and a child. They were probably . . . from the intelligentsia. They smiled, they greeted me. They were happy."[110] Zhirinovsky's comments underlined the general sense that belonging to the Russian in-group was not contingent only on one's ethnicity but also on knowledge of the Russian language and culture and being able to comply with social norms. The 2003 amendment to the 2002 law and the Compatriots' Resettlement Program were meant to attract these people who were welcome and needed in Russia.

But in late modernity, as people were moving according to their own calculations and best economic prospects, the state could not choose which migrants it wanted to attract. Those migrants that the society wanted were not necessarily those that the economy attracted. The Russian federal government and local bureaucracy chose to ignore this reality. They continuously favored control over flexibility and did not address the broader context of late modernity. For the rich and well connected, this had few consequences, as they could buy citizenship and even belonging from the very highest political echelons, as was the case of Depardieu. But for poor migrants and laborers, the strict regulations pushed them deeper into the shadows. A representative of the Russian Union of Foreign Workers in Construction described this on Russian television: "These people [labor migrants] are working invisibly, but [they are] working. . . . Building sites are fenced. We do not see the people [who work there]."[111]

For many Russians, like their counterparts in the West, the economy's need for migration was easier to ignore than to deal with the complex situation that neoliberal globalization posed. Bauman noted in his last interview in 2016 that in the West, too, people preferred to omit the unpleasant realities of migration, until this was no longer possible.[112] These internal tensions in Russia between the public's desire for order and stability and the economy's need for migration are likely to intensify in the coming years due to the impact of the coronavirus pandemic on Russia's demography and economy. These grim forecasts exemplify how the global context presents an enormous challenge in the field of migration and citizenship, which defied simple solutions of migration control and order.

The analytical framework of fluid Russianness helps to understand and explain Russian realities, while allowing for the Russian case to be considered as part of the broader global context. Russia was not the only country that struggled to find stability and normality in the field of citizenship in recent decades. In the late modern globalized world, where the movement of labor and capital across national borders was intensifying, governments felt the increasing need to control who was in and who was out.

In 2015, following a wave of Middle Eastern and North African migration into Europe, the debate on migration became highly charged. The Hungarian prime minister Victor Orban, a sympathizer of President Putin and a known critic of immigration, went so far as to say that immigration was threatening Europe's Christian heritage.[113] By 2016, for the first time since the Second World War, there was talk of "fortress Europe," questioning the continuation of freedom of movement into and across the continent.[114] But this debate was hardly new. In the United Kingdom, immigration had dominated election campaigns since 2000 and was the main topic during the Brexit campaign, which aimed to pull the United Kingdom out of the European Union. In 2006 the French presidential contender Nicolas Sarkozy argued that "selective immigration . . . is the expression of France's sovereignty. It is the right of our country."[115] In this context, the Russian experience was hardly unusual, and its government's policies and subsequent failures, specifically since 2000, should be viewed as part of a broader trend where national governments grappled with migration in the globalized world.

This explanation, provided through the conceptual framework of fluid Russianness, reveals several important points. First, these findings contribute to the academic debate on Russian citizenship, as it provides a significant explanation for Russians' dissatisfaction with their citizenship policies in the 2000s and the 2010s. Unlike what scholars have been observing so far, Russian citizenship and the identification that it projects are not abnormal or ambiguous. It is a late modern experience with some specifically Russian elements. Like elsewhere in the globalized late modern world, citizenship became fragmented, and identification, more flexible. And like elsewhere in this world, the Russian public demanded that its government fix the situation of fluid citizenship and identification. Second, these calls, and the stricter policies that often ensued, were expressions of the intrinsic internal dialectic of late modernity, where increased freedoms lead to insecurity, which, in turn, leads to calls to curb those freedoms. But curbing freedoms in a deregulated system where the economy relies on the rapid movement of people and capital across borders is counterproductive and often impossible. Hence, controlling policies often lead to illegal behavior by poor labor migrants who migrate illegally, and by the rich who buy their way out, while the majority of the population is left with the unending sense that something is wrong with migration and citizenship policies.

In this situation, where the incurable internal contradictions of late modernity have been pointed out as unresolvable, why do governments, including the Russian government, engage in stricter citizenship and migration policies? The answer is twofold. First, the modern concept of sovereignty, one of whose pillars is the right to legislate and execute policies within given borders, is still a central element of politics. In this way, scholars of late modernity, Bauman included, were correct to point out that modernity has not finished, and we are not living in postmodernity. States are deeply modern political units, and they continue to execute their sovereign rights for stricter migration policy because this is what they are meant to do—to rule and govern over a specific population within their borders. As long as nation-states remain the political units that order our lives, they will keep legislating stricter policies and try to create order by anchoring the late modern fast-moving world.

Second, very often, in the absence of actual solutions, migration policies in the global world have become a symbolic field of policy that are meant to satisfy populist sentiments and project state power.[116] In everyday life, migration control has mainly made people more vulnerable to discrimination and abuse.[117] This is a sort of imitation of order and stability, which gives people a short respite from the lingering feeling of anxiety that late modernity brings with it (along with the liberties that it promotes). This imitation and performance of security and stability, which are substitutes for the longed-for state of solidity, have been expressed in discourse, and in practice too, which the next chapters consider.

Part Two

Fluid Words

Discourse on National Identification

CHAPTER 3

Media Discourse in the 1990s

In 2003, the late Mikhail Lesin, a key figure in post-Soviet Russian media, explained that in his view "only 5% of the population [are active people] and . . . the majority of the population . . . are not able to form their own approach to life."[1] The media, in his opinion, "helps them by performing an intermediary function."[2] Lesin's views attested to the unique place that the mass media holds in Russia. As shown in the previous chapter, post-Soviet Russia experienced transformations that were consequences of both the postimperial condition and the new context into which it was transforming—globalized late modernity. In these circumstances of parallel transitions into freer and more liberal settings, the media had become central in constructing a new sense of self and society.

Unlike the previous chapter, which focused mainly on state-level actors—the government, the legislative branch, and law enforcement agencies—this chapter considers broader processes. It looks at the formation of national identification in Russia, as expressed by the Russian media elite in the polylogue that it formed and its interactions with historical and political developments. To consider these interactions, this chapter focuses on several questions: How was the post-Soviet Russian national identification expressed through words and in texts? What discourses were formed, and how did they interact with economic, social, and political developments in Russia? Did these discourses reflect a late modern experience described in this work as fluid Russianness?

This chapter shows that Russian media discourse reflected both a late modern tendency for inclusive identification, as well as elements of ethnic Russianness, such as the Russian language and Orthodox Christianity.

This chapter examines texts from the liberal *Moskovskiye Novosti* and *Nezavisimaya Gazeta*, from the *Novaya Gazeta* of 1993, and from *Izvestia*. These texts and various statements therein will be considered as socially contingent acts using the methods of the Russian twentieth-century speech and literature theoretician Mikhail Bakhtin and of critical discourse analysis (CDA). Bakhtin noted: "Any utterance . . . has . . . an absolute beginning and an absolute end; its beginning is preceded by the utterances of other, and its end is by others' responsive utterances."[3] Following this thinking, this chapter uses tools provided by CDA, which was influenced by Bakhtin's writing.

CDA studies statements as relational (focusing on social relations), dialectical (considering relations that are interconnected), and interdisciplinary.[4] It asserts that authors of texts are in constant interaction and dialogue with each other, as well as with readers, even without their knowledge. In this process, certain discursive boundaries are formed, and words become fixed with meaning. They become the central axes around which other expressions are positioned, and they interact with the historical context in which they are being uttered—in our case, with late modernity.[5] Hence, the media clippings in this chapter are considered as a polylogue that was in interaction with the diachronic development of the Russian society.

Russian Media in the 1990s—a Polylogue on Freedom and Security

Between 1989 and 1999, the Russian media experienced new freedom from state censorship but was strained in economic resources. During that period, four main discourses dominated the social polylogue on national identification in Russia—national idea as a periphery, the discourse of loss, the search for a national idea, and the discourse of war. All four discourses related to late modernity in two ways. First, they emerged as the Soviet authorial voice was fading away. The end of state censorship over texts meant that different discourses interacted freely with each other and reflected the new historical and political circumstances of a liberal social polylogue. Second, all of them related, in some way, to the broader overarching discourse of flexibility that had been dominating the global neoliberal arena since the 1980s, where, due to economic and social changes in the late modern period, flexibility became a fundamental concept.[6] This discourse views economic performance uninterrupted by state institutions as a desirable state for human relations. The discourse of flexibility dictates easy adjustments and lightness not only in the economic sphere but also in national affiliations, which are expected to be more flexible. Hence, there is a preference for more inclusive and civic identifications.

National Ideas as Phenomena of the Periphery

In the early 1990s, when Russia became independent, surprisingly the media scarcely discussed Russian national identification. When the media did discuss it, the topic was rarely addressed in positive terms. In the context of this chapter, which deals with words and texts, that point of departure of relative silence seems rather odd—especially if we take into consideration the centrality of the question of citizenship at the time. Members of the Russian cultural and media elite often explained that in the early 1990s, they were focused on economic and democratic transition rather than the formation of national identification.[7] The main goal was to distance the new Russian state from the communist Soviet tradition, not to create a new national ideology.[8] Yeltsin also saw Russia's breaking away from the Soviet Union as an act of freeing itself from the communist ideology, not an act of national liberation.

This approach was the result of an unexpected incidental ideological alliance between pro-Soviet approaches and Western thinking. In Soviet imperial thinking, nationalism was regarded as a dangerous peripheral phenomenon that threatened the union. These attitudes were linked to the geopolitical realities of the land-based empire, where nationalism had been considered both peripheral and dangerous. National sentiments and, even more so, national revolts threatened the imperial existence. Hence, in the Soviet and later Russian discourse, the term *nationalism* had negative associations.[9] Billig noted that in Western nation-states, too, national separatists were found in the outer regions of states, where extremists "lurked on the margins of political life."[10] He pointed out that "from the perspective of Paris, London or Washington, places like Moldova, Bosnia and Ukraine," where guerrilla figures were fighting to establish their new homelands, "are peripherally place. . . . This makes nationalism not merely an exotic force, but a peripheral one . . . the property of others."[11] Osipov explained this affinity by noting that both Soviet and Western thinking originated from frameworks of modernist social engineering, which resulted in similar views of nationalism in Soviet/Russian and Western perspectives.[12] Hence, for the Moscow and Leningrad elites, due to their common philosophical origins, Moldova and Ukraine were as much a periphery as they were for Paris and London.

As a result of this thinking, identification or belonging to the Russian national group was not considered mainstream topics for media discussion in Russia in the early 1990s. Newspapers surveyed for this chapter barely mentioned phrases like "Russian national idea" or "Russian identification." When national ideas and national ideologies were discussed, they mainly referred to foreign (or otherwise peripheral) phenomena. Other ethnic groups, primarily in the former Soviet republics and in Russia's peripheral regions, had national ideas that were mostly portrayed as belligerent and dangerous and were usually discussed in connection to the suppression of minorities and ethnic strife.

The Russian media in the early 1990s was overflowing with reports on national movements and conflicts on the Soviet periphery. Indeed, there was plenty to report on. The Soviet Union disintegrated along national-administrative lines, and some newly independent states perused aggressive nationalizing policies. In 1989–1993, conflicts erupted between Armenia and Azerbaijan in Nagorno-Karabakh, in Georgia's South Ossetia and Abkhazia, in Moldova and Transdniestria, and between different groups in Tajikistan. Within Russia, ethnic tensions were rising between the federal central in Moscow and regional elites, many of whom were non-Slavic, like the Tatars. Conflicts also broke out between groups in the Russian North Caucasus—the Ossetians and the Ingush. In other former Soviet republics, like the Baltic states, Ukraine, and Kazakhstan, nationalizing policies in the spheres of citizenship, language, and education threatened to trigger violent responses from Russian minorities. These events were the objective materials with which the Russian media constructed the discourse that portrayed national identification as a peripheral and often dangerous phenomenon.

Examples of this discourse are countless. A good place to start is the Caucasus, where in 1991 the ultimate international symbol of Soviet brotherhood—victory over Nazi Germany—was allegedly under threat. In January 1991 *Izvestia* reported that Armenian Second World War veterans were protesting the possible removal from the official calendar of Victory Day over Nazi Germany (May 9). The article was published under the title: "Who wants to cancel Victory Day?" ("Kto hochet otmenit' Den' Pobedy?"). A letter signed by multiple veterans read: "We want to remind those who try to belittle the historical role of the great victory of the Soviet people in the Great Patriotic War, which saved . . . Armenia from the repetition of the 1915 genocide . . . our nation's contribution to the great victory—one of the brightest pages of the centuries-old Armenian history."[13] The article also noted that the veterans were deeply concerned and offended by certain deputies from the local soviet who resisted the inclusion of Victory Day in the official national calendar of Armenia.

Although the genre of this article was reportage, which should be informative and neutral, it was openly opposed to the idea of canceling the official celebrations of Victory Day. It contained only statements made by the veterans, while those who were in favor of canceling the celebrations were not given a voice. They were not even given any agency—they remained anonymous actors whose sole intention was to hurt war veterans. This was also expressed in the title of the article—"Who wants to cancel Victory Day?" The answer was not given in the article, but the mystique created by the title was thin. Quite obviously, the plan of those who wanted to "belittle the historical role" of the Soviet people were anonymous nationalist forces lurking in the dark, looking for an opportunity to unleash their destructive agenda.

That article used the unique place of the memory of the Second World War in the Soviet Union and in Russia. It flagged the two Soviet myths of the war—the supranational victory and the place of veterans. Consequently, the article labeled national ideologies as a negative force that splits society, insults veterans' feelings, and undermines human solidarity, placing it on the periphery, in Armenia. The negative approach described here probably stemmed from pro-union feelings and the traditional imperial aversion to national ideologies, yet it also flags some universal ideas—harming elderly veterans and human solidarity.

Another example came from the conflicts in Georgia, which dominated the news in 1989–1993. War broke out in South Ossetia and Abkhazia, while clashes ignited in other parts of Georgia. In early January 1992, Zviad Gamsakhurdia, former Soviet dissident and the first elected Georgian president, was deposed and forced to leave the country. On January 16, 1992, *Moskovskiye Novosti* commented on these events. An article laid serious accusations against Gamsakhurdia. It referred to his role in the bloody events of April 9, 1991, when the Soviet army clashed with peaceful demonstrators in Tbilisi, killing twenty people and injuring many. The article accused Gamsakhurdia of knowingly sending demonstrators to their deaths, by not ordering them to withdraw despite knowing that the military was about to move on them. The newspaper wrote:

> Gamsakhurdia was forgiven for his role in those events. What for? Why [did] the Georgians have strong sympathy for this person? Maybe because of [his] dissident past? Hardly . . . Gamsakhurdia "took" [the elections by] other [means]. He gave an outlet to offended national feelings, offering a simple and clear slogan: "Georgia—for Georgians." Power obtained with this mandate could not have turned otherwise but into a genocide in South Ossetia, bloody clashes in Abkhazia and Adjara, the

expulsion from Georgia of Avars, oppression of Armenians and Azerbaijanis and the refusal to allow Meskhetian Turks to return to their homeland.[14]

This commentary placed Gamsakhurdia and Georgia as peripheral nationalist entities. In this article, national feelings have clouded the judgment of the Georgian people. They were so smitten by the simple appeal to their offended national pride that they forgave Gamsakhurdia for his crimes. What followed was allegedly unavoidable, as the article deterministically pointed out that things "could not have turned otherwise." The logical conclusion of the article was that appealing to national feelings necessarily leads to genocide, massacre, bloody clashes, and the oppression of minorities. This part also served as a warning to Russians to avoid toying with the idea of a monoethnic state, as some were doing. This text portrayed national feelings as dangerous and placed them on the post-Soviet periphery—perpetrated by and affecting those who reside there. The Georgian people, a nation on the periphery, responded to "simple and clear slogans" that led to strife among peripheral national groups—Ossetians, Abkhaz, Adjar, Avars, Armenians, Azerbaijanis, and Meskhetian Turks. Unlike in the previous article, here Soviet-imperial ideas were less clearly set; it more closely resembled a post-Soviet liberal rejection of national ideology.

This reporting was not confined to the Caucasus. A similar attitude was observed in *Nezavisimaya Gazeta* relating to ethnic Russian expressions of national identification. The newspaper reported about a Direct Line with Yeltsin—a Russian political tradition when the president answers questions from ordinary citizens. The conversation was quoted as follows:

[GALINA VLADIMIROVNA]: Galina Vladimirovna, engineer, Novosibirsk. I am concerned about an issue. Why does our government not have people of Russian nationality?

[YELTSIN]: In the government? You don't say!

[GV]: Yes, I am judging by last names. I was offended. I am a deeply Russian person [*Russkiy chelovek*], a Siberian, and I feel that there are no Russian people. This is a sore point.

[YELTSIN]: Yes, most, in my opinion, are Russian. Vorobyov, is he not Russian?

[GV]: Gaidar, Burbulis . . .

[YELTSIN]: Burbulis is not [in] the government.

[GV]: I'm just saying.

[YELTSIN]: I'll explain. Burbulis grandfather is from the Baltics, and his mother was Russian.

[GV]: You just want to say that he is not Jewish. But this still does not mean that there are [ethnic] Russians [Russkiy] in the government. We, the Siberians, feel very strongly about this. . . . I look at it with pain.

[YELTSIN]: Well, we will conduct an investigation . . . and publish it.[15]

Appalled by this conversation, *Nezavisimaya Gazeta* (NG) ran an editorial titled "National composition of the government subject to examination—hopefully, the president was joking": "NG is not even surprised by the 'apologetic' tone of the President and not by the conclusion of the conversation—on the investigation into the government's national composition. . . . We are surprised that the President allowed himself to seriously discuss such issues."[16]

The editorial went on to quote a conversation they had been told about between two exiled Russian writers, Irina Berberova and Sergey Dovlatov, who presumably had the conversation while in exile before the collapse of the Soviet Union. In one of their conversations, Dovlatov mentioned to Berberova that in the Russian state, key posts should be held by Russian (Russkiy) people. Berberobva corrected him: "In the Russian [*Rossiskaya*] state key posts should be held by NORMAL [*normalniye*] people."[17]

In this the Direct Line exchange, the peripheral nationalist was a Russian woman from Siberia, while *Nezavisimaya Gazeta* revealed its bias against national identification. The newspaper did not condemn the woman, although she made offensive remarks against officials who were Russian citizens. In a similar manner, the newspaper did not criticize the president for not deploring the comments or alerting the woman that her remarks were inappropriate. According to *Nezavisimaya Gazeta*, the president should have ignored her comments completely and not responded. The subtext was that it was expected from a woman from the periphery to make nationalist and racist comments. However, the president should not have engaged her, since her comments were unacceptable. In quoting the conversation between Dovlatov and Berberova, *Nezavisimaya Gazeta* ruled on appropriate (and inappropriate) forms of identification. It noted that the only acceptable form of identification in the multiethnic Russian (Rossiskaya) state was "normal people" (*normalniye ludi*). This attested that the media elites viewed an acceptable Russian national identification only as one that was flexible and highly inclusive.

A review of the texts that dealt with national identification in the early 1990s revealed that they did not address Russian national identification as an appropriate topic for discussion. National identity was viewed as a negative phenomenon that belonged in the periphery and had no place in the civilized center.

The consequences of national ideologies were also highlighted—they were risky and often led to violence. Nationalist sentiments within Russia were also portrayed as illegitimate. Hence, the center was called on to promote a civic-liberal-inclusive agenda. The discourse of national ideas as a peripheral phenomenon served as an ethical and linguistic delineation of *us*—the liberal-minded Russian center, where national feelings and identification were inclusive and flexible—and *them*, the peripheral nationalists. It echoed the meta discourse of neoliberalism—the discourse of flexibility, when people are called to adopt more flexible and inclusive identities.

The Discourse of Loss

In tandem with the discourse that underlined the dangerous and peripheral nature of national ideology, loss had become the focus of another strong discourse of the early 1990s. This discourse underlined the hardship of the early years after the collapse of Soviet Union. While the elite concentrated on democratic and economic transition, living standards deteriorated, and security and stability eroded. The sense of loss was perhaps the most dominant feeling in this period, and it included many different losses—economic instability, security in the face of rising criminality, and food insecurity, as well as political instability and conflicts in the former Soviet states. The strongest association of loss was with national identification—loss of pride, loss of status, loss of motherland. This discourse remained central and important throughout the post-Soviet period, underlying the feeling that Russian national identity was in crisis and that measures should be made to reveal, reinvent, or remedy it.

The media reported and commented on the difficulties that Russian people experienced when seeking new formative ideas and on the negative consequences for society attendant to the feelings of loss. These texts appeared from 1992, with the realization that the union was gone forever and with it the positive things it had represented—a feeling of predictability, normality, and belonging.

In April 1992, *Izvestia* ran a long article on the feelings of loss among Soviet military men stationed in a military base in Belorussia. The title was "God forbid to see you across the frontline" ("Ne day bog uvidet'sya cherez liniyu fronta"). The men were being dismissed as the former Soviet republics started to form their national armies. Many men described the loss of communist ideology as a painful experience; they were left with no real ideological alternatives except national ones, which, from the reporter's point of view, were vague: "It should be noted that after the dismissal of the communist ideology, officers were given no other [ideological] choice, but national idea. . . . All [Soviet ideas] are things of the past. What [came] instead? National idea."[18] The loss of ideology, in military settings, had very practical implications, like to whom to swear allegiance: "We asked every officer—what state do you serve? The answer, pensive, [came with] a shrug 'I don't know.'"[19] The article related that Soviet officers experienced the territorial integrity of the Soviet Union in a very real way—a vast landmass that they swore to defend and across which they moved from one base to another, together with their families. The article described this loss: "The dissolution of the concept of the Soviet Union, for him [the officer], is not a political or geographic fact, but a personal tragedy."[20] Not only did the officers lose a sense of ideological orientation, retaining only a vague sense of whom they served and which land they defended, but they also lost the sense of who was a friend and who was a foe. As the article's title suggests, these officers expressed their fear that in the future they might be ordered to fight each other. This must have been a deeply disorientating experience for those who until recently were brothers-in-arms: "When an officer leaves the base, departs to his native country, he tells his co-servicemen 'God forbid to see you across the frontline.' Sounds like a joke, but it . . . acquires a sinister meaning."[21]

This text expressed the multifaceted and extensive sense of loss in former Soviet societies. The feelings of loss were enhanced since the article dealt with military men. The contrast between the might of the Soviet army and the current situation of its former officers was stark. Left behind, while the changes were happening in the urban centers, they were depicted as weak and helpless. Their glory was gone, and the future was uncertain. Interestingly, the subtext of the article also reflected the previously described discourse of national ideas as a negative force. It presented an adverse image of national ideology and placed the blame for the feeling of loss on nationalists, who had caused the collapse of the Soviet Union. This was an interesting take on events that allowed the two discourses to work synergistically rather than clash, though it would not always work in that way.

In 1993 the sense of loss became ever deeper, as Russia underwent an extreme political crisis. At that point Yeltsin was fighting political rivals from all sides. He had pushed forward reforms and a new constitution, which he had struggled to pass through the Supreme Soviet (the predecessor of the State Duma). The political deadlock resulted in the bloody events of October 1993, in which over a hundred people were killed.

In August 1993 *Nezavisimaya Gazeta* published an interview with a former top general of the KGB, Leonid Shebarshin. He was concerned with the new weakness in which Russia found itself from a national security point of view.

He predicted that the sense of loss would evolve into a national reassertion. The interviewer asked, "Will Russia be able to get out of the position in which it finds itself now?" Shebarshin answered:

> Predicting [is] difficult. This uncertainty, tension, anticipation of a social explosion, had lasted about one and a half years. How long can such a situation [continue]? . . . I do not know. In my opinion, one thing is clear: Russia will be saved [by] the revival of the self-identification [*samosoznaniye*] of the Russian nation [Russkiy *narod*). The only question is who will lead it. One of the current leaders? This I doubt.[22]

This text pointed out that feelings of loss could not forever remain open-ended. Once too many voices said that something was lost, other voices would try to retrieve it. Shebarshin's solution was the "Russkiy narod," an ethnic delineation of identification, which is exclusive and bears the promise of clear and solid and predictable demarcation. Shebarshin presented a counterargument to discourse, which avoided solid expressions of national identification by describing them as peripheral and dangerous; they provided only inclusive acceptable forms of identification, which were harder to grasp. This was the unavoidable evolution of the two prevalent discourses in the Russian polylogue from a parallel understanding of reality into a confrontation. Shebarshin's interview should be considered part of a broader development that was taking place in Russian society.

Both discourses in the early 1990s—national identification as a periphery and the discourse of loss—were responding to the government's retreat from people's lives. They responded to the fact that the state had stopped narrating the story of collective belonging in Russia. As in other places in the globalized late modern world, Russians were left to their own devices and were expected to create their own meaning. The first discourse—nationalism as a periphery—adopted the Western liberal approach to nationalism, viewing it as a destructive force, on the fringes of state and society. This discourse viewed identification favorably only when it was articulated in the broadest and most inclusive way. The second discourse—the discourse of loss—focused on the hardship and suffering experienced by individuals, who adopted that new system of values. These individuals gained freedom but lost many other emotional and material properties—the certainty that a strong national ideology lent and a narrative that helped to understand one's place in the world. The discourse of loss emphasized the most important shortcoming of late modernity—that being on your own, in a rapidly changing world, without sources of authority that anchor identity, could be daunting and tiresome.

In Russia freedom and loss created two competing and conflicting interpretations of events. For instance, the Russian literary critic and publisher Irina Prokhorova, in the book she edited *1990: Russians Remember a Turning Point*, remembered: "I spent three unforgettable days on the barricades defending the Russian government's White House during the 1991 August coup attempt, and came away from that experience a free, no longer Soviet, person."[23] Another writer in the same book, Sergey Karnaukhov, who had lived in the peripheral regions of Tula and Irkutsk, called 1990 the year of the "Funeral of Food."[24] These were two parallel interpretations of events, but a causal link between them could easily be made. The sense of loss could easily be pinned on those who pushed national ideology to the periphery and labeled it dangerous. This revealed the internal dialectic of late modernity—openness and inclusiveness—which rejected strong national affiliations but also created deep insecurity and a sense of loss. The suffering described in the Russian media was not uncommon in globalized neoliberal Western societies, where the constant and endless need to adjust to new realities, which is the essence of being flexible, created a sense of insecurity.

This late modern dynamic made the discourse of loss particularly prone to manipulation by extreme ideologists. Indeed, from 1993 the open-ended sense of loss, which was not directed at pinning blame on someone, gave way to nationally infused politics of the new Russian opposition. Its adherents used the discourse of loss for a reactionary call to a more solid sense of identity. In December 1993, Vladimir Zhirinovsky won 22 percent of the vote and, together with Gennady Zyuganov, formerly of the National Salvation Front and by 1993 of the Communist Party, who also relied on nationalistic messages, had considerable influence in the Duma. Both promoted toughening Russia's position vis-à-vis the West, a more assertive stance toward the former Soviet republics, and a stronger sense of national pride (which often included racist verbal attacks on migrants and Jews).

In 1994 Zhirinovsky was quoted addressing the difficult position of ethnic Russians in the former Soviet republics, for which he blamed Russia's traditional Others—the Jews:

> The orchestras playing the same song, "Russians get out!" are being directed by the same conductors, the same provocateurs. . . . The same provocateurs in Russia itself have persistently moved into the most prestigious and well-paid professions—scholars with grants, writers, composers, film directors, lawyers, journalists and so on—the Jews.[25]

By the mid-1990s, the government could no longer ignore these political uses by far-right and Communist politicians of the discourse of loss. In 1996, the year when he had to fight Zyuganov in the presidential elections, Yeltsin, for the first time, made his own move to address the issue of national identification.

In Search of a National Idea

In July 1996, after his hard-won victory, Yeltsin asked Russia's leading scholars from the Russian Academy of Sciences to find, within a year, a new national idea. At the same time, *Rossiskaya Gazeta* announced a competition for its readers to come up with a new national idea and set the prize at $2,000. It is unclear what Yeltsin was aiming to achieve with this call to action, since he never addressed his intentions. That call did not have any implications for policy; nor did it raise Yeltsin's popularity. In fact, in practical terms, it was a flop. The Academy of Sciences never submitted any paper on this matter. Nor did *Rossiskaya Gazeta* pick any suggestions from the public.

Yeltsin's call received mixed responses from the media. Many claimed that a national idea should not be ordered from above. Some of these responses echoed the discourse of national identification as a dangerous periphery. For instance, in July 1996 *Izvestia* published an editorial under the title "Russia does not need another state ideology," which stated: "Anyone who watched the formation of the newly independent states knows that 'national ideas' result in turmoil, strife and blood."[26] Yeltsin's move was, however, still smart enough to steal some wind from nationalist and Communist politicians who dominated the debate on national identification. Yeltsin's aide, Gregoriy Satarov, explained the idea behind the request:

> We are talking about the development of a certain universal formula related to common values and uniting all people. . . . Please note that the President voiced the idea after saying that we cannot, after the presidential elections, divide the country into losers and winners. . . . The president does not say: "I will give you a national idea," but on the contrary, he asks: "Find it."[27]

It is clear from this statement that Yeltsin's administration was unable and did not intend to provide substantive input on the issue of national identification. Instead, Yeltsin stuck to a liberal and open-ended approach—asking people to launch a conversation on national identification, which was more acceptable for the media elites. The *Izvestia* editorial quoted above, which was overall critical of the initiative, concluded more leniently, stating: "The country needs a nationwide spiritual guidance that can consolidate society and thus strengthen the state."

This initiative started a new discourse in the Russian media that can be summed up in what became a catchphrase: "There is a national idea." This was a sort of popular deliberation, where for the first time it became acceptable to reevaluate Russian national identification—to discuss (and criticize) the new Russian ways of life, to reminisce about the old ones, and to express ideas about what Russia should become. This deliberation and the ideas that were raised showed that Russia had become part of the temporal context of globalized late modernity. One of the strongest themes that featured in this discourse was economic progress as a national idea. This was unsurprising, as the country was undergoing sweeping economic reforms, which had far more impact than the political reforms of democratization. It also resonated with both late modern elastic identifications and the neoliberal discourse of flexibility—an agenda that focuses on economic development, with national affiliation becoming more flexible and fluid.

The Economy as a National Idea

A good example of the subnarrative of "the economy as a national idea" was published in a 1998 interview with the governor of Leningrad Oblast, Vadim Gustov. Its title was "Vadim Gustov: We do not need any extra rubles from the government" ("Vadim Gustov: Ot Pravitel'stva Nam Ne Nado Ni Odnogo Lishnego Rublya"). Gustov, a rebranded Communist *nomenklatura* politician, spoke in neoliberal terms of self-reliance and a pragmatic economic approach. The interview went as follows:

> [INTERVIEWER]: Some think that only a national idea can really unite the [Russian] Federation?
>
> [VG]: You know, in its pure form, this idea [belongs to] yesterday. Russia today is at the stage of entry into the European and world market system. This factor cannot be ignored. The Leningrad region is, theoretically, at the intersection of enormous cash flows that will affect us, if we are able to create a decent complex of ports. . . . Our ports will be able to bring one and a half billion dollars a year. In this situation, it would be wise to talk of the national idea, [that is,] an economic one.[28]

Gustov embraced the neoliberal idea as a formative theme of the nation. For him, national identification was a thing of the past—the new national idea must be an economic one. His point of reference was local—his oblast. But his thinking was global, as his aim was to join the European and world economy. It underlined the devolved sense of power in Russia in the 1990s. An appropriate local national idea was grounded on utilizing the geographical position of the oblast and its ports that stretched across the Gulf of Finland, to redirect and enjoy the cross-border flow of capital. This economic national identification forfeited any substantive attachments that were unique to Russia. It was a stark manifestation of the neoliberal discourse of flexibility. The Leningrad region did not need ideas of national belonging and social affinity. What it did require, according to Gustov, was flexibility. It had to adjust itself and to flourish from the profits that such behavior reaped. It showed that people like Gustov accepted the central place of flexible economic performance in the life of the state and its citizens.

In 1998 Sergey Kirienko, the former Russian prime minister who at the time of writing serves as the Deputy Chief of Staff of the Presidential Administration, presented a similar vision of the economy as a Russian national idea:

> In our country, 61% of the population—now it's my favorite figure—are people who do not need state paternalism and rely on their own means. . . . It is a very significant change in consciousness. . . . In general, the idea of the fatherland does not attract as an all-national [idea]. . . . I believe that a strategy of national competitive advantages can become such an idea.[29]

Kirienko was proud that Russians were fending for themselves. For him, the state, nation, and fatherland were things of the past. He was a new neoliberal Russian who looked to the future and believed in making his own fortune. The nation, for him, was an enterprise that should have "competitive advantages." This was an economic logic, which envisioned society as a series of monetary exchanges rather than a nation tied in unbreakable blood brotherhood. National attachments were quantifiable and changeable—they were not based on blood, religion, history, or language but on the ability to compete in the free market. This vision exhibited a high level of inclusiveness—anybody who could compete effectively could become part of the national group—yet it also created a dislocation, for if somebody could not compete flexibly, he or she was out.

A different approach to the economy as a national idea was published in *Izvestia* in August 1998. Rustam Afidjamov, an Azerbaijani-born Russian journalist, wrote about the role of the middle class in Russia's national idea. He referred to it in Russian as *midl* (a Russian pronunciation of the English word *middle*). He reminisced about his experiences as a young person in the late-Soviet period—having to drive from one place to another to obtain a coffee machine. The long drive in a Soviet Zhiguli car to the big city with his friends from the Komsomol, a Communist youth organization, was cold. Since then, he had come up in life and was making an honest living. This, in his opinion, was his way to identify with Russia and as a Russian. He wrote:

> I did not become a bandit and a swindler. I tried to pay taxes and staff salaries. I really worked very hard to save up for an apartment and a warm car. I became "Midl." Because this is the ideology of the middle class: a little envy and a lot of work for the coffee machine and an electric iron. Maybe this is the national idea—to live normally, to envy and work. To earn and consume.[30]

Afidjamov's idea of national belonging revolved around a microeconomy and consumption culture. He outlined an inclusive, open-ended type of belonging—a banal experience, which was expressed in everyday practices. Furthermore, he revealed that in Russia, as in other neoliberal societies, identification was often expressed through consumerism.

National Ideas in the Open-Ended Polylogue

Apart from the economy as an expression of national identification, other texts suggested a plurality of themes and ideas, which were in line with trends in the globalized era. Some suggested universal values (human rights, common sense, and Russia as a nation of ideas) or specific activities (sports and films). This polylogue charted a new inclusive and adjustable experience that started to present the contours of late modern Russian national identification—fluid Russianness.

Many authors tried to create a mental bridge between the Soviet past and Russia's contemporary realities. They suggested ideas and themes from the Soviet past that could have been appropriated in post-Soviet Russia to recreate continuity of identity. For instance, in 1996 *Izvestia* published an article on the Russian understanding of common senses (*zdravyy smysl*):

> [In the Soviet Union] ordinary people . . . simply ceased to regard formal laws that were contrary to common sense [zdravyy smysl]. And created a shadow rule of law, a shadow code of life, based not on legal norms, but on the norms of common sense. . . . It was the most important, if not the final, victory over the doctrine. . . . Moral consciousness, enlightened patriotism and private economic interest—the three components of the people's ideology . . . What else to look for, if the formula is already suggested by the national ideology of Russian life?[31]

This text titled "There is a national idea" connects the late-Soviet and the post-Soviet period. The sociologist Alexei Yurchak noted that in the late-Soviet period people ceased to follow state ideology yet did not resist it. They lived alongside the Soviet doctrine. They expressed their belonging to the large community of the unaffiliated and apolitical individuals in the term *normal'ny chelovek* (a normal person)—somebody who is neither ideological nor a dissident.[32] Normal'ny chelovek lived according to the shadow rule of law and what is described here as common sense (zdravyy smysl). They continued to perform their duties as Soviet citizens but did not ascribe ideological content to this performance. The text from *Izvestia* argues that this set of values, an inclusive-centrist approach to identification, continued to serve as a core unifying idea in the post-Soviet period. This is strongly linked to Afidjamov's article about the ideology of the middle class, or as he calls it, the midl. Such a banal identification allowed a practical way to identify with post-Soviet Russia, to fit in with the new economic and social circumstances, and at the same time to reinstate continuity of identity and ontological security.

Another attempt to reinstate the continuity of identity was through the remembrance of the victory in the Second World War as a central idea around which the national collective could unite. In 1997, the publicist and current member of the Moscow city Duma Yevgeny Bunimowich wrote in *Novaya Gazeta*: "Is this [victory] not the phantom pain, phantom memory, that . . . is the national idea?"[33] Bunimowich suggested that the continuity of identity could be reinstated via the memory of the Second World War, which in the Soviet Union, at least since 1965, was molded into the Soviet metanarrative that underscored unity for a righteous cause.[34] The magnitude of devastation caused by the war was as close as possible to a national, all-encompassing experience of tragedy. Bunimowich was bringing back to the fore this inclusive sense of unity where loss made sense and had an outlet—the greatest victory in the battle of good against evil.

Fluid Russianness and Nikita Mikhalkov

In 1998, the famous Russian filmmaker Nikita Mikhalkov, who in the 1990s became one of the most vocal commentators on national identification, described his take on Russianness. In the interview, he revealed central axes around which Russian national identification was discussed in the 1990s. He began with the discourse of loss and stressed the prevailing disappointment with freedom and liberal democracy, stating: "Freedom! And what to do with it? Do not really know."[35]

Mikhalkov also shared his terminological distinctions between nationalism and patriotism, putting forward an inclusive multiethnic agenda for Russia:

> What distinguishes patriotism from nationalism? Nationalism is when self-affirmation is pressing on someone else, and you love at the expense of another. Patriotism is when you love and do not interfere with another's love to his [country]. I have *schi* [traditional Russian soup] and you *chebureki* [Central Asian pastries]. And you have matzo [Jewish unleavened bread] and you *Shashlyk*[Caucasian barbecue]. Tell me how you make it.[36]

He went on to explain the importance of religion and attachment to the land in his vision of Russianness:

> I am convinced that Orthodoxy is the foundation of our country. Because here the majority is Orthodox Christians. But one day near Nizhny Novgorod I got to a Tatar village. [There I saw] birch trees, a field—and a mosque.... Somehow it is strange to see a mosque in the middle of the Russian landscape! ... [I ask,] How long [did the] Tatars live here? Eight hundred years, they respond. That's it! My question was removed forever. If for people who practice Islam, this landscape is native—this river, these fish, this birch, this field—they grew up here, how can I think that these people do not fit into my landscape? They fit, simply because they are my brothers.[37]

Mikhalkov concluded his vision: "For me, the national idea is to have a reason, the ability and the basis upon which to recover the dignity of the state [*vernut' strane dostoinstvo*]."[38] This text was different since Mikhalkov, unlike the authors quoted earlier, was aspiring to a semiofficial ideological and political position in society and considering entering politics. Mikhalkov expressed several popular themes in the media discourse. First, he connected with the discourse of loss, underlining the widely felt disappointment granted by liberal democracy, due to the sense of loss that it brought about. Second, he tapped into Soviet terminology and made a distinction between nationalism and patriotism. By doing so, he made his vision accessible to the wider public and circumvented the discourse of national ideology as a dangerous periphery, which viewed nationalism as an aggressive ideology. Patriotism, according to Mikhalkov, was supposedly a pacified ideology that envisioned an inclusive nation, where one's love of country did not impinge on the feelings of others. His views firmly tied Russian identification to the multiethnic composition of the state. Mikhalkov called for an inclusive, banal patriotism that was expressed in everyday practices. For him, belonging was expressed in such simple things as food, living side by side, loving the same landscapes, and being proud of the Russian state. Third, this identification was also underpinned by certain historical and cultural constants, as he was convinced that Orthodox Christianity played an important role in Russia.

Mikhalkov's inclusive approach of belonging demonstrated that by the end of the first decade of Russian independence, Russian identification was starting to take shape in the direction of fluid Russianness. Yet his bottom-line definition of the Russian national idea—"to recover the dignity of the state [vernut' strane dostoinstvo]"—showed that his inclusive Russian identification could turn aggressive. Although Mikhalkov spoke in very general terms, this comment suggested that his vision could easily be used to justify forceful action.

The discourse surrounding the search for a national idea reflected the new national experience that was forming in Russia. Russia entered the globalized late modern context, which became the relevant framework for considering national identification in Russia, mainly through economic themes. At the same time, it was marked by the desire to create continuity of identity by remembering Soviet historical events, such as the victory in the Second World War. It was also supplemented with specific ethnic elements, such as Orthodox Christianity, which tied people to a particular Russian national experience. As Mikhalkov's comment showed, however, the aggressiveness that had started to appear in the polylogue in 1993 was also present. By 1999 a full-blown aggressive discourse of war was emerging.

The Discourse of War in Yugoslavia

At the turn of the millennium, the war in Yugoslavia and NATO's bombings of Belgrade, gave rise to a belligerent discourse on national identification among the Russian political elite. Russian politicians from various parties reacted aggressively to the bombing of the Serbian capital, flagging Russian-Serbian kinship based on Slavic origins. The Duma, dominated by Zhirinovsky's nationalistic Liberal Democratic Party of Russia (LDPR) and Zyuganov's Communists, pushed for a Russian military intervention and concurrently applied political pressure on Yeltsin and tried to impeach him. Yeltsin came under serious pressure to respond. He, in turn, threatened the United States with war in Europe, should they deploy ground troops.[39] His remarks raised concerns for the first time since the end of the Cold War about the possibility of a nuclear exchange.[40]

The Russian media elite resisted this discourse. They reverted to the discourse of nationalism as a dangerous periphery and presented its danger as a potential tool for political rallying. In April 1999, *Izvestia* wrote:

> Yugoslav hysteria clearly demonstrated that national myths are easily converted into profitable electoral slogans. This awakened [feeling], which is erroneously called "national consciousness," can erode from the Russian brain the remnants of common sense [*zdravogo smysla*] and become dangerous for the health of the nation, the political system and the economy.... Now for the sake of uniting the nation and for avoiding impeachment, the regime is ready for anything. And this "anything" suddenly fits the dominant public mood—Serb-brothers against bastards-NATO-Americans.... This is the national idea.[41]

The "awakened" national mood was rejected by *Izvestia* and was described as a negative and fake show of unity achieved by creating an external enemy. They accused the political elite of manipulation, geared toward winning elections or avoiding impeachment. They also depicted this mood as irrational and dangerous to the inclusive values that define the "health of the nation"—common sense, which was also viewed as a possible national characteristic, as well as the democratic political system and free-market economy. All of this had been sacrificed, according to *Izvestia*, to suit the public mood and serve the populist dichotomy of "us-brothers" against "them-bastards." Here newspapers were already bound to report from the center and could not position that nationalistic mood on the outskirts of the country and society. By 1999 the center of the nation had been influenced by an "erroneous national consciousness."

These new aggressive expressions might be seen as a divergence from the flexible and inclusive identifications that had been described in the discourse of the national idea and charted the contours of fluid Russianness. Billig observed, however, that flexible, inclusive, and banal identification in Western democracies did not mean that these identifications always remained pacified. The tendency of Western democracies to view violent outbursts of nationalism as confined to peripheries was a fallacy. In fact, unifying the nation in times of war and conflict continued to have an appeal in late modern liberal democracies. As Billig noted: "Crises, such as the Falkland, or the Gulf Wars, infect a sore spot, causing bodily fevers: the symptoms are an inflamed rhetoric and an outbreak of ensigns."[42] In Russia, the war in Yugoslavia served as a reminder that even if Russians were adjusting to the globalized late modern world, the unifying power of identification with the national group through war was still strong.

A Late Modern Russian Discourse

During the decade between 1989 and 1999, the discourse on Russian national identification underwent a remarkable change. From an almost complete rejection of national ideas in the early 1990s, by 1999 Russian national identification had become a widely discussed topic with aggressive nuances. The initial rejection of national ideas as peripheral and dangerous grew into a sense of national loss and dislocation, with calls for the national identity to be fixed and remedied. The discourse surrounding a search for a national idea was an answer to those calls and an attempt to have a free and wide-ranging polylogue on what it meant to be Russian in post-Soviet and late modern times. It charted the counters of fluid Russianness and showed preferences for inclusive ideas and flexible identities that could fit with the new globalized times. Moreover, it showed an interest in specifically Russian features, like the Russian Orthodox Church, which anchored the free-flowing sense of Russianness. But as the decade drew to a close, Russian society was reminded that flexible identifications were no guarantee for a pacified discourse. The war in Yugoslavia awakened an aggressive and divisive political discourse in Russia, which was not going away.

By August 1999, Russia had a new prime minister, Vladimir Putin, who marked the beginning of a new phase in the debate on national identification in the Russian media. Since 2000, the debate had intensified, and Russian national identification became one of the most visited themes in the Russian media. Interestingly, many ideas raised in the discourse from 1996 onward had been picked up in the 2000s by the new regime in the Kremlin. They were turned into pillars of the resurgent authorial voice and the government discourse on national identification.

CHAPTER 4

Media Discourse under Putin
Fluid Words and Fluid Screens

In August 1999 Yeltsin explained his choice to appoint Vladimir Putin as prime minister: "I have decided to name this person, who is, in my opinion, able to consolidate society. . . . He will be able to unite around himself those who are to renew Great Russia in the new twenty first century."[1] Unifying and renewing Russia became Putin's main stated task. For this purpose, Putin strove to divert the media discourse from the metanarrative of flexibility to a government-led discourse of stability. This effort aimed to put an end to the period of transition and to the feelings of dislocation and loss that it had brought about. A stable and unified national identity was meant to be an important remedy for the perceived and real losses during the 1990s. To change the metanarrative, the Kremlin began an aggressive campaign to change media power relations—from a free press to a government-controlled and obedient sector. These policies had only partial success, however, revealing the strengths and weakness of the Kremlin's efforts, as well as the limitation of controlling media discourse in the late modern era.

This chapter will analyze texts from the liberal *Novaya Gazeta*, as well as *Izvestia*, which from 2003 adopted the government line. Due to the growing role of television in Russia in the 2000s, it will also investigate broadcasts of the talk show *Poyedinok*, which was broadcast on Russian Channel 1 (formally K bar'yeru! on NTV), hosted by Vladimir Solovyov. Solovyov started as a liberally leaning media personality, but over the years he turned into one of the most fervent supporters of the Kremlin, and his show became a tool for the development and dissemination of government discourse.

Putin's Quest for Power and the Discourse of War

Putin's rise to power relied on the unifying power of war within Russia's borders—in Chechnya. Putin's appointment as prime minister coincided with the serious deterioration of the situation in Chechnya, when Chechen separatists invaded the neighboring republic of Dagestan. Putin decided on a swift and forceful course of action to repel the Chechen fighters. There were many theories, some of which were substantiated, that suggested that Putin's intervention in Chechnya was planned to help him consolidate his hold over the government and to boost his leadership.[2] Although Putin's intentions may never be revealed, it is important to note that in 1999 Putin had to work hard to win the support of the Russian public and Russian elites, and the war in Chechnya was an important element in his quest.

The Russian media responded negatively to Putin's rallying. It resonated with the discourse of the national idea as a dangerous endeavor, which was dominant in its recent reporting on the war in Yugoslavia. It depicted Putin's war in Chechnya as a political game, fought for his personal political gains. In November 1999, *Izvestia* published the following text:

> Russia needs a new national ideology—the Prime Minister said on Wednesday.... [He] noted the indisputable: the old ideology has been destroyed, and the new has not been created—"We have a lot to offer in terms of ideology. It should be based on patriotism in its best sense."... But somehow ... [the] appeal to patriotism was [caused by] the explosions in Buinaksk, Moscow, Volgodonsk[3] and the fear of their recurrence.... Unfortunately, there is almost never a rise of patriotic consciousness without an image of the enemy.... However, while the Prime Minister has the backing support of favorable public opinion, it sharply differs from the mood in the West. But Putin withheld the attack [and] ... made it clear that he was not going to listen to teacher-like conversations with the West ... anti-Caucasian and anti-Western sentiment—the solid alloy from which the shields and swords for electoral stadia are forged today.[4]

In this article, the main tenets of Putin's introduction of a new nationally infused political agenda were fleshed out. It noted that Putin was on a quest for a new ideology, to replace the debunked communist one. Putin's ideology was based on "patriotism in its best sense"—resonating Soviet typology of positive patriotism versus negative nationalism. But the author contrasted Putin's claims with his own understanding of the situation—that Putin's appeal was not based on constructive feelings of belonging, but on fear disseminated by the terrorist attacks on apartment blocks in Buinaksk, Moscow, and Volgograd and by creation of an image of the enemy, be it Caucasian or Western. According to this article, anti-Western and anti-Caucasian sentiments were the two pillars of Putin's national ideological orientation and quest for public support. This article underlined an important point—the reciprocal nature of the relationship between Putin and the public. Putin did not impose his own ideas, but provided ideological and emotional outlets for existing exigencies.[5]

The appeal of war was one such exigency that the Russian public craved, before Putin introduced it. The sample of media clippings used in the previous chapter and in this one showed that the national rallying around war began approximately six months before the war in Chechnya when it focused on Yugoslavia. The close timing and similar discursive patterns of the two arenas (Yugoslavia and Chechnya) were instructive of the Russian public's mood at the end of the previous millennium. Politicians were using aggressive national rhetoric and the Russian public, generally, responded favorably. The media, in both cases, resisted the trend. There is no evidence that Putin or his advisors decided to focus his prime ministership on Chechnya following the debate on Yugoslavia. But the Russian public's receptiveness to the rhetoric around Yugoslavia may have helped them see the popular appeal of a military campaign. This reciprocal relationship with audiences became one of the most important characteristics of the government-backed discourse, which was highly reflexive and receptive. In the Chechen campaign, Putin harnessed support by providing the public with what they had seemed to desire—a strong flagging of the nation through military means in which identification could be crystallized. In this episode, Putin for the first time played the role of a national facilitator.

This did not mean that there was no objective security problem in Chechnya and that the intervention served purely political ends. On the contrary, Chechnya became volatile before Putin was appointed prime minister and designated successor to Yeltsin. Hence, it is completely possible that the Chechen campaign would have taken place even without Putin at the helm. Yet the rallying, the intensive publicity, the language used, and the national and political argumentations to justify this campaign, all demonstrate that the military operation in Chechnya was packaged to fit a specific public need for a strong sense of national unity.

The Introduction of the Discourse of Stability and the Authorial Voice

As in other cases of rallying around a conflict, after a while the heightened mood calmed down. National identification went back to being flagged from time to time, and expressed in more banal ways. Although the war on terrorism and other flagging of war themes continued, the media discourse started to feature the new government-backed 'discourse of stability' and the government's authorial voice. Yet this discourse appropriated themes from the post-1996 discourse and continued to feature the experience of fluid Russianness.

A very strong theme of national identification was, very much like in the 1990s, the economy as a unifying national endeavor. In April 2000 *Izvestia* ran the following commentary, underlying the importance of the economy for Putin's unifying measures:

> Vladimir Putin is excited. The results of the first quarter are so blissful that the president-elect spoke about the Russian economy with delight, using the most flattering epithets. Economic growth, which according to official results amounted in the first quarter to more than 9 per cent, was called by the head of state "stable," "good" and "enormous" . . . If the latter definition is fully consistent with the truth, and the second - only partially, and the first is an obvious exaggeration . . . Nevertheless, economic growth becomes the main [issue] for Putin's ideology and national idea, and a criterion for the efficiency of officials . . . [6]

Although this article was part of the forming counter-discourse to the government's discourse of stability (Putin's efforts were doubted and belittled), it is an important text for understanding the contours of the new government discourse. For Putin, economic growth was focal point around which he could harness popular support. First, the economy as a national idea was already a popular sub-discourse from mid-1990s. However, in the government-backed discourse of stability the economy played a different role from the 1990s discourse. In the 1990s, the economy was part of the neoliberal globalized free market, which was unpredictable and needed constant elasticity on the part of the individuals, as expressed in the discourse of flexibility. Putin's thinking inferred a modernist approach that if the economy was run effectively, it would lead to stability. By doing so the government-backed discourse subverted the theme of economy into a new context, where Russia would be experienced as a "stable" entity, in contrast to the transition period of the 1990s.

Putin attached the idea of a successful economy to the idea of efficient government. Efficiency and effectiveness became central points. This was Putin's promise to the Russian people—an effectively controlled state that was ruled by pragmatic laws with a foreseeable outcome. This image of stability and effectiveness which was generated from the discourse on the economy transcended the economic context and became a defining feature of political and social life, and the heart of the discourse of stability. Peter Pomerantsev, a British journalist of Russian origins, remarked in his book *Nothing is True and Everything is Possible* that the image of the President, as developed by Putin, was that of an "effective manager."[7] The term effective was placed at the center of the discourse, closely linked to the term stable. Pomerantsev wrote: "'Effective' becomes the raison d'être for everything . . . 'Our relationship is not effective' lovers tell each other when they break up."[8] Putin expressed these ideas in an interview to *Izvestia* in July 2000: "In Russia, there is shortage of effective state power—that's a fact . . . As a result . . . we have, perhaps, the freest society—unfortunately, even free from law, order and morality . . . Yes, there is a favorable external environment, which we use . . . But there is another [thing]—consistent, persistent and deliberate actions of the state . . ."[9]

This abstract reveals the logical chain behind the government's discourse. First, the previous Russian government had suffered from loss of effectiveness. By doing so Putin tapped into the well-established and popular discourse of loss. Second, he underlined the popular causal link between the failure of the state system and liberal values. This focused the attention on the consequences of late modernity of freedom that leads to insecurity. This linkage was powerful because it revealed a real shortcoming of the late modern system, where freedom was not always a pleasant experience and often led to a sense of loss. It made it easier for Putin to argue that freedom was not necessarily a good thing and law and order were more important to society. Putin also linked up morality with law and order. This was a response to early claims that his vision lacked spirituality, as an integral part of Russian national identification. He signaled that he was not merely a pragmatist who was implementing major domestic reforms, but also an ideologue who cared about the morality of the people. Last, Putin defied claims that Russia's economic growth was due to factors unrelated to his efforts—specifically rising oil prices. He stressed that the state was reassuming its responsibilities through "consistent, persistent and deliberate" activity.

Many parts of the interview addressed national identification. For example, the interviewer asked which social forces supported Putin. His answer was a highly inclusive one—"The multinational Russian people (*Rossiyskiy narod*) . . ."[10] This answer signaled that he did not reject Yeltsin's civic approach and referred to Russia's multinational composition and identity. He implied that there was no fundamental change in the approach to national identification, as was also seen in citizenship legislation, where Putin never tried to insert an ethnic clause for eligibility, and that there would be no ethnic or other ideological reorientation.

Putin concluded the interview by tying national ideology and unity to his reforms' success: "I am convinced that now the outlines of a new national ideology are already determined. If the society, the people, will be willing to follow basic common objectives—this will mean the success of the reforms that are underway."[11] This interview outlined the basics of the government's discourse of stability: Putin would reinstate a strong state, while he would not diverge from the civic model of national identification. He asked the Russian people to give up some of their freedoms and unite behind him so that he could stabilize Russia and lead it to success.

The Old-New Anthem and the Performative Shift

A similar dynamic of discourse of stability and counter-discourse by media elites was manifested in the debate around the Russian anthem, which also revealed the deeper meanings of the transformation in the discourse on Russian national identification. Since 1990 the Russian anthem was a melody by the nineteenth-century composer Mikhail Glinka, called Patriotic Song. In 2000 Putin proposed to reconsider the Patriotic Song as a national anthem. He set up a working group that looked into several options—devising lyrics for the 'Patriotic Song' melody; choosing a new anthem; or reinstating the Soviet anthem with new words.[12] Putin was reported to favor the last option from the outset. This was the option that the working group chose, and it was adopted by a Presidential Decree in December 2000.[13] The Unbreakable Union, which had been the Soviet Union's anthem for 46 years, was reintroduced as the new anthem with lyrics re-written by the original writer, Sergey Mikhalkov (father of the film-maker Nikita Mikhalkov). The process leading to this decision sparked a heated public debate.

In October 2000 *Novaya Gazeta* published the following:

> Excited like a schoolboy, Nikita Mikhalkov describes on television the new version of the national idea, the search for which he was engaged in for several years now. It turned out there is not one idea, but two. And both are good. Just now Nikita Sergeyevich delivered them to the President in the Kremlin, and now he shares them with us. The first idea—Orthodoxy... The second idea—even better. It [is] expressed, by chance, (and even twice—in the 1930s and 1970s) by a close relative of Nikita

Sergeyevich—Sergei Vladimirovich Mikhalkov. To quote the famous director and caring son:—And I told the President that he [his father], if asked to do so, will not refuse to write the national anthem once more . . .[14]

Novaya Gazeta, a liberal publication generally averse to discussions of national ideology and reintroduction of elements from the Soviet past, took a particularly critical stance. The text belittled Mikhalkov and his efforts in the field of national ideology. The article used satirical style to ridicule Mikhalkov's idea and referred to him as "excited schoolboy." His idea, besides orthodoxy, was to allow his father, Sergei Mikhalkov, the writer of the original Soviet anthem, to write the new lyrics for the reintroduced anthem. *Novaya Gazeta* defined this as self-serving, and an attempt to acquire the sympathy of the new president. The article refers to the fact that Sergei Mikhalkov wrote the anthem twice, once in the 1940s, when the lyrics were edited personally by Stalin, and once more in the 1970s when the references to Stalin were removed. This draws a parallel between Soviet times and Putin's Russia, when the Mikhalkovs, father and son, offered their creative services to ingratiate themselves with the regime.

Last, *Novaya Gazeta* brought up a stylistic important point: "Under the Bolsheviks people lived [in] *perelitsovkoy* [remaking of objects/ideas] . . . Putin and his love for the masquerade . . . revived *perelitsovka* as a style. It is because this is what he was taught in the KGB, and, apparently, because he does not have his own ideas. But something needs to be done . . ."[15] This article noted that Putin revived a certain style that was common in Soviet times. However, they dismissed it as a shallow populist move that could not have real bearing on Russian society ("something needs to be done"). The reintroduction of the Soviet anthem was indeed popular in the public, and even Yeltsin criticized Putin for "following the mood of the people" in this issue, rather than promoting his own agenda.[16] *Novaya Gazeta* and Yeltsin saw the reintroduction of the Soviet anthem as a response to the growing nostalgia and heightened nationalistic mood, and underestimated the importance of this move.

However, the move signified a deeper symbolic shift and in fact began a process of reconciliation of different parts of Russian history and acceptance of continuity from Soviet times.[17] It was part of Putin's ideological quest for stability and normalization and as British historian Richard Sakwa puts it, an "attempt to reconcile the various phases of Russian history, especially over the last century."[18] The anthem was adopted into a law together with two other national symbols—the national emblem (the double-headed imperial eagle) and the three-color national flag. These symbols represented both imperial and post-Soviet Russian history—thus linking between the three historical periods.

Putin commented that the old-new anthem was "an important indication that we finally managed to bridge the disparity between past and present."[19]

In this framework, the subtext of *Novaya Gazeta*'s comment about Putin's KGB past, as a man who could not be trusted, was useless. Putin spoke openly about his past in the Soviet Union's security services. Not only was Putin proud of his own service, many of the people he brought to power were his former KGB colleagues, the *Siloviki*.[20] This was a source of pride in his personal Soviet history that allowed others to take pride in their Soviet history and to reconstruct continuity of identity. The reintroduction of the anthem encouraged Russians to take pride in the Soviet past, such as the Soviet victory in the Great Patriotic War, when the first version of the Unbreakable Union was introduced.[21] This was not a simple lapse back into old patterns, but a coping mechanism for the difficulties that were posed by both the collapse of the Soviet social order and the new social circumstances of flexibility, where identities were less well-defines. Putin was helping Russians to reproduce continuity of identity and to restore ontological security.

The return of Soviet *perelitsovka*, which was mentioned in the *Novaya Gazeta* article in connection to the new anthem, signaled another deep change in Russia. It was a restoration of Soviet discursive techniques that had shaped power relations in society in the late-Soviet period. Yurchak noted that after the 1950s the Soviet discourse experienced hypernormalisation. It became increasingly fixed and underwent a shift in which "the performative dimension took precedence."[22] This allowed actors to have power delegated to them once they reproduced *"in form* acts and utterances of ideology."[23] In the Soviet times this meant that as long as people spoke using certain terms in certain contexts, the power of the authorities was bestowed on them and they could go on in their daily tasks—managing employees at the workplace, conducting youth club Komsomol gatherings, and speaking in public. Putin's *perelitsovka* of the anthem, the use of the old tune, created the performance of a great state with a glorious history.

Putin reproduced this discursive style that was familiar in Russia and was easily absorbed by society. For example, using terms such as effective and stable would make people feel secure and part of the in-group. This hypernormalized language and made interactions in the society more predictable. By reintroducing this style, Putin was bridging and reconciling not only between different phases of Russian history, but also between different historically contingent discursive styles. As the next several sections in this chapter will show, these discursive techniques were used in new ways. They were adapted for the new post-Soviet era and became ever more sophisticated over Putin's years in power, revealing their potency as political tools, as well as their limitations.

The Kremlin's New Media Tools

In 2002 an *Izvestia* article outlined the new political discourse in Russia and its constitutive elements and the place of the media in its dissemination:

> The population, including the intelligentsia (or "intellectual elite"), is so tired of politicians that with the greatest pleasure it is watching on television endless football, hockey, boxing, etc . . . They interpret the signals coming from the authorities in their own way, assuming that the Uvarov triad "Orthodoxy, Autocracy, Nationality" will be reformulated and transformed into a "Vertical of Power, Sport, Orthodoxy." The government tests the state ideology specifically on TV. And soon on the sixth button [of the remote control] we will be shown what the national idea actually looks like and whether it provides the answer to all possible questions or just for one: "what's the score?"[24]

This snappy text underlined that Putin's construction of national identification had captured the attention of the Russian population, including the intellectuals. The newspaper even likened it to the so-called official nationality which was formulated as early as the 1830–40s by the Minister of Education of Nicholas I, Sergey Uvarov. This sent a message to the reading audience, which was familiar with Uvarov's triad and the historical context of Nicholas I's reign, which signified Russian conservatism. In its reincarnation, the triad mixed between such serious themes as the Federal center's governance, dubbed as vertical of power and Christian Orthodox religion, and trivial lay themes of sports.

But most importantly, the text underlined the Kremlin's campaign to assert control over the media and specifically over television, which was underway since 2000. The sixth button mentioned in the text was TV-6, a Moscow-based television channel, owned by the oligarch Boris Berezovsky that was shut down in January 2002. Its license was given to a sports television channel and when viewers turned on their televisions, instead of TV-6 they discovered sports programs.[25] *Izvestia* itself came under increased pressure from the Kremlin to align with the government, threatened to lose its name, which was supposedly a state-owned brand. In March 2002 (a month after the above quoted text was published) Putin visited the newspaper's office together with his Media Minister Lesin, who was notorious for his creative measures to exert political and economic pressure as tools to subvert media outlets.[26] After the visit the newspaper shifted the editorial line towards pro-Kremlin reporting.

The Kremlin's takeover the media began in 2000–2001 when the state-owned Gazprom took over the NTV channel, Russia's most professional TV channel, and dismissed its editor-in-chief, Yevgeny Kiselev.[27] These events signified a shift in power relations between the media and the government that had far reaching consequences on the development of language. The nature of this shift was discussed on April 3, 2001 during an emergency televised sit-in moderated by Kiselev.[28] He asked the audience: "what would Russia look like after NTV?"[29] Historian Yuri Afanasiev, referred to Putin's address to the Federal Assembly, which focused on the terms stability and effectiveness: "If we take what is being said as the departing point, namely that stabilization was achieved and now there is gradual progress . . . this false starting point . . . can only gain foothold without such phenomena as NTV. . . . In one way this is a lie, in another way it is perfidy (*verolomsvo*)."[30] This was an important distinction between lies and the much stronger Russian word of *verolomsvo*, implying consciously undermining someone's trust, acting in bad faith, and perpetrating deceit. Lillia Shevtsova, a Russian social scientist noted: "I think that we are entering the period of imitation—imitation of parties, of NTV, imitation of a strong state."[31] Indeed, perfidy (*verolomsvo*) and imitation, which are also closely related to the term of *perelitsovka* that was mentioned in the 2001 *Novaya Gazeta* article, were important discursive techniques that were used to shape political discourse and to manage political reality.

Fluid Russianness and Government Discourse

Before this chapter proceeds into an investigation of the Kremlin's new discursive techniques, this section will present a few media clippings of the continued evolution of fluid Russianness in the government's discourse of stability. These exemplify the variety of themes that circulated in the Russian media, reflecting an inclusive identification with supplementing ethnic elements.

In 2003, Putin met with university students, winners of an essay competition themed "My home, my city, my country." He stated: "When an empire falls, it is difficult to find a simple and yet profound idea, which would be able to unite the nation above economic, national, ideological, political and generational divides. . . . Perhaps the only idea of this kind—the real connection that would not split society—love for the mother tongue and involvement in the 'big' history of the country through a link with the history of 'small.'"[32]

In this talk, Putin tapped into feelings of loss in the Russian society—the fall of the empire—which caused divide and dislocation throughout society. The remedy for that perceived loss, in his opinion, was by underscoring the role of the Russian language. The mobilizing power of Russian language was both an exclusive and an inclusive element. On the one hand, the Russian language was an ethnic Russian element. By promoting Russian as an element of identification with the nation, Putin was embedding ethnic Russianness as one of the pillars of Russian national identification. Language, however, was in some ways an inclusive element, since command of the language could be acquired and then serve as a path for admission into the national in-group. As part of elevating the Russian language as an expression of identification, in 2005 the Russian government recognized it as the official language of the Russian Federation, to ensure the "protection and development of language culture."[33]

As part of the attempts to bridge between the post-Soviet Russian people and Russia's history, a new holiday from the Tsarist era was reintroduced to the national calendar. In 2005 the government restored a Tsarist-era holiday, which was celebrated around November 4.[34] This holiday replaced the Anniversary of the October Revolution (November 7, which in 1996 was renamed The Day of Accord and Conciliation). This move is discussed at length in chapter six, but the debate is instructive for the development of the government's discourse of stability. In 2004 *Novaya Gazeta* published an article on this topic: "Maybe next year November 7 will be excluded from the holiday calendar. Instead, November 4 will be made a holiday - in memory of how the Nizhny Novgorod merchant Kozma Minin and Prince Dmitry Pozharsky who drove the Poles and Lithuanians out of Moscow in 1612 . . . Vladislav Surkov said that 'we need to create a strong state to build a strong nation.' And now the Russian Orthodox Church took the initiative to go back from October 1917 to November 1612."[35]

This text rightly noted that removing the old holiday in favor of the new Unity Day was a big symbolic step. The decision was part of a government policy to bridge between different chapters in Russian history and to reinstate continuity of identity. This step linked ethnic Russian (*Russkaya*) history with post-Soviet civic Russian (*Rossiskaya*) history. The government, with the backing of the Russian Orthodox Church, supplemented the national discourse with ethnic elements that would express Russianness—the old kingdom's military victory and the Orthodox symbolism of the state. Importantly, in the post-Soviet era, due to a deliberate policy by the Russian Orthodox Church, Orthodox Christianity became closely associated by the public with ethnic Russianness.[36]

The decision to remove the day that celebrated the 1917 Revolution, however, had ideational goals that went beyond supplementing national identification with ethnic Russian themes. It introduced the government's discourse of stability in relation to national identification. Putin was projecting that post-Soviet uncertainty—which was likened to the sixteenth-seventeenth century Time of Troubles in Muscovite Russia, when Russia had no legitimate ruler—was over. He signaled that the time of transition, arguably an ongoing process that started with Peter the Great's modernization, had also come to an end.[37] The image of the 1917 revolution did not fit the discourse of stability and was rejected on the grounds that this was not a desirable form of political development. Putin's ideology of stability, packaged for media consumption by his top aide, Vladislav Surkov, connected between the image of strong state and a strong nation. The vertical of power, which was meant to increase governance was also set as a tool to construct a strong national identity.

Surkov's Newspeak

In 2006, Surkov introduced another term into the government discourse—"sovereign democracy." Sovereign democracy was an expansion of the earlier concept of vertical of power, which referred to strengthening the state in the domestic arena. Sovereign democracy encompassed domestic as well as foreign policy themes of stability. It argued for a different type of political development in Russia—one that allowed more powers to the executive domestically and was no longer anchored in Western models of liberal democratic transition.

The debate around this term showed the prevalence of the discursive techniques of perfidy, imitation and *perelitsovka* that were mentioned earlier. They became powerful tools that were increasingly used in the Russian media by the government to manage public opinion, and eventually became its pitfall.

In February 2006 Surkov gave a speech titled "Russia is an Independent Subject of History—Our Russian Model of Democracy is Called Sovereign Democracy."[38] *Izvestia*, which was already aligned with the government line, exemplified the use of authorial voice, perfidy and imitation to promote the idea of sovereign democracy:

> Of all European values, the idea of sovereignty—especially sovereignty of the nation-state—[is] the most closely related to the traditional political values of Russia. . . . In the 1990s there was no freedom for patriotic-minded intellectuals, for those who were trying to save the Russian culture and national identity. . . . The arrival of Putin to power in the summer of 1999 entailed the restoration of independence and sovereignty for

those who like and want to use the ensuing freedom for the blessing of Russia, for the benefit of the Russian majority, loyal to the Motherland, who does not think of life outside of it . . .[39]

This article was not simple propaganda to legitimize Russia's divergence from democratic transition, but a sort of Orwellian newspeak, further deepening of use of authorial voice, perfidy and imitation. The text manipulated the meaning and context of terms such as value of freedom and the worth of liberal democracy. The author claimed that the introduction of liberal democracy did not bring about freedom, at least not to those Russians who regard themselves as "patriotic-minded intellectuals." Putin, conversely, according to the author, gave those people the opportunity to use their freedom by restoring independence and sovereignty. In this text Putin was a true democrat, who strengthened the state and gave back the "Russian majority" their rights. This article argued that by taking freedom away from people Putin was freeing them. It emptied the terms *sovereignty* and *democracy* of their meaning.

The article showed the manipulation of political language in Putin's Russia, where argumentation included blurring terms, emptying their original meaning, and prioritizing performative elements—keeping the trappings of democracy, but undermining its system of values. However, these techniques were a double-edged sword—it gave the government command over the discourse, but it was also made political debate unstable, or fluid, which was fundamentally irreconcilable with its own efforts to increase the sense of stability. These trends were even more evident on Russian federal television, where the government focused most of its attention.

Fluid Screens—The Rise of The Federal Television

The events around NTV in 2000–2001, described earlier, exposed a decision by the Kremlin to use television as its tool of choice for constructing the authorial voice and delivering the discourse of stability to the public.[40] Television's unique features meant that the Kremlin could not simply reintroduce Soviet discursive techniques. Soviet techniques were more appropriate for texts—speeches, ritualized conventions or censored and pre-recorded televised broadcasts. In post-Soviet Russia discourse was produced in live televised broadcasts, which required far more innovation and became a new type of manipulation where the medium was the message. This section will turn to Vladimir Solovyov's *Poyedinok*, which was a prime venue for the development of the new discursive techniques.

It was intriguing that Putin chose television in the first place as an instrument to generate an authorial voice. Television is a reflexive tool that is constantly self-conscious and relies on a sender-receiver mechanism.[41] Without capturing the audience's attention, televised broadcasts have no meaning. Hence, television had to remain interesting and entertaining, and Soviet-style censorship was out of the question. Instead, politics were imitated. Pomerantsev recalled a meeting where a political TV presenter said: "We all know there will be no real politics. But we have to give our viewers a sense that something is happening. They have to be kept entertained. . . . Politics has got to feel like . . . like a movie."[42] In this system the relevant market imperatives of television were kept, while a looser (in comparison to Soviet times) system of censorship was maintained through levers of state-owned companies who owned the channels, as well as instructions from the presidential administration to editors, called *temniki* from the Russian word *tema* (theme).[43]

Poyedinok—A Fluid Duel

Vladimir Solovyov's live political talk show *Poyedinok* (Duel), formerly called *K Bar'eru* (To the barrier), was in many ways a product of the political struggles in the Russian media, as well as an important player in forming the authorial voice in the new televised settings. The format of a verbal duel first appeared on Russian television in 1999 on NTV, hosted by NTV's Kiselev. The show was called *Glas Naroda* (Vox populi) and was a highly praised talk show. After Gazprom's takeover of NTV, *Glas Naroda* appeared for a while on liberal TV-6 and TVS. *Poyedinok* appeared on TVS in 2002, as a liberal political talk show. In 2003 TVS was taken off air by the government. *Poyedinok* moved to the already government controlled NTV and aired under the name *K Bar'eru*, where it aligned with the government. During these years the show was in a unique position, as Russian television did not feature many political talk shows.[44] In 2010 the show moved to Channel-1, Russia's second largest channel, again under the name *Poyedinok* and became a focal point for political discourse in Russia and a model for a growing segment of political talk shows on Russian television.[45] Solovyov had become one of Russia's most popular media personalities and an influential public intellectual.

Poyedinok used both imitation and perfidy (*verolomsvo*). The format reeked of free speech, but there was no place for free expression. Like in the Western format, *Poyedinok* mixed politics and entertainment through a seemingly lively and frank conversation.[46] It was broadcasted live and as the name of the show suggested, it was a one-on-one verbal duel, dealing with pertinent social and political issues. The "duelists" were politicians, social or cultural figures, including government representatives, members of the approved opposition (LDPR, Communists, the nationalist Rodina party) and members of the unapproved nationalist and liberal opposition. The studio had a raised glass stage with two barriers behind which each participant stood. The participants, some of whom did not receive airtime on federal news broadcasts, took center stage in this show.[47]

Nevertheless, this was an imitation of free speech. Anti-government participants were often treated unfairly, which undermined their ability to perform well. They were not informed of the theme of the show in advance and encountered hostile atmosphere in the studio (booing and provocative questions from paid persons in the audience).[48] The winner of the duel was chosen by the viewers via telephone. In most cases, this was the figure closer to the government line. Moreover, a judge or a jury, usually persons aligned with the government line, commented on the performance of the duelists from the studio.

Perfidy was another important discursive technique that was used on *Poyedinok*. The show constantly blurred terms, such as democracy, liberalism, and even ethnic Russian (*Russkiy*), and disseminated mistrust. This mechanism helped the government keep the audience passive. The British social scientist Andrew Wilson noted that the imitation of politics, which he called virtual politics, required passive audiences.[49] For hybrid authoritarian regimes, like Putin's Russia, to continue to govern, citizens should be willing to forfeit their civil and political rights.[50] This could be achieved by undermining people's trusts in their ability to make sense of politics and to impact the social world around them. In *Poyedinok*, once all political terms and concepts were ruled to be untrustworthy, the government's authorial voice and its discourse of stability, became the only rational option. This was an intentional breaking of people's trust in politics, or in Russian—*verolomsvo*.

Verolomsvo as a Discursive Technique

Among the many manifestations of the shapeshifting nature of the debate in Solovyov's show, a pivotal one was the increased sense of withering away of political orientation. In December 2008, the show featured Vladimir Zhirinovsky, who was a frequent guest, and Boris Nadezhdin, leader of the Russian liberal opposition party, Just Cause.[51] The show discussed the constitutional reforms of 2008, which extended presidential and parliamentary terms.

Zhirinovsky began his performance by calling Nadezhdin a "democratic worm." Nadezhdin, in response, noted: "Vladimir Wolfowich, you have confused something. Liberal Democratic is the name of your party and not mine.

Mine is called Just Cause." This kick-started a debate that strongly resonated the fragmented nature of broadcasted political discussions in Russia. Accusations about responsibility for Russia's ills were traded at length, when the discussion took a sharp turn.

Nadezhdin accused Zhirinovsky of selling his parliamentary support to the government since Yeltsin's times. Zhirinovsky, agitated, turned to Solovyov accusing Nadezhdin of lying, and called him a scoundrel. Solovyov sarcastically added "and a worm," heightening the tense atmosphere. Zhirinovsky continued to swear. At some point Solovyov tried to calm him down. Not only did Zhirinovsky not calm down, he ordered his guard to "take this scoundrel and kick him out of the studio." A large man entered the stage and approached Nadezhdin. Solovyov physically shielded Nazehdin, while exclaiming "this is a [TV] program!" Nadezhdin, looking stunned, mumbled "have you lost your mind?" Severe-looking Solovyov called the NTV guards to the stage. Five large men entered the stage, while Zhirinovsky yelled at them "take this beast away." Solovyov tried to physically separate Zhirinovsky from Nadezhdin, while the former continued to curse. The scene ended by Solovyov calling a recess. In the interval, commentators in the studio calmly discussed the participants' performance.

When the participants returned from the recess, Solovyov addressed the incident in the following way: "I understand that you hold the deepest contempt for each other, but I asked you to stay for one reason—because the citizens of Russia are unfortunately deprived of many political formats, they have no opportunity to hear their political leaders and to understand what is the essence of things . . . I would suggest continuing in order to deliver to the people, to your voters, your point of view." The debate continued with the following exchange:

> NADEZHDIN: Nobody explained to the people [the government's decisions . . .], you are a member of parliament, please explain them.
> ZHIRINOVSKY: [. . .] I agree, [. . .] but we are not the government.
> NADEZHDIN: But you are a deputy.
> ZHIRINOVSKY: But we tell them the same thing you tell them. What do you blame us for?[52]

This episode was extraordinary in many respects, but also very symptomatic of the televised debate that the show produced. From the very start the term democracy and who was a democrat was scrutinized. Zhirinovsky used it as a derogatory term. Nadezhdin, who represented a party that cherished democratic values, did not stop him. In Russia, a society that had been building its state institutions such a conversation was ruinous to a stable sense of national development and identification. After the collapse of the Soviet Union, Russian democrats, such as Nadezhdin, claimed they had a national vision for the country's development—a free market economy and liberal democracy. This was a Western path of development, which had strong consequences for the type of national identification that developed in Russia. Hence, twisting the term democracy and comparing its advocates—Nadezhdin and the Union of Rightist Forces—to Zhirinovsky, resonated Surkov's blurring of sovereign democracy. It deliberately confused not only political orientation but also the orientation of national identification.

Solovyov's appeal to continue the show for the sake of pluralistic debate revealed his biased approach. He had a vested interest in the political circus that unfolded in the studio. The extreme language used, the loss of meaning and agency and the threat of physical violence had nothing to do with a pluralistic debate. This show's purpose was to undermine political alternatives to the current regime. The ideological credibility of two opponents was tarnished—they were in fact one and the same. They were also made to look ridiculous, vapid and irresponsible. This was in sharp contrast to the leadership in the Kremlin.

Fluid Russianness on *Poyedinok*

The second decade of Putin's regime, and especially since Putin returned for his third term as president in 2012 after switching briefly with Dmitry Medvedev, was marked by an increase in the importance of national issues on the political agenda. This trend was growing for years and by 2010 things had come to the fore. This was reflected in the selection of discussion topics on *Poyedinok*. In 2010 several episodes of *Poyedinok* dealt with issues linked directly with national identification in Russia. These episodes showed how, on one the one hand, the government responded to pressure from the nationalist right in Russia by shifting its approach towards more exclusivist nationally-infused agenda. But, on the other hand, used its techniques of blurring and disorientation in order not to divert too much from the contours of fluid Russianness that developed in the Russian society.

In November 2010 Poyedinok focused on migration to Russia, which, as described in chapters one and two, was closely linked to conceptions of national identification. The show featured the conservative Russian journalist Mikhail Leontyev and the Jewish Azerbaijani-born film director Yuli Gusman. The following discussion took place at the very start of the program:

> GUSMAN: I was born in the city of Baku where the words "friendship of the people," "man to man - friend, comrade and brother," were not

> just slogans of the CPSU, but a real fulfilment of life . . . This problem [with migrants] in the country in which we lived [together] for seventy years . . . seems invented and disgusting.
>
> LEONTYEV: I was born in the Soviet Union, I did not like the political regime . . . but the country as a whole was to my liking. . . . These people, they are for me . . . my compatriots. All of them. Including the Tajiks . . . Armenians, Moldovans, Western Ukrainians and so on. . . . And what happened with them is in some way our fault. The country was destroyed by the Russians (*Russkiye*) . . .[53]

This show was supposed to present contesting views on a very serious matter—migration and Russian national identification. However, there was actually no disagreement in this exchange, although the basic views of the discussants and the moderator were quite different. Gusman and Leontyev both stressed the common past as a rudimentary building block in the post-Soviet Russian experience. Gusman argued for a humanistic approach towards migration, which is perched on Soviet concepts like "friendship of the people."[54] Leontyev, who was invited to the program on an anti-migration ticket, also referred to migrants as his compatriots, resonating an inclusive approach to Russianness. Leontyev's approach was imperialist as he noted that he felt responsibility for the fate of the most unpopular compatriots, such as the Tajiks and Western Ukrainians. Both men's views converged on the revisited memory of the Soviet past.

This performance represented an expression of fluid Russianness, while it also reproduced the government's authorial voice, as it resonated Putin's assertion from 2005 that the collapse of the Soviet Union was a catastrophe.[55] Yet Gusman and Leontyev's expressions blurred very basic assumptions regarding migration in Russia. First, there was confusion about who belonged to the national in-group and who was an outsider. While some commentators on the show described migrants as different and threatening, people who were not needed and unwanted, many others, including Gusman and Leontyev, saw them as lost brothers from a previous life who had been mistreated. It was also not clear who was the perpetrator and who the victim.

The fact that the show did not present two approaches to migration, with no expertise or data, enhanced the sense of instability in the field of migration. These unanswered questions demonstrated the fragmentation of the debate, while the format of the show allowed for the imitation of political debate on one of the most serious topics in Russian political life. Such a show curbed any opportunity for people to form their opinion on migration and scrutinize (or support) the government's policy, which, as shown in the previous chapters, was very problematic. It also increased the pervading sense of dislocation and complicated feelings of national belonging.

A Nationalist Turn in Russian Politics?

At the end of 2010 the national issue reached a boiling point when Moscow experienced mass ethnic riots on Manezh Square, which caught the government off guard. On 11 December 2010 between 5,000 (police estimate) and 12,000 (experts estimate) demonstrators flooded the center of Moscow under the slogans "Russia for the Russians—Moscow for Muscovites" and "Moscow is not the Caucasus."[56] The events were prompted by the murder on 6 December of Spartak FC fan Egor Sviridov by men of Caucasian origin. The perpetrators were arrested, but five out of the six were released the same night.[57] Spartak fans demonstrated for several days after the event and on 11 December, a day after Sviridov's funeral, mass demonstrations of ultra-right groups broke out.[58] These events posed an acute need to address tensions of what were perceived as deriving from increased migration to Russia.[59] *Poyedinok* devoted two shows to riots. Both featured the blurring of terms in the participants' argumentations and in Solovyov's moderation.

The first show featured playwright and director Mark Rozovsky, who was accepted in government circles, and writer Alexander Prokhanov, who was associated with nationalist circles.[60] In these settings Prokhanov was poised as the oppositional participant. The mood in the studio was grim. To underline that the show was broadcasted in an emergency format, instead of studio commentators the show featured public addresses by President Dmitry Medvedev, Prime Minister Vladimir Putin, and Russian Orthodox Church Patriarch Kirill. They provided embodiments of the authorial voice. Yet, these appearances by the "holy trinity" of political and moral authority in Russia did not anchor the debate in any meaningful way. During the show, Rozovsky and Prokhanov continuously described the fragmented late modern reality of post-Soviet Russia. This may have served the purpose of deflecting criticism from the government, but also reinforced the sense of helplessness and underscored that Russia was neither more stable nor more secure.

> ROZOVSKY: Russia for the (ethnic) Russians (*Russkiy*)—who can argue with that? Only in Russia Russians (*Russkiy*) are Russians themselves, Udmur, Tatars, Jews, Chukchas and even Chechens . . .
>
> PROKHANOV: We have to admit that inter-ethnic strife (*mezhnatsionalia rozn'*) is a terrible reality in Russia. . . . We need to honestly look this

truth in the eyes and to say that in the centre of this terrible problem is the Russian question (*Russkiy vopros*).

ROZOVSKY: Let's start from the fact that I am a fan of Spartak. . . . But I am precisely a fan, not a fanatic. I remember football in Soviet times when in our team from the left side played Meskhi from the right Metriveli, Simonyan played for Spartak. . . . All these are people who have non-Russian (*Russkiy*) surnames. . . . And now I went to a football [game] and Spartak played against, I think, Nalchik.⁶¹ I remember how the fans' gallery chanted: *"Russkiy* forward," *"Russkiy* forward"* [emphasizes aggressively] and at the end . . . Welliton scored a fantastic goal.⁶² Our reality is completely different . . . if there were no provocateurs. . . . We would have lived in a different reality. . . . I consider you responsible for what happened in our country. . . . Do you not feel responsibility? You, personally! (Rozovsky points at Prokhanov)

PROKHANOV: You Mr. Mark Grigorievich a person that hates all that is Soviet and . . . suddenly you are reminiscing about Soviet brotherhood. . . . The reality is as follows: In the Soviet times the Russian nation (*Russkiy narod*), I repeat the Russian nation, was busy. Mainly it served in the Army . . . Russian people worked on gigantic factories that produced ships and airplanes . . . and the main place where [ethnic] Russians worked was in building the mega-machine of the state, the imperial state, all of that the democrats . . . have taken away from the Russian people. . . . These people passed to their grandchildren this energy of protest. . . .

The debate exhibited high levels of fragmentation of the political discourse. Prokhanov tried to anchor the debate and used the term "inter-ethnic strife," which was a legal-official term. Rozovsky informally represented the government in the debate and helped Solovyov blur terms and deflect criticism away from the government. He immediately blurred the meaning of ethnic Russian (*Russkiy*). The blurring of terms related to ethnic purity served the government, as it undermined the rioters' demands for ethnically pure Russia. In fact, Solovyov made this blurring of the term *Russkiy* in his essay from 2009 "We are Russians—god is with us" ("*My russkiye - s nami' bog*").⁶³ This statement by Rozovsky could have been planted by Solovyov to test the reconstruction of the term *Russkiy* on larger audiences, or could have been on Rozovsky's own initiative. In any case, Rozovsky revealed himself as a pro-government participant. Rozovsky played along with Solovyov, when presenting the current globalized experience where football clubs have players from a variety of countries. This revealed to Spartak's football fans who rioted on Manezh, that Prokhanov represented in the debate, as misguided. They chanted for an ethnically pure cause, but their football club was multinational.

Very importantly, this show presented competing conceptions of reality. Notably, Solovyov did not interrupt the exchange between Rozovsky and Prokhanov about what was real in Russia. Solovyov's non-interference exposed that this discussion served the show's aim to manage public opinion. The debate on what was real in Russia blurred the certainty with which one can construct a valid counterargument to the Kremlin. If reality itself was questionable and uncertain, open to alternative interpretations, public opinion could be directed, or at least deflected from forming a viable opposition to the Kremlin. This was particularly important in the context of this show, since it was noted by scholars that the Kremlin was caught by surprise by the Manezh riots.[64] There was no official line to promote and the content was produced according to previously established conceptions, rather than around a pronounced government line. As a result, in this dialogue Solovyov did not feel the need to direct the debate towards a specific conclusion and a certain new blurring of concepts could be examined (like the blurring of the term *Russkiy*). The show benefited from a debate that seemed energized and entertaining, while the demands of the rioters on the streets were purposely blurred by the debate about what was real in Russia. This was a late-modern trend, when different conceptions of reality in the society co-exist.

The second show about the Manezh riots featured Vladimir Zhirinovsky and liberal politician Leonid Gozman. The judge on the show was Nikita Mikhalkov, underlining the high status he acquired since the 1990s as an arbiter on issues of national identification. Solovyov opened the show:

> We stopped feeling that we are one nation (*narod*). . . . After the events on the Manezh square it became clear that the slogans "we are Russians (*Russkiy*)" and "Russia for the Russians (*Russkiy*)" are supported not only by the disorderly youth. For some these are the signs of growing national self-understanding, to others these are frightening expressions of Nazism. On Monday . . . the President said that Russian (*Rossiyskaya*) identity is necessary for Russia. . . . What is the face of Russian (*Rossiyskaya*) nationality and should [ethnic] Russians (*Russkiy*) be defended in Russia?[65]

In comparison to Solovyov's negative attitude to the rioters on the previous show, these remarks demonstrated that *Poyedinok* shifted in its approach. This reflected the evolution of the government's approach over time, which at least partially accepted the claims of the football fans and took their side.[66] For the

CHAPTER 4

most part, participants presented familiar arguments about the place of ethnic Russians in Russia and the debate about the ethnic versus civic character of the Russian national group. In the intervention, Mikhalkov, ruled that the debate was "empty," while Solovyov emphatically agreed and explained, once again, that the aim of the program was "to show the people for whom they vote" (although Gozman's party was not permitted to run in the elections). In this context, it seemed that the hidden agenda of the show as a manager of public opinion was partially revealed—to disqualify politicians and political ideas in the eyes of the public.

The only cathartic moment was a comment made by a young man in the audience who identified himself as a son of white immigrants, born in San Francisco and educated in a "super patriotic" environment. He shared memories of his childhood in a "conserved Tsarist atmosphere," where there was no understanding of *"Russkiy* and *not-Russkiy,"* but of *"Rossiyane* and citizens of the Russian Empire." He professed that he moved to Russia from the US and that he had been working in Russia for twenty years, but received his passport only the previous year. He shared his experience and noted that there were many ways to circumvent the bureaucratic system. He noted that "we are pushing away the law obeying [people] and attracting law breaking [people]" to come to Russia. He said that he wanted to be treated similar to "other nationalities that are residing on *our* territory" (emphasis in italics mine) and asked why there is no system to incentivize Russian-speaking people to come to Russia. He stressed that he got a "vaccine" in his education which allowed him to overcome the difficulties in moving to Russia and declared that he self-identified as a *"Rossiyane"* who wants to live in his homeland. Solovyov delighted by his gust's testimony, noted that that the "vaccine" he mentioned was "love of motherland and pride in its history and traditions."

After the young man finished his comments the following discussion regarding citizenship laws in Russia took place:

ZHIRINOVSKY: We submitted an amendment to the law on citizenship, to automatically give [ethnic] Russian citizenship. It didn't pass . . .
GOZMAN: SPS[67] submitted this amendment about ten years ago.
ZHIRINOVSKY: Right.
GOZMAN: It didn't pass. So what?
ZHIRINOVSKY: It didn't pass. Why do we blame each other?
SOLOVYOV: So don't blame each other. Say what to do.
ZHIRINOVSKY: [Ethnic] Russians cannot come here, because they face the obstacles that are being erected.
SOLOVYOV: The obstacles are erected by other [ethnic] Russian officials.

ZHIRINOVSKY: From FMS, MVD.[68]

GOZMAN: Crimes against our country are committed not by the Tajiks, Afghans, Vietnamese and so on. Crimes against our country are committed by those officials who created the corrupt system. Who are trading our rights for money and sell them to the highest bidder. These are the enemies of the country and we should fight them and not the Tajik.

SOLOVYOV: I agree.[69]

In this show, public opinion was managed in several ways. First, Solovyov aligned the show with the government line and reproduced the authorial voice. He then moved to disqualify the participants as ideological alternatives. This was done by allowing Mikhalkov, as a representative of the regime, to act as a judge on the show. Mikhalkov evaluated and commented without being questioned. The exchange between Zhirinovsky, Gozman and Solovyov's comments was another example of distortion of political stances as a technique for public opinion management. In this instance, Zhirinovsky's LDPR and Gozman's SPS, two opposite poles of the Russian political arena, merged once again. Gozman tried to differentiate himself as an anti-government speaker when he spoke about the "corrupt system." But this move was undermined by Solovyov who actually joined in by agreeing with Zhirinovsky and Gozman in order to reinforce the blurring of political stances. This was a surprising consensus. As was discussed in the previous chapters, the automatic issuing of passports to Russians was a controversial political issue that could have had far-reaching consequences for domestic and foreign policies. Solovyov maneuvered the debate in a way that eroded political differences and disqualified the political debate.

Second, the show presented a commentator whose story was questionable and probably was fabricated.[70] A government official from the Federal Migration Services (FMS) who was in the audience, was thoroughly surprised by the young man's claims that it took him almost twenty years to gain citizenship (especially as he was from the United States and had means). This US-born patriotically minded Russian reproduced the authorial voice in his own style. He underlined central tenets of inclusive identification in the form of a unifying civic identification as a *Rossiyane*, with supplementing elements of attachments to the Russian land as a national home and the centrality of the Russian language. He also, like Rozovsky in the previous show, blurred the term *Russkiy*, when he said that for him, as a true patriot and son of white immigration, that term was meaningless. Yet his comments about "our territory" and about the need to defend ethnic Russian's rights in Russia, revealed the

CHAPTER 4

government's new approach to the subject. This commentator represented the government's turn towards favoring a more ethnic and stronger articulation of Russianness.

A year later, in January 2012, after a period of increasingly ethnically-infused discourse promoted by pro-government figures, Putin articulated his vision in printed press.[71] Putin's article titled "Russia: The National Question" ("*Rossiya: natsional'nyy vopros*") in *Nezavisimaya Gazeta*, gave the presidential seal of approval to the increased use of the term *ethnic Russian—Russkiy*, with a new meaning. Putin defined the national in-group in the following way: "The rod that binds the fabric of this unique civilization [of the historical Russian state] is the Russian people, Russian culture (*Russkiy narod, Russkaya kul'tura*). . . . The Russian people are state-forming [people] (*Russkiy narod yavlyayetsya gosudarstvoobrazuyushchim*). The great mission of the Russians is to unite and cement civilization . . . to bond Russian Armenians, Russian Azerbaijanis, Russian Germans, Russian Tatars."[72]

Putin's use of the ethnic terms of Russian identification—*Russkiy* was a concession to nationalist groups, who demanded stronger ethnically-based national identifications. However, at the same time, he blurred the meaning in the same way as it was done the year before on *Poyedinok* saying that *Russkiy* are also Tatars, Armenians and Azerbaijanis, which made it lose its exclusionary properties. This was obviously politically beneficial for the Kremlin, as it can allow solidifying of national identification without paying the price of excluding other ethnic groups from the national in-group.

Putin's article from 2012 showed how perfidious political language became in Russia, as well as the important function that television broadcasts and specifically *Poyedinok* played in this process. Although, as this chapter exemplified, the manipulation of language happened not only in televised broadcasts, but also in print media, television had an important function. As the debates in *Poyedinok* demonstrated, such platforms were a convenient testing ground. Televised talk shows are flexible formats. They can mix humor, sarcasm and even mockery in a serious conversation. They are also not meant to be listened to assiduously and they assume that people are listening in while doing other things at home.[73] These characteristics allowed *Poyedinok*, despite its origins as a Western format that was meant to serve values such as free speech, to develop as a dissemination vehicle for the manipulation of language. It also allowed to float on federal television the possibility of blurring of key political terms. As a result, Poyedinok became a sort of laboratory for the development of discursive techniques in the new televised circumstances. It created an imitation of politics and made discursive techniques that originated in

Soviet time to fit the new reflexive media environment. Solovyov was rewarded generously for his role in this effort and became a leading figure in the Russian state media, decorated with numerous state medals and received growing airtime on the radio and on television, including a lucrative one-on-one interview with the president in 2018.

But these techniques had an internal flaw, which revealed their limitation. In the new late modern context, they could not extinguish the opposition. A counter-discourse continued to co-exist side by side with the government-backed discourse. This counter-discourse was critical of the government and exposed the inherent tensions in propagating stability by undermining people's trust in the world around them. The volatility of language that the techniques of imitation and perfidy produced became a major source of criticism by the opposition and a glaring gap in the core of the government's claim of stabilization. The next section will consider more closely the critical counter-discourse that was formed in Russia as a response to the government's discourse of stability.

Resistance to the Discourse of Stability

From the early 2000s, a counter-discourse had developed in parallel to the government discourse of stability on national identification. At first the counter-discourse was mainly a response to Putin's rising popularity and his ability to rally, in war and in peace, parts of the Russian elites and the people. This counter-discourse emerged in parts of the media, which were still free to express their disdain. It featured critical commentary of the government's actions in Chechnya and resonated the discourse of nationalism as a dangerous endeavor, some of which were presented earlier. Other commentary challenged more fundamental tendencies in the Russian society, like nostalgic yearning for Soviet times, which was a source for Putin's rising popularity despite the diversion from liberal democracy.

In July 2000, for instance, an article titled "Conflicts are our fortune" appeared in *Izvestia*. This was an interview with the philosopher Eugenie Stepanov. As the title suggested, Stepanov disapproved of Putin's rallying of the Russian nation under the banner of unity. He attacked the nostalgic memory of the simple and peaceful Soviet past, and Putin's promise to reinstate stability and end the confrontation in society: "Recently, we have lived, according to party leaders, in a cloudless society. . . . Forced unanimity was the essence of society. Contradictions were driven inwards . . . a society without conflict cannot happen at all . . . the Russian people are used to transfer responsibility for everything that happens to the government. And then they are surprised that they are doing badly . . ."[74]

Stepanov dismissed the nostalgic view of a stable and peaceful Soviet society. He reminded that in Soviet times anonymity was achieved through suppression. Problems and disagreements were hidden away but did not disappear. For him, conflicts in society were natural. Stepanov addressed the state-society relationship in Russia. The Russian public, in his opinion, lapsed back to a historical pattern of transferring responsibility. In his view this relationship was not workable. Stepanov's article undermined Putin's plan at its very core, as he stated that the premises that Putin put forward in his political agenda could not materialize. Putin asked people to renounce some of their freedoms so he can govern effectively. However, Stepanov asserted that by doing so the Russian people condemned themselves to failure.

As the years went by, this counter-discourse focused on the flawed internal logic created by the government's discursive techniques aimed at undermining of language in order to create stability. This came down to the fact that in the globalized late modern context, where people and information travel freely, the government's choice to play with the meanings of words, like sovereign democracy or ethnic Russian (*Russkiy*) was ever more problematic.

In the Soviet Union, the gap between the codified performances acceptable by the regime and the reality in which people lived could be kept in-check by tools of censorship, surveillance and coercion. In the post-Soviet context, this was no longer the case. This gap became apparent to critics of the regime and, to some extent, was also apparent to the wider public. From the end of Putin's first term, and increasingly after the end of his second term in 2008, criticism pointed out that the quest for a clear and strong unified concept of identity was not materializing. Life was still fast-paced and unpredictable, the economy, which relied on high oil prices, was by its own nature unstable, and national identification persistently felt like it needed repair.

An interesting sub-theme of the counter-discourse pin-pointed specifically the mix between entertainment and politics on Russian television and the president's image, which was packaged in celebrity culture themes. It described Russia more like an entertainment show, run by and for the prestige of the president. This image was far from the 'strong' and 'solid' national identity that Putin promised to deliver. Instead, commentators described Russia as an outrageous fusion of pop and politics that had little to do with ordinary people's lives.[75] In February 2004, *Novaya Gazeta* published the following text:

Pre and post *Novy God* (New Year's Eve) TV orgiastic outburst, among other things, reincarnates—in the spirit of the triumph of United Russia—the triumph and domination of one united show-clan, [which] whether you like it or not, makes [one] a little obsessed with the embodiment of the clan in one person who—obviously!—cannot be followed without admiration.

Our enduring penchant for the cult creation, [and notice] of each and every whim and silliness of those whose cult is being created, is cloned to become the common law. In particular, the one that is called Alla Borisovna[76] (an analogue - flattering to the male-politician - Vladimir Vladimirovich). . . . Actually, she (Alla Borisovna), together with the completely surrendered to pop culture television, are our present ideology. The sought-after "national idea."[77]

The Russian New Years' celebration—*Novy God*—a secular Soviet tradition, still the most cherished celebration of the year, was described here as the vulgar triumph of popular culture. Federal television reproduced the triumphant performances that celebrated the political culture of United Russia, Russia's dominant political clan, to elevate another clan—show business. In this case too, television strived for unanimity and conformity regarding the admiration of a particular member of the clan that personified the clan in its entirety. In the world of popular music it was Pugacheva (Alla Borisovna) and in politics it was Putin (Vladimir Vladimirovich). The author concluded that this was not an imitation of the political culture in the world of popular music, but that it was the political culture itself—the present ideology and national idea. The blurring between the political world and the world of popular culture, a blurring between the serious and the trivial, between truth and lies, heightened the sense of dislocation in Russian society. Politics was a show, an imitation produced by the media and packaged for media consumption. The situation *Novaya Gazeta* described was anything but a solid experience of national identity, and enhanced a sense of loss and disorientation.

In 2007, an article from *Novaya Gazeta* pointed towards the mixed signals that the government was sending on national identification—specifically the continued use of economic themes and at the same time the enhanced emphasis on religiousness and Orthodox Christianity. The title of the article was "Orthodoxy is ineffective" (*"Pavoslaviye neeffektivno"*): "Orthodoxy . . . is an ineffective, artificial ideology that does not even have the mythological reserve that the Bolsheviks had at one time. In any case, Orthodoxy cannot contribute to the project of a 'competitive person' put forward the government." This article uses the terms that were introduced by the government, revealing their limited capability to shape people's identification. They could not hide the simple facts that neither the reorientation of the economic language toward a more stable and predictable image, nor strengthening of religious Orthodox themes could stop the sense that life in Russia remained in flux.

During 2010–14, voices of dissent grew louder and even the government-controlled *Izvestia* texts were seasoned with sarcastic criticism. In 2012–2013 *Izvestia* reported several times on a modern art competition that took place in Moscow under the titled "The national Idea of Russia." The winner of the competition received a financial award and was sent to represent Russia at the Venice Biennale. In December 2012 *Izvestia* quoted the competition organizers: "According to the organizers, today Russia needs a new unifying idea, but it cannot be composed from the remains of the past, nor imposed from outside. The idea should be created by Russians themselves."[78]

The competition's organizers reproduced a well-established notion that was part of the government discourse of stability—"today Russia needs a new unifying idea." But the competition did not follow the government line and called for pluralistic and popular action through which the idea would be created. At some point *Izvestia* reported sensationally that one proposal expressed Russian national idea as a pile of manure and another presented a portrait of Russian scientist Mikhail Lomonosov, painted with crude oil, to represent Russia's economic dependency on natural resources.[79] This showed that despite all government efforts the social polylogue did not feature a sense of stability, but rather dismay and internal fracture.

The political reality in Russia was transforming radically. In late 2011, liberal and nationalist protests in Bolotnaya Square in Moscow were led by Russia's opposition leader Alexey Navalny chanting "a party of crooks and thieves" about the Russian governing elite. The protests showed that the scheme to deceive the Russian public into passivity through an elaborate sequence of discursive tricks had failed. Pomerantsev perceptively conveys this in his book: "'Effective,' 'stability' no one can quite define what they actually mean, and as the city surges and transforms everyone senses things are the very opposite of stable and certainly nothing is 'effective,' but the way Surkov and his puppets uses them, the words have taken on a life of their own and act like falling axes over anyone who is in any way disloyal."[80]

The discursive techniques of imitation and perfidy, which blurred the meanings of terms, until nobody "can quite define" them had further destructive impacts on the sense of stability in the society. The use of volatile language and the promise of making life more stable were irreconcilable. Unlike in late-Soviet times of "developed socialism," when the state did not demand from citizens high levels of ideological fervor, in Putin's Russia the imminent threat of being labelled as disloyal was constantly present and its use was arbitrary. As Irina Prokhorova noted on *Radio Echo Moskvy* in 2013: "[our] country is absolutely torn. Society is fragmented, in society in general it is no longer understood what is good, what is bad."[81] Prokhorova's concern was not only with the society being torn, but also with the fact that basic concepts of bad and good became blurred, which was a consequence of a highly illusive political discourse.

In 2014 the Russian government responded finally and aggressively to these challenges by rallying the nation to war in Ukraine. The annexation of Crimea and the separatist war in East Ukraine were meant to remedy historical injustices and unite the nation behind the government. But in the absence of deeper change in Russia, which would have removed it from the late modern globalized context, such efforts were unlikely to resolve the regime's long term problems. These themes are exemplified in the discourse in *Poyedinok's* episodes around the crisis in East Ukraine and the annexation of Crimea.

The Maidan Square Protests (2013–14)

The events on Maidan Square in Kiev were the greatest challenge to the government's discourse. The protests calling for Ukraine's integration with Europe, which led to the Russian annexation of Crimea and an armed conflict in South-East Ukraine, touched Russian national identification in a particular way. Ukraine was considered culturally close to Russia with a large community of ethnic Russians and Russian speakers. A democratic Ukrainian revolution could spill over to Russia and boost a pro-Western national development agenda. This was very worrying for the Russian government since the Moscow protests in Bolotnaya Square in 2011–2012 had a similar agenda.

Poyedinok addressed the events in Ukraine in three episodes. They demonstrated that the show continued to use the discursive techniques of imitation and *verolomsvo* during the crisis and in some ways, these techniques were brought to an extreme. The first program aired on 23 January 2014 and addressed the protests on Maidan Square. The second show, in an emergency format, ran on 27 February 2014 and focused on events in Crimea. The third, which aired after the annexation of Crimea, on 4 April 2014, discussed Russia's deteriorating relations with the West. This was also the last show of *Poyedinok* that had aired for over a year, when the show went on a long and unexplained break from broadcasting.

116   CHAPTER 4

Maidan Square, January 2014

On 23 January 2014 Solovyov opened the show by saying that the Maidan protests were hijacked by ultra-nationalist elements and described the situation in Kiev as uncontrollable.[82] Footage from Kiev was televised at the beginning of the show. It showed the center of Kiev in flames, a zone of urban warfare with Molotov bottles being thrown at policemen. The discussants were Dmitry Kiselev, Russia's most important news presenter and head of the state news corporation Russia Today (*Rossiia Segonia*), and Gennady Gudkov, a politician who was closer to the opposition. The two were prominent figures in Russia, and from the highest tier of professional and political echelons. Choosing such senior participants demonstrated the seriousness with which the production treated the events in Ukraine.

Solovyov began by asking who was responsible for the events in Ukraine. The opening statements were overall similar, addressing Ukraine as a brotherly country. Kiselev noted that it was senseless to blame President Yanukovych's Ukrainian government, which cooperated with Russia. Gudkov blamed the Ukrainian government for "not starting an *effective* dialogue with the protesters" (emphasis in italics mine). Kiselev compared Ukraine to Libya, saying: "Gaddafi was not an ideal leader, but what did the opposition do? It turned [the country] into a desert where tribes wonder around killing each other . . . the danger that such a thing could happen with Ukraine exists." Gudkov's answer was rather surprising. He said: "I will not argue with my opponent, as surprising as it may seem." His statement revolved around the need for political dialogue, before mass protests could escalate into revolution. In response to this statement Solovyov said: "So with whom should the government lead a political dialogue? With *Benderovtsy*,[83] who say: we will kill Jews, Russians and Poles? It will be a great dialogue! . . . The dialogue could not happen with me. I am a Jew! It will be a short dialogue." Kiselev moved to explain that "unfortunately the system that emerged in Ukraine is that the incoming governments reproduces the vices of the previous [government]." Kiselev continued to describe relations between the government and the oligarchs in Ukraine, concluding that in Ukraine everyone is in opposition and "no one builds Ukraine." Solovyov noted that the system in Ukraine, as explained by Kiselev, reminded him of Russia in the 1990s. Gudkov's response was once more "I absolutely agree, by the way, with my opponent, as strange as it may sound."

This episode of *Poyedinok* was a forceful example of management of public opinion and enforcement of the government's discourse through imitation and perfidy. The objectives were twofold: first, to blur the protesters' political affiliation, and second, to dissuade the Russian people from following the example of the protest. Kiselev and Solovyov, two of Russia's strongest orators left Gudkov, himself a seasoned speaker, with very little room for maneuver. Solovyov attacked the ideological side of the protest on Maidan Square. Although the protesters in the Maidan Square were pro-Western and demanded transparency and economic cooperation with Europe, the Russian Government narrative identified the protests as an extremist nationalist-fascist movement.[84] This was important in order to paint their cause as illegitimate and to warn the Russian public from showing understanding to their demands. It resurrected the 1990s discourse national idea as a dangerous periphery and warned the Russian people that similar protests in Russia would generate conflict along national lines.

Kiselev engaged in perfidy (*verolomsvo*)—breaking people's trust in the political system. His aim was to undermine the rationale behind democratic political contestation. His assertion was that political competition in Ukraine did not produce better and more responsible governments. Rather, successive governments replicated each other, making the political atmosphere unconstructive. The link between democracy, popular action, and accountability were purposely weakened. Kiselev's argument intended to sow confusion in the Russian public about their ability to better the situation through a change of government. This is an important technique to sway people away from protesting and trying to overturn the government.[85] If people did not believe that free and fair elections brought about positive change or more accountability, they would lose the incentive to participate in elections or topple through unrest a non-democratic regime, even if they felt that its performance was unsatisfactory. Kiselev's words showed how blurring political terms allowed the government to enhance its legitimacy. Gudkov's response showed that he did not resist this system, but tried to make his arguments within the discursive framework set by the government—he used the term effective, called for avoiding revolutions and often agreed with what his opponent was saying. Whether Gudkov was aware of it or not, he allowed the blurring to continue, which undermined his ability to put his point across.

Crimea, February 2014

The second and third shows dedicated to Ukraine were more restrictive in format, showing the production's self-awareness of ongoing erosion in its ability to direct and manage public opinion using the same discursive tools, in the heightened emergency circumstances. On 27 February, a few weeks before the annexation of Crimea, the show aired in an emergency format, no longer featuring two ideological opponents, but an open studio hosting public and political figures from Ukraine and Russia. The representatives from Ukraine, with one representative from Crimea, were all pro-Russian to varying degrees. The representatives from Russia were almost exclusively pro-government figures. The only prominent guest who represented a more critical line towards Russia's policies was Nikolai Zlobin, a Russian historian and journalist who worked and lived for many years in the US. Zlobin was critical of the Kremlin in the past, but leaked US State Department cables identified him as "United Russia-connected."[86]

The debate had not allowed even the slightest alternative view to be voiced. The main question was how Russia should respond to the supposedly illegal situation that emerged in Ukraine after the toppling of President Yanukovych. At the same time Solovyov underlined that the only legal actions were those of Crimea, which was defending itself from the illegitimate coup in Kiev. When Zlobin addressed the theme of the illegality of potential foreign intervention that could undermine Ukraine's territorial integrity, Solovyov instructively responded "now all we need to do is to understand what is meant by 'intervention.'" The same legal terminology was used in Putin's address to the Federation Council after the annexation of Crimea less than a month later.[87] In this show there was frequent use of the term *Russkiy*, rather than *Rossiyane*. By the end of the show Solovyov announced: "we have unanimity about Crimea."

The aim of this program was to show a multiplicity of voices, which were similar, yet seemingly argued with each other. In many ways, this show, which from the start was an imitation of an open debate, crossed the line completely and became a support rally for Crimea. The choice to run the show in this format hinted at the war-like situation that emerged in Crimea that demanded a display of national unity. The chosen format was closer to the new format of another show hosted by Solovyov since 2012 called This Evening with Vladimir Solovyov (*Vecher c Vladimirom Solove'vm*). In that format, the debate was held between several speakers and was even easier to blur political orientation, as the show presented multiple views, most of which agreed with each other and can easily work together against selected few critics.

Russia and the West, April 2014

The third episode that aired on April 4, a few weeks after the annexation of Crimea and the launching of Western sanctions against Russia, focused on the clash between Russian and Western values.[88] The show returned to its original format of a duel. The contenders were Alexander Prokhanov, who represented anti-Western nationalist opinions, and Nikolai Zlobin, who represented a pro-Western liberal line. Prokhanov identified his core value as a "higher Godly justice," which was spiritual, transcendental, and divine. Zlobin argued for an individualist approach, associated with the liberal West, where the human and his needs were core values. Very quickly though it became clear that Zlobin did not intend to represent Western values on the show. He retreated from defending the US, explained that he only tried to describe the point of view of the West, while he himself "does not blame Russia . . . [and] criticizes the US very much." One of the commentators on the show, who identified with the nationalist agenda, told Zlobin mid-show, "you switched sides, you should come to our side." To make sure that the right ideas were received by the public Solovyov noted by the end of the show: "For me it is clear that a man without spirituality is a beast." Solovyov sided with Prokhanov's point of view, resonating a sharp turn in government's line to radicalized nationalist and religious-spiritual agenda instead of economic development (which was expected to stall under the pressures of Western sanctions). Yet, Zlobin's cover was blown and the imitation was over.

Solovyov's format was unable to withstand the pressures of the turbulent days of March-April 2014 in its original format. During the crisis, *Poyedinok's* production experimented with new formats and constellations, while continuing to use the techniques of imitation and perfidy. The new formats were evidently a more appropriate for the changing political situation, where the blurring of terms can be managed more easily than in a one-on-one debate. In fact, Tolz, together with social scientist Yuri Tepper, found that since 2014 Russian television featured a growing number of political talk shows, which managed the public's opinion for the government.[89] However, these talk shows featured formats that were closer to *Poyedinok's* emergency format on Crimea or Solovyov's show *Vecher with Vladimir Solovyov*, where there are multiple speakers. In a counter-intuitive twist such debates present a more fertile ground for blurring because these formats do not have to present two opposing views.[90] Hence, *Poyedinok's* suspension in 2014 and its subsequent end in 2015 did not signify a failure of Sovovyov's efforts. On the contrary, the technique of blurring continued in a format that was perfected by Solovyov, although his original format had been exhausted and was no longer a useful tool to produce perfidy.

A Fluid Russian Discourse

When Putin came to power as an Acting-President at the end of 1999, Russia was a divided society, fatigued by years of difficult economic reforms and political instability and plagued by deep social insecurity. Liberal democracy and a globalized free market economy failed in the eyes of the Russian people to provide assurances for a better future and became increasingly discredited. Putin understood the media's crucial role in national mobilization, as a tool for creating a sense of security and stability. His first step was to mobilize the nation to go to war in Chechnya. Contrary to the first Chechen War, which was seen as a failure, the war in 2000 was seen in the context of increased security and stability, strengthening law and order and going back to normality. This almost instantly won him tremendous popularity and, propelled by a wave of support from wider society and the political elite. Putin became the most powerful man in Russia. In 2000 the Governor of Novgorod region, Mikhail Prusak, said "all of us together—the collective Putin."[91]

Nevertheless, media discourse analysis at that period of *Izvestia*, *Novaya Gazeta*, and Vladimir Solovyov's talk shows demonstrates that fluid Russianness continued to dominate as the experience of national identification in Russia. National identity became one of the most discussed issues in the Russian media, which echoed the government line that it was of utmost importance for Russia. Security, effectiveness and stability, as a mean to reinstate a unified national identity, became main themes around which Putin constructed the government's authorial discourse of stability. But the content and ideas which the government promoted rarely diverged from what had already been discussed in the discourse on the search for a national idea in the second half of the 1990s, and formed the contours of fluid Russianness. Putin borrowed inclusive ideas—most of which were already floated in the media in the second half of the 1990s—like development of the economy, themes from the shared Soviet history, the Russian language and supplementary themes of Orthodox Christianity. This aimed to make identification both inclusive and to supplement it with specifically Russian themes. In fact, under Putin the government served as facilitator of a debate that had already been taking place under Yeltsin.

In terms of form, however, the debate diverged from the 1990s when discussions had an open-ended nature. The government cracked down on the free press and reintroduced a Soviet discursive style that was adapted to new circumstances. The president's authorial voice was reproduced by government officials, public figures, and journalists. It was individualized and stylized to create a discourse describing life in Russia as more stable and secure. Similar to the Soviet hypernormalisation of language, the reproduction of the government discourse and the authorial voice undergone a performative shift, where representations increasingly dominated social life. These were imitations that allowed the government to manage public opinion and to gain popularity. However, as the Russian society transformed in the post-Soviet period, Soviet discursive techniques needed further adaptation. One such adaptation was that public opinion was increasingly managed through televised broadcasts.

In this period, the government relied more heavily on television, which gained popularity in the 1990s, to construct the discourse. For television to be useful for the regime it had to be interesting—it had to feature a debate, to be provocative, and imitate a political discussion. This was exactly what was done in the talk show *Poyedinok*. The show's format represented free speech and liberal agenda, but it served very well illiberal values and managed public opinion to accept the government's agenda. Putting up this imitation was necessary. Otherwise, the sender-receiver mechanism would not have worked because people would have switched off. In *Poyedinok*, discursive techniques of imitation made truth and lies irrelevant categories. The moderator, Solovyov, actively undermined or passively allowed others to undermine clear conceptions and terms. This was not a simple lie, it was perfidy—*verolomsvo*. It was the undermining of people's trust in their own ability to comprehend the world and to act in it. In this discursive atmosphere of deep distrust, public opinion could be managed in a direction favorable for the regime.

This success and popularity of the regime's discursive and performative mechanisms can at least partially be attributed to the profound shortcomings of the political and economic system that Russia embraced in the 1990s and the discourse of flexibility that accompanied it. Giddens noted that one of the results of anxiety, caused by disruption of routines and lack of ontological security, was to identify with a strong leader.[92] Bauman added that the fragmentation of social institutions and the demand for flexibility precipitate the rise of charismatic authoritarian leaders, who promised the public to protect them in return for some of their rights.[93] Hence, Putin's success in the reintroduction of the authorial voice can be seen as a phenomenon that is embedded in the late modern reality. This was an authentic rejection of the insecurities that globalization brought about. Once people are being left on their own, with uncertain identities and in ever-changing reality, they seek security in the form of charismatic authoritarian leaders whose authorial voice can help them make sense of reality.

However, this mechanism had its limitations. In the late modern context of freer media and faster means of communication, the use of the authorial voice and the performances that accompanied it did not produce the same sense of normality as it did late-Soviet times. Despite government control over the media, it could not silence all the voices, and the discourse on Russian national identification remained a polylogue, in which many voices, including the government's, interacted with each other. Within this polylogue a counter-discourse developed, which criticized the government's efforts in constructing national identification and pointed the fallacies spoken by the authorial voice. Hence, the secure and stable uniformity of language that was formed in late-Soviet times could not be achieved.

Moreover, cracks started to appear on what seems to be the most heinous internal tension and self-destructive element of this mechanism, where increasing the sense of stability was achieved by undermining the very essence of politics. Early in Putin's presidency, the Russian liberal pollster Yuri Levada said that Putin "is a mirror in which everybody, whether communist or democrat, sees what he wants and hopes to see."[94] This style where everyone saw what they want to see had exacerbated the sense of instability. A system that relied on the dissemination of mistrust and manipulation of people by undermining their trust and presenting politics as a series of deceptions can only work for so long. It undermined the ability of the opposition—Gozman, Gudkov, or Nadezhdin—to question the government discourse, but it also created a persistent sense of instability and did not resolve the sense of loss in the society. By 2011–2013, the flaws within the government discourse of stability, which made people feel the very opposite of stable, were crystallized.

The government's effort to counter these challenges were revolved around the annexation of Crimea and the war in East Ukraine. Solovyov became a commanding general in what the director of Levada-Centre, Lev Gudkov, characterized as the "battle between television and the refrigerator"—the tension between deteriorating living conditions in Russia and the government's call for ideological patriotic mobilization.[95] Solovyov demonstrated professional mastery in managing public opinion in crisis by experimenting with new formats, such as multi-participant shows. For his contribution during these years Soloviev was rewarded and despite *Poyedinok's* suspension Solovyov became a key figure in the Russian media.[96] Indeed, television helped the Russian government to withstand the stresses of 2011–2014 and salvage Putin's popularity.[97] However, several years after the heightened patriotic feelings around the annexation of Crimea, the mobilization drive stalled and alienation dominated the Russian polls.[98] Meanwhile, displeasure grew online, in the evolving and expanding Russian-speaking cyberspace—Runet—and among the younger generation of Russians.[99] This resentment by young Russians manifested itself in ongoing political protests in the late-2010s and early 2020s.

It is important to note that the discursive mechanisms in the Russian media and on *Poyedinok* were not an ahistorical, exceptional acts, limited to the Russian experience. Surprisingly for Westerners, the use of reflexive tools to create a government discourse in authoritarian states through imitating supposedly liberal formats was fairly easy. This was the case since television production in the West was already based on the pretense of freedom. Television studios were producing versions of reality that were carefully designed to imitate free speech and open-ended discussions. Virtual politics were not restricted to Russia or the former Soviet Union. As Fairclough noted in his analysis of British political talk shows, this format relies on creating a certain pretense.[100] The craft of the talk show moderator is to create a facade of a frank, private, and often even intimate conversation, that is also light and entertaining. This is far from what is happening in the studios and both the host and the guests do not treat it as a free and open conversation, but a virtual expression of freedom of speech.[101] Hence, Putin did not constitute a complete roll-back of global trends. Rather this virtuality has been subverted in Russia, using late-Soviet discursive techniques, for illiberal ends.

Hence, the examples from this chapter can be instructive of a much wider phenomenon in the late modern world. The English documentarist, Adam Curtis, who explained President Trump's victory, borrowed Yurchak's term "hypernormalisation" as the name and theme of his film. He made a specific reference to the type of manipulation that developed in Russia, as very similar to the discourse that developed in the US on Trump's campaign. He noted that the Kremlin under Putin, and specifically Vladislav Surkov, understood that "the version of reality that politics [in the West] presented to the people was no longer believable . . . that you can play with reality constantly shifting and changing and in the process, undermine and weaken the old forms of power."[102] Understanding these late modern realities in Russia allow us both to narrate the Russian story as part of a broader late modern globalized context and to enrich the Western understanding of late modernity with examples from Russia.

Part Three

Fluid Times
Practices of the Russian National Calendar

CHAPTER 5

From the Soviet Calendar to Russian Calendars

National calendars represent a collectively imagined past (memorable events, historic dates), projected future (Judgment Day, redemption), and how societies perceive their present social essence.[1] They stand, according to the German historian Reinhart Koselleck, at the intersection of biological time and social-historical time and "punctuate social life."[2] During the punctuations of time—on holidays—individuals perform certain practices that the sociologist Emil Durkheim described as repetitive acts that reinforce values and beliefs and reaffirm identity.[3] This makes national calendars related to both the conception of time and the practical dimension of individual agency—how individuals act in the social world and by doing so construct identification.

In post-Soviet Russia something seemed broken in the functions of the national calendar. On June 12, 1991, Yeltsin declared the sovereignty of RSFSR. The date was acknowledged as a national holiday and psychologically was meant to distinguish between the Soviet and post-Soviet periods, as well as to celebrate Russia's independence and transformation to democracy. Yet in the post-Soviet period, only 1–3 percent of respondents to Levada-Center polls named it the most important holiday (see table 3). Even by 1999, 28 percent of respondents did not know what holiday fell on June 12.[4] This could not have happened in previous periods. In nineteenth-century Russia, there would not have been a person who identified as a Russian and who

Table 3 Which of the following holidays is the most important for you? (%)

	1992	1998	2000	2002	2004	2005	2010	2012	2014	2015	2016	2017
December 31, Novy God	79	82	81	79	83	81	78	81	76	80	83	77
Birthdays of relatives and close friends	41	38	34	28	35	30	37	36	48	44	44	46
May 9, Victory Day	25	29	34	30	29	32	36	33	36	42	38	43
Your birthday	43	37	37	37	30	31	33	39	43	42	41	38
Pascha	30	29	32	26	23	28	31	29	33	27	25	25
January 7, Orthodox Christmas	18	23	16	19	22	26	19	19	20	15	15	17
March 8, International Women's Day	17	28	23	27	20	23	18	20	18	19	19	16
February 23, Day of the Defender of the Fatherland	–*	–*	–*	12	10	12	9	12	12	10	10	11
Your saint's name day	–*	–*	–*	2	3	2	4	2	5	4	5	5
May 1, Spring and Labor Holiday	5	5	5	13	8	6	4	6	6	7	6	5
Wedding anniversary	–*	–*	–*	4	4	5	2	5	6	3	3	4
January 14, Old Novy God	–*	–*	–*	–*	–*	–*	–*	–*	–*	–*	–*	4
Kurban-Bayran (Eid El-Adha)	–*	–*	–*	3	2	3	3	3	3	5	3	3
June 12, Russia Day	1	2	2	3	3	3	3	3	1	3	2	2
November 4, Day of National Unity	–*	–*	–*	–*	–*	–*	1	1	1	1	≤1	1
Russian Constitution Day	–*	1	1	1	1	1	1	1	≤1	1	1	1
December 25, Catholic Christmas	–*	–*	–*	–*	–*	1	1	1	1	1	≤1	≤1
Difficult to answer	6	2	3	2	2	2	2	≤1	1	1	2	2
Number of respondents	1,834	1,600	1,600	1,600	1,600	1,600	1,600	800	800	800	800	1600

Source: Levada-Center.
Note: Answers are ranked in descending order; hence, the total sum exceeds 100 percent.
*Option not included in the poll.

missed Orthodox Easter (Pascha), and in Soviet times, masses of people participated in November 7 and May 1 celebrations. So what went wrong in post-Soviet Russia?

This chapter argues that the difficulties experienced in the formation of a unified post-Soviet Russian calendar were tied to the temporal context of late modernity. Several scholars have provided theoretical explanations for this phenomenon. Koselleck attributed complications in the collective memory to the fact that modernity removed the certainty of a prophetic future—Judgment Day—in favor of a less certain scientific prognosis.[5] And if the future was

FROM THE SOVIET CALENDAR TO RUSSIAN CALENDARS 129

uncertain, so was the past and the present. In late modernity, this was further complicated, as prognosis became ever more obscure.[6]

Pierre Bourdieu's *Outline of a Theory of Practice* and Anthony Giddens's structuration theory informed this problem from the perspective of practices and social power relations. They argued that practices are reproduced in the interaction between individual agency and the social system (the state, the religious community).[7] In late modernity, Giddens noted, there was a systemic power shift toward individual agency, while the state withdrew from the monopoly over the production of ideology (and thus prognoses of the future). In this temporal context, people became more empowered to choose which holidays they celebrated and how. Hence, as opposed to Durkheim's understanding of holiday rituals that bound communities, the sociologist Amitai Etzioni noted that holidays do not only unify the community.[8] In late modernity, holidays often become contested, and competing calendars emerge.

This chapter shows that as Russia entered the late modern era, it experienced the obscurity of the future and shift of power toward individual agency, which resulted in multiple and competing calendars. Yet this experience of fragmentation of the calendar had elements that were tied to the collapse of the Soviet Union and to Russian history, culture, and religion. Hence, this chapter evaluates whether the Russian national calendar denoted identification that matched the framework of fluid Russianness, as an inclusive and flexible late modern identification with supplementing cultural and ethnic Russian elements.

To that end, this chapter begins by considering the Soviet calendar, which was dominated by modernist thinking with a prognosis of a utopian future set as "the radiant future of communist society" (in Russian, *svetloye budushcheye kommunisticheskogo obshchestva*). The analysis considers the social implications of the removal of the Soviet calendar and looks at processes of fragmentation of the national calendar in the 1990s under Yeltsin's government. The chapter looks at how the Russian national calendar and its practices were transforming from the collapse of the Soviet Union until Putin came to power; what kind of practices developed in Russia; and whether they represented a specific type of identification.

In this analysis the chapter focuses on the practical dimension of individual agency (unlike previous chapters, which focused on legislative and discursive dimensions). It illustrates how individuals themselves construct identifications in late modernity in the specific cultural context. To illustrate these experiences, the chapter uses diverse primary materials, such as opinion polls conducted by the Levada-Center and VTSIOM, entries from blogging platforms, and materials gathered on several research trips to Russia in 2013–2017.

The Soviet Calendar

Before examining the post-Soviet annual calendar and its practices, it is important to sketch the Soviet annual system of holidays and its practices, since they were a mental and emotional departure point for many Russians and informed the post-Soviet experience in two ways. First, the Soviet national calendar had a deeply modernist logic, in how it structured the past and projected a prognosis of the future. This produced an internally logical understanding of historical time within which Soviet people could form a comprehensive world view. In comparison to the Soviet calendar, late modern calendars are far more fragmented. Second, as Bourdieu's practice theory suggests, despite the authoritarian nature of the Soviet state, the practices of the calendar were not an entirely top-down process. Especially in the late-Soviet period, they acquired personal meaning for Soviet citizens. In this period, individuals could perform practices of the calendar and feel secure about their position in the society and identification with the collective Soviet group.[9] Hence, the Soviet calendar was not an annual set of practices that was forced on the population but part of a social system that provided anchoring and a basis for predictable social interactions between the state and the public and between individuals.

The Soviet set of holidays represented a Marxist-Leninist interpretation of history. By the 1980s, there were eight national holidays: Red Army Day (February 23), International Women's Day (March 8), Cosmonautics Day (April 12), International Labor Day (May 1), Victory Day (May 9), Anniversary of the Great Socialist Revolution (November 7), Day of the Constitution (October 7), and Novy God (New Year's Eve, December 31). Out of those, Red Army Day and Cosmonautics Day were not days of rest, while on International Labor Day and the Anniversary of the Great Socialist Revolution, Soviet citizens received two days of rest.[10] For Novy God, the day off work was designated January 1. In addition, there were professional celebratory days, for instance, Teacher's Day (first Sunday of October), which were not days of rest. Each of these holidays symbolized an understanding of historical time and was positioned in relation to the bright communist future.

The most important state holiday that symbolized a breakthrough in communist history was the anniversary of the October Revolution—November 7. As the Soviet rhyme went: "den' sed'mogo noyabrya—krasnyy den' kalendarya" (November 7 is the red day of the calendar). It divided history between the tsarist and Soviet eras, celebrated the Bolshevik military victory in the civil war, and projected the future victory of achieving a worldwide communist utopia. A military parade was held in Red Square, and demonstrations took place in cities. People who worked in large state companies and factories and members of the Komsomol—the Soviet youth organization—were required to march in the procession with red flags, ribbons, red carnations, and balloons.¹¹ Despite the state-sanctioned manner with which the holiday was conducted, people remember that the festive public atmosphere was often accompanied by voluntary celebrations—families with children went to watch the parade, and celebrations continued in private settings at home and among friends with merriment and drinks.

The detachment from deep ideological meanings of Soviet holidays like November 7 was reinforced in the late-Soviet period. In the mid-1960s, the Soviet statesman and unofficial Communist Party ideologue Mikhail Suslov announced the time of "real socialism" (*real'nyy sotsializm*).¹² At that time, citizens' adherence to Marxist-Leninist ideology was assumed but, at the same time, was not aggressively required by the state. As Yurchak described, people who participated in the parades on May Day (May 1) and the Anniversary of October Revolution (November 7) viewed them as ritualized performances and "paid little attention to the slogans."¹³ This did not mean that these rituals were insignificant. Yurchak noted that "participating in these acts reproduced oneself as a 'normal' Soviet person," bearing the possibility that later one would engage in activities that ran contrary to these acts.¹⁴ Hence, on Soviet holidays like November 7, citizens often made performative acts without attaching ideological meaning to them. Even if one did not feel attached to the specific day, the festive atmosphere dictated certain practices, which, once performed, encouraged the sense of belonging to the Soviet in-group.

Cosmonautics Day, which celebrated Yuri Gagarin's space flight, did not have popular practices but had a strong resonance in both the official and personal spheres. For the Soviet state, this holiday symbolized a victory over the United States in the space race. Moreover, Gagarin's flight was no regular victory. It was a scientific victory, the peak of Soviet modernist admiration of science. It was a reification of the Soviet promise of a bright communist future, when the Soviet state would reach the stars through scientific progress. Yet this holiday transcended top-down Soviet propaganda and channeled personal identifications with the Soviet group. As Yurchak noted, the promise of a bright future around images of Soviet cosmonauts produced a sincere and very pleasant sense of belonging among the Soviet people.¹⁵ This was evident in post-Soviet recollections. The Nobel laureate Svetlana Alexievich wrote: "My father would say that he personally started to believe in communism after Gagarin went into space. We're the first! We can do anything! That's how my mother raised us."¹⁶ A post-Soviet history magazine, *Istorik*, reminisced about the day of Gagarin's landing: "[We] believed in a man, believed in science that could improve the world. [We] believed in progress, that tomorrow would open new horizons, unheard of opportunities."[17] These recollections pointed to the importance of a collective vision of the future for generating identification. In post-soviet Russia, Gagarin's portraits can still be spotted.

Military Soviet holidays also evolved over time and acquired specific meanings for Soviet citizens, which sometimes diverged from state ideology. In the militarized Soviet society, the armed forces were celebrated, in addition to November 7, also on Red Army Day (February 23, when Leon Trotsky established the Red Army) and on Victory Day (May 9). But by the late Soviet era, Red Army Day, which originally had a clear militarized message, had turned into a gender-based holiday that celebrated manhood. Although about a million women served in the Soviet Army in the Second World War, in 1945 they were rapidly demobilized, excluded from the military, and required by the state to perform the dual social role of mother and worker.[18] Mandatory male conscription meant that after the war, the military was associated with manhood, which was in turn militarized. On Red Army Day, wives and children greeted husbands and fathers with presents and cards. Thematically, it corresponded more with International Women's Day rather than with Victory Day, as both reinforced Soviet conservative gender roles.[19]

International Women's Day had been celebrated in tsarist Russia sporadically since 1913 as one of the Bolshevik's days of protest. It gained a prominent place in the postrevolutionary Soviet calendar partly because it sparked the February 1917 revolution.[20] Yet its practices evolved over time together with women's changing roles in society. In the 1930s, after the early revolutionary liberating policies, patriarchal hegemony was reinstated to stop the falling birth rates and social fragmentation caused by years of revolution and civil war.[21] Women's integration into the workforce continued and was assisted by the provision of childcare facilities and communal dining.[22] This happened in private settings, too, as the Soviet cookbook *The Book of Tasty and Healthy Food* noted: "It is necessary to create a habit in the population and a taste for the semi-finished products. . . . These products . . . expand the woman's release from domestic work for more productive and creative work."[23] In this time the image of the Soviet woman as a worker and a mother was formed.[24] International Women's Day remained a working day, and women were greeted with flowers and presents by male colleagues in professional settings.

During the "real socialism" of the 1960s, greater state resources were shifted from the communal to the private realm, and the family played an ever greater role.[25] As part of this trend, in 1965 International Women's Day became a nonworking day, which had implications for its social function.[26] The fact that women were no longer celebrated at work but at home represented a societal shift in women's position—from the laboring women to the 1970s–1980s female image as beautiful and revered.²⁷ The holiday was celebrated by giving women gifts, chocolates, and spring flowers (mimosas). Men sometimes took upon themselves to perform some domestic roles, but women often complained that a day off work meant another day of domestic work. These practices reinforced conservative gender roles and tried to manage tensions in a society where gender equality had stalled. But the late-Soviet society of the 1970s–1980s was also a more secure experience. The growing personal sphere made it possible to live outside of big ideologies and politics, which Yurchak described as "living lightly" (*zhili legko*) or living "outside" (*vne*).²⁸ Hence, gender-based celebrations like Army Day and International Women's Day now acquired a strong personal side, a day when people greeted their loved ones in the private realm, without the interference of the state and without adhering to political ideas.

Victory Day (Den' Pobedy, May 9) practices also evolved over time and became fixed in Brezhnev-era "real socialism."²⁹ After 1945, Victory Day was not a public holiday. Veterans marked it in smaller circles by visiting cemeteries. Stalin wanted to diminish the memory of the war for a variety of reasons, not the least because of the millions who died due to his stern military approach. The only statewide celebrations were after-dark fireworks.³⁰ Victory Day only became a nonworking day (like International Women's Day) in 1965, and a military parade took place, which also symbolized a shift in its narrative and meaning.

The practices of Victory Day went beyond the celebration of a military victory to a broader articulation of a collective pan-Soviet identification. Yearly celebrations did not include a military parade (except on the anniversaries in 1965 and 1985), but party leaders paid their respects at the Tomb of Unknown Soldier in different cities; veterans marched on the main streets and afterwards met in parks, danced to music, and were greeted by children with flowers.³¹ These practices were performed in the public sphere and were followed meticulously. This qualified as what the historians Eric Hobsbawm and Terence Ranger called "invented traditions," since they were fairly recent rituals that were laden with deep historical meaning.³² They symbolized the Brezhnev-era narrative, which was a story about suffering and perseverance that circumvented Stalin's role and focused on the veterans.³³ The veterans became symbols of unity between government and people and between the Soviet Union's different nationalities and ethnicities.³⁴ The young generation was expected to pay the mythic debt owed to the heroism of veterans and to the Soviet people. It was not the simple celebration of a military victory, but as the Soviet song "Den' Pobedy" (Victory Day) says, "it is joy with tears in our eyes" ("eto radost' so slezami na glazakh"). It also inserted a strong personal element into the celebrations, when the celebrating veterans were often family members, colleagues, or teachers.

Another holiday that symbolized most late-Soviet gravitation to the personal sphere was Novy God (New Year's Eve, December 31), which was nonreligious and nonideological and was celebrated at home or with one's closest family and friends. Novy God practices were nascently formed in the mid-1930s. After the revolution, the Bolsheviks wanted to get rid of the bourgeois and religious traditions of Christmas and New Year's Eve—the fir tree (*yëlka*), Father Frost (Russian Santa Claus), and gift exchanges—and in 1929 the fir tree was banned.[35] But by the 1930s, the needs of the Soviet state were changing, and Novy God came to serve the Stalinist return to family values.[36] The evolution of Novy God practices was also tied to the state's changing approaches toward consumerism and food. Since the mid-1930s, the Soviet state ended food rationing and encouraged urban elites to develop a new type of consumerism to boost industry.[37] Through books and magazines, it guided new Soviet urbanites (specifically women) on how to consume, cook, serve, and celebrate in a modern, rational, and Soviet manner.[38] As part of these trends, in 1935 the fir tree was rehabilitated, together with Father Frost and gift exchanges, and Novy God became a nonreligious tradition and a children's winter festival. It emerged as a nationwide celebration in private gatherings, banquets, festivals, decorations, and theater and circus shows.[39]

In the 1950s–1980s, the state further promoted themes of abundance and Soviet consumerism, and Novy God food practices were consolidated. The holiday menu became fixed with staples that reflected the desire to present a plentiful table, as part of the state's promotion of abundance, but also adapted to Soviet realities of food shortages.[40] The codified celebratory menu included Oliv'ye or meat salad (*salat* Oliv'ye or *myasnoy salat*), fish in marinade, *seledka pod shuboy* salad (literally, "herring under a fur coat"), caviar, Soviet champagne, wine, spirits, citrus fruit, chocolates, and cakes. The 1952 edition of *The Book of Tasty and Healthy Food* expressed the desire to present newly achieved culinary richness and thus for the first time had a special section that taught how to set a festive table, with an accompanying photo.[41] Although this book featured ingredients that were unavailable to the public, it also had recipes that were simpler versions of pre-Soviet dishes as substitutes for the holiday menu. For instance, Oliv'ye salad was a French dish that originally included smoked quail eggs, shrimp, and crab meat.[42] *The Book of Tasty and Healthy Food* had a simpler version of meat or sausage salad, which also included potatoes, cucumbers, celery, cornichons, apple, and mayonnaise.[43] These recipes, and the colorful photos that accompanied them, provided demonstrations for how to celebrate in the private realm in a Soviet manner. It was an important expression of belonging that went beyond a mere celebration of the New Year. It was a type of normality that was both collectively Soviet (everybody celebrating at the same time the passage of time), as well as personal (celebrating with one's family and friends and in one's own apartment).

Starting in the 1960s, television became an important vehicle for disseminating Novy God practices. In the most practical way, television provided people with information about when the new year commenced (midnight), and it also created demonstrations of Novy God celebrations.[44] On December 31, besides the address by the general secretary of the Communist Party, Soviet television broadcast holiday variety shows and New Year's films. The most famous entertainment show was *Goluboii Ogonek*, which started broadcasting in 1962, with the New Year's Eve broadcast being the most important.[45] The show featured a concert, which was a Soviet carnival where strict social hierarchy was broken in favor of light entertainment music, and humoristic performances.[46] Importantly, the setting of *Goluboii Ogonek* was that of a café with little festive tables around which members of the Soviet elite gathered (actors, musicians, cosmonauts, and representatives of the national republics).[47] These small tables practically demonstrated the Soviet festive table and the practice of small-scale private gatherings during the holiday. On a deeper level, this show presented the evolving social essence of a society that was moving toward a settled apolitical order, in which the personal sphere (celebrating around a small table) and nonideological life (spending time with friends, enjoying music and humor) were a formative experience of belonging to the in-group.

In addition to TV shows, the New Year's movie developed as a television genre that was consumed during Novy God celebrations at home. The most popular Soviet New Year's movie was *Ironiya sud'by, ili S logkim parom!* (The irony of fate, or enjoy your bath!) (1976). The film also became a demonstration of practices and channeled a certain projection of social realities in the late-Soviet period. It tells the story of two single people, Zhenia and Nadia. Zhenia, intoxicated after a pre–Novy God celebration at the bathhouse (*banya*) in Moscow, accidently boards a flight to Leningrad. Not realizing that he is in a different city, he tries to get home but ends up in Nadia's apartment, who lives at the same address as him but in Leningrad.

The movie was mildly critical of Soviet uniformity, but at the same time it was a personal and touching love story. It began with "In bygone days when someone found themselves in a strange city, he felt lost and alone. . . . But it's all different now. A person comes to a strange city and feels at home there. . . . All staircases look the same . . . standard apartments furnished with standard furniture and standard locks cut into featureless doors." Yet amid the Soviet uniformity of large apartment buildings and standard keylocks (Zhenia managed to open Nadiya's apartment in Leningrad using his key from Moscow), there was the possibility for magically meeting someone special. The film takes place within Soviet apartments, around kitchen tables, living-room sofas, and the festive Novy God table, underlining the importance of the personal sphere in people's lives.[48] Nadia's Novy God table, like the festive table in *The Book of Tasty and Healthy Food* and the small tables in *Goluboii Ogonek*, demonstrated the practice of Novy God and a representation of Soviet identification. This was an articulation of life where state-sanctioned uniformity still left enough space, even the literal space of an apartment or a kitchen table, for people's personal miracles.

Soviet holiday practices exhibited a specific type of identification that developed in the late-Soviet era. The Soviet state provided a strongly established and well-settled annual set of practices with a strong internal logic. Each holiday channeled ideological meaning, ordered the past, and projected the radiant Soviet future. It was clear which practices the state expected individuals to perform. But in the late-Soviet period, the fact that society was defined as having achieved socialism allowed individuals to build personal lives and identify as Soviet citizens without strongly adhering to the ideology. Hence, by the late-Soviet era, practices had a new nonideological meaning of belonging. The personal sphere that was encouraged by the state and was evident in holiday practices was a projection of the nonideological social essence and identification as normal (Soviet) people. This personal sphere was physical, in the form of an apartment, and metaphysical in the form of living lightly and being vne (outside). Hence, celebrations that had strong personal components, like International Women's Day, and specifically Novy God, in fact channeled a sense of belonging that was quite stable and secure for the late-Soviet generation.

Post-Soviet National Calendars in the 1990s

The collapse of the Soviet state shattered the feelings of belonging and sense of security that stemmed from the practices of the Soviet calendar. In September 1992, the Russian government designated seven all-national public holidays: New Year's celebrations (January 1–2), Orthodox Christmas (January 7, which was the only religious day of rest), International Women's Day (March 8), May 1–2 renamed from International Worker's Solidarity Day to Spring and Labor Day, Victory Day (May 9), Day of Declaration of State Sovereignty of the Russian Federation (June 12), and Anniversary of the October Revolution

(November 7).⁴⁹ While the post-Soviet calendar kept a certain skeleton of Soviet holidays, as five out of seven national holidays were Soviet holidays, they stopped serving the same social purpose. Without the Soviet ideology to order the past and project the future, celebrating these holidays became illogical and no longer served as unifying and binding events for the national in-group. This opened a large vacuum for creating new ways of life in Russia. It was not clear which direction this new experience would take.

The new Russian government, led by Boris Yeltsin, anchored Russia's development to a neoliberal free-market economy, but it had no clear prognosis of what its future would look like. New political elites argued for respect for plurality of practices and against the production of a new ideological set of values.⁵⁰ Consequently, they did not attempt to generate an ideology that would guide life in place of the defunct Soviet calendar, a task that was left to the individuals themselves. Hence, the disintegration of the national calendar was not only the result of the collapse of the Soviet system but also of the embrace of new neoliberal and late modern forms of thinking of the new government and elites.

In the absence of new collective frames of reference, three parallel sets of holidays emerged in Russia—political holidays, personal-local holidays, and Orthodox Christian religious holidays. The first set—political holidays—included old Soviet political holidays, which after the collapse of Soviet ideology acquired new and contested meanings, and new democratic holidays. This, apart from resulting from the collapse of the Soviet Union, was also in line with the late modern trend where holidays become contested, as political memory becomes more pluralistic and open to different interpretations. The second set consisted of personal and local holidays that had a strong appeal in post-Soviet Russia, while the third were from the religious Orthodox Christian calendar, promoted by the Russian Orthodox Church, which channeled ethnic Russian exclusivist identification and could suggest a return to a more solid exclusivist identity.

The Political Calendar

The commemoration of historical holidays was particularly problematic, as they were tied to the evaluation of the past and to the construction of collective memory. After the demise of Soviet ideology, memory became one of the most complex and contested issues in Russian society. Nascent Russian civil society was overwhelmed with newly declassified historical documents, which became the basis for completely opposite interpretations of the past. The scholar Nurit Schleifman describes it in the following way: "At present it is impossible to talk about a dominant Russian memory. The meaning of Russia's past, or rather its narrative, is in a process of continuous deconstruction, reshaping and negotiation by various social and political groupings."[51]

Giddens's structuration theory can explain this process as a result of the collapse of the Soviet social system and the empowerment of individuals' agency to decide which practices they wanted to reproduce and how to perform them. This resulted in competing interpretations of commemorative days, as people were deciding for themselves how to interpret historical events. In this situation, holidays stopped performing the Durkheimian purpose of binding communities together. Instead, memory, remembrance, and commemoration as a political practice became an arena for political contestation. Yet this contestation of memory had a distinct sense of Russianness, since it was a result of the imperial and authoritarian collapse that precipitated the reevaluation of Russian history.

There were three main political holidays in 1990s Russia—Victory Day (May 9), the Anniversary of the October Revolution (November 7), and Russian Independence Day (June 12).

Victory Day (May 9), which emerged as a popular post-Soviet memorial and political holiday, did not escape controversy and contestation of memory. In the post-Soviet calendar, according to the Levada-Center, in 1992 Victory Day ranked the fifth most important holiday for Russians (third, excluding personal holidays like birthdays), and by 1998 it became the fourth most popular holiday, in public holidays second only to Novy God. After the collapse of the Soviet ideology and hence the Brezhnev-era narrative of victory, liberals, communists, and nationalists competed over the articulation of the meaning of this day.[52] This was extremely detrimental for the practice of this holiday, because in Brezhnev's era it was performed in the public sphere and led by official figures. In an atmosphere of discord and contestation, it was unclear how the holiday should be performed.

In 1992–1994, a series of competing practices undermined the holiday's unifying capability. Liberals contested the memory of victory on grounds of

Table 4 Which of the following holidays is the most important for you? (%)

	1992	1998	2000
May 9, Victory Day	25	29	34
June 12, Russian Independence Day	1	2	2
November 7, Anniversary of the October Revolution	–	7	–

Source: Levada-Center.
Note: Partial results; for full results, see table 3.

tragic details of the human price of victory that had been silenced in Soviet times but emerged during glasnost and in the post-Soviet period. For instance, in 1992 members of the Supreme Soviet inquired about Russians who fought in the allied armies, usually escapees from German POW camps. Upon returning to the Soviet Union, they were labeled enemies of the people and interned in camps until Stalin's death. Yeltsin wanted to distance the memory of the war from militaristic themes and focus rather on peaceful memories.[53] Instead of events at the Tomb of Unknown Soldier near Red Square, he decided to pay respects on Poklonnaya Gora (outside the city center) and return to the center later to personally greet veterans.[54] But the communists and nationalists perceived this contestation of the Soviet narrative as an attempt to undermine the memory of national achievements. The communist newspaper *Trudovaya Moskva* (Workers' Moscow) wrote: "False democrats robbed the people of [their] victory."[55] Rumors spread that communists and nationalists planned violent clashes in central Moscow to protest Yeltsin.[56] This fear partly materialized when communist protesters tried to block Yeltsin's route from Poklonnaya Gora back to the Kremlin.[57] This undermined the sense of unity that this holiday had channeled in Soviet times, as this contestation left public spaces in disarray.

In 1993–1994, the political discord around Victory Day intensified, when a series of competing ceremonies were held on the same day in Moscow. Yeltsin and government officials held ceremonies on Poklonnaya Gora, while opposition leaders conducted their own ceremonies in the center of Moscow.[58] Practically, in the absence of mutually agreed physical places where the public could pay respects to fallen soldiers and greet veterans, the mythic debt could not be redeemed, and the holiday's practice could not be reproduced. At this point, instead of communists complaining about the loss of victory because of a liberal-democratic questioning of the narrative, democrats complained that the opposition was dividing the public and the veterans and politicizing the holiday.[59] The disunity around this holiday was evidently unpleasant to both sides of the political map.

By 1995, the fiftieth anniversary of the victory, Yeltsin was set to resolve this matter. On May 9, 1995, Yeltsin commenced a military parade on Poklonaya Gora, which was decorated with the colors of the Saint George military decorations, and a veterans' parade on Red Square.[60] Observers of the 1995 parade on Red Square noted that it was an odd event. (It was organized by a supporter of the 1991 coup, and Yeltsin stood on top of the Lenin Mausoleum with Soviet symbols decorating Red Square.)[61] In a notable gesture, Yeltsin unveiled a statue of Marshal Zhukov outside the Kremlin. Since Zhukov was also culpable of the high human price incurred by the military effort, placing his statue was a clear sign that Yeltsin was departing from early attempts to articulate a peaceful message.[62] These moves worked to partially suppress revisionist historical inquiries and quell protests by communists and nationalists. Most importantly they practically allowed the resumption of Brezhnev-era practices. Once ceremonies were consolidated, the mythic debt to the veterans, as a symbol of national unity, could be paid.

The continued popularity of Victory Day and how disagreements were resolved offered an insight into which practices the Russian public deemed appropriate to reproduce. The process of contestation of this holiday seemed to have been unpleasant for the various social and political actors. Once Yeltsin reinstated Soviet-era practices in the public sphere, despite continued disagreements, the different actors fell in line. Victory Day's popularity showed that it was not only a Soviet holiday but could also articulate post-Soviet unity; it had all-national and supranational inclusive elements embodied by the war veterans. The veterans were a personal reminder of the many lives the war had touched. Moreover, the holiday's projection of the future was also very fitting. In a society overburdened with a deep sense of loss, Victory Day provided a relieving belief that loss can lead to greatness.

Yet reconciliation of this sort could not be achieved with other political holidays. The two most important such dates were the Anniversary of the October Revolution (November 7) and the Day of Declaration of State Sovereignty of the Russian Federation (June 12). The unified public practices of celebrating the Anniversary of the October Revolution (November 7) began to unravel even before the collapse of the Soviet Union. This holiday, which was celebrated in the public sphere in Soviet times, no longer projected a nationwide message. Different interpretations of the Soviet past by liberals and communists turned public spaces into arenas of protest, and the holiday's popularity during the 1990s was not high (7 percent [see table 4]).[63]

In 1990–1991, liberals used November 7 to demand further democratization, while communists protested Gorbachev's reforms. In 1990, although the Soviet state still organized November 7 celebrations, in the atmosphere of glasnost, competing demonstrations sprang up, with slogans like "November 7—a Day of National Tragedy."[64] A year later, in 1991, a month before the collapse of the Soviet Union, the same situation reoccurred. In Moscow, in tandem with the last state-sponsored parade, liberals and anti-Gorbachev communists protested.[65] A spontaneous gathering of about 10,000 communists took place near Lenin's monument in Revolution Square in Moscow.[66] They held slogans like "Hands off Lenin" and "Dermo-kratia" (Shit-ocracy).[67] Fifteen protesters

FROM THE SOVIET CALENDAR TO RUSSIAN CALENDARS 141

crawled across Moscow's ring road to mark the disgraceful transition from a socialist to a capitalist market economy.[68] Democrats held a protest in remembrance of the victims of the Soviet regime. They marched from Lubyanka Square (headquarters of the KGB) to the site of the Church of Christ the Savior (which was demolished in 1931). Due to early links between the Orthodox Church and liberal audiences, the protest concluded with a prayer, and protesters held a banner reading, "Forgive us, crucified Russia."[69]

After the collapse of the Soviet Union, communists used this day to protest Yeltsin's government. On November 7, 1992, communists held a demonstration calling for Yeltsin's resignation.[70] The protests were rather small and disorganized since the Communist Party was banned. In October 1993, the Communist Party became legal again, and in 1994–1995, the profile of the Anniversary of the October Revolution was substantially raised as a day of political mobilization for the communists. By the mid-1990s, the communists had become a fierce opposition to Yeltsin, together with the nationalists. In the 1996 presidential elections, the contestation between liberals and communists reached a boiling point when the head of the Communist Party of the Russian Federation (CPRF), Gennady Zyuganov, threatened Yeltsin's presidency.

In 1996, after Yeltsin won the presidential elections, he tried to resolve the political tension around November 7, and issued a decree to rename the holiday as the Day of Accord and Reconciliation.[71] He wanted to offer a holiday that respected and honored the victims of the revolution, civil war, and political repressions.[72] This was part of Yeltsin's broader attempt to reconcile Russian society after a divisive and aggressive presidential campaign, which many considered to be unfair. Yet the holiday did not acquire new practices. Communists continued to protest on that day. Meanwhile, liberal demonstrations were no longer seen on that day in the late 1990s.

The demise of Soviet ideology in the early 1990s shattered the Soviet understanding of the Anniversary of the October Revolution and its practices. The demonstrations that were taking place were the very opposite of Soviet practices on November 7, when this day signified Soviet normality—routinely going to a parade and later drinking with friends. This normality was gone forever, and neither the communists nor the liberals offered anything of that sort on the day. This, very much like early celebrations of Victory Day, was a manifestation of the fragmentation of the national calendar in late modern circumstances, where the government no longer ideologically ordered time and people were left to decide which practices they reproduced and how. Yet, unlike with Victory Day, the discord around November 7 was never truly resolved, and instead, the Anniversary of the October Revolution became irrelevant to the wider public. As Russia moved away from its communist past, this holiday failed to channel messages that transcended the Soviet ideology and did not appeal to the wider public.

Unlike old Soviet holidays that in 1990s became days of political discord, new holidays that were introduced by the government were mostly ignored. In 1992, for instance, only 1 percent of the respondents regarded the Day of Declaration of State Sovereignty of the Russian Federation (June 12)—Russian Independence Day—as the most important holiday.[73] The low popularity of the holiday continued throughout the 1990s. In 1998 it was most important for only 2 percent of respondents. In 1997–1999 the Levada-Center asked: "June 12 is a holiday. Do you know for sure what holiday is celebrated in Russia on this day?" Only 47–51 percent answered correctly. About a quarter did not know which holiday took place on that date, and 10–12 percent said that they did not consider it a holiday.

This was an odd result as this holiday could have become a symbol for many things in Russia. On the one hand, it fit well the framework of fluid Russianness—it is inclusive and thus could have become a nationwide celebration. On the other hand, it represented the collapse of the Soviet Union, so it could have become a day of protest for and against democracy. However, it had one major flaw—it organized the past in an illogical way. The Russian activist and photo blogger Ilya Varlamov noted this important error in his photo album *A Walk around Moscow in 1993*. In the background of one photo, there is a banner reading, "With Independence Day [greetings], Dear Russians [Rossiyane]." Varlamov noted: "June 12 . . . note [the banner] congratulating Muscovites on Independence Day. This is a mistake. Russia has never been dependent on anyone, so we cannot celebrate Independence Day."[74] Varlamov pointed out that most Russians did not consider that national independence had been won in 1991, the holiday made no sense for them, and this made them apathetic toward it. This situation was cyclical—as not many people regarded this as a holiday that had a logical interpretation of history, it did not punctuate social time. As a result, it was not celebrated.

This analysis of the political set of holidays that emerged in post-Soviet Russia shows that while, indeed, political holidays became contested, Russians did not treat them similarly. Victory Day, which was initially contested, was reconciled and continued to be popular in Russia. Yeltsin did not force individuals to participate in the celebrations. He merely provided a platform for the unified celebration, and individuals chose to join in. Meanwhile, the Anniversary of the October Revolution (November 7) became a day of protest that could not be resolved, and Russian Independence Day was largely ignored.

This variance could be explained through the lens of Giddens's theory of structuration. As Russians became more empowered to choose which holiday practices to reproduce, they chose holidays that had a personal appeal. This became an important criterion for popular holidays in the neoliberal late modern era, when identity is generated by the individual agency. Since the personal meaning of Soviet normality on the Anniversary of the October Revolution was pointless outside the Soviet ideology, this holiday was not reproduced. As for Russian Independence Day, the new Russian regime did not create a narrative that involved the agency of Russian individuals, how they contributed to the emergence of a new Russia, and where was it heading. In contrast, victory in the Second World War involved people's private histories and had a clear personal connection to individuals' lives. In a privatized and personalized post-Soviet society, this type of narrative, evidently, was key for the successful reproduction of holiday practices. The importance of private appeal emerged even more vividly in next set of holidays that developed in Russia—personal and local holidays.

The Personal-Local Calendar

Personal-local holidays included Novy God (which was a family holiday in Russia), birthdays (of relatives and one's own), and International Women's Day (March 8), which had been celebrated as a personal holiday since late-Soviet times and honored feminine beauty. Moreover, besides these personal holidays, a new holiday emerged in Russia in the 1990s, which was not recorded by the Levada-Center but which from people's testimonies became popular in Russia—City Day (Den' goroda)—and has been celebrated in different cities in Russia since the 1990s.

These were holidays whose practices were focused on the private or local sphere. The preference for these holidays was in line with both late-Soviet trends gravitating toward the personal sphere as well as a common trend in late modern societies in the West. While in the Soviet era the private sphere signified a retreat from big ideologies, in late modernity the personal sphere was a refuge from the whirlwind swings of deregulated economies and global forces that were given almost free rein.[75] In this global world where people were expected to construct their identification themselves, they often opted to construct it around the individual sphere. This construction involved consumer practices, foods, and civic practices that blended cultures and traditions. These trends in Russia revealed it as a society of rising individualism.

An example for preference of the private over the public realm was illustrated in the one day of the year that remained most important to most

Table 5 Which of the following holidays is the most important for you? (%)

	1992	1998
December 31, Novy God	79	82
Birthdays of relatives and close friends	41	38
Your birthday	43	37
March 8, International Women's Day	17	28

Source: Levada-Center.
Note: Partial results; for full results, see table 3.

Russians—Novy God (New Year's Eve, December 31). In the 1990s, around 80 percent of Russians considered it the most important holiday. Its late-Soviet practices were reproduced and reformulated in the post-Soviet context. It continued to be a secular holiday, and celebrating it denoted identification with the broadest possible group—all those who celebrate the arrival of the new year. It also continued to be a private holiday, celebrated in a particularly Russian way—with family or friends and usually at home. Similar to the late-Soviet practice, Russian celebrations were accompanied by children's carnivals, music performances, and films usually broadcast on television and watched at home. This holiday emerged as a unique example of a strong secular tradition that exemplified continuity from late-Soviet times, based on a sense of normality that stemmed from personal relationships. In post-Soviet Russia, a new sense of normality developed; while the state took a step back from ordering the ideological public sphere, individuals continued to perform their sense of Russianness in their private spheres.[76]

In changing political and social circumstances, Novy God became a signifier of continuity. Television served as an important tool in this regard. Broadcasts of pop music concerts, banquets, and masquerades created a festive apolitical and nonreligious atmosphere in most Russian homes. The *Goluboii Ogonek* entertainment program, which for a short period in the late 1980s changed its name to New Year's Festive Performance (*Novogodneye prazdnichnoye predstavleniye*), was reintroduced in 1997 under its old name.[77] According to the program's producers, this was done to create continuity and provide some stability for viewers.[78] Although Western Christmas-season films penetrated the Russian market, watching *Ironiya sud'by, ili S logkim parom!* was reproduced as a Novy God tradition. The traditional televised address by the head of state, the Russian president, also persisted. In 1998 the NTV channel took an outstanding step, when instead of President Yeltsin, it broadcast an address by a puppet of Yeltsin from the popular political satire show *Kukly* (Dolls). It was perceived as a terrible mockery, which tainted the tradition of

FROM THE SOVIET CALENDAR TO RUSSIAN CALENDARS   145

Novy God. Evidently, it was the only time that such a joke was made.[79] Symbolically, Putin acceded to power on December 31, 1999, and his first speech as acting president to the Russian people was his Novy God address.

Novy God was also a flexible tradition that could open Russia to cultural influences from both Western traditions and Eastern symbols.[80] For instance, Russians became interested in Chinese zodiac signs, identifying each year with one of twelve zodiac animals, which decorated Novy God celebrations and postcards. Western features of Christmas also became popular. For example, the color red came to be used as a symbol of the holiday season. Non-Christian minorities in Russia could adapt Father Frost (Ded' Moroz) to local traditions, as part of renegotiations of center-periphery relations. In Tatarstan, he is known as Kysh Babay (Winter Old Man), and his snow maiden (in Russian Snegurochka) is called Kar Kyzy, while in the Republic of Sakha-Yakutia in the Russian Far East he is called Chys Khan, and the snow maiden, Khaarchana. The Russian scholars Natalya Radchenko and Tatiana Kuzmina noted that in the freer cultural context, minorities in Russia started incorporating their own mythical and cultural symbolism in Novy God celebrations. For instance, in Sakha-Yakutia, locals incorporated the god of winter in Novy God celebrations.[81] The holiday's secular traditions allowed groups from different backgrounds to articulate their cultural traditions.

International Women's Day (March 8), which by the late-Soviet period was no longer an ideological holiday, also remained important in the post-Soviet national calendar. In late-Soviet time, March 8 became an all-national celebration of beauty, honoring one's mother, wife, female colleague, or friend. The holiday also had seasonal symbolism, as it was the first spring holiday and was celebrated with flowers. Evidently, this holiday remained attractive in the post-Soviet period and ranked among the ten most important days of the year. According to the Levada-Center, in 1992, 17 percent of respondents marked it the most important holiday, and in 1998, its popularity rose to 27 percent.

The personal elements of March 8 had additional functions in the post-Soviet context, allowing it to fit with the new ways of life, as well as specifically Russian elements. This holiday fit well with the consumer culture that had become an important feature in late modern calendars in free-market societies. In the new circumstances that lacked a clear interpretation of the past and prognosis of the future, consumer culture became a tool and a coping mechanism to reproduce practices of the national calendar and to construct identity.[82] In Russia, consumerism was nascent, and living conditions were still very difficult, but the ideological trajectory was set toward a free-market economy, and consumer practices were an integral part of it. For instance, in one of the first issues of the fashion magazine *Vogue Russia*, in March 1998 the cover story was about the "best presents for March 8."[83] Moreover, this holiday reproduced gender-based normality that reflected a specifically Russian understanding of order in society. This expressed a sense of Russianness as a supplementing element of identification.

Another trend of late modern globalized societies, which was observed in Russia in the 1990s, was the rise of localism and the redefinition of center-periphery relations. While Soviet calendric practices evolved mostly in the interaction between the center in Moscow and the citizens, after the collapse of Soviet Union, identification was also generated on the local level—in regions, republics, and towns. One such manifestation was the rise of a new holiday—City Day (Den' Goroda). The city of Moscow led the way in establishing the practice, but it was not confined to the national capital. Other cities—large ones like the capital of Tatarstan, Kazan, and small ones, like Zheleznogorsk in Siberia—started to celebrate their own special days.[84] Although this did not manifest a preference for the personal sphere, because City Day was celebrated in public spaces, it was tied to a specific locality, unlike nationwide celebrations.

Varlamov recalled the particularly lavish celebrations of Moscow's 850th anniversary in 1997. Behind this event stood Moscow's mayor, Yuri Luzhkov. He was seen in many photos from the events, including the opening ceremony, where he hosted Yeltsin and the head of the Orthodox Russian Church, Patriarch Aleksei II. During the celebrations, Luzhkov toured the city on huge trucks that carried singers and entertainers. A large puppet of Luzhkov decorated the carnival.[85] This underlined the central place of local leadership during the 1990s. During that decade, Luzhkov became a popular leader, with municipal housing program, charities, media outlets, and development projects. Hence, while Yeltsin was a global leader, Luzhkov provided people with real solutions to everyday matters, ranging from welfare services to alternative practices of belonging.

Varlamov noted that celebrations were freestyle, inclusive, and diverse, befitting a society that was Westernizing and joining the globalized world. Street carnivals presented a mix of different messages, including the US flag. Some attractions were sponsored by Western companies, like "Nestle Town."[86] It was not, however, a simple party that celebrated Moscow life in a globalized style. The slogan that led the celebrations—"Moscow, Russia's True Value"—articulated that the local had a deep national sense of Russianness. This sort of renegotiation of local identity was part of a larger renegotiation of the place of localities in Russia. Schleifman pointed out that the demise of the centralized dictatorial regime in Russia inevitably led to a "discussion about the essence of Russianness, local identity and center-periphery relations."[87] In this context, City Day in Moscow articulated that being a Muscovite had its own specifically Russian value.

The personal set of holidays that emerged in post-Soviet Russia featured many of the coping mechanisms that were observed in Western societies. This meant that the personal Soviet holiday practices became instruments that helped people feel belonging in a society in flux. Post-Soviet Novy God practices, for example, were individual reflexive constructions of identification and a kind of mechanism for coping with the problem of ontological insecurity that occurs with the removal of state-sponsored ideology and routines. Moreover, in this persistent insecurity, Bauman pointed to the rising role of consumer culture, which was seen in March 8 practices. He found "a 'mutual fit' . . . between the inanities of the consumer market and the incongruities of the task which individuals are presumed to perform on their own. . . . The marriage between the two protagonists has been made in heaven."[88] Hence, the commercial aspect of March 8 can also be seen as a coping mechanism for the articulation of identity, when it had to be defined by individual agency.

Last, the reformulation of the center-periphery dynamic was also a global trend, which made Russian City Days not a uniquely post-Soviet practice but a manifestation of the late modern experience. Bauman elaborated that "on the fast *globalizing* planet, politics tend to be passionately and self-consciously *local*" (italics in the original).[89] He explained that while being unable to influence global forces, people resorted to political frameworks over which they could exert some influence—"my city, my community, my chapel."[90] In Russia, while the economic system was deregulated and the national political system hesitant or incapable of drawing people together, local politics became crucial in providing frameworks of reference. Hence, the preference for the practices preformed in the personal sphere, consumerism, and localism should be seen as mechanisms for coping with Russia's new late modern insecurities.

The Religious Orthodox Russian Calendar

Analysis of the historical and private sets of holidays showed that practices that became popular in post-Soviet Russia denoted an inclusive and individualized identification with the national in-group. Victory Day was a supranational holiday, Novy God had a secular tradition, and even International Women's Day emerged as a commercial celebration, like Valentine's Day in the West. Yet during the 1990s, there was a spike within Russian society in religious belief and identification with the Russian Orthodox Church, which put into question the inclusive tendencies of Russian national identification. Identification with Orthodox Christianity rose from 16 percent in 1989, to above 30 percent in 1990, to around 50 percent in 1995, and remained at approximately the same level until 2000.[91] Belief also consistently increased, and this was evident in the rising popularity of Pascha (Easter) and Rozhdestvo (Orthodox Christmas).[92]

This trend can suggest a rise in exclusivist ethnic Russian identification. This is because the type of identification that was promoted by the post-Soviet Russian Orthodox Church was overwhelmingly ethnically based and necessarily exclusivist. The sociologist Boris Dubin noted that in the 1990s there was "an actual merger for the greater, if not for the overwhelming, majority of the population between the semantics of 'Orthodox' and [ethnic] 'Russian' ('*Russkogo*')."[93] The Church moved toward exclusionary visions of identification, and as another scholar of Orthodox Christianity, Alexandr Verkhovsky, noted, it promoted "extremely mythologized notions about the pre-revolutionary Orthodox monarchy."[94] As a result, the Russian Orthodox Church represented exclusionary religious and ethnic identification.[95] Although other denominations and religions exist in Russia, most notably Sunni Islam and Orthodox Old Believers (Staroobryadtsy), mainstream Orthodox Christianity has been the biggest and the most privileged religious denomination.[96] Hence, it is the focus of religious calendars in this chapter.

This section evaluates whether the mode of religious worship in the 1990s indeed reflected an adherence to the Orthodox Church rituals and denoted an exclusivist national identification or whether the situation was closer to what happens in late modern societies. In this context, *how* people performed religious practices is material to this analysis, specifically since, as the sociologist Amitai Etzioni noted, in the current age religious practice is often performed as selective observance of religious rituals.[97] Unlike in the Durkheimian understanding of religious rituals, Etzioni pointed out that in recent decades people had more freedom to choose which rituals were relevant to their lives and were "cherry picking."[98]

The Russian Orthodox calendar has several main holidays that are celebrated according to the Julian calendar (used in Russia before 1917). Unlike in Western Christianity, where Christmas has been established as the prime holiday, in the Orthodox calendar the most important holiday was Pascha (Easter). Pascha, the resurrection of Christ, was celebrated on the last Sunday of the Velikiy Post (Great Lent), a strict seven weeks' long Lent, which was another important practice of the Orthodox calendar.[99] Velikiy Post started after the festive week of Maslenitsa, which originally was a pagan spring festival and the main carnival in pre-Soviet times. In Orthodox Christianity, this week was marked by festivities and carnivals and included practices like eating blini, cheese- and butter-rich dishes, fish, and drinking wine, while meat was forbidden.[100] Other important holidays included Christmas (Rozhdestvo, January 7), the Christening of Christ (January 19), the Feast of the Ascension, Pentecost, Dormition of the Mother of God (August 28), and the Feast of the Cross (September 27). Following the Orthodox calendar required performing a complex system of rituals as well as frequent church attendance.

Levada-Center polls show certain trends of religious worship in Russia.[101] Out of the entire calendar of Orthodox holidays, the only two holidays that were popular enough to be ranked by the Levada-Center in 1992 and 1998 were Pascha (Easter) and Orthodox Christmas (Rozhdestvo). This already suggests that most Russians did not adhere to the Orthodox calendar to punctuate social time and were selectively observing Orthodox holidays. In terms of the popularity of holidays, in 1992, 30 percent of Russians responded that Pascha was the most popular, and 18 percent indicated Orthodox Christmas (see table 6).[102] In 1998 Pascha was most important to 29 percent of the population (together with Victory Day), while Rozhdestvo was most important to 23 percent.[103] These results showed these two Orthodox holidays to be very important for Russians.

In terms of rituals performed during the holidays, the Levada-Center offered some instructive insights. In 1997–1999, it asked, "Will you celebrate Pascha? If so, which of the following will you or your family do?" It then offered a list of rituals. Most respondents indicated that they would celebrate Pascha, but they intended to follow religious rituals selectively. About 70 percent said that they would be painting eggs—a tradition that symbolizes Christ's empty tomb. The second most popular practice (about 40–45 percent) was baking a traditional Pascha cake, called *kulich*. The third and fourth most popular practices were either to host people (30 percent) or to be hosted (25 percent), and the fifth was buying kulich (16 percent in 1997, 21 percent in 1999). Following the same trend, rituals that required more commitment to religion scored relatively low. The practice of consecrating kulich cakes, which requires going to church and performing a religious ceremony, received 13–18 percent in 1997–1999. In the same period, only 7–11 percent indicated that they would attend a vigil.[104]

Table 6 Popularity of Orthodox Holidays, 1992–1998 (%)

	1992	1998
Pascha	30	29
Orthodox Christmas	18	23

Source: Levada-Centre
Note: Partial results; for full results, see table 3.

Hence, in terms of the performance of rituals during Pascha—the most important and most popular Orthodox holiday in Russia—there was an evident selective observance. The most popular rituals were softer expressions of Orthodox Christianity, which could be tagged as supplementary elements of identification. These practices would have been acceptable even in Soviet times, when religion was suppressed. Painting eggs was practiced by older generations and was tolerated. The same can be said of baking kulich cake (and even more so of those who only intended to buy a kulich). In the 1952 edition of *The Book of Tasty and Healthy Food*, there is a page-long recipe for baking a kulich.[105] This was an obvious indication that the Soviet regime did not see these traditions as particularly religious and threatening to the secular order. The same can be said about other practices that scored high—sharing meals with friends and family. The limited popularity of rituals that required more religious commitment further underlined that in the 1990s, despite a rise in affiliation with Orthodox Christianity, relatively few Russians followed the Church's rituals.

Religious practices for other holidays featured similar trends. In 1997–1998, the Levada-Center asked, "Have you celebrated [Orthodox] Christmas this year, and if so, in what way?" Among respondents, 58 percent said that they celebrated by sharing a meal with family and friends, 25 percent watched a broadcast of religious service on television, while only 8 percent participated in a service.[106] This showed that an overwhelming number of respondents celebrated the religious holiday in a nonreligious way, and a large portion performed the religious practice in a distanced manner—participating from afar by watching televised broadcasts. In 1997, in response to a survey about practices during Velikiy Post (Lent), 73 percent of respondents said that they would not change their eating habits, while 20 percent said that they would give up some prohibited foods (meat, spirits). To a similar question about Maslenitsa, 68 percent said that they would make blini, 37 percent said that they would go to visit family or host guests, 16 percent intended to participate folk celebrations, 48 percent said that they would continue to eat meat (which is forbidden during this week), and 16 percent did not intend to celebrate Maslenitsa. Here again, the trend was clear—Russians related to the Orthodox calendar but preferred rituals that required less religious commitment, like making blini or sharing a meal.

Polls about church attendance and other religious rituals in Russia in the 1990s showed similar results. During this decade, church attendance was gradually rising, although *frequent* church attendance remained low (see table 7). The Levada-Center indicated that in 1991 67 percent of respondents said that they never attended church, 6 percent said they attended less than once a year, about 18 percent once a year or a few times a year, while approximately

FROM THE SOVIET CALENDAR TO RUSSIAN CALENDARS 151

Table 7   Church Attendance in Russia, 1991–1998 (%)

	1991	1998
Never attended church	67	61
Less than once a year	6	16
Once a year or a few times a year	18	18
Frequent attendance (more than once a month)	6	6

Source: Levada-Center
Note: Partial results.

6 percent said they attend church more frequently.[107] By 1998, according to the Levada-Center, nonattendance declined to 61 percent, 16 percent attended less than once a year, 18 percent once or a few times a year, and 6 percent attended frequently. The striking fact here is that throughout the 1990s, the majority of Russians never attended church. This meant that in no way could Orthodox Christianity have been considered a central element of Russian identification. Yet the fact that by 1998 about 40 percent of the population attended church infrequently (most likely on Orthodox holidays and personal occasions like weddings, christenings, or for lighting candles) suggests that this was a supplemental element in ordering life in Russia.

Practices of the Orthodox religious calendar that were performed by Russians showed that they did not adhere to the Orthodox Christian annual set of holidays as a system that punctuated social time and denoted an exclusivist ethnic identification as was articulated by the Church. In fact, a rise in people's beliefs was not necessarily tied to involvement with institutions of the Church. Similar to European countries, levels of belief and religious affiliation in Russia were remarkably higher than levels of worship and church attendance.[108] Also, in line with what took place in Western counties, in the new post-Soviet context Russians engaged in selective observance. They preferred rituals that did not require much religious commitment. The Church gained strength but was unable to win over other nonreligious forces that the globalized new era unleashed. Hence, the Orthodox calendar served as an additional denotation of Russianness that was supplementary to inclusive and individualized elements and together formed the experience of fluid Russianness.

Late Modern Russian Times

This chapter reveals Russia as a telling case of social and psychological implications of time-related issues on practices of individual agency in the transition from classical to late modernity. The Soviet calendar had a modernist logic. It had a clear system of dates that punctuated time, ordered the past, and projected a progress-oriented prognosis of the radiant communist future. These practices were shaped through interactions between individuals and the social system, despite the authoritarian conditions. Similar to discourse in late-Soviet society, performative adherence to state-sanctioned practices became a nonideological sign of normality.[109] The collapse of the Soviet Union took away the socialist modernist calendar and its sense of normality with it. Instead of a new unified calendar, however, in the globalized late modern context what emerged were multiple understandings of the past and no unified projection of the future.

The national calendar in Russia demonstrates the relevance of the analytical framework of fluid Russianness—a civic and inclusive identification with supplementing ethnic elements. If one considers the most popular holidays in Russia in the 1990s—Novy God, birthdays (one's own and one's loved ones), Victory Day, and Pascha, closely followed by Orthodox Christmas and International Women's Day, these holidays denoted an experience of inclusive Russianness, with supplementing religious Orthodox elements, expressed in individualized and mundane practices. This was the experience that formed fluid Russianness.

For instance, the practices of Victory Day, which were intimately bound to themes of debt owed to war heroes who symbolized victory through perseverance, made this supranational holiday appealing to the Russian public. Holidays that had a stronger personal component, such as Novy God and International Women's Day, remained popular but turned into coping mechanisms to deal with the lack of state-guided orientation. Pascha and Orthodox Christmas supplemented inclusive identification with more solid exclusive elements of ethnic Russianness. By taking the same actions on a yearly basis to preserve and develop these traditions in Russia, ordinary Russians engaged in the process of the production and reproduction of their experience of belonging to the in-group. This effectively became the new post-Soviet Russian normality.

This annual cycle of holidays did not form a unified and synced calendar in the same way that the Soviet calendar was perceived. The thee post-Soviet sets of holidays stood in contrast to the well-ordered Soviet set of practices, which, even in their nonideological performative version, represented clear collective interpretations of the self as normal and Soviet. The experience of Russianness that stemmed from the post-Soviet calendar was not endorsed by the government or any other social actor. Moreover, collectively these holidays had neither a clear evaluation of the past nor a projection of the future.

Hence, the post-Soviet calendar was still fragmented and disorderly. It did not provide a solid, easily attainable shorthand as to how to perform Russianness in a predictable way. This departure from a firm punctuation of time through the routines of the Soviet calendar to a more amorphic collection of different holidays that were celebrated in individualized and tacit ways became unpleasant and reinforced the general sense of loss across society. This feeling was at the center of the construction of the national calendar in the second decade of Russian independence.

CHAPTER 6

Putin's National Calendar
A Solid Experience or Floating Ice?

The Russian anthropologist Svetlana Boym noted that by the late 1990s, Russians were looking for a "convincing plot of Russian development that will help make sense of the chaotic present."[1] This was also the case with the formation of the national calendar. It seemed that the calendar had lost its internal logic and was not useful in binding society and denoting a unified national identity. President Putin understood that in order to counter that loss and create a feeling of belonging, he would, among other things, have to articulate a common narrative of the past and a projection where Russia was heading. Both could be achieved through the national calendar. Indeed, from 2000 Putin initiated numerous changes to the annual cycle of holidays, promoting two categories of holidays—military and religious (mainly Orthodox Christian). In this process, some holidays were abandoned, while others were introduced and encouraged. The move was meant to put an end to the contested and competing calendars and to crystallize an accepted popular calendar around which a more secure and stable identity could take shape.

This chapter investigates the formation of the Russian national calendar in the 2000s, in light of Putin's efforts, and its impact on national identification. It examines primarily the two themes around which the national calendar was meant to become more unified and project a clearer sense of national identification: militaristic holidays and religious Orthodox Christian holidays. The promotion of these holidays had some unexpected consequences. Personal and local holidays are also reviewed—they were not necessarily promoted by the government but remained popular in Russia and showed that the Russian population continued to reproduce practices outside the government-promoted calendar.

The Military Calendar

Putin became president just a few months after the increase of aggressive rhetoric around the war in Yugoslavia and on the back of a military operation in Chechnya in 1999. Against this background, military holidays became one of the pillars around which Putin tried to unify the calendar. To do so, several new military holidays were introduced. In 2002 Putin reinstated February 23, formerly Red Army Day, as Defender of the Fatherland Day.[2] The Russian Duma had tried to reestablish this holiday in the late 1990s but failed.[3] Under Putin, the holiday was hollowed of its Soviet ideological context (the birthday of the Red Army) and refashioned as a day celebrating the achievements of the military and the men serving in the armed forces and security agencies.[4]

In 2003 the Duma approved a list of military anniversaries to be marked in the armed forces, and among them was the liberation of Moscow from the Polish occupation in 1612.[5] A year later, in 2004, the end of the Polish occupation of 1612 became a national holiday—Unity Day (November 4)—and replaced the Anniversary of the October Revolution (November 7). This removed the communist day of protest, which was part of the competing political calendars of the 1990s, and expunged the symbol of revolution, which did not fit the government's discourse of stability. Unity Day (November 4) represented the return of the strong Russian state, since the end of the Polish occupation of Moscow in 1612 was also the end of the Times of Trouble, when Russia did not have a legitimate leader.[6] Hence, Unity Day positioned Putin as the leader who ended instability and reinstated a strong and stable Russian state. Moreover, since it had been a religious holiday in tsarist times, its reintroduction was linked to Orthodox Christianity and represented continuity between pre-revolutionary and post-Soviet history.

In 2006, Putin signed a further decree: On the Establishment of Professional Holidays and Memorable Days in the Armed Forces of the Russian Federation.[7] This was a list of memorable days, which celebrated professional units in the army. They were meant to be celebrated only in the armed forces. One holiday in this decree, however, became particularly popular and started to be celebrated in the public sphere—the Day of Airborne Forces (Den' Vozdushno-desantnykh voysk, or in short, Den' VDV, August 2).

These main legislative acts meant that there were three national military holidays—Victory Day, Day of the Defender of the Fatherland, and Unity Day—and numerous other memorable military dates in the Russian calendar. The following considers how those holidays were celebrated and what sort of national identification they denoted.

Victory Day (May 9)

The holiday that received most attention from the government and gained most traction in the public was Victory Day. Putin's speech at the Victory Day parade on May 9, 2000, the fifty-fifth anniversary, confirmed his intention for ever more vigorous mythmaking of the victory as a symbol of national unity, along the lines of the Brezhnev-era narrative. Putin described the war as a great trial to "our statehood, people's spirit, cohesion of comradeship."[8] He addressed the traditional role of the veterans on this holiday and linked it to a projection of a successful future for Russia: "Dear front-line soldiers [*frontaviki*], with you we got used to winning. . . . It will help the young generation to build a strong and flourishing new state."[9] He also connected honoring veterans to the "sacred duty to honor the memory of fathers," which stressed the personal dimension of the holiday.[10] Indeed, in 2000 veterans had an important role in the celebrations, as they marched in the parade alongside the serving military.[11] Putin also mentioned the role of the "brotherly republics," with whom the supranational victory was achieved. It was a reminder of the holiday's inclusiveness and continuity with Soviet history.[12] From 2001, the orange and black pattern, the colors of the Saint George military decoration, were ever more apparently used as symbols of Victory Day.

Public responses to the themes of Victory Day were overwhelmingly positive, and by the 2000s and 2010s, it had become the most popular militarized holiday. If in the 1990s its popularity was 25–29 percent, in the 2000s–2010s the holiday received 30–36 percent approval. In 2005 it overtook birthdays and ranked as the second most important holiday, and in 2015 it had a record 42 percent popularity (see table 8). This was not entirely connected to the government's endeavors. Victory Day's importance had been rising since the 1990s. To some extent, the government's promotion of Victory Day practices, very much like the themes within the government discourse, was a facilitation of trends already unfolding in Russia, regardless of the government's efforts.

Despite growing popularity, contestation and conflict around Victory Day surfaced once more. It happened around the ongoing insurgency in the

Table 8 Popularity (and Ranking) of Military Holidays 1992–2015 (%)

	1992	1998	2000	2002	2004	2005	2010	2012	2014	2015
Victory Day (May 9)	25 (5)	29 (4)	34 (3)	30 (3)	29 (4)	32 (2)	36 (3)	33 (4)	36 (4)	42 (3)
Day of the Defender of the Fatherland (February 23)	_*	_*	_*	12 (9)	10 (8)	12 (8)	9 (8)	12 (8)	12 (8)	10 (8)
Unity Day (November 4)	_*	_*	_*	_*	_*	_*	1	1	1	1

Source: Levada-Center
*Option not included in the poll.

Caucasus. In the early 2000s, Russia sustained terrible terrorist attacks, and on May 9, some particularly brutal incidents took place. On May 9, 2002, a bomb exploded at the Victory Day parade in the town of Kaspiysk in the Caucasian republic of Dagestan, killing forty-three people and injuring more than a hundred.[13] In 2004, also during the Victory Day parade, a terror attack took place in Grozny, the capital of Chechnya. The president of the republic, Akhmet Kadyrov, father of the current president, Ramzan Kadyrov, was killed, together with more than fifty people.[14] Victory Day, which was supposed to exhibit an all-national inclusive Russian unity, was tainted by terrorism. Targeting Victory Day celebrations underlined the insurgents' divergent interpretation of the holiday. During the Second World War, Stalin accused the Chechens of collective treason, and in 1944, they were brutally deported to Central Asia.[15] In the 1990s, the Chechen national leadership strongly denied the accusations of treason. By the 2000s, the Chechen leadership turned to Salafi Islam and targeted Victory Day parades as symbols of the Russian military.[16] This was a reminder that there was no one victory for all in Russia and that certain parts of Russia were not unified with the federal center.

Besides these bloody contestations, Victory Day practices had other challenges. From 2005, late-Soviet Victory Day practices faced a major practical problem—the veterans, around whom celebrations revolved, were growing fewer in number. In 2005, veterans still participated in the celebrations. (They were driven during the parade on military trucks.) With the years, they had grown too old and too few to perform their role during the holiday. How does one continue to celebrate a holiday without its main symbol and the focal point of its practice? The desire to keep reproducing Victory Day called for innovation. Increasingly, props that helped people celebrate in new circumstances were produced in an interaction between the government and the public; an evolution of Brezhnev-era practices began.

One such example of a new Victory Day prop was the Georgian ribbon. The Georgian ribbon was invented in 2005 as part of the Russian news agency RIA Novosti's online commemoration project—Den' Pobedy (Victory Day).[17] There RIA Novosti invented a symbol—a black-and-orange striped ribbon (the colors of Saint George military decoration) to mark the anniversary. RIA Novosti called on the public to embrace remembrance by wearing the ribbon: "If you cherish your ancestors' contribution to the Allied cause, tie a ribbon on your bag, around the collar, or on anything you like, and wear it as long as you like.... The tiny ribbon is worn as a symbol of patriotism, which ... does not demand spectacular action."[18]

The ribbon had vast potential as a mnemonic tool. As veterans were dying, the Georgian ribbon could symbolically replace the medals worn by them. It was also a simple and mundane way to identify with the nation, which matched the growing trend in late modern societies for banal nationalism. This was expressed by RIA Novosti, as it claimed that one could perform a small deed to show patriotism and, by doing so, recall great actions for the nation. Yet it also had a latent aggressive potential, as a physical demarcation of *nash* (ours) versus *ne nash* (not ours). In 2005–2007, the ribbon became increasingly popular during the May 9 celebrations.

Another new Victory Day practice was conceived in 2007, in Tyumen, Western Siberia. A resident of the town, Gennady Ivanov, suggested holding a procession in which participants would carry photos of deceased veterans and fallen relatives.[19] This idea materialized under the name the Victors Parade (Parad Pobediteley), and it was held in Tyumen for several years.[20] Like the Georgian ribbon, this too was a practice that aimed at circumventing the fact that veterans were growing fewer. It was a personalized practice, where each participant was asked to carry photos of *his* or *her* relatives. By 2009 several cities across Russia held processions of this sort under various names, and by 2012 the idea was picked up by local television journalists in Tomsk in Siberia, who organized a well-publicized procession and renamed it the Immortal Regiment (Bessmertnyy polk).[21] As the historian Mischa Gabowitsch noted, the Immortal Regiment was neither a top-down nor a bottom-up initiative but rather a horizontal movement that spread this new commemorative practice across Russia.[22]

In 2008, Victory Day displayed more elements recalling late modern trends. During the parade, President Medvedev and Prime Minister Putin wore Georgian ribbons.[23] The troops were treated to a new uniform, designed by Russia's top fashion designer Valentin Yudashkin.[24] Yudashkin's involvement with the military underlined the fraternization between militarism and popular culture in Russia.[25] Victory in the Second World War and military matters were repositioned in society. They were no longer heavy topics of conversation but also a light and fashionable affair. This mix between high and low culture, fashion and patriotism, was a postmodern turn and could be considered an expression of banal nationalism. Banality did not, however, mean pacifism. Amid deteriorating relations with the West and former Soviet states, for the first time since Russia's independence, heavy military hardware was displayed at the Victory Day parade.[26] Indeed, just a few months later Russia went to war with Georgia.

By 2013–2014 the Russian government fully embraced the new Victory Day practices. The Georgian ribbon and the Immortal Regiment, which the government appropriated, became new all-national and supranational practices of Victory Day. The dissemination of Georgian ribbons by volunteers became an international operation that went beyond the borders of Russia to former Soviet states and countries with Russian-speaking populations, such as Germany and Israel. A similar thing happened with the Immortal Regiment, which became—in 2015, the seventieth anniversary of victory—one of the leading commemorative events in Russia. According to the Levada-Center, in 2015 an overwhelming 63 percent saw the initiative favorably, 82 percent knew what it was, and 25 percent said they would like to take part, with an extra 37 percent saying they were likely to want to take part.[27] Indeed, about half a million participants marched in 2015 in Moscow, among them President Putin, who held a photo of his father.[28]

During those years, the new popular practices of Victory Day had a dual use. In the short run, they were used by the government for mobilizing support for the Annexation of Crimea and the war in East Ukraine. The Georgian ribbon and the Immortal Regiment were used as instruments for national mobilization to show support for the government and legitimize its actions after the Crimean campaign. The Georgian ribbon became a physical marker of consensus over Russia's actions in Crimea and Ukraine and the new militaristic mainstream, showing who was really nash (ours) and supported the slogan "Krym nash" (Crimea is ours).[29] The Immortal Regiment was used by the government to mobilize society behind Russia's narrative of victory, in contrast with the narrative of the new regime in Kiev, which Russia labeled fascist.

In the long run, these new practices were badly needed because by 2010s the number of veterans had become so few. The Georgian ribbon and Immortal Regiment processions, where photos of veterans were carried and people wore Georgian ribbons and dressed in Soviet Army uniforms, were positioned to fully replace the veterans. They were popularized by state-owned media and on social networks, where the government held photo competitions and pop stars and celebrities popularized the practices by posting images of the ribbons and photos of their relatives who had fought in the war.³⁰ These novel, cyber-based practices of Victory Day denoted an inclusive and mundane Russian national identification and became extremely popular.³¹ For instance, by performing individualized and cyber-based practices of Victory Day, MC Doni, who in everyday life may have been a misfit and not Russian enough, uploaded a photo of his grandfather in uniform and was instantly marked as nash (ours). Doni, while using cyber technologies, could write his own inclusive narrative of Russianness around Victory Day—a narrative in which he belongs. This example defies the dichotomy of pro- and antigovernment practices, as individuals reproduced the new practices not only as a mean of supporting the government but also to create belonging that fit the late modern era.³²

These new performances, which were in sync with late modernity and banal nationalism, channeled a different type of memory from the Brezhnev-era narrative. They signified a memory that was cleaner and less burdened with loss. Participants in the Immortal Regiment carried photos from their family albums and their association and belonging with the nation stemmed from their own personal history.³³ This shifted the focal point of the practice to individual agency. It was no longer a performance centered on the mythicized agency of veterans. In the post-Crimean atmosphere, when the new government in Ukraine was described as fascist, those who marched in the Immortal Regiment performed the heroic duty of defending the memory of the war from real and imagined fascists. The inconceivable heroism of risking one's life and defeating Nazi Germany was replaced with the mundane practice of joining a procession and fighting—not in a real war but in a political polemic and propaganda war.

Within the same trend, the new practices of memory were also cleansed of suffering and became increasingly upbeat rather than sad. The vanishing veterans gave way to their photos. People could casually wear a Georgian ribbon, instead of hard-won medals. People dressed up in Soviet Army uniforms and turned it into a carnival, where love of country could be shown by imitating great deeds, without performing them. This alteration in memory was recorded by Levada-Center polls. Respondents were asked, "What feelings do you have about Victory Day?" In 2015, there was a spike in those who said it is primarily a happy day (59 percent). The Russian public no longer treated it as the Soviet song "Den' Pobedy" (Victory Day) says, "it is joy with tears in our eyes" ("eto radost' so slezami na glazakh"); the burden of war was lifted, and only victory remained. In the following years, the government encouraged more practices of a similar nature, like building a mock Reichstag that the new militarized youth movement Yungvardiya could storm.³⁴

It was not by chance that these new practices of memory were crystallized around the annexation of Crimea. Crimea was Russia's first New Generation War (Voyna novogo pokoleniya), a theoretical military term for a late modern type of war, a war where the use of kinetic force is reduced to minimum.[35] Acting in the sphere of plausible deniability and using communication technologies such as live media broadcasting, the Russian government constructed a clean war that was easily consumed and applauded from the comfort of one's living room. This was barely a Russian or a new phenomenon. In the West, reporters who covered the war in Iraq in 2003 recalled that "the war was set up to be filmed and recorded by the media," as part of the Pentagon's perception management.[36] This was treated as "militainment," which used music and graphics to make the war more appealing and easier to support.[37] In Russia too, the war in Crimea, as well as the memory of the Second World War, no longer had the same gruesome and unpleasant connotations. The narrative of military victory changed, and now it was no longer loss that led to greatness. The new greatness could be achieved effortlessly and cleanly. The New Generation War victory in Crimea and the new memory practices of Victory Day were a match made in heaven. They expressed how deeply Russian national identification was influenced by late modern trends.

This analysis shows that not only did Victory Day remain contested; at least in the early 2000s, its new practices channeled late modern trends. While the government encouraged militarized holidays, in many ways it was a facilitator for grassroots (or horizontal) initiatives. These new practices of Victory Day were expressions of banal, mundane, and individualized national identification. Hence, the identification that developed in Russia around Victory Day was not necessarily more militarized and unified but a late modern and banal identification.

Day of the Defender of the Fatherland (February 23)

The Day of the Defender of the Fatherland (February 23) was the second most popular holiday out of the three national military holidays but with nowhere near the popularity of Victory Day.[38] Putin gave the holiday a purely military tone. For instance, in 2002 Putin marked the holiday by visiting wounded servicemen.[39] The government encouraged educational and militarized activities on this holiday through the Program for the Patriotic Education of Citizens of the Russian Federation (Patrioticheskoye vospitaniye grazhdan Rossiyskoy Federatsii).[40] However, in the early 2000s this message seemed misplaced. Unlike in Soviet times, society was freer, and the military, despite a relative rise in popularity, was a controversial institution in many respects. Recent wars in Afghanistan and the First Chechen War were viewed as disastrous.[41] Moreover, the Russian army was associated with grave internal abuses of power and bullying (*dedovshchina*). Dodging the draft became widespread, and the Russian ombudsman admitted that many of those who were drafted were not fit for service.[42] In these circumstances, the army was not necessarily a celebrated institution. In later years, the image of the Russian military improved due to successful military reforms and following the bloodless annexation of Crimea. Yet, similarly to its Soviet-era practices, this holiday did not celebrate the armed forces.

For those who did celebrate the holiday, its reproduction looked more like an excuse for masculine activities. For instance, a school in Rostov held a family activity called "Daddy and I—a sporty family," where young children dressed as little sailors ran, jumped, and danced with their fathers. This was a relatively militarized event. Other events were more mundane. In Sochi and in Dubna (a town near Moscow), martial arts clubs used the day for competitions. In Nizhny Novgorod, an off-road riding competition was held, while a group of hikers from the Ural region decided to share on a local news website their celebrations of the holiday on the ice of Lake Baikal. These practices reinforced gender relations in the society and marked what was regarded as masculine in Russia. Even more importantly, like on International Women's Day (March 8), commercialization became a main feature of the holiday, with recommendations for presents as well as special sales events for manly products, such as cars.[43] Hence, while the official agenda of the day was military, its popularity was not high, and its practices were reflected and reproduced mainly in mundane ways and through commercialism.

Here too, competing interpretations of the day existed. For the Chechens, this was a day of memory and sorrow: Stalin had chosen Red Army Day (February 23) to begin the deportations of the Chechens in 1944.[44] In 1956 Khrushchev exonerated them, and they began to return to the Caucasus.[45] In post-Soviet Chechnya, demonstrations against Moscow's policies and commemorative events were held on that day.[46] Since 2012, Moscow-backed Ramzan Kadyrov ordered that the Day of the Defender of the Fatherland be celebrated on February 23, together with the rest of the Russian population. The day of mourning for the deportations was moved to May 10, the date of his father's burial in 2004.[47] Yet Chechens looked for ways to circumvent the ban through private practices of mourning on February 23, like posting on social networks and leaving their doors open (a Caucasian ritual of mourning).[48]

These varied interpretations of the Day of the Defender of the Fatherland meant that after the reintroduction of the holiday in 2002, it had several interpretations in Russia. The official interpretation celebrated military servicemen. The wider public reproduced practices that were not necessarily tied to military themes but rather, like in Soviet times, represented manhood and were often celebrated through commercial practices. The Chechen minority view diverged altogether, as they continued to mourn the deportations that had traumatized their community. This was another example that in the late modern context multiple and competing calendars could not be completely scrapped.

In fact, the date that marked a mass celebration that was linked to the armed forces in Russia became the Day of the Airborne Forces (August 2), popularly known as Den' VDV. But this was a slightly different celebration from what the government envisioned. The date was designated as a memorable day in 2006.[49] Den' VDV commemorates the establishment of the Airborne Forces in 1930 and celebrates the fighters in one of the toughest forces in the Russian army. This day was meant to be celebrated in a very proper and dignified manner—meetings of the blood brotherhood of the blue berets (airborne forces members) in cemeteries to lay flowers. In 2006, as a sign of the increased closeness between the army and the Russian Orthodox Church, the authorities organized a Christian Orthodox service in Moscow, accompanied by a *krestnyy khod* (an Orthodox Christian procession) and a liturgy.[50] A music concert was organized in Gorky Park in Moscow.

Although not a day off work, it became very popular. While some participants came out with families to celebrate and remember their fallen brothers-in-arms, for most former and current paratroopers this day became a yearly carnival of rowdy behavior. It featured heavy drinking, fights, public disorder, and public sexual acts. In line with the carnivalesque spirit of the holiday, the celebrating forces used their nickname—"Uncle Vasya's troops" (in Russian, Voyska dyadi Vasi, which had the same abbreviation as the Airborne Forces: VDV)—named after Soviet general Vasily Margelov, "Uncle Vasya," who established the Soviet airborne troops. In Moscow, Novosibirsk, Irkutsk, and other smaller cities, mass brawls, attacks on ethnic minorities, bathing in fountains, and other disorderly conduct were reported.[51] Photos of the events show people in white-and-blue striped T-shirts, khaki military trousers, and blue berets looking intoxicated, often bleeding, singing in fountains. The events were so disturbing to the public order that in 2016 Moscow local authorities wanted to move the celebrations from Gorky Park in the city center to Patriot Park on the outskirts.[52] In several cities, celebrators were heavily guarded by police to ensure disorder did not spill over. This was far from the wholesome patriotic image the holiday was meant to project and was a different and competing interpretation of this celebration—a carnival.

The meaning of carnival as a social phenomenon has been discussed in several studies. Most famously, the historian Natalie Zemon-Davis noted that carnivals, where people play fool and marry, are "not mere 'safety valves'" but that "festive life can, on the one hand, perpetuate certain values of the community . . . and on the other hand criticize political order."[53] The carnival of Den' VDV was, as other such events, a "safety valve"—a day to blow off steam. This was probably also the reason that the authorities did not move the celebrations to the city outskirts. However, as Zemon-Davis noted, such events have deeper meaning. Den' VDV also represents a negotiation over the meaning of normality in post-Soviet Russian society and the government-promoted image of military-patriotic (and religious) morality. Putin's image of a sober security services officer, a sportsman, and a pious Christian is not necessarily the image of Russian military men. Den' VDV challenged conceptions of this military image. It revealed the government's return to security and stability as untrue and boring. Instead, Den' VDV presented a distorted-carnival mirror of the government's wholesome military image in Russia, which was in fact rowdy and raucous. Hence, it became another example of the competing interpretations of memorial days, which were common in the late modern context and remained so in Russia in the 2000s.

Unity Day (November 4)

The situation was even more extreme with Unity Day (November 4), which also did not escape controversy. Despite the government's backing, this holiday was barely known to the population. The president together with the heads of major religions in Russia marked the day by laying flowers at the Monument to Minin and Pozharsky, the heroes of the 1612 campaign. This was a public show of interfaith national unity in Russia. Concerts were organized in Moscow and other major cities. But polling results showed that at no point did this holiday receive more than 1 percent popularity. Most people did not even know the holiday's name. In 2005, only 8 percent of respondents knew what holiday was taking place on November 4, while 33 percent thought it was the Day of Reconciliation and Accord (the post-1996 name for the Anniversary of the October Revolution, November 7). In 2012, still 25 percent thought it was the Day of Reconciliation and Accord. Although the number of those who recognized the date as Unity Day was rising (from 8 percent in 2005 to 43 percent in 2012), in 2012 still 48 percent of respondents either misconceived or bluntly did not recognize the holiday.[54] When asked whether respondents intended to celebrate November 7 or November 4, around 60 percent of the respondents said that they would celebrate neither.

In contrast to the general apathy toward this holiday, Unity Day became the holiday of far-right groups. From 2005 far-right groups organized Russkiy March on November 4—a procession of far-right and racist groups in Russia.[55] This marked the holiday as a day of political protest, extreme ideologies, and opposition to the government—messages that were all contrary to the government's initial plans for the day. Right-wing protestors, the pro-Kremlin youth movement Nashi (Ours), and the antifascist left-wing movement Antifa clashed on this day.[56] Moreover, even within the right-wing movements there was discord. By 2007 there were multiple protests of right-wing groups in Moscow. The researcher Denis Zuev noted that "in 2009 no less than five marches were organized by different groups representing different ideological frames, from fundamentalist Russian Orthodox to national socialist and competing versions of patriotism."[57] Although by the 2010s the government accepted some ideas that were raised by nationalist groups that protested on Unity Day (such as Neo-Eurasianism), Russian nationalists remained competitors with the government, and Unity Day was their rallying date.

Unity Day was meant to curb competing political calendars that developed in the 1990s around the communist day of protest on November 7. But, in fact, it produced another type of protest that was no less challenging. Unity Day became a holiday that underlined disunity, ethnic tensions, and competing interpretations of love of country and belonging to the national in-group. This underlined the continued fragmentation of the national calendar and the presence of competing and contested calendars in Putin's Russia, which characterize late modernity.

A "Morality Turn"? The Religious Calendar

Military and religious themes were intertwined in the effort to create a unified national calendar that reflected a stable national identification. The Russian Orthodox Church understood the need to work with the government to make sure its calendar worked synergistically with government-promoted militarized themes. For instance, in 2003, a Church press release stated: "The Primate of the Russian Orthodox Church and the Head of the Russian State congratulated each other on the holiday of the Bright Resurrection and Victory Day."[58] Despite the odd coupling between the resurrection of Jesus Christ and victory over Nazi Germany, they were blended as the new sanctities of post-Soviet Russian society. The scholar of Russian nationalism Marlene Laruelle termed this a "morality turn" in Russian politics—the increased debate on the role of traditional values in Russia's national identity.[59]

The symbiotic connection between President Putin and the Russian Orthodox Church materialized instantly. Putin developed a close relationship with the head of the Russian Orthodox Church, Patriarch Alexei II (and later Patriarch Kirill); the president attended services and was involved in the affairs of the Orthodox Christian world. On his inauguration in 2000, Putin sought the blessing of Patriarch Alexei II. In 2003 he got involved in the process of reconciliation between the Moscow patriarchate and the Russian Orthodox Church abroad.[60] He attended every Pascha service starting in 1999 in the Church of Christ the Savior, except for 2003, which he spent in Tajikistan. He attended Orthodox Christmas services in churches and monasteries across Russia's regions and in 2007 celebrated Orthodox Christmas in Jerusalem.[61] By mid-2000 Putin became known for his traditional values, had a strong standing in the Orthodox world, and was described by Patriarch Alexei II as a "[true] Orthodox Christian."[62] Photos of him attending Christian services on holidays became tools for the elevation of the Christian Orthodox calendar to a semiofficial level.

This was accompanied by the gradual acceptance and endorsement of Orthodox-civilizational approaches, such as adherence to traditional values, recognition of Russia's special path, and Russia as the heart of a unique civilization.[63] This culminated in the 2010s, but even beforehand, Russia had positioned itself as the defender of conservative values. These approaches legitimized the divergence from a democratic transition to the introduction of sovereign democracy. It was explained by Russia's special path as a truly Christian nation, while democracy and liberal values were Western and foreign to Russia.[64] These ideas expressed exclusive identification and were in many cases aggressive.

Rejection of Western liberal values and encouragement of traditional and family values allowed for the forming of partnerships with other traditional actors abroad and at home. Domestically, Putin developed relationships with the heads of other "traditional religions" in Russia, such as the chief mufti of Russia, Rawil Gaynetdin, and the chief rabbi of Russia, Berl Lazar.[65] From Putin's point of view, these relationships showed Russia's greatness. In a meeting with Rabbi Lazar, Putin stated: "It's good that we have such a big country, a multinational country, and a holiday like the New Year is celebrated here several times."[66] Hence, the government's support for religion was not limited to Orthodox Christianity, and alliances based on conservative and religious values were encouraged.

Interfaith cooperation between "traditional religions" was also used to suppress other minority groups in society. Here the LGBTQ community served as a scapegoat. For instance, at an interfaith roundtable at Kazan's Hall of Culture in Tatarstan, the archpriest of Kazan, Vladimir Samoilenko, said: "We, all of us, will not put up with attempts to legitimize homosexual weddings. . . . I know I speak for my Jewish and Muslim colleagues, too."[67] This representative statement repositioned the issue of identification from an ethnically exclusive one, which stemmed from Orthodox identification, to a broader struggle by a coalition of religious leaders against liberal conceptions of flexible identifications, primarily LGBTQ. Although the depth of this alliance should not be overestimated, it allowed the Russian government certain flexibility in approaching other religious groups, when the general atmosphere was increasingly exclusivist and aggressive.

The portrayal of the liberal West as a new common enemy with its LGBTQ agents of subversion within Russia culminated around an annual celebration of the LGBTQ community—the Gay Pride parade. In 2006, LGBTQ activists planned to mark May 27, the thirteenth anniversary of the repeal of act 121, which banned homosexuality in the Soviet Union, with the first Gay Pride parade in Moscow.[68] Yet this started a chain of events that revealed the depth of the Orthodox Church's penetration into the politics of Russia. Around this pretext, an attack on LGBTQ rights was launched in the name of protecting the traditional family. The conflict was colored in civilizational themes—the sinful West against the truly Christian Orthodox Russia. In 2007, Moscow's mayor called the parade a "satanic rite."[69] Society supported these moves, and anti-LGBTQ sentiment in the public rose significantly. (From 2007 to 2013, the number of people who viewed homosexuality negatively rose from 21 to 54 percent.)[70] It became common in the 2010s to refer to Western Europe as "Gay-ropa," which turned into a general derogatory term for the liberal West.

To articulate proper traditional and Orthodox conceptions of love, a new Orthodox Christian holiday was introduced (although it did not become a national holiday). From 2008, Dmitry Medvedev's wife, Svetlana Medvedeva, who is a devout Christian, was promoting the Day of Peter and Fevronia (July 8). In Orthodox Christianity, Peter and Fevronia were the patrons of family, love, and faithfulness, and the holiday was meant to celebrate traditional and family values. This was an alternative to Valentine's Day, which became popular in Russia, as well as a conservative rearticulation of family and gender in Russia.[71] In 2008, Medvedeva elaborated on the values and gender roles projected by this holiday: "I think for women this holiday is especially meaningful. A woman must by nature strive for humility. Its purpose is to keep peace and love in the family."[72] This holiday promoted the notion that conservative gender roles were somehow historically tied to Russian heritage. Although the holiday never became widely popular, its banal symbolism—a daisy—and other greetings circulated on social networks on July 8.

CHAPTER 6

Against this background, it is important to examine the extent to which these processes precipitated a change in Russian identification toward a more exclusive Orthodox-based identity. Specifically, did these processes result in increased worship and the punctuation of time by the Orthodox calendar, or did selective observance, which is common in late modern societies, persist in the 2000s and 2010s? This would make clear whether Russian identification continued to develop along the lines of other late modern societies or became more exclusivist and based on Orthodox religious values.

In the 2000s, opinion polls showed that Orthodox Christian religious affiliation grew in Russian society. Levada Center polls showed that from 1996 to 2002 the number of respondents who considered themselves Orthodox Christians rose from 50 to 56 percent and remained around that level until 2005.[73] In 2005, polls showed that about 60 percent of Russians identified as Orthodox Christians. These figures rose steadily, peaking at almost 80 percent in 2009 and stabilizing at around this figure through 2012.[74] The proportion of individuals who identified as Muslim gradually grew as well, reaching 7 percent in 2012.[75]

Responses regarding religious worship among believers were mixed. Poll results showed an increase in church attendance between 1998 and 2003 (see table 9).[76] The number of people who never went to church decreased from 61 to 46 percent and remained so into the 2010s. But people did not report frequent church attendance either, which suggests that they did not perform regular religious worship and did not follow religious rites. The results can suggest that people participated in religious ceremonies in church (weddings, christenings, attendance during holidays) or went individually to light candles but did not perform deeply religious rituals, which would have required more regular attendance. Indeed, in 2012 when asked about the purpose of attending church, most people said that they went to church to light a candle and not for a specific religious service. Another illustration of this is a very slight increase over the years in the performance of receiving Holy Communion, an important religious ritual. By 2015 more than 61 percent of those who identified as believers never received Holy Communion.

Results of religious worship and performance of religious rituals during holidays were also mixed. In the 2000s there was no increase in the popularity of Pascha.[77] The popularity of Orthodox Christmas grew from 16 percent in 2000 to 26 percent in 2005 but then went down again to 19 percent in 2010–2012 (see table 10). As in the 1990s, other Orthodox Christian religious holidays were not popular enough to be recorded by the Levada-Center. As for Muslim holidays, the Levada-Center recorded that since 2002 the Muslim holiday of Eid al-Adha, known in Russia under its Turkish name Kurban-Bayram,

Table 9   Church Attendance in Russia 1998–2011 (%)

	1998	2003	2007	2011	2017	2019
Never went to church	61	46	43	45	33	37
Less than once a year	16	18	17	12	16	13
At least once a year or a few times	18	30	17	29	35	33
Once or a few times a month	4	5	8	8	10	7
Weekly attendance	2	2	2	4	3	5

Source: Levada Center.

Table 10   Popularity of Pascha and Orthodox Christmas, 1992–2012 (%)

	1992	1998	2000	2002	2004	2005	2010	2012
Pascha	30 (4)	29 (4)	32 (4)	26 (6)	23 (5)	28 (5)	31 (5)	29 (5)
Orthodox Christmas	18 (5)	23 (6	16 (6)	19 (7)	22 (6)	26 (6)	19 (6)	19 (7)

Source: Levada-Center.
Note: Partial results.

received 3–5 percent. This showed that religious holidays did not gain primacy as dates that punctuated social time and denoted a religious, ethnically based, exclusivist identification.

In terms of rituals during holidays, selective observance persisted. During Pascha, the most popular ritual remained that of painting eggs (72 percent in 2000, 75 percent in 2006, and 69 percent in 2013). Russians continued to like kulich cakes, but during the 2000s, while the number of those who intended to bake kulich was going down, the number of those who intended to buy one was going up.[78] This suggests the penetration of commercial practices into holiday rituals. The only deeply religious performance that increased in popularity was consecrating kulich, which increased from 14 percent in 2000 to 26 percent in 2006 and remained at around 20–25 percent in the 2010s. The same increase did not happen with vigils, which remained at around the same level of popularity as in the 1990s. During Velikiy Post (Lent), there was a slight rise in nonobservants and a decrease in partially observant practices. Contrary to this trend, on Maslenitsa, the spring festival a week before Lent, there was an increase in observance (a decrease in those who intended to eat meat) from 48 percent in 1997 to around 30 percent in the early 2000s.[79] It is interesting that Russian were more likely to observe Maslenitsa than Velikiy Post. Velikiy Post was far more important from a religious point of view, while Maslenitsa was a festive holiday that was originally pagan. This may suggest that Russians preferred a festive holiday over religious repentance.

Overall, these results suggest that Russians continued to perform selective observance and that there was no significant change in the place occupied by religion and religious rituals in individuals' lives. Despite the government's increased involvement in and encouragement of religious institutions, deeply religious rituals did not become more common. It suggests that while the president—who was photographed attending services—served as a mnemonic tool of the Orthodox calendar and elevated it to a semiofficial level, the Russian public continued to "cherry-pick" religious practices like in the 1990s. These findings reveal, like the government's militarized calendar, the morality turn as a relatively thin layer of ice, which did not fundamentally change the public's relationship with religion. The reproduction of religious rituals showed less commitment to religious tenets and more cultural affiliation with Orthodox Christianity. Hence, Orthodox Christianity remained a supplemental element of ethnic Russianness in an overall late modern experience of fluid Russianness.

These findings suggest that the ostracization of the LGBTQ community should not be considered a symptom of a society that was becoming more religious and conservative. Rather, it was an attempt to firmly delineate an in-group by a process of othering a traditionally vulnerable minority in Russia. The LGBTQ community was a scapegoat used by an unstable coalition of political actors whose interests were fundamentally at odds with each other. For the Russian Orthodox Church, it was a populist rallying point for a society that, otherwise, was not growing more religious. For non-Orthodox actors, it was a common denominator around which they could unite, as the political climate was changing toward exclusive visions of identity, which might impinge on their rights too.

Personal Holidays and Statist Ideology

The last section of this chapter turns the spotlight on personal and local holidays that persisted through the 2000s and signified the continued importance of the private sphere. The Russian cultural critic Daniil Dondurey noted that Russians' continued preferences for personal and private holidays is important, especially since in the 2000s it was assumed that the public favored statism.[80] The most important holiday during this period remained Novy God, an apolitical and personal holiday to which people continued to strongly relate. Another interesting local new holiday discussed here is Monstratsiya.

Novy God

According to the Levada-Center, in the 2000s and 2010s about 80 percent of respondents considered Novy God the most important holiday in the year. Its popularity surpassed by far all other holidays and memorial days. After Novy God, the most popular holidays were personal events (birthdays), which scored around 40 percent. This illustrates the continuation of a previous trend, and Novy God continued to be a focal point in the Russian national calendar. As for celebrations, Levada-Center polls showed that Russians continue to prefer celebrating Novy God in private settings, at home (over 70 percent of respondents).[81] As for the holiday rest days, again most respondents said that they intended to stay at home and do housework/projects.

In those years more holiday practices evolved. For instance, writing postcards, which had been very popular in Soviet times, was adjusted to new technological and commercial realities, and Russians often preferred more instant ways of greeting friends and family—like text messaging.[82] Yet postcards did not completely lose their appeal, and new trends appeared, like preferences for unique one-of-a-kind handmade postcards or DIY postcards.[83] Internet marketplace websites like Yarmarka Masterov (similar to the Etsy marketplace website in the United States) offered hand-made, personalized, and one-of-a-kind presents themed for the new year.

There was also interest in reinventing the Soviet-era Novy God menu, to reflect new tastes and rising living conditions. A Russian lifestyle and cooking guru with a heavy presence on social media, Nika Belotserkovskaya, published the cookbook *Everything for under the Fir Tree: My Favorite Recipes for the Celebratory Table* (*Vso pod yëlku: Moi lyubimyye retsepty k prazdnichnomu stolu*). The title of the book revealed a known truism of continuity of the Russian national calendar—there was only one celebratory table, and it was the Novy God table. But the content of the book showed an evolution of practices. On the book's cover appeared a photograph of Belotserkovskaya in a nostalgic Soviet military *ushanka* hat and a large fur coat hanging off her shoulder, showing a fashionable, revealing dress—an expression of the mix of traditions and the evolving image of Russian life.

The content of this book was obviously an attempt to sketch this new sense of Russianness and to cater to new tastes. The book included photos of Soviet-era Novy God foods, like mandarins and caviar. Yet, Belotserkovskaya noted in her Introduction that the book contains no recipe for the traditional Soviet salat Oliv'ye, as "you will probably have your own." This book included recipes of traditional Russian foods, which were not staple Novy God foods, like borscht, schi soup (meat and cabbage), and an Orthodox Christmas cake.[84] At the same time, the book was stylized with red-color ornaments, mirroring Western Christmas traditions, and included foreign dishes like lasagna, tagliatelle, and focaccia.[85] Belotserkovskaya's book was not a masterpiece of carefully balanced ideological, cultural, and culinary advices like the Soviet *Book of Tasty and Healthy Food*. It was a late modern selection—a fragmented assemblage of tastes, fashions, and trends. The flexible framework of Novy God allowed for this type of adaptation, without taking away the important place that this holiday had in Russian life.

In 2007 a sequel to the legendary film *Ironiya sud'by, ili S logkim parom!* was released. It featured the same actors, as well as a new generation of popular Russian young actors, who played their sons and daughters. Although this movie did not gain the same status as the original film from 1976, it underlined the flexible elements of Novy God, which can be reproduced over time. The film mixed Soviet-era traditions and features of post-Soviet life. The apartments, in the same Soviet-era blocks, were decorated for Novy God with staple celebratory tables. But the new protagonists were different. They were global-minded, refrained from drinking, drove expensive Japanese cars, had cell phones, and planned American-style marriage proposals, which included a large diamond ring. It also featured a diasporic element, as one of the characters emigrated to Israel and called on Novy God to greet her friends in Russia. In the film, as in reality, Novy God transcended not only the change from Soviet to post-Soviet regimes but also the move from one country to another. Notably in Israel, a Jewish country, Novy God had gained a semiofficial status, and one Israeli website noted: "As there is more than one way to be Israeli—there is more than one way to celebrate a Novy God."[86] As the development of the original film to its sequel showed, this holiday's flexibility made it a symbol of inclusiveness not only for post-Soviet Russians but to others of the late modern globalized world.

The 2015 New Year's movie *Strana OZ* (Land of Oz) portrayed a different perspective of post-Soviet Russian Novy God. In this dark comedy, Lenka, a young girl from a village in Siberia, comes to the big city Yekaterinburg, to work as a saleswoman in a kiosk. Her Novy God night turns into a destitute and dangerous journey where she meets various unsavory types (drug-addicted businessmen, prostitutes in snow maidens' dresses, and low-life pseudo-intellectuals). The movie purposely negates the accepted conventions of Novy God practices: most scenes are set outside, on the cold streets; none of the characters are celebrating Novy God at home; none of them have families, and there is no festive table in sight. They are lonely, lost, and often violent people. The movie does not completely diverge from the Novy God genre, however, as Lenka does find love in the end (after sustaining a gunshot wound from drive-by shooting). This movie showed that although the tradition of Novy God lives on—even in these gruesome circumstances, Lenka experienced her private miracle—the experience of Russian life is fragmented, and reality can be contested by competing narratives.

Non-Soviet Localism—Monstratsiya (May 1)

Localism has come under pressure during the Putin regime, but it has not ceased to create its own understandings of Russianness. In 2004 Putin initiated far-reaching federal reforms in Russia, which severely weakened local executives in the federal regions of Russia. The pretext for this reform was the deadly terrorist attack in Beslan, which was blamed on insufficient security provisions in the regions. But the real motivation for this move was to strengthen the federal center as part of the vertical of power and to reverse processes of localism that had emerged in the 1990s. In this political context, City Day (Den' Goroda), which became a popular local tradition in the 1990s, was hollowed of its deeper political meanings as a negotiation over identification between the center and the periphery.

Interestingly, in the same year, a new local practice emerged in Novosibirsk. There, since May 1, 2004, students and young people had carried out a yearly *monstratsiya*—a wordplay produced by removing the *de-* prefix from *demonstratsiya* (demonstration), which were heavily sanctioned in Russia. Artem Louskutov, a local street artist, and his fellow students created a new unique practice, which he claimed was a protest against the "absurdity of Russia's political life."[87] It was a very colorful event, which gained much support as part political act and part artistic (often surreal) personal expression. It also carried elements of localism, and Louskutov often underlined that it was a peripheral tradition, removed from the political power struggles of Moscow. One of the slogans Louskutov promoted was "Here it's not Moscow" ("Zdes' vam ne Moskva").

Starting in 2004, every May 1 "monstrators" dressed up in colorful street fashion, often appearing in costumes. They carried slogans that were weird and absurd. They had no real political meaning—one girl dressed in black-and-white stripes held a placard that read, "Racoons are also people." Another girl with a flower in her hair and a painted face held one reading, "Give me the keys to ward no. 6 and I'll hide there from all the psychos."[88] Each participant was dressed uniquely, and each slogan was unique, showing their individuality and original artistic expression. The organizers also noted that each year's Monstratsiya proceeded under a different slogan because "the world is different every day and it changes the context around monstratsiya." For instance, in

2008 the main slogan, carried on a large banner, read, "Do not teach us how to live, or [else] we will teach you." In 2012, it was "We are like you, but better."[89]

Monstratsiya has a carnival dynamic that featured both a safety valve as well as a deeper meaning. Local and federal governments were suspicious about and even hostile to this event. In 2009 Monstratsiya celebrations were dispersed by police, and the organizer, Louskutov, was arrested.[90] However, the authorities never completely cracked down on this tradition, which as of 2010 was taking place in more cities across Russia and in former Soviet republics. It was a safety valve that allowed young Russians, raised in the late modern context with all the reflexive tools and fashions that accompanied it (from increased consumerism to daily use of internet and social media), an individualized form of celebrating.

However, Monstratsiya has a deeper meaning as a striking example of the proliferation of late modern practices in Russia's periphery. The practices of Monstratsiya (slogans, costumes) were very personalized and stood as a testament to the interest of young people in performing competing and contested practices on the defunct Soviet holiday of May 1. To some extent, Monstratsiya was a political expression of displeasure with the regime in Moscow. For instance, in 2014 the Novosibirsk Monstratsiya celebration marched under the slogan "Ad Nash" (Hell is ours) and challenged the new consensus of "Krym Nash" (Crimea is ours). In the same year, Louskutov also tried to organize a Siberian independence march, to reveal the Kremlin's hypocrisy when dealing with Crimea. Yet Monstratsiya is also a sign of a deeper change—of a new generation, which is neither Soviet nor post-Soviet but non-Soviet.[91] These young Russians have lived their entire lives in a context that was both Russian and very much late modern. Evidently, for them competing and contested calendars are natural and normal, making Monstratsiya their own non-Soviet normality.

A Russian National Calendar? Political Technologies of the National Calendar and Their Limits

In conclusion to this chapter, one should acknowledge that in the 2000s, the Russian government accomplished the construction of a unified national religious-militarized calendar that had a coherent internal logic. This was an important and complicated task, and it managed to reinstate a sense of a centrally controlled punctuation of social time. Military holidays were part of the broader processes of securitization in Russia. Orthodox holidays also made sense, as for centuries the Church had positioned itself as a pillar of a strong Russian state—another theme that was promoted across the board.

As citizenship, migration, the media, and discourse became focused on security and stability, so did the order of historical and social time. In this context, these holidays made sense and reinforced each other and the main message of Putin's regime. In Putin's Russia, historical victories linked up the different phases of Russian history and, most importantly, charted a prognosis of the future: after years of suffering, triumph awaits. Yet, as in other late modern societies, Putin's vision of the future was never fully articulated and remained a vague image of greatness that relied on the past. The American historian Timothy Snyder called this type of futureless reorganization of time the "politics of eternity."[92] This was part of a political technology that was meant to recreate a sense of stability in highly volatile late modern circumstances.

This was a particularly useful political technology as it implemented tools that fit well with the fragmentation of contemporary life. The government promoted popular grassroots practices that allowed the Russian public to identify with the nation in banal and understated ways, like wearing the Georgian ribbon on Victory Day or taking part in the Immortal Regiment procession. These practices became widespread, since they were relevant to people's projection of their contemporary social reality of commercialism, information technologies, and flexible economic relations. As part of the same political technologies, Putin's personal military and Christian image was popularized along the lines of celebrity culture.[93] On Victory Day, he assumed a personal role in the Second World War myth—the son of a veteran and a native of Leningrad, the besieged Hero City.[94] The Day of the Defender of the Fatherland represented a militarized manhood, which was associated with the president's image fishing or riding a horse, shirtless, in khaki military trousers. Around Unity Day, he was positioned as the man who ended years of transition and political weakness, from the post-Soviet Time of Troubles to the reestablished strong state. And on Pascha and Rozhdestvo, he attended religious sermons in Russia and abroad. Pop songs were written about Putin, his image in uniform appeared on T-shirts, cell phone covers, advertisements, and annual calendars.[95] This was once more a banalization of patriotic performances, which made them more popular but also more transient.

Similar trends were seen in devotion to Orthodox Christianity. While wide segments of the Russian public proclaimed devotion to Orthodox and conservative values and supported the protection of family values, including the repression of LGBTQ rights, religious worship remained scant. In the 2000s people continued to perform selective observance and preferred religious practices that required less commitment. This revealed the government's efforts as a skin-deep experience that provided a fleeting moment of stability in a social system that was overwhelmingly fast changing and unstable.

The new patriotism's transient nature reminds us of the fact that it was a result of political technology and not a fundamental shift in the way Russians identified with the national in-group. If we follow the metaphor of fluids, this technology produced a thin layer of rapidly formed ice on top of a volatile and constantly shifting fast-paced reality. Ice is an appropriate metaphor for the stabilization of the national calendar, since it was a temporary and precarious stability that allowed relief from earlier fully fledged contestations of the national calendar. But Russia was still part of the late modern temporal context, and these technologies did not alter the systematic shift in power relations within Russian society, when individual agency was free to decide which holiday practices to perform and how. Using this freedom, individuals continued to reproduce holidays that denoted inclusive and banal forms of identification and made fluid Russianness—an inclusive identification with supplemental ethnic and cultural elements—a durable and relevant analytical framework for Russian national identification.

As the last empirical chapter of this books draws to a close, I would like to point out an interesting social dynamic that Putin's desire for the stability of the national calendar in Russia revealed, a situation where, on the one hand, society gravitated toward government-endorsed practices that reinforced security and stability—as a refuge from the dislocation that followed the collapse of the Soviet system and the absence of new frames for orientation. And yet, on the other hand, without a fundamental shift in the organization of social and political life, late modernity penetrated all spheres of life and continued to be the constitutive experience of this time. Hence, despite people's attraction to the sense of stability and security offered by the government, they continued to reproduce practices that denoted late modern identifications. This social dynamic demonstrated how intrinsically tied together were the two elements that formed the dialectic of global late modern times—the liberating realities and the longing for stability and security.

These findings go beyond the idea that "two Russias" were emerging, or at least that Russia had two parallel, competing, and even contested paths of development—one that embraced the liberal and globalized developments of late modernity and one that opposed it. Stephen Hutchings and Vera Tolz in *Nation, Ethnicity and Race on Russian Television: Mediating Post-Soviet Difference* warned against the dangers of internal disintegration—of Russia literally becoming "two Russias and then multiple Russias."[96] But, as was shown here, we might also consider a situation in which late modernity intrinsically produces both flexible and fast-changing realities *and* the longing for a solid articulation of identity. They are two sides of the same coin that form the dialectic of late modernity and should both be considered within its context.

Epilogue

Fluid Russia: Lessons, Implications, and Prospects for the Future

Pelevin's post-Soviet odyssey ends with his protagonist Tatarsky discovering Russia's best guarded secret—the political system is a simulation, invented for media consumption by an advertising agency. Tatarsky is shown to the simulation's control room. There at the heart of Russia's new political system "there are no furniture.... Hanging on one wall was a picture of Yuri Gagarin.... The opposite wall was covered with ... numerous identical blue boxes." Tatarsky asks, "What is it?" His guide explains, "A 100/400 render-server," a computer that "can render up to one hundred primary politicians and four hundred secondary politicians." Stunned, Tatarsky asks whether US politicians are also produced by a computer. "Sure," he is told, "Reagan was animated all his second term." But the Russian newly acquired know-how is outstanding. "Our screenwriters are ten times as good. Just look at the rounded characters they write. Yeltsin, Zyuganov, Lebed. As good as Chekhov."[1]

It is fitting to conclude this book, which dealt with many aspects of imitation, manipulation, and simulation, with Tatarsky's final disillusionment with the new globalized Russian life. It is also an appropriate ending because Pelevin highlighted that what was wrong with post-Soviet Russia was linked by an umbilical cord to the same features in the West. In recent years this has become strikingly evident.

This book set out to rethink Russian national identity in the post-Soviet period. It inquired whether it was a late modern experience, an inclusive identification with some ethnic and cultural supplemental elements, referred to as fluid Russianness. This hypothesis was ambitious. The main body of literature and the self-understanding of many Russians still maintains that Russian national identity is crisis ridden, divided, and lost. In March 2018, Michael Khodarkovsky, an American historian of the Russian empire, wrote for the *New York Times*: "Where does the Russian empire end and the Russian nation begin? . . . These have always been the principal questions in Russia's perennial search for its national identity, and still there is no clear answer in sight."[2] In 2015, the Russian social scientist Lillia Shevtsova described for the *American National Interest* Russia's post-Soviet dominant narrative of humiliation and its self-ascribed "Weimar syndrome"—an identity that is informed by geopolitical collapse that it feels bound to redeem.[3] Whether framed as a perennial weakness, as Khodarkovsky presented it, or a novel dislocation that became an excuse for belligerent behavior, as Shevtsova described it, Russian national identity has been consistently designated as an outlier that does not fit the norm.

To rearticulate Russian national identification as a normal experience, this book relied on the theoretical framework of late modernity. This theory described the far-reaching consequence for national identities from the temporal shift between classical and late modernity. In late modernity, theorists concurred that the nation-state had conceded to global forces and was no longer the most important arbiter that ordered people's lives and generated national identity. As a result, national identities were generated on the individual level and became weaker, more fragmented, and inclusive. To test this hypothesis in Russia, this research investigated three dominant spheres of life that helped people construct and express their self-identification and sense of belonging to the collective: citizenship legislation, media discourse, and holiday practices. This triangulation aimed to explore the cross-sphere impact of late modernity on national identification in Russia and the possibility of the emergence of fluid Russianness. If that was affirmed, Russian national identification should no longer be considered abnormal or perennially difficult—at least no more than other national identifications in the late modern world.

Interestingly, besides the challenge of reformulating the focus on Russian national identification, during the course of the research for this book, the benchmarks for identification in the globalized West were shifting as well. National identities, which in the West had been pronounced dead or dying, have been vigorously reanimated.[4] The passing of national identities, or at least their transformation into more fluid concepts, was intrinsically tied to globalization. As national identity was decreasing in importance, globalization was celebrated.[5] In the globalized world, Russia's continuing grappling with national identity and Putin's national mobilization seemed misplaced and anachronistic, often linked to the Weimar Russia scenario. But by the end of 2014, things seemed to be changing. The British commentator Gideon Rachman admitted: "In recent years any writer who predicted that nationalism was the wave of the future would have been regarded as an eccentric. . . . However, it became increasingly clear that nationalism is back."[6] In the following years, the rise of far-right and far-left parties across Europe, the nationally infused UK vote to leave the European Union (one of the institutions most associated with globalization), and Donald Trump's election in the United States reinforced this feeling. As the pendulum was swinging toward nationalism, obituaries of globalization were now appearing.[7]

Putin's national rallying was now seen in a new light, as ahead of the curve, leading the charge of an ever more national world. Putin's pivot to articulate a firmer national identity in Russia, after years of being considered backward and lost, together with his political technologies and virtual politics, seemed to be increasingly relevant for understanding trends in the globalized West.[8] It posed an even more complex set of problems for this book. In this global context of firmer national identifications, can we still speak of flexible identifications, especially in Russia?

The findings of this book tell a nuanced story about national identification in Russia. The three parts present how life in Russia transformed along the lines of late modern neoliberal trends and how these trends and their shortcomings affected Russian national identification. In the 1990s, Russia opened up to the globalizing world. Borders were opened, censorship was lifted, and Marxist-Leninist ideology was cast aside. Individuals were freer to travel, to live where they wanted, to express what was on their minds, and to perform whatever practices they saw fit. As a result, migration increased, and citizenship became a less well-defined and focal institution that confirmed national identity; the media featured an open-ended polylogue with strong neoliberal themes, such as the discourse of flexibility; historical memory became problematic, and holidays were practiced in an assortment of ways. In these conditions, a much freer and more flexible identification of Russianness developed.

Notwithstanding the above developments, elements of Russian identification were shaped due to uniquely Russian conditions. In the newly formed post-Soviet migration space, ethnic Russians and Russian speakers, who had been left beyond the borders of Russia due to the collapse of the Soviet Union, were critical to the development of Russian citizenship legislation. In media discourse, elements of Russian culture, language, and Orthodox Christian religion were reminders that identification was not only flexible and inclusive, but also Russian. Similarly, the Russian public became interested in the practices of the Christian Orthodox calendar as a supplemental ethnic and cultural feature of identification. Together, the global trends of late modernity and the unique Russian elements of culture, language, and religion formed fluid Russianness.

But alongside shaping national identification, late modernity's disruptions and shortcomings were revealed. In the 1990s, globalization and neoliberalism brought to Russia freedom that was never seen before. However, at the same time, these trends required endless flexibility and adaptability. The requirement for flexibility fragmented social institutions that in the late-Soviet era had formed citizens' routines and created a sense of stability, security, and belonging. The Soviet citizenship and residency registration (propiska) systems were falling apart. Russia was overwhelmed with what seemed like uncontrollable migration and, therefore, vague demarcations of its citizenry. The media discourse featured a deep sense of loss and disorientation. The discourse concerning the search for a national idea, which developed from 1996, was open-ended and felt dispersed. It lacked the government endorsement that prevailed in Soviet times, in the form of the regime's authorial voice. Instead of the Soviet modernist calendar, which clearly projected a "radiant communist future," the national calendar became contested. The different holidays in the calendar contradicted each other, and there was no clear and unified projection of where Russia was heading. This fragmentation of institutions accentuated the sense of loss.

This heightened sense of loss and the fragmentation of institutions in the 1990s were often associated with the collapse of the Soviet Union, but they were not necessarily entirely tied to the collapse. The problem that the Russian public faced was that the post-Soviet social institutions that emerged instead of the Soviet ones were far less stable. They were in line with late modernity's focus on change, progress, and choice. This, as Giddens observed in his theory, disrupted routines of continuity of identity and created ontological insecurity.[9] Hence, while power shifted toward individuals and liberated them, it also left them to cope alone with the external forces of a fast-changing world. Russia's early unpleasant encounter with globalization shed light on a common blind spot regarding national identification in the global late modern world—that is, the assumption that freedom on a global scale is always a welcome experience. Despite the freer experience of the 1990s, the Russian public was disillusioned with the consequences of the state's withdrawal from people's lives.

Putin's rise to power and popularity should be understood within this social, political, and temporal context and the heightened sense of loss it produced. When Putin came to power in late 1999, it seemed that the ills of the neoliberal globalized system were more noticeable in Russia than the positive impact it generated. Putin's government took far-reaching steps to counter the dislocation and instability in citizenship, discourse, and holiday practices. It introduced a new citizenship law that was meant to create a normal migration and citizenship policy. Putin subjected the media to his authority, reintroduced the Soviet-era authorial voice, and constructed a discourse of stability. Although this discourse incorporated many of the 1990s national identification themes, it no longer had an open-ended nature. Putin also introduced numerous changes to the national calendar. He endorsed military and Orthodox Christian holidays that denoted a more exclusively defined Russian national identification. His government used various techniques that reinforced a sense of security in different spheres of life in Russia. This revisionism did not intend to counter the collapse of the Soviet Union; instead it addressed the social and psychological consequences of global neoliberal transformations. Putin had some success in that process. His popularity rose, but the limitations of his efforts were also revealed.

This book showed that fluid Russianness prevailed despite the push for firmer national identification in the 2000s and 2010s for several reasons. First, fluid Russianness endured between the 1990s and the 2000s–2010s because there was much continuity between the two periods, as the new government incorporated 1990s policy trends and themes. In citizenship legislation and implementation, the legal gray zone that undermined the institution of citizenship in the 1990s was not really countered and persisted into the 2000s–2010s. In discourse, themes that were raised as unifying in the mid-1990s discourse, such as the economy, were incorporated in the 2000s–2010s into the government's discourse of stability. Moreover, the commercial imperatives of television did not change, and it had to remain engaging and interesting for viewers. In the national calendar, the government promoted holidays that were already gaining popularity in the 1990s, like Victory Day and Orthodox Pascha and Christmas. This underlined that Putin's Russia did not emerge in December 1999 when he became acting president. It was a product of the dialectic struggle within Russia, which was a consequence of globalization, the dislocation that it ensued, and its consequent rejection. Putin had a central role in this process, but not as its perpetrator, rather as a talented and capable facilitator for the deficit of ontological security. By doing so, he played on the integral late modern dialectic of security and freedom. If Yeltsin brought freedom, Putin's inevitable role was to reinstate security.

Second, fluid Russianness remained appropriate because Putin did not remove Russia from the late modern context. In the field of citizenship, while gaining a Russian passport became more difficult, the new and freer migration space continued to exist. Strict regulations clashed with the new trends of freedom of movement and flexible international labor markets. Instead of stopping migration, new regulations pushed underground the countless people who had arrived in Russia or into the legal gray zone—a precarious legal status where their rights were impinged. Moreover, when the government tried to control migration by attracting desirable groups of migrants—for example, compatriots—to strategic regions, the policy failed miserably. This showed the limits of controlling migration in a globalized world and a free-market economy. In media discourse, attempts to silence the popular polylogue on national identification and gain control over the discourse achieved partial results. The government did not have full control over the media, and a counterdiscourse developed, which focused on the fact that Russian life and identification was not stabilizing. As for the national calendar, despite the endorsements of militarized and Orthodox Christian holidays, the public continued to have different and competing meanings for holidays that diverged from the government agenda. Putin did not remove Russia from the late modern context and did not stop the flow of people, capital, and information. Hence, the social outcomes of late modernity could not be undone and were not reversed.

Last, the fluid Russianness framework was still useful for understanding identification in Putin's regime, since this regime often used reflexive tools of late modernity. This was especially evident in the media and in the construction of the national calendar. On the one hand, the use of reflexive tools made his actions more popular. But on the other hand, they also inhibited the stabilization of life in Russia and contributed to further fragmentation of social institutions and an ever-deepening sense that life was unpredictable and unstable. In the media, especially in televised debates, hegemony over discourse was achieved through blurring terms. In this process, the government's discourse of stability was promoted, but it undermined people's sense of security and trust in what was being said. It may have served the government's short-term goals of suppressing political opposition and keeping television popular, but it did not promote the overall goal of furthering stability. In the realm of practices of the national calendar, this was evident in the government's promotion of late modern mundane and individualized performances, like the Georgian ribbon and the Immortal Regiment. These practices became hugely popular and ostensibly supported the government's militarized calendar. But their focus had shifted to individual agency and reinforced the late modern trend. The social essence that these practices denoted was not firmer national identification and unity but what Bauman described as the "individualized and privatized" versions of identity that were brought about by globalization.[10] This analysis revealed that Putin's stability was a superficial experience that did not fundamentally alter identification in Russia.

These outcomes revealed fluid Russianness as a far more durable and enduring experience of Russian national identification. This was not merely an identification that developed in the freer situation in the 1990s, but it continued in the 2000s when the regime ostensibly tried to put an end to these trends. Even in the aftermath of the annexation of Crimea, when describing Russian national identification as flexible became ever more challenging, this book has shown that fluid Russianness remained relevant. In fact, the annexation of Crimea itself was a new type of war—bloodless and constructed for media consumption—in line with the global trend. Hence, its popularity should also be considered as part of these trends rather than a revanchist national awakening.

These findings allow us to break away from the paradigm in which Russian identification is either weak and flawed or strong and belligerent. This paradigm provided little intellectual benefit and deepened fear of Russia. While alarmism over Russia's policies is not without grounds, this book places Russia's policies within the broader temporal context. This allows a clearer picture of what has been taking place in Russia. While the regime diverged from liberal democracy, engaged in the suppression of freedoms, and pursued an aggressive foreign policy, other global realities continued. Migratory flows became an integral part of life in Russia, and citizenship lost its prime place as a signifier of identification. Russians moved according to where their best prospects were. Very often they lived in cities with migrant communities and were more likely to know people who lived in different countries and experienced traveling beyond Russia's borders. This changed their perception of self-identification and how they related to the national in-group. They experienced a much freer media space. Despite the government's control of the media, alternative options, such as *Novaya Gazeta* and the Dozd television channel, meant that the social polylogue still existed. In the growing Russian blogosphere, which was touched on in chapters 5 and 6, alternative views flourished and turned into popular actions, like Novosibirsk's annual Monstratsiya.

These conclusions contest the supposition that the rejection of freedom and globalization necessarily leads to a full roll-back of its trends. In the 2000s–10s, Russia did not return with the pendulum movement from openness and globalized liberalism to the other end—complete closeness and belligerent nationalism. Instead, a third option unfolded—one where fluid Russianness, a more fragmented and flexible version of globalized late modern identification, continued to exist in more restricted circumstances. To reinforce a sense of stability, which would imitate solid institutions and a strong state with a unified national identity, the regime used political and media technologies. This was an imitation that provided the Russian public with a welcome sense of stability, without removing Russia from the globalized context. This imitation, which has been widely discussed by analysts and scholars of Russia, was not mere manipulation of a politically uneducated and passive Russian public.[11] It was a more complex system within which the Russian government simultaneously fought and embraced global trends. It used televised talk shows and the internet, which are reflexive tools that encourage action in the social world. At the same time, it engaged in breaking people's trust (referred to here as *verolomsvo*)—that is, aiming to erode people's belief in their ability to bring positive change through political action. These are contradictory trends, but in Russia they coexist.

This apparent mixing of globalized-open and restrictive-nationalist trends opens the way to reconsider the assumption that Putin's reassertion of a firmer identity divided the Russian public into two well-defined camps.[12] Namely, it might suggest that society is not divided into those who are a liberally minded, pro-West, and proglobalization opposition and those who are progovernment, nationalist revanchists who oppose Western globalization. This is not to say that there are not oppositionists and government supporters but rather that individuals could mix practices that feature openness and a globalized lifestyle together with performances that reflected alignment with a progovernment reinstatement of stability. They could perform a variety of actions that supported Putin's project for reassertion of stronger national identification. For instance, they could watch *Poyedinok*, wear the Georgian ribbon, and say that they adhere to the Orthodox Christian faith. But by doing so, they are consuming media from a reflexive tool, expressing identification in a mundane and individualized manner, and engaging in selective observance, like their counterparts in the West. This means that they would be stating that they supported Putin's project, yet at the same time, their actions reflected a social essence that was reflexive and open to globalized trends, individualized and mundane. As the organizer of one of the Kremlin's youth projects concluded, "In Russia there are hundreds of thousands of young, modern, patriotic people ... [who] have Putin on their t-shirt and an iPhone in their pocket."[13] This should draw our attention to a situation where the liberal and the illiberal, the globalized and the isolationist, can coexist side by side. Evidently, such hybridity is common in Russia.

These intricacies of Russian politics and society can help to make better policy decisions vis-à-vis Russia. Russia's divergence from liberal democracy and more recently its aggressive foreign policies were perceived in the West as the whims of a lawbreaking regime that needs to be punished, while helping the suppressed Russian masses to push back and fight against it. Such views miss the realities of life in Russia and are doomed to fail. Punishing the Russian elites by cutting them off from the indulgences of the global world has proven very difficult and has not led to a change of heart in the Kremlin. When Surkov was asked how he would be affected by Western sanctions, he said, "The only things that interest me in the U.S. are Tupac Shakur, Allen Ginsberg, and Jackson Pollock. I don't need a visa to access their work. I lose nothing."[14] Surkov may not have assets in the West like others in the Kremlin's inner circle, but he captured the point that isolating people from the global world is not an easy task. His response also revealed how Western policies failed to capture the hybrid character of contemporary Russian identifications—one can be a fan of Western popular culture and a top Kremlin ideologue. There are no obvious demarcations between those who are on the side of the illiberal Kremlin and those who are proliberal West.

This book calls for Western decision makers to see the profound impact of global politics on Russia. Russian society is on an almost irreversible path of convergence with the global world, but the gaps and shortcomings of globalization, as well as Russia's unique historical circumstances, slowed this process and sidetracked some of its elements. In such circumstances, a better approach would be to engage Russia in a dialogue that acknowledges the grievances that Putin's regime raises against neoliberal globalization—that the constant call for flexibility is a source of anxiety. Such an approach would intensify the vanishing attraction of Putin's regime, as a self-professed guarantor of stability and security. It can also start a broader discussion on how to fix the global system to benefit more people.

This research should account for its own limitations. The two most important ones are context and time. First, there is a scenario where, in case of a change in the global context, Putin's project to solidify Russian national identification might go beyond its shallow nature and result in a deeper transformation in Russia, which will render fluid Russianness irrelevant. Such a scenario could become more likely due to external changes in the global context, such as an international conflict, deadly pandemic, or a large-scale natural disaster. In this case, the international borders will be closed, and at least temporarily, the flow of capital and people across them would halt. This type of isolation will, over time, inevitably have an impact on forms of identification with the national in-group. Second, time is another factor that might affect the relevance of fluid Russianness. This is a less radical scenario, but if we accept that the stabilization of national identification takes time as a process of internal negotiation within society, a new, firmer consensus can emerge in Russia over time. In this scenario, which was recently endorsed by the Russian ethnographer Valery Tishkov, as time passed Russia would become more ready to embrace a collectively agreed unified identification.[15] There is no way for this research to provide answers that can predict the likelihood of these scenarios. Hence, as national identification continues to evolve, the scope of this book cannot, nor does it intend to, determine the future course of this evolution.

As a growing number of examples from across the global world suggest, lessons from Russia can be instructive to the broader study of national identification in late modernity and for a global approach to a worldwide neoauthoritarian wave. This is especially timely as global economic performance is slowing down and social dislocation is biting deeper into the developed world. The British journalist and author Paul Mason noted (in this case about Moldova), "It's in these edge places of the world that we can watch the economic tide receding—and trace causal links between stagnation, social crisis, armed conflict and erosion of democracy."[16] This book has shown that the shortcomings of globalization were not merely linked to the changing economic tide of globalization but to deeper faults of late modernity that have been eroding core issues. They undermined institutions and routines that provided individuals with ontological security. Russia was particularly vulnerable and may have been patient zero in such an experiment. It was poorer, the dislocation that globalization ensued was in deep contrast to the Soviet system, and the change occurred particularly fast. As a result, the Russian experience was a quick and painful baptism by fire with the ins and outs of the late modern globalized system. Examples from around the world show that Russia's response was not abnormal and that it was not alone.

In recent decades, a number of neoauthoritarian regimes have challenged the postwar global order in a similar manner as Putin's regime in Russia—from the Philippines to Turkey, from Hungary to Venezuela. There are many similarities between these regimes. Their leaders are often sympathetic to each other and learn from each other's experience. On the international arena, many of them see Putin as an inspiration and a true global leader. At home they try to limit the consequences of globalization by restricting the spectrum of acceptable identifications and by strengthening a centrally approved national identity. By the mid-2010s, such ideas were more common in Western democratic politics. Most famously such themes were reflected in President Donald Trump's rhetoric and politics, which won him sympathy in the Kremlin. Putin congratulated Trump's victory by underlining the ideational affinity with his campaign: "A significant part of the American people has the same ideas [as us] . . . people who sympathize with us about traditional values. . . . The newly elected president subtly felt the mood of the society . . . although no one believed, except us, that he will win." These affinities and mutual sympathies between these regimes have resulted in them being considered together as part of a global trend of receding globalization and the growing worldwide wave of nationalism and populism.

The findings of this book call for researchers not to consider antiglobalist and illiberal rhetoric within the simplistic binaries and pendulum movements of rising globalization and receding national identity. Instead, the current struggle between liberal and illiberal points of view should be studied as two sides of the same coin, since the globalized system often simultaneously produces both freedom and longing for security. The dialectic between the two shapes identification with the national in-group, which is often manifested in mixed or hybrid ways. This book presents a perspective that overcomes the pendulum movement between globalization and nationalism. The two are bound together and nourish each other rather than standing as two poles.

Russia and its leader were cited as vicious perpetrators of illiberal trends around the world. They were accused of manipulating the global system into submission to national zeal. Yet this book has presented an explanatory model in which the global system has intrinsically produced events such as those in Putin's Russia and has allowed them to develop within the global context. They are not an outside attack on globalization but a dynamic that is internal to the system. This dynamic, which has been observable in Russia over the course of three decades, has increased openness and produced calls for security and stabilization. This is not a mere retreat from globalization but rather a change into new forms that combine elements of openness and calls for more closeness. As the global world moves forward, these findings can be instructive beyond the realm of Russian studies.

NOTES

Introduction

1. Victor Pelevin, *Babylon*, trans. Andrew Bromfield (London: Faber, 2000), 4.

2. *Generation P* is an alternative title of Pelevin's *Babylon*; Anthony Ramirez, "International Report; Pepsi Will Be Bartered for Ships and Vodka in Deal with Soviets," *New York Times*, April 9, 1990.

3. George W. Breslauer, *Gorbachev and Yeltsin as Leaders* (Cambridge: Cambridge University Press, 2002), 149.

4. Kremlin (website), "State of the Nation Address," last modified April 25, 2005, http://en.kremlin.ru/events/president/transcripts/22931.

5. Maria Nikiforova, "Prezident Proshelsya Po Ryurikovskim Mestam," *Nezavisimaya Gazeta*, July 18, 2003.

6. Thomas De Waal, "The Short Road to Nostalgia," *Moscow Times*, August 1, 1994.

7. Kremlin (website), "Direct Line with Vladimir Putin," last modified April 17, 2014, http://eng.kremlin.ru/news/7034.

8. Vera Tolz, *Russia* (London: Arnold, 2001); Marlene Laruelle, *Russian Nationalism and the National Reassertion of Russia* (London: Routledge, 2009); Eduard Ponarin, *Security Implications of the Russian Identity Crisis* (PONARS Eurasia, policy memo 64, Washington, DC, June 1999); Anne Applebaum, "Russia's Ongoing Identity Crisis," *Telegraph*, September 22, 2002; Serguei Oushakine, *The Patriotism of Despair: Nation, War, and Loss in Russia* (Ithaca, NY: Cornell University Press, 2009).

9. Applebaum, "Russia's Ongoing Identity Crisis."

10. Tolz, *Russia*; Valery Fyodorov, "Russian Identity and the Challenges of the Time," Valdai Discussion Club, August 19, 2013, http://valdaiclub.com/culture/61340.html. See also Vera Tolz, "Conflicting 'Homeland Myths' and Nation-State Building in Postcommunist Russia," *Slavic Review* 58, no. 2 (1998): 268.

11. Karen Barkey and Mark Von Hagen, eds., *After Empire: Multiethnic Societies and Nation-Building: The Soviet Union and the Russian, Ottoman, and Habsburg Empires* (Boulder, CO: Westview, 1997).

12. Laruelle, *Russian Nationalism*, 2; Yitzhak M. Brudny, *Reinventing Russia: Russian Nationalism and the Soviet State, 1953–1991* (Cambridge, MA: Harvard University Press, 1998), 259.

13. Laruelle, *Russian Nationalism*.

14. Rogers Brubaker, *Nationalism Reframed: Nationhood and the National Question in the New Europe* (Cambridge: Cambridge University Press, 1996), 135; Steffen Kailitz

and Andreas Umland, "Why the Fascists Won't Take Over the Kremlin (for Now): A Comparison of Democracy's Breakdown and Fascism's Rise in Weimar Germany and Post-Soviet Russia," Higher School of Economics (Moscow), Working Paper No. 14, 2010, http://dx.doi.org/10.2139/ssrn.1659929; Anatol Lieven, "The Weakness of Russian Nationalism," *Survival* 41, no. 2 (1999): 53; Niall Ferguson, "Look Back at Weimar—and Start to Worry about Russia," *Telegraph*, January 1, 2005.

15. Roger Cohen, "Russia's Weimar Syndrome," *New York Times*, May 1, 2014; Alexander J. Moytl, "Will Putin's Invasion Backfire?," comment on *Ukraine's Orange Blues* (blog), World Affairs, March 3, 2014, http://www.worldaffairsjournal.org/blog/alexander-j-motyl/will-putins-invasion-backfire.

16. Pal Kolsto and Helge Blakkisrud, eds., *The New Russian Nationalism: Imperialism, Ethnicity and Authoritarianism 2000–2015* (Edinburgh: Edinburgh University Press, 2016).

17. Gulnaz Sharafutdinova, *The Red Mirror: Putin's Leadership and Russia's Insecure Identity* (Oxford: Oxford University Press, 2020).

18. Oushakine, *Patriotism of Despair*.

19. Kirill Kobrin, *Postsovetskiy Mavzoley Proshlogo* (Moscow: Novoye literaturnoye obozreniye, 2017).

20. Zygmunt Bauman and Benedetto Vecchi, *Identity: Conversations with Benedetto Vecchi* (Cambridge: Polity Press, 2004), 12.

21. Ronald Grigor Suny points to the complexities of applying the term *empire* to the Soviet Union. This issue is not addressed in this research, but its conceptual implications are taken into account; see Ronald Grigor Suny, "The Empire Strikes Out: Imperial Russia, National Identity, and Theories of Empire," in *A State of Nations: Empire and Nation-Making in the Age of Lenin and Stalin*, ed. Ronald Grigor Suny and Terry Martin (Oxford: Oxford University Press, 2001), 23–66.

22. Hugh Seton-Weston, "Russian Nationalism in Historical Perspective," in *The Last Empire: Nationality and the Soviet Future*, ed. Robert Conquest (Stanford, CA: Hoover Institution Press, 1986), 17.

23. Seton-Weston, "Russian Nationalism," 17; Liah Greenfeld, "The Formation of the Russian National Identity: The Role of Status Insecurity and Ressentiment," *Comparative Studies in Society and History* 32, no. 3 (1990): 549–51; Marc Raeff, *Origins of the Russian Intelligentsia: The Eighteenth-Century Nobility* (New York: Harcourt, Brace & World, 1966), 170–71.

24. Yuri Slezkine, "The USSR as a Communal Apartment," *Slavic Review* 53, no. 2 (1994): 420.

25. Brubaker, *Nationalism Reframed*, 110; Valeri Tishkov, "The Russian People and National Identity," *Russia in Global Affairs*, no. 3 (2008), https://eng.globalaffairs.ru/articles/the-russian-people-and-national-identity/; Slezkine, "Communal Apartment," 421.

26. Tolz, *Russia*, 1; Alexei Yurchak, *Everything Was Forever, until It Was No More: The Last Soviet Generation* (Princeton, NJ: Princeton University Press, 2006), 161.

27. Laruelle, *Russian Nationalism*, 39.

28. Andrzej Walicki and Hilda Andrews-Rusiecka, *A History of Russian Thought from the Enlightenment to Marxism* (Oxford: Clarendon, 1980), 92.

29. Walicki and Andrews-Rusiecka, *History of Russian Thought*, 95–97, 104–5.

30. Marlene Laruelle, *Russian Eurasianism: An Ideology of Empire* (Baltimore: Johns Hopkins University Press, 2012), 1.

31. Geoffrey Hosking, "Slavophiles and Westernizers in Russia," Valdai Discussion Club, March 21, 2012, http://valdaiclub.com/a/highlights/slavophiles_and_westernizers_in_russia/; Laruelle, *Russian Eurasianism*, 2.

32. Breslauer, *Gorbachev and Yeltsin*, 150.

33. Valeri Tishkov, Zhanna Zayinchkovskaya, and Galina Vitkovskaya, *Migration in the Countries of the Former Soviet Union* (Global Commission on International Migration, Geneva, September 2005).

34. Slezkine, "Communal Apartment," 422.

35. Slezkine, 422.

36. Brubaker, *Nationalism Reframed*, 50; Brudny, *Reinventing Russia*, 7.

37. Anders Aslund, *Russia's Capitalist Revolution: Why Market Reform Succeeded and Democracy Failed* (Washington, DC: Peterson Institute for International Economics, 2007), 89.

38. Brubaker, *Nationalism Reframed*, 139; Tolz, "Conflicting 'Homeland Myths,'" 269.

39. Laruelle, *Russian Nationalism*, 4; Richard Sakwa, "Regime Change from Yeltsin and Putin: Normality, Normalcy or Normalisation?," in *Russian Politics under Putin*, ed. Cameron Ross (Manchester: Manchester University Press, 2004), 18.

40. Brudny, *Reinventing Russia*, 27.

41. In tsarist Russia, October 22 (November 4 according to the Gregorian calendar) was the Day of Our Lady of Kazan, and according to Russian tradition, on that day in 1612 Russian forces defeated the Polish-Lithuanian occupiers of Moscow, ending the Time of Troubles.

42. RFE/RL, "Legko li byt' natsionalistom?," January 25, 2016, YouTube video, 54:56, https://www.youtube.com/watch?v=NEiMDO2Cwec.

43. Kremlin (website), "Meeting of the Valdai International Discussion Club," last modified October 18, 2018, http://en.kremlin.ru/events/president/news/58848.

44. Azar Gat and Alexander Yakobson, *Nations: The Long History and Deep Roots of Political Ethnicity and Nationalism* (Cambridge: Cambridge University Press, 2012).

45. Benedict Anderson, *Imagined Communities: Reflections on the Origin and Spread of Nationalism* (London: Verso, 2006); Ernest Gellner, *Nations and Nationalism* (Malden, MA: Blackwell, 2006).

46. Eric J. Hobsbawm and Terence O. Ranger, *The Invention of Tradition* (Cambridge: Cambridge University Press, 2012), 263; Gellner, *Nations and Nationalism*.

47. Anthony D. Smith, *Myths and Memories of the Nation* (Oxford: Oxford University Press, 1999), 9.

48. Anderson, *Imagined Communities*, 7.

49. Gellner, *Nations and Nationalism*, 62.

50. Anthony Giddens, *Modernity and Self-Identity: Self and Society in the Late Modern Age* (Cambridge: Polity, 1991), 12; Zygmunt Bauman, *Liquid Times: Living in an Age of Uncertainty* (Cambridge: Polity, 2007), 1.

51. Giddens, *Modernity and Self-Identity*, 2.

52. Giddens, *Modernity and Self-Identity*, 2.

53. William Davies and Aditya Chakrabortty, *The Limits of Neoliberalism: Authority, Sovereignty and the Logic of Competition* (Los Angeles: Sage, 2017), 5.

54. Giddens, *Modernity and Self-Identity*, 28.

55. Bauman, *Liquid Times*, 1.

56. Giddens, *Modernity and Self-Identity*, 28; Bauman and Vecchi, *Identity*, 18; Bauman Zygmunt, "Identity in the Globalizing World," *Social Anthropology* 9, no. 2 (2001): 125, http://dx.doi.org/doi:10.1111/j.1469-8676.2001.tb00141.x.

57. Giddens, *Modernity and Self-Identity*, 2.

58. Bauman and Vecchi, *Identity*, 29.

59. Bauman and Vecchi, 22.

60. Michael Billig, *Banal Nationalism* (London: Sage, 1995), 8.

61. On the challenges to security in the late modern age, see Ulrich Beck, *Risk Society: Towards a New Modernity* (London: Sage, 1992); Zygmunt Bauman, "Wars of the Globalization Era," *European Journal of Social Theory* 4, no. 1 (2001): 11, http://dx.doi.org/10.1177/13684310122224966.

62. Anthony Giddens, *A Contemporary Critique of Historical Materialism* (London: Macmillan, 1981), 193.

63. Bauman and Vecchi, *Identity*, 29.

64. *Oxford English Dictionary Online*, s.v. "Identification," accessed April 5, 2018, http://www.oed.com/view/Entry/90995?redirectedFrom=identification#eid.

65. The term *nation* in English has two corresponding words Russian. The first is *narod*, which refers to the lower estates of tsarist Russia, that is, the Russian people. The second is *natsiya*, which refers to civic and liberal conceptions of nationhood. See Alexei Miller, "Istoriya ponyatiya 'natsiya' v Rossii," Otechestvennyye zapiski 46, no.1 (2012): 162–186. https://strana-oz.ru/2012/1/istoriya-ponyatiya-naciya-v-rossi.

1. The Unmaking of the Soviet Project

1. Svetlana Alexievich, *Secondhand Time: The Last of the Soviets* (London: Fitzcarraldo Editions, 2016), 23.

2. For a discussion on whether the Soviet Union constituted an empire, see Oxana Shevel, "The Politics of Citizenship Policy in Post-Soviet Russia," *Post-Soviet Affairs* 28, no. 1 (2012): 115, http://dx.doi.org/10.2747/1060-586X.28.1.111; Dominic Lieven, "The Russian Empire and the Soviet Union as Imperial Polities," *Journal of Contemporary History* 30, no. 4 (1995): 607–36, http://www.jstor.org/stable/261085; Yuri Slezkine, "Commentary: Imperialism as the Highest Stage of Socialism," *Russian Review* 59, no. 2 (2000): 227–34, http://www.jstor.org/stable/2679754.

3. Shevel, "Politics of Citizenship," 111.

4. George Ginsburgs, *From Soviet to Russian International Law: Studies in Continuity and Change* (The Hague: Martinus Nijhoff, 1998), 156–76.

5. George Ginsburgs, "From the 1990 Law on the Citizenship of the USSR to the Citizenship Laws of the Successor Republics (Part I)," *Review of Central and East European Law* 18, no. 1 (1992): 5.

6. The Soviet takeover of the republics in 1940 was presented by the Soviet government as an outcome of the Baltic governments' decision to join the union. In fact, it was a predesigned plot, which was outlined in the secret protocols of the Ribbentrop-Molotov Pact. Soviet rule ended in 1941 when the Germans occupied the Baltic states. However, in 1945, when the Soviets expelled the Germans, they claimed that it was legally sound to reinstate the pre-1941 situation. The Soviet claim for the Baltic states was never fully internationally recognized, most notably by the United States.

7. Jonathan Steele, *Eternal Russia: Yeltsin, Gorbachev and the Mirage of Democracy* (London: Faber, 1994), 155.
8. Steele, *Eternal Russia*, 155.
9. Rogers Brubaker, "Citizenship Struggles in the Soviet Successor States," *International Migration Review* 26, no. 2 (1992): 270.
10. In Estonian, the restoration of independence was "Eesti taasiseseisvumist," and in Lithuanian, "Lietuvos nepriklausomos valstybės atstatymo."
11. Ginsburgs, "Part I," 20.
12. Ginsburgs, 22.
13. Archie Brown, *The Gorbachev Factor* (Oxford: Oxford University Press, 1996), 303; Steele, *Eternal Russia*, 189.
14. Steele, *Eternal Russia*, 189–90.
15. Ginsburgs, "Part I," 28.
16. Steele, *Eternal Russia*, 230.
17. Federal Law of the RSFSR No. 1948-1. "O grazhdanstve RSFSR," Congress of People's Deputies of the RSFSR, November 28, 1991, item 13.
18. Federal Law of the RSFSR No. 1948-1, item 13-1. Legal scholars defined the term *zero option* as the default option, under which all residents on the territory of a newly formed state are granted citizenship. Historians have noted that the zero option has not been as widely used over history as the name may suggest.
19. Federal Law of the RSFSR No. 1948-1, item 13-2; Galina K. Dmitrieva and Igor I. Lukashuk, "The Russian Federation Law on Citizenship," *Review of Central and East European Law* 19, no. 3 (1993): 270.
20. Federal Law of the RSFSR No. 1948-1, items 14–17.
21. Dmitrieva and Lukashuk, "Russian Federation Law," 280.
22. Patrick Weil, "Access to Citizenship: A Comparison of Twenty-Five Nationality Laws," in *Citizenship Today: Global Perspectives and Practices*, ed. Thomas Alexander Aleinikoff and Douglas B. Klusmeyer (Washington, DC: Carnegie Endowment for International Peace, 2001), 17–36.
23. Valery A. Tishkov, "What Is Russia? Perspectives for Nation-Building," comment on Valery Tishkov's blog, accessed October 5, 2017, http://valerytishkov.ru/cntnt/publikacii3/knigi/the_mind_a1/what_is_ru.html.
24. George Ginsburgs, "From the 1990 Law on the Citizenship of the USSR to the Citizenship Laws of the Successor Republics (Part II)," *Review of Central and East European Law* 19, no. 3 (1993): 233.
25. Federal Law of the RSFSR No. 1948-1, item 18.
26. Dmitrieva and Lukashuk, "Russian Federation Law," 282.
27. Federal Law of the RSFSR No. 1948-1, items 18-3 and 18-4.
28. This item overlapped and contradicted item 13-2, which stated that such people would be directed to the recognition path. In 1996 this unclarity within the law was politicized. It is discussed later in this chapter.
29. Federal Law of the RSFSR No. 1948-1, items 19 and 19-3-1.
30. Federal Law of the RSFSR No. 1948-1, items 19 and 19-3-1.
31. Service of State Statistics, "Obshchiye Itogi Migratsii Naseleniya Rossiyskoy Federatsii," accessed May 19, 2014, http://www.gks.ru/wps/wcm/connect/rosstat_main/rosstat/ru/statistics/population/demography/#.

32. Federal Law of the RSFSR No. 1948-1, items 18-3 and 18-4.
33. Elena Samoilova, "Vkladysh Do Vostrebovaniya," *Kommersant*, February 10, 2003.
34. Ginsburgs, *From Soviet to Russian*, 172.
35. Ginsburgs, 172.
36. The perceived interests of Russians and Russian speakers in the republics lay with keeping the Soviet Union together, as was seen in the Russians' protests in the Baltic republics. Attitudes may, however, have been different across communities. For instance, in the 1991 referendum on Ukraine's independence, "yes" won a majority in the most Russian populated areas of Donetsk and Crimea (albeit with much lower margins than in other parts of Ukraine). Hence, it is more likely that the Russian and Russian-speaking communities in the republics were more heterogenous in relation to the possible independence of the republics. See Chrystyna Lalpychak, "Over 90% Vote Yes in Referendum; Kravchuk Elected President of Ukraine," *Ukranian Weekly*, December 8, 1991.
37. Ginsburgs, *From Soviet to Russian*, 174–75.
38. Ginsburgs, 174–75.
39. Federal Law of the RSFSR No. 1948-1, item 19-2.
40. Permanent registration could be acquired only at a proven permanent residency address (ownership or long-term rental contract), while temporary registration could be acquired at any address.
41. Ginsburgs, *From Soviet to Russian*, 163.
42. Ginsburgs, 165–66.
43. Moya Flynn, *Migrant Resettlement in the Russian Federation* (London: Anthem, 2004), 91.
44. Federal Law of the Russian Federation No. 5242-1, "On the Right of Citizens of the Russian Federation to the Freedom of Movement, the Choice of a Place of Stay and Residence within the Russian Federation," the Supreme Soviet, 1993, item 3.
45. Federal Law of the Russian Federation No. 5242-1, item 3.
46. For more on Moscow's weakness vis-à-vis the federal regions in the early 1990s, see Cameron Ross, *Federalism and Democratisation in Russia* (Manchester: Manchester University Press, 2002). For the continued practice of propiska, see Ginsburgs, *From Soviet to Russian*, 165–66.
47. Tishkov, Zayinchkovskaya, and Vitkovskaya, *Migration*.
48. In 1941, Soviet heavy industry and its work force was moved east, and some people stayed after the war. In 1954, the Virgin Lands Campaign, a program of land development, was initiated by Khrushchev. As a result, in Kazakhstan, for instance, between 1926 and 1959 the Slavic population increased from 20.6 percent to 42.7 percent of the total population. See Sebastien Peyrouse, *The Russian Minority in Central Asia: Migration, Politics and Language* (Kennan Institute, occasional paper 297, Washington, DC, 2008).
49. Peyrouse, *Russian Minority*; Brubaker, "Citizenship Struggles," 275; Flynn, *Migrant Resettlement*, 14.
50. Tishkov, Zayinchkovskaya, and Vitkovskaya, *Migration*.
51. Alexander Osipov, "Chto v Rossii oznachaet ponyatiy 'regulirovanie migratsi'?," in *Migratzia I Natsionalnoe Gosudarstvso*, ed. Tatyana Baraulina and Oksana Karpenko (St. Petersburg: Center for Independent Social Research, 2004), 42.

52. Osipov, "Chto oznachaet ponyatiy," 42.
53. Tishkov, Zayinchkovskaya, and Vitkovskaya, *Migration*.
54. Osipov, "Chto oznachaet ponyatiy," 43.
55. Brubaker, "Citizenship Struggles," 280.
56. Enterprise Estonia, "Citizenship," Estonia.eu website, last modified 2014, accessed April 11, 2014, http://estonia.eu/about-estonia/society/citizenship.html.
57. Kristine Krume, "Checks and Balances in Latvian Nationality Policies: National Agendas and International Frameworks," in *Citizenship Policies in the New Europe*, ed. Rainer Baubock, Bernhard Perchinig, and Wiebke Sievers (Amsterdam: Amsterdam University Press, 2007), 71.
58. Marika Kirch and Aksel Kirch, "Ethnic Relations: Estonians and Non-Estonians," *Nationalities Papers* 23, no. 1 (1995): 43–45, http://dx.doi.org/10.1080/00905999508408348.
59. Kirch and Kirch, "Ethnic Relations."
60. Karen Dawisha and Bruce Parrott, *Russia and the New States of Eurasia: The Politics of Upheaval* (Cambridge: Cambridge University Press, 1994), 74.
61. Sebastien Peyrouse, "Nationhood and the Minority Question in Central Asia: The Russians in Kazakhstan," *Europe-Asia Studies* 59, no. 3 (2007), 481, http://dx.doi.org/10.1080/09668130701239930.
62. Peyrouse, "Nationhood," 490.
63. Peyrouse, *Russian Minority*.
64. Peyrouse.
65. Steele, *Eternal Russia*, 156.
66. Steele, 156.
67. General Lebed was the secretary of the National Security Council (1996–1998) and governor of Krasnoyarsk Krai (1998–2002). In the early 1990s, he was seen by many as a possible contender for the presidency of Russia, although he did not stand for elections against Putin in 2000. He died in a helicopter crash in 2002.
68. materik.ru, "Dokumental'naja khronika bor'by protiv ugolovno-politicheskih Ppesledovaniy Russkogo pravozashhitnika B.F. Suprunjuka Kazahstanskimi Vlastyami," accessed October 12, 2017, http://observer.materik.ru/observer/N18_94/18_21.htm.
69. The agreement was unilaterally revoked by Turkmenistan in 2003. This caused much suffering to Russians who lived in Turkmenistan and had to decide whether to become foreigners in Turkmenistan or to renounce their Russian citizenship. See Peyrouse, *Russian Minority*.
70. Federal Law of the Russian Federation No.5206-1, "O vnesenii izmeneniy i dopolneniy v zakon RSFSR "o grazhdanstve RSFSR," the Supreme Soviet, June 17, 1993.
71. In Russian: "Za litsom, sostoyashchim v grazhdanstve Rossiyskoy Federatsii, ne priznayetsya prinadlezhnost' k grazhdanstvu drugogo gosudarstva." See Ginsburgs, *From Soviet to Russian*, 177.
72. A forced migrant was a person who had Russian citizenship or was eligible for Russian citizenship and was forced to leave their place of residence. Forced migrants were entitled to an allowance, assistance in transportation fares, accommodation, and free medical assistance. A refugee was a person who was not entitled to Russian citizenship, but the provisions for them did not sharply differ from the provisions for

forced migrants. See Federal Law of the Russian Federation No. 202-FZ , "On Introducing the Amendments and Addenda to the Law of the Russian Federation on the Forced Migrants," Federal Council of the Russian Federation, December 20, 1995.

73. Ginsburgs, *From Soviet to Russian*, 175.
74. Ginsburgs, 178.
75. Ginsburgs, 182.
76. Ginsburgs, 225.
77. Thomas De Waal, "'Yeltsin Doctrine' Planned in Ex-USSR," *Moscow Times*, August 11, 1994.
78. De Waal, "Yeltsin Doctrine"; Victor Khamraev and Gleb Cherkasov, "Dmitriy Rogozin obyavil ul'timatum prezidentu Kazakhstana a stranam SNG posovetoval dogovorit'sya o yedinom grazhdanstve," *Segodnya*, February 18, 1994.
79. Flynn, *Migrant Resettlement*, 41; Federal Law of the Russian Federation No. 13-3f, "O vnesenii izmeneniy v federal'nyy zakon o "grazhdanstve Rossiykoy Federatsii," Federal Council of the Russian Federation, February 6,1995..
80. Ginsburgs, *From Soviet to Russian*, 184.
81. Ginsburgs, 225.
82. Ginsburgs, 201.
83. Ginsburgs, 201.
84. Rainer Bauböck, "Studying Citizenship Constellations," *Journal of Ethnic and Migration Studies* 36, no. 5 (2010): 848, http://dx.doi.org/10.1080/13691831003764375.
85. Ginsburgs, *From Soviet to Russian*, 233.
86. Ginsburgs, 237.
87. Ginsburgs, 240.
88. Flynn, *Migrant Resettlement*, 77.
89. Osipov, "Chto oznachaet ponyatiy," 45.
90. Osipov, 45; Svetlana Ganushkina, "Detey bezhentsev vse chashche otkazyvayutsya brat' v Rossiyskiye shkoly," interview by Olga Zhuravleva and Ilya Rozhdestvensky, *Dnevnoy Razvorot*, Radio Echo Moskvy, July 28, 2015, https://echo.msk.ru/programs/razvorot/1592682-echo/.
91. Ginsburgs, *From Soviet to Russian*, 212.
92. Ginsburgs, 213–15.
93. Taras Kuzio, "Russian Passports as Moscow's Geopolitical Tool," *Eurasia Daily Monitor* 5, no. 176 (2008), https://jamestown.org/program/russian-passports-as-moscows-geopolitical-tool/; Lada L. Roslycky, "Russia's Smart Power in Crimea: Sowing the Seeds of Trust," *Southeast European and Black Sea Studies* 11, no. 3 (2011): 300, http://dx.doi.org/10.1080/14683857.2011.590313.
94. According to Estonian sources, by 1996, out of roughly 500,000 stateless Russians and Russian speakers, 88,000 received Estonian citizenship, 85,000 acquired Russian citizenship, while 70,000 moved to Russia. See Enterprise Estonia, "Citizenship." These figures, which Russian sources claimed to be too low, show that by 1996 in Estonia there were still 250,000 stateless people. In Latvia, the Citizenship Law was only enacted in 1996, and by 1999 only 23,858 persons out of the 700,000 stateless people were naturalized as Latvian citizens. See Krume, "Checks and Balances," 85.
95. Krume, 71–72; Law of the Republic of Latvia No. 10 "On the Status of Those Former USSR Citizens Who Do Not Have the Citizenship of Latvia or That of Any

Other State," Latvian Saeima, April 25, 1995; The Venice Commission, *Consequences of State Succession for Nationality* (Strasbourg: Council of Europe, 1998).

96. Krume, "Checks and Balances," 85.

97. Postanovleniye Konstitutsionnogo Suda RF ot 16.05.1996, "Po delu o proverke konstitutsionnosti punkta 'g' stat'i 18 zakona Rossiyskoy Federatsii 'o grazhdanstve Rossiyskoy Federatsii' v svyazi s zhaloboy A. B. Smirnova," Constitutional Court of the Russian Federation, 1996, No. 12-P.

98. Postanovleniye Konstitutsionnogo Suda RF.

99. Ginsburgs, *From Soviet to Russian*, 242.

100. Ginsburgs, 242.

101. Postanovleniye Konstitutsionnogo Suda RF.

102. By the 2000s Baburin became a marginal politician, although he was a candidate in the 2018 presidential elections (where he received 0.16 percent). For Baburin's profile, see Lenta.ru, "Baburin, Sergei," October 19, 2014, https://lenta.ru/lib/14159613/; Dawisha and Parrott, *New States of Eurasia*, 63.

103. Postanovleniye Gosudarstvennoy Dumy Federal'nogo Sobraniya Rossiyskoy Federatsii O proyekte federal'nogo zakona N 96003602-2, "O vnesenii izmeneniy i dopolneniy v preambulu i stat'i 2, 12, 13 i 18 Zakona Rossiyskoy Federatsii o grazhdanstve Rossiyskoy Federatsii," Federal Council of the Russian Federation, 2003, No. 3931-III.

104. Sergey Baburin, *Mir Imperii. Territoriya, Gosudarstva I Mirovoii Poryadok* (Moscow: Yuridichiskiy Tsentre, 2005).

105. Baburin, *Mir Imperii*.

106. Stenogramma Zasedaniy 18 Fevralya 1998, State Duma, 1998.

107. Draft federal law of the State Duma of the Federal Assembly of the Russian Federation No.462-2, "O Vnesenii Izmeneniy I Dopolneniy V Preambulu I Stat'i 2, 12, 13 I 18 Zakona Rossiyskoy Federatsii O Grazhdanstve Rossiyskoy Federatsii," State Duma of the Federal Assembly of the Russian Federation, June 13, 1996.

108. Federal Law of the Russian Federation No.99-F3, "O gosudarstvennoy politike Rossiyskoy Federatsii v otnoshenii sootechestvennikov za rubezhom," Federal Council of the Russian Federation, 1999.

109. Federal Law of the Russian FederationNo.99-F3, "O gosudarstvennoy politike Rossiyskoy Federatsii," item 1.

110. Shevel, "Politics of Citizenship," 140.

111. Shevel, 140.

112. Federal Law of the Russian Federation No.99-F3, "O gosudarstvennoy politike Rossiyskoy Federatsii," item 11; Osipov, "Chto oznachaet ponyatiy," 30.

113. By 2010 a significant part of the population in Transdniestria, Abkhazia, and South Ossetia held Russian passports. See Oksana Antonenko, "Frozen Uncertainty: Russia and the Conflict over Abkhazia," in *Statehood and Security: Georgia after the Rose Revolution*, ed. Bruno Coppieters and Robert Legvold (Cambridge: MIT Press, 2005), 220.

114. Progovernment members of the Duma underlined in the debates that automatic recognition of Russian citizenship would infringe on the rights of former Soviet citizens since the prohibition of dual citizenship in most former Soviet republics would have an adverse impact on Russia's relations with former Soviet states and put

a serious economic burden on Russia, due to obligations to social rights. See Stenogramma Zasedaniy 18 Fevralya 1998.

115. Tishkov, Zayinchkovskaya, and Vitkovskaya, *Migration*.

116. Service of State Statistics, "Obshchiye Itogi Migratsii"; Tishkov, Zayinchkovskaya, and Vitkovskaya, *Migration*.

117. Ginsburgs, *From Soviet to Russian*, 225.

118. Peyrouse, *Russian Minority*; Ginsburgs, *From Soviet to Russian*, 227.

119. Peyrouse, "Nationhood," 295.

120. Calculated according to data provided by Peyrouse, which indicates that by the end of the 1990s there were about 6.1 million Russians in Central Asia. See Peyrouse, *Russian Minority*.

121. Olga Lazareva, "Russian Migrants to Russia: Choice of Location and Labor Market Outcomes" (paper presented at the 11th IZA European Summer School in Labor Economics, Lake Ammersee, Germany, May 12–18, 2008).

122. Lazareva, "Russian Migrants to Russia"; Charles M. Becker, Erbolat N. Musabek, Ai-Gul S. Seitenova, and Dina S. Urzhumova, "The Migration Response to Economic Shock: Lessons from Kazakhstan," *Journal of Comparative Economics* 33, no. 1 (2005): 120, http://dx.doi.org/10.1016/j.jce.2004.12.003.

123. Tishkov, Zayinchkovskaya, and Vitkovskaya, *Migration*; Service of State Statistics, "Mezhdunarodnaya Migratsiya," accessed May 19, 2014, http://www.gks.ru/wps/wcm/connect/rosstat_main/rosstat/ru/statistics/population/demography/#.

124. Flynn, *Migrant Resettlement*, 90.

125. See Migration Policy Institute, "Migration Policy Institute Homepage," accessed February 12, 2018, https://www.migrationpolicy.org.

126. Yasemin Nuhoglu Soysal, *Limits of Citizenship: Migrants and Post-National Membership in Europe* (Chicago: University of Chicago Press, 1994).

127. Soysal, *Limits of Citizenship*; Bauböck, "Studying Citizenship Constellations."

128. Osipov, "Chto oznachaet ponyatiy," 25.

129. Tishkov, Zayinchkovskaya, and Vitkovskaya, *Migration*.

130. Ganushkina, "Detey bezhentsev vse chashche."

131. Osipov, "Chto oznachaet ponyatiy," 28.

132. Ginsburgs, *From Soviet to Russian*, 238.

133. Personal interview. Source asked to remain anonymous.

134. Ginsburgs, *From Soviet to Russian*, 241.

135. Ginsburgs, 241.

136. Osipov, "Chto oznachaet ponyatiy," 30.

137. Tishkov, Zayinchkovskaya, and Vitkovskaya, *Migration*.

138. "Krakh Chetvertogo Internatsionala," editorial, *Izvestia*, August 26, 1993.

139. Tishkov, Zayinchkovskaya, and Vitkovskaya, *Migration*.

140. Flynn, *Migrant Resettlement*, 13; Osipov, "Chto oznachaet ponyatiy," 35.

141. Ayelat Shachar noted in her book that developed societies, following the free flows of migration in earlier stages of globalization, introduced strict measures to control the free movement of people. See Ayelet Shachar, *The Birthright Lottery: Citizenship and Global Inequality* (Cambridge, MA: Harvard University Press, 2009). This was also one of the main arguments raised by such thinkers as Noam Chomsky. He claimed that in neoliberal globalization, while capital could move freely, people were

restricted in movement. See csc302, "Discussion on Globalization," October 30, 2006, YouTube video, 10:58, https://www.youtube.com/watch?v=AHJPSLgHemM. For a general overview of these processes in Europe, see Jef Huysmans, "The European Union and the Securitization of Migration," *Journal of Common Market Studies* 38, no. 5 (2000): 751–77, http://dx.doi.org/10.1111/1468-5965.00263.

142. Flynn, *Migrant Resettlement*, 88.

143. Flynn, 10.

2. Seeking Stability in a Fluid Russia

1. Oxana Shevel, "Russian Nation-Building from Yel'tsin to Medvedev: Ethnic, Civic or Purposefully Ambiguous?," *Europe-Asia Studies* 63, no. 2 (2011): 179, http://dx.doi.org/10.1080/09668136.2011.547693.

2. This regulation was a follow-up to an internal regulation from 1997, which was not put into force before 2000. See V. C. Chernyavsky, *Instruktsiya ot 22.08.2000 o dokumentirovanii vidami na zhitel'stvo* (Moscow: Ministry of Interior, 2000, No. 1/15651).

3. Osipov, "Chto oznachaet ponyatiy," 42.

4. Osipov, 42.

5. Alexander Zhuravsky and Olga Vykhovanets, "Compatriots: Back to the Homeland," Russian International Affairs Council, May 31, 2013, https://russiancouncil.ru/en/analytics-and-comments/analytics/compatriots-back-to-the-homeland/.

6. Federal Law of the Russian Federation No. 62-FZ, "On Citizenship of the Russian Federation," Federal Council of the Russian Federation, 2002.

7. Federal Law of the Russian Federation No. 62-FZ, item 13-1.

8. Federal Law of the Russian Federation No. 115-FZ, "Concerning the Legal Status of Foreign Citizens in the Russian Federation," Federal Council of the Russian Federation, July 25, 2002; Shevel, "Russian Nation-Building," 185.

9. Federal Law of the Russian Federation No. 115-FZ, item 5.

10. Federal Law of the Russian Federation No. 115-FZ, item 8-2.

11. Federal Law of the Russian Federation No. 115-FZ, item 8-3.

12. Sakwa, "Regime Change," 17.

13. Kremlin (website), "Excerpts from an Interview Granted to the Media in the Krasnodar Region," last modified September 17, 2002, http://en.kremlin.ru/events/president/transcripts/21722.

14. Kremlin (website), "Excerpts from an Interview."

15. Edwin Bacon, Bettina Renz, and Julian Cooper, *Securitising Russia: The Domestic Politics of Vladimir Putin* (Manchester: Manchester University Press, 2006), 11.

16. Valerii Grebennikov quoted in Shevel, "Politics of Citizenship," 203.

17. Stenogramma Zasedaniy Soveta Federatsii, Federal Council of the Russian Federation, May 15, 2002.

18. Bacon, Renz, and Cooper, *Securitising Russia*, 126.

19. Valery A. Tishkov, "Zakon O Grazhdanstve, Immigratsii I Mezhetnicheskiye Otnosheniya," on Valery Tishkov's blog, accessed October 5, 2017, http://www.valerytishkov.ru/cntnt/publikacii3/publikacii/zakon_o_gr.html.

20. Tishkov, "Zakon O Grazhdanstve."

21. Tishkov.

22. Service of State Statistics, "Mezhdunarodnaya Migratsiya."

23. Igor Terent'yev and Olesya Volkova, "Skrytaya ugroza: Rossiya okazalas' na poroge 'demograficheskoy yamy'," *RBC*, February 3, 2016, https://www.rbc.ru/society/03/02/2016/56b1c3b69a7947bf91c297ce.

24. According to the 1989 census, the population of RSFSR was 147 million people. By 1993 the number rose to 148.6 million, but since then the numbers have decreased. In 2000, 145.5 million people lived in Russia. In percentages, this meant that the natural decline was about 5 percent, while the recorded figures in totality put the decline at about 2 percent.

25. Osipov, "Chto oznachaet ponyatiy," 38.

26. Osipov, 38.

27. Kremlin (website), "Excerpts from an Interview."

28. Stenogramma Zasedaniya Soveta Federatsii.

29. Shachar, *Birthright Lottery*.

30. Fedor V. Russkikh, "Grazhdanstvo Rossii ne podtverzhdayetsya... Priklyucheniya 'inostrantsa' v Rossii—1 Oktyabrya 2002g," Pravda.ru, October 1, 2002, https://www.pravda.ru/politics/837513-grazhdanstvo_rossii_ne_podtverzhdaetsja_prikljuchenija/.

31. It is important to note that the 2002 law had not come into force yet, as it was signed in May 2002 and Russkikh applied to exchange his passport in April the same year. It showed, as was mentioned in the instructions sent to the Ministry of Interior in August 2000, that the police were enforcing the new citizenship policy before it came into force.

32. Russkikh, "Grazhdanstvo Rossii ne podtverzhdayetsya."

33. Russkikh.

34. Kremlin (website), "President of Russia Address to the Federal Assembly," last modified May 16, 2003, http://en.kremlin.ru/events/president/transcripts/21998.

35. Kremlin (website), "President of Russia Address."

36. Kremlin (website), "President Vladimir Putin Signed a Law on Introducing Amendments and Additions to the Law," last modified November 13, 2003, http://www.en.kremlin.ru/events/president/news/29736.

37. Kremlin (website), "President Vladimir Putin Signed."

38. Valery A. Tishkov, "Rossii Nuzhny Novyye Zhiteli," comment on Valery Tishkov's blog, last modified November 1, 2006, http://www.valerytishkov.ru/cntnt/novye_publikacii/rossii_nuz.html.

39. Lidiia Grafova, "Nado Legalizovat' Migrantov!," *Novaya Gazeta*, November 13, 2008.

40. Caress Schenk, *Why Control Immigration? Strategic Uses of Migration Management in Russia* (Toronto, University of Toronto Press, 2018).

41. Kremlin (website), "President Vladimir Putin Held a Meeting with the Cabinet," last modified June 3, 2002, http://en.kremlin.ru/events/president/news/27124.

42. The program was announced in 2006, but the amendment to the 2002 Citizenship Law was made in 2008.

43. Decree of the President of the Russian Federation No. 637, "O merakh po okazaniyu sodeystviya dobrovol'nomu pereseleniyu v Rossiyskuyu Federatsiyu sootechestvennikov, prozhivayushchikh za rubezhom (vmeste s 'Gosudarstvennoy programmoy po okazaniyu sodeystviya dobrovol'nomu pereseleniyu v Rossiyskuyu

Federatsiyu sootechestvennikov, prozhivayushchikh za rubezhom')," Presidential Administration, June 22, 2006.

44. Zhuravsky and Vykhovanets, "Compatriots."

45. Gosudarstvennaya programma po okazaniyu sodeystviya dobrovol'nomu pereseleniyu v Rossiyskuyu Federatsiyu sootechestvennikov, prozhivayushchikh za rubezhom, Administrativnyye Protsedury, Federal Migration Services, 2009.

46. Zhuravsky and Vykhovanets, "Compatriots."

47. Zhuravsky and Vykhovanets.

48. Federal Law on Citizenship of the Russian Federation (as amended by Federal Laws No. 151-FZ as of November 11, 2003; No. 127-FZ as of November 2, 2004; No. 5-FZ as of January 3, 2006; No. 121-FZ as of July 18, 2006; No. 296-FZ as of December 1, 2007; No. 328-FZ as of December 4, 2007; No. 163-FZ as of October 1, 2008; No. 301-FZ as of December 30, 2008; No. 127-FZ as of June 28, 2009), Federal Council of the Russian Federation, 2009.

49. Decree of the President of the Russian Federation No. 637, items 14 and 19.

50. Decree of the President of the Russian Federation No. 637, items 14 and 19.

51. Decree of the President of the Russian Federation No. 637, items 19 and 20.

52. Gosudarstvennaya programma po okazaniyu sodeystviya dobrovol'nomu pereseleniyu, 2009.

53. Gosudarstvennaya programma po okazaniyu sodeystviya dobrovol'nomu pereseleniyu v Rossiyskuyu Federatsiyu sootechestvennikov, prozhivayushchikh za rubezhom, Federal Migration Services, 2012.

54. Zhuravsky and Vykhovanets, "Compatriots."

55. Zhuravsky and Vykhovanets.

56. For instance, regarding the one-time allowance, if the condition of residency for two years was not met, the allowance had to be returned. See Gosudarstvennaya programma po okazaniyu sodeystviya dobrovol'nomu pereseleniyu, 2009.

57. Since 2007, compatriots who resided in Russia without citizenship were also allowed to participate in the program. See Decree of the President of the Russian Federation No. 637, items 5–16

58. Gosudarstvennaya programma po okazaniyu sodeystviya dobrovol'nomu pereseleniyu, 2009.

59. Gosudarstvennaya programma po okazaniyu sodeystviya dobrovol'nomu pereseleniyu, 2009.

60. Gosudarstvennaya programma po okazaniyu sodeystviya dobrovol'nomu pereseleniyu, 2009.

61. Olga Zeveleva, "Political Aspects of Repatriation: Germany, Russia, Kazakhstan. A Comparative Analysis," *Nationalities Papers* 42, no. 5 (2014): 808, http://dx.doi.org/10.1080/00905992.2014.916663.

62. Natalia Zubarevich, "Gastarbaytery v rossiyskoy ekonomike: plyusy i minusy," interview by Marina Koroleva, *Bolshoi Dozor*, Radio Echo Moskvy, February 12, 2014, https://echo.msk.ru/programs/dozor/1256500-echo/.

63. Zeveleva, "Political Aspects of Repatriation," 819.

64. Vladimir Dergachev, Eugeni Safronov, and Dimitri Evstifeev, "V Rossiyu s lyubov'yu," Gazeta.ru, April 1, 2014, https://www.gazeta.ru/politics/2014/04/01_a_5972817.shtml.

65. Dergachev, Safronov, and Evstifeev, "V Rossiyu s lyubov'yu."

66. "Poyedinok. Efir Ot 20.01.2011," broadcast on January 20, 2011, on Rossiya1. https://russia.tv/video/show/brand_id/3963/episode_id/91907/video_id/91907/viewtype/picture/.

67. Irina Ilina, "Ne problema, a konkurentnoye preimushchestvo," Cogita!Ru, October 25, 2012, http://www.cogita.ru/grazhdanskaya-aktivnost/migranty/5-i-konkurs-esse-migraciya-i-integraciya-migrantov-v-evrope-i-rossii/irina-ilina.

68. Zeveleva, "Political Aspects of Repatriation," 821; Shevel, "Russian Nation-Building," 187.

69. EurActiv.com, "France Tries to Attract Higher Qualified Immigration," May 4, 2006, http://www.euractiv.com/innovation/france-tries-attract-higher-qualified-immigration/article-154938.

70. Zhuravsky and Vykhovanets, "Compatriots."

71. Zhuravsky and Vykhovanets.

72. The figures provided to Romanovsky are so low that they make one question the authenticity of figures provided in 2014, which claimed that 150,000 people participated in the program. See Roman Romanovskiy, "Khotyat Li Russkiye Domoy?," Cogita!Ru, November 1, 2012, http://www.cogita.ru/grazhdanskaya-aktivnost/migranty/5-i-konkurs-esse-migraciya-i-integraciya-migrantov-v-evrope-i-rossii/hotyat-li-russkie-domoi.

73. Romanovskiy, "Khotyat Li Russkiye Domoy?"

74. Romanovskiy.

75. Romanovskiy.

76. A saying commonly attributed to the nineteenth-century writer Mikhail Saltykov-Shchedrin.

77. Osipov, "Chto oznachaet ponyatiy," 44.

78. Osipov, 44.

79. Federal Law of the Russian Federation N0.71-f3 "O vnesenii izmeneniy v Federal'nyy zakon 'O grazhdanstve Rossiyskoy Federatsii' i otdel'nyye zakonodatel'nyye akty Rossiyskoy Federatsii," Federal Council of the Russian Federation, April 20, 2014; Svetlana Antushenina, "Grazhdanstvo po sobesedovaniy," Lenta.ru, April 21, 2014, https://lenta.ru/articles/2014/04/21/grajdanstvo/.

80. Dergachev, Safronov, and Evstifeev, "V Rossiyu s lyubov'yu."

81. Antushenina, "Grazhdanstvo po sobesedovaniyu."

82. Antushenina.

83. Antushenina.

84. Antushenina.

85. Antushenina.

86. Kremlin (website), "Agreement on the accession of the Republic of Crimea to the Russian Federation signed," last modified March 18, 2014, http://en.kremlin.ru/events/president/news/20604.

87. Kremlin (website), "Agreement on the accession of the Republic of Crimea to the Russian Federation signed."

88. Kremlin (website), "Agreement on the accession."

89. Interestingly, Yarosh did not mention that 1.56 million people was about half the population of Crimea in 2014. It is known that some people already had Russian passports before the annexation. They probably did not amount, however, to half the

population of Crimea. See Eva Hartog, "Want to Become a Russian in Crimea? Join the Queue," *Moscow Times*, July 9, 2015.

90. Hartog, "Become a Russian."

91. Hartog.

92. Nedicom.ru Advocates, "Kak poluchit' Rossiyskiy pasport bez propiski v Krymu I Sevastopole?," accessed June 29, 2015, www.nedicom.ru/fakt-prozhivaniya-v-krymu.

93. Anastasia Vityazeva, "Hiding Dual Citizenship Now a Criminal Offense in Russia," Russia Beyond the Headlines, August 12, 2014, https://www.rbth.com/society/2014/08/12/hiding_dual_citizenship_now_a_criminal_offense_in_russia_38929.html.

94. Vityazeva, "Hiding Dual Citizenship."

95. Svetlana Bocharova and Farida Rustamova, "Vstupil v silu zakon o vtorom grazhdanstve," *RBK*, August 4, 2014, https://www.rbc.ru/politics/04/08/2014/5424a089cbb20f749dbbc29d.

96. Eleonora Tafuro Ambrosetti, "Russia's Great Disease: The Demographic Decline," Italian Institute for International Political Studies (ISPI), Commentary, Milan, November 4, 2019, https://www.ispionline.it/en/pubblicazione/russias-great-disease-demographic-decline-24313; Yuliya Starostina, "Pochemu Rossii mozhet grozit' sokrashcheniye naseleniya vervyye za 10 let," *RBK*, July 12, 2018, https://www.rbc.ru/economics/12/07/2018/5b477cdc9a794726717db27c.

97. *Kommersant*, "Mnogopasportiynaya Sistema," February 7, 2020.

98. Blackstar is the name of the rapper Timati's production company.

99. Ravshan and Dzhamshut are comic characters portraying Central Asian laborers on the Russian TNT channel.

100. Doni, "Doni feat. Natali—Ty takoy (Prem'yera klipa, 2015)," October 29, 2015, YouTube video, 3:37, https://www.youtube.com/watch?v=5Fix7P6aGXQ.

101. Dergachev, Safronov, and Evstifeev, "V Rossiyu s lyubov'yu."

102. Dergachev, Safronov, and Evstifeev.

103. Dergachev, Safronov, and Evstifeev.

104. Kim Willsher, "Gerard Depardieu's Tax Move to Belgium Divides France," *The Observer*, December 22, 2012.

105. Kremlin (website), "Ukaz o priyome v grazhdanstvo Rossiyskoy Federatsii," last modified January 3, 2013, http://kremlin.ru/events/president/news/17275.

106. Tom Parfitt, "Gerard Depardieu Pleased at Russian Citizenship," *The Telegraph*, January 3, 2013.

107. US Department of the Treasury, "Treasury Sanctions Russian Officials, Members of the Russian Leadership's Inner Circle, and an Entity for Involvement in the Situation in Ukraine" (press release, Washington, DC, March 20, 2014), https://www.treasury.gov/press-center/press-releases/Pages/jl23331.aspx.

108. Atossa Araxia Abrahamian, *The Cosmopolites: The Coming of the Global Citizen* (New York: Columbia Global Reports, 2015), 14.

109. Alice Tidey, "Depardieu Throws House Party for New Belgium Neighbors," CNBC, August 26, 2013, https://www.cnbc.com/id/100987661.

110. Vladimir W. Zhirinovsky, "Migratsiya," interview by Yuri Kobaladze and Svetlana Sorokina, *V Kruge Sveta*, Radio Echo Moskvy, August 27, 2013, https://echo.msk.ru/programs/sorokina/1143798-echo/.

111. "Poyedinok. Efir Ot 25.11.2010," broadcast on November 25, 2010, on Rossiya1.

112. Al-Jazeera, "Zygmunt Bauman: Behind the World's Crisis of Humanity," July 3, 2016, https://www.aljazeera.com/program/talk-to-al-jazeera/2016/7/23/zygmunt-bauman-behind-the-worlds-crisis-of-humanity.

113. BBC, "How Is the Migrant Crisis Dividing EU Countries?," September 19, 2015, https://www.bbc.co.uk/news/world-europe-34278886.

114. Stephan Lhene, "The Tempting Trap of Fortress Europe," Carnegie Europe, April 22, 2016, http://carnegieeurope.eu/2016/04/21/tempting-trap-of-fortress-europe-pub-63400.

115. Ozden Ocak, "Immigration and French National Identity under Neoliberalism: Sarkozy's Selective Immigration Politics as a Performance of Sovereignty," *Patterns of Prejudice* 50, no. 1 (2016): 82–95, http://dx.doi.org/10.1080/0031322X.2015.1127642.

116. Schenk, *Why Control Immigration?*, 209.

117. James F. Hollifield, *Immigrants, Markets, and States: The Political Economy of Postwar Europe* (Cambridge, MA: Harvard University Press, 1992), 139.

3. Media Discourse in the 1990s

1. M. Lesko, "Pechat' ministra Lesina," *Kar'era*, June 2, 2003.

2. Lesko, "Pechat' ministra Lesina."

3. Mikhail Bakhtin in Gary Saul Morson, *Bakhtin: Essays and Dialogues on His Work* (Chicago: University of Chicago Press, 1986), 93.

4. Norman Fairclough, *Critical Discourse Analysis: The Critical Study of Language* (London: Routledge, 2010), 3.

5. Lilie Chouliaraki and Norman Fairclough, *Discourse in Late Modernity: Rethinking Critical Discourse Analysis* (Edinburgh: Edinburgh University Press, 1999), 4.

6. Chouliaraki and Fairclough, *Discourse in Late Modernity*, 3.

7. Hasan Guseynov, "The Shock of Irrevocability," in *1990: Russians Remember a Turning Point*, ed. Irina Prokhorova (London: McLehose, 2013), 48.

8. Irina Prokhorova, ed., *1990: Russians Remember a Turning Point* (London: MacLehose, 2013), 1.

9. Laruelle, *Russian Nationalism*, 4.

10. Billig, *Banal Nationalism*, 5.

11. Billig, 5.

12. Alexander Osipov, "The Background of the Soviet Union's Involvement in the Establishment of the European Minority Rights Regime in the Late 1980s," *Journal on Ethnopolitics and Minority Issues in Europe* 15, no. 2 (2016): 65, http://www.ecmi.de/fileadmin/downloads/publications/JEMIE/2016/Osipov2.pdf.

13. Sergey Bablumian, "Kto khochet otmenit' den' pobedy," *Izvestia*, January 3, 1991.

14. *Moskovskie novosti*, "Posledniy privet Gruzii ot SSSR," January 19, 1992.

15. *Nezavisimaya Gazeta*, "Natsional'nyy sostav pravitel'stva podvergnut ekspertize: Budem nadeitsya chto prezident poshutil," July 4, 1992.

16. *Nezavisimaya Gazeta*, "Natsional'nyy sostav pravitel'stva podvergnut ekspertize."

17. *Nezavisimaya Gazeta*.

18. Nikolai Andreev and Victor Litovkin, "Ne day bog uvidet'sya cherez liniyu fronta," *Izvestia*, April 14, 1992.
19. Andreev and Litovkin, "Ne day bog uvidet'sya."
20. Andreev and Litovkin.
21. Andreev and Litovkin.
22. Rodion Morozov, "Leonid Shebarshin: Ya znayu, chto inostrannyye razvedki narashchivayut deyatel'nost' protiv Rossii," *Nezavisimaya Gazeta*, August 18, 1993.
23. Guseynov, "Shock of Irrevocability," 148.
24. Guseynov, 148.
25. Thomas De Waal, "Zhirinovsky Sets Signature to Anti-Semitic Statement," *Moscow Times*, December 10, 1994.
26. *Izvestia*, "Ocherednaya gosudarstvennaya ideologiya Rosii ne nuzhna," July 17, 1996.
27. Stepan Kiselev, "Grigoriy Satarov: Natsional'naya Ideya—Eto Nevol'no," *Izvestia*, July 19, 1996.
28. Vladimir Borodin, "Vadim Gustov: ot pravitel'stva nam ne nado ni odnogo lishnego rublya," *Izvestia*, May 13, 1998.
29. Alexander Sadchikov, "Sergey Kiriyenko: Kto ne protiv nas, tot s nami / Byvshiy prem'yer pobyval v redaktsii izvestia predlozhil svoyu obshchestvennogo dogovora," *Izvestia*, December 22, 1998.
30. Rustam Afidjamov, "Midl i natsional'naya ideya," *Izvestia*, August 15, 1998.
31. Lev Timofeev, "Naivnaya formula pobedy," *Izvestia*, August 9, 1996.
32. Yurchak, *Everything Was Forever*.
33. Yevgeniy Bunimovich, "Voyny ne zakanchivayutsya. Oni prosto stanut pamyat'yu," *Novaya Gazeta*, June 23, 1997.
34. Nina Tumarkin, "The Great Patriotic War as Myth and Memory," *European Review* 11, no. 4 (2003): 600, http://dx.doi.org/10.1017/s1062798703000504.
35. Valeri Kichin, "Nikita Mikhalkov: Tak Konchayutsya Smutnyye Vremena," *Izvestia*, July 1, 1998.
36. Kichin, "Nikita Mikhalkov."
37. Kichin.
38. Kichin.
39. CNN, "Yeltsin Warns of Possible World War over Kosovo," April 9, 1999, http://edition.cnn.com/WORLD/europe/9904/09/kosovo.diplomacy.02/.
40. BBC, "Russian Anti-US Feeling Grows," April 24, 1999, http://news.bbc.co.uk/1/hi/world/europe/327202.stm.
41. Andrey Kolesnikov, "Posledneye pribezhishche," *Izvestia*, April 10, 1999.
42. Billig, *Banal Nationalism*, 5.

4. Media Discourse under Putin

1. Karen Dawisha, *Putin's Kleptocracy: Who Owns Russia?* (New York: Simon & Schuster, 2014), 201.
2. Dawisha, *Putin's Kleptocracy*; Masha Gessen, *The Man without a Face: The Unlikely Rise of Vladimir Putin* (New York: Riverhead Books, 2012), 33–37; Olessia Koltsova, *News Media and Power in Russia* (London: Routledge, 2006), 217–18.

3. Explosions in the apartment buildings in September 1999, which killed 293 people.

4. Valeriy Vzyhutovich, "Mezhdu Terekom i Potomakom," *Izvestia*, November 6, 1999.

5. For more on the reciprocal nature of Putin's regime, see Samuel A. Greene and Graeme B. Robertson, *Putin v. the People: The Perilous Politics of a Divided Russia* (New Haven, C: Yale University Press, 2019).

6. Andrey Kolesnikov, "Okna rosta," *Novaya Gazeta*, April 25, 2000.

7. Peter Pomerantsev, *Nothing Is True and Everything Is Possible: Adventures in Modern Russia* (New York: Public Affairs, 2014), 66.

8. Peter Pomerantsev, *Nothing Is True*.

9. *Izvestia*, "Vladimir Putin: Rossiya ne dolzhna byt' i ne budet politseyskim gosudarstvom," July 14, 2000.

10. *Izvestia*, "Vladimir Putin: Rossiya."

11. *Izvestia*.

12. Guy Chazan, "Putin Favours Restoring Soviet National Anthem," *Guardian*, October 15, 2000.

13. Chazan, "Putin Favours."

14. Andrei Chernov, "Yel'tsin pokhoronil perestroyku, Putin reanimiroval perelitsovku," *Novaya Gazeta*, October 23, 2000.

15. Chernov, "Yel'tsin pokhoronil perestroyku." The Russian term *perelitsovka* literally means to remake something (clothing, for example) by turning it inside out, so the outer layer, or the front, is new. The essence of the object did not change, but it was remade to look fresh. The article referred to Soviet times, when people had to adjust themselves and change their opinions and words according to political changes.

16. BBC, "Yeltsin Attacks Putin over Anthem," December 7, 2000, http://news.bbc.co.uk/1/hi/world/europe/1059784.stm.

17. Laruelle, *Russian Nationalism*, 7.

18. Richard Sakwa, *Putin: Russia's Choice* (London: Routledge, 2008), 49.

19. Sakwa, *Putin: Russia's Choice*, 49.

20. Laruelle, *Russian Nationalism*.

21. J. Martin Daughtry, "Russia's New Anthem and the Negotiation of National Identity," *Ethnomusicology* 47, no. 1 (2003), http://dx.doi.org/10.2307/852511.

22. Yurchak, *Everything Was Forever*, 78.

23. Yurchak, 79.

24. *Izvestia*, "Kakoy Shchet?," February 4, 2002.

25. BBC, "Putin Blamed for TV Shutdown," January 22, 2002, http://news.bbc.co.uk/1/hi/world/europe/1775302.stm.

26. Lenta.ru, "Putin v gostyakh u Izvestia: govorili pro Sankt-Peterburg, SSHA, TV-6 u smertnuyu kazn," March 13, 2002, https://lenta.ru/news/2002/03/13/izvestia.

27. NTV's takeover was due to financial troubles that were precipitated by debt collection from state-owned debtors and an episode of denial of advertising brokerage services by the firm formally owned by Mikhail Lesin, Putin's minister of media. See in Koltsova, *News Media and Power*, 194–95.

28. globoball, "Itogi s Evgeniem Kiselevym—Ekstrenny vypusk ot 03 Aprelya 2001 goda," July 18, 2015, YouTube video, 2:15:52, https://www.youtube.com/watch?v=fD9hU8fkwBo.

29. globoball, "Itogi s Evgeniem Kiselevym."

30. Kremlin (website), "Annual Address to the Federal Assembly of the Russian Federation," last modified April 1, 2001, http://en.kremlin.ru/events/president/transcripts/21216.

31. globoball, "Itogi s Evgeniem Kiselevym."

32. *Izvestia*, "Vladimir Putin prinyal finalistov konkursa studencheskikh sochineniy," June 6, 2003.

33. Federal Law of the Russian Federation No. 53-FZ, "About the State Language of the Russian Federation," Federal Council of the Russian Federation, 2005.

34. In tsarist Russia, October 22 (November 4 according to the Gregorian calendar) was the Day of Our Lady of Kazan. According to Russian tradition, on this day Russian forces ended the Polish-Lithuanian occupation of Moscow at the end of the Time of Troubles in 1613.

35. *Novaya Gazeta*, "Novyye Russkiye prazdniki," November 11, 2004.

36. Boris Dubin, "Massovaya religioznaya kul'tura v rossii (Tendentsii v gody 1990-Kh Godov)," *Vestnik obshchestvennogo mneniya*, no. 3 (2004): 37, https://cyberleninka.ru/article/n/massovaya-religioznaya-kultura-v-rossii-tendentsii-i-itogi-1990-h-godov.

37. Sakwa, *Putin: Russia's Choice*, 49.

38. Vladislav Surkov, "Surkov: In His Own Words," *Wall Street Journal*, December 18, 2006, https://www.wsj.com/articles/SB116646992809753610.

39. *Izvestia*, "Ideologiya suverennoy demokratii," April 21, 2006.

40. Lenta.ru, "Putin v gostyakh."

41. Stephen C. Hutchings and Natalia Rulyova, *Television and Culture in Putin's Russia: Remote Control* (London: Routledge, 2009), 24.

42. Pomerantsev, *Nothing Is True*, 6.

43. For more on power relations and government control, see Hutchings and Rulyova, *Television and Culture*, 3–12. In 2013 the Russian hacker ring Shaltai Baltai leaked numerous emails and communications between television producers and government officials. See Rosbalt, "Glavnye slivy Shaltaya-Boltaya," January 31, 2017, https://www.rosbalt.ru/russia/2017/01/31/1587547.html.

44. Vera Tolz and Yuri Teper, "Broadcasting Agitainment: A New Media Strategy of Putin's Third Presidency," *Post-Soviet Affairs* 34, no. 4 (2018): 380, http://dx.doi.org/10.1080/1060586X.2018.1459023.

45. Lenta.ru, "Vladimir Soloviev pereydet na kanal Rossiya 1," August 12, 2010, https://lenta.ru/news/2010/08/12/vsoloviev/.

46. Fairclough, *Critical Discourse Analysis*.

47. The Russian liberal politician Leonid Gozman, who participated in the show, recalled that it was the only format in which he was allowed to freely speak on federal television and that he felt that it had profound public resonance. Leonid Gozman, pers. comm., 2018.

48. Leonid Gozman, pers. comm.

49. Andrew Wilson, *Virtual Politics: Faking Democracy in the Post-Soviet World* (New Haven, CT: Yale University Press, 2005), 35, 41–42.

50. Joakim Ekman, "Political Participation and Regime Stability: A Framework for Analyzing Hybrid Regimes," *International Political Science Review* 30, no. 1 (2009): 27, http://dx.doi.org/doi:10.1177/0192512108097054.

NOTES TO PAGES 101–110

51. Just Cause was formerly known as the Union of Rightist Forces. For a video of the show, see antik.ws, "Boris Nadezhdin i Vl. Zhirinovskiy K Bar'yeru!," September 18, 2011, YouTube video, 1:01:38, https://www.youtube.com/watch?v=b3fXeuIn7e8&t=1608s.

52. antik.ws, "Boris Nadezhdin."

53. "Poyedinok. Efir Ot 25.11.2010."

54. Hutchings and Tolz mentioned that this term, originally coined by Stalin to represent a pan-Soviet unity and discredited by the end of the Soviet period, made a comeback as a positive concept on Russian television. See Stephen Hutchings and Vera Tolz, "Fault Lines in Russia's Discourse of Nation: Television Coverage of the December 2010 Moscow Riots," *Slavic Review* 71, no. 4 (2012): 880, http://dx.doi.org/10.5612/slavicreview.71.4.0873.

55. In 2005, Putin famously called the collapse of the Soviet Union a catastrophe. See BBC, "Putin Deplores Collapse of USSR," April 25, 2005, http://news.bbc.co.uk/2/hi/4480745.stm.

56. Emil Pain, "Events in Moscow 11th December 2010: Political Crisis," *Russian Analytical Digest*, no. 93 (March 10, 2011), https://www.files.ethz.ch/isn/127703/Russian_Analytical_Digest_93.pdf.

57. RIA Novosti, "Ubijstvo futbol'nogo bolel'shhika Egora Sviridova: hronika sobytiy," December 6, 2013, https://ria.ru/20131206/981951049.html.

58. RIA Novosti, "Ubijstvo futbol'nogo bolel'shhika."

59. Hutchings and Tolz, "Fault Lines"; Stephen Hutchings, Vera Tolz, and Elisabeth Schimpfoessl, "Race and Ethnicity in the Russian Media: Rights, Responsibilities and Representations; Public Debate, the Frontline Club, London, Thursday 18 October 2012," *Russian Journal of Communication* 5, no. 3 (2013): 302, http://dx.doi.org/10.1080/19409419.2013.819462.

60. "Poyedinok. Efir Ot 23.12.2010," broadcast on December 23, 2010, on Rossiya1, https://russia.tv/video/show/brand_id/3963/episode_id/91904/.

61. Capital of the mainly Muslim republic of Kabardino-Balkaria.

62. Welliton Soares de Morais is a Brazilian football player who plays for Spartak FC.

63. Vladimir Solovyov *My—Russkiye! S Nami Bog!* (Moscow: Eskimo, 2009).

64. Hutchings and Tolz, "Fault Lines."

65. "Poyedinok. Efir Ot 20.01.2011."

66. Hutchings and Tolz, "Fault Lines."

67. Soyuz pravykh sil (Union of Rightist Forces), the previous name of Just Cause party.

68. FMS is Federal Migration Service; MVD is Ministry of Interior.

69. "Poyedinok. Efir Ot 20.01.2011."

70. The audiences in the show are usually paid for their participation and expected to help the production to promote the desired message. Gozman, pers. comm.

71. For the increasing use of ethnically based articulations of Russian national identity, see Yuri Teper, "Official Russian Identity Discourse in Light of the Annexation of Crimea: National or Imperial?," *Post-Soviet Affairs* 32, no. 4 (2016): 378, http://dx.doi.org/10.1080/1060586X.2015.1076959.

72. Vladimir V. Putin, "Vladimir Putin. Rossiya: Natsional'nyy Vopros," *Nezavisimaya gazeta*, January 23, 2012.

73. Fairclough, *Critical Discourse Analysis*.
74. Yuri Medvedev, "Konflikty—nashe bogatstvo," *Izvestia*, July 26, 2000.
75. Helena Goscilo and Vlad Strukov, *Celebrity and Glamour in Contemporary Russia: Shocking Chic* (London: Routledge, 2012).
76. Alla Borisovna Pugacheva, a Soviet and Russian popular musical performer, started her career in 1965 and continues to perform to this day. She enjoys an iconic status in the Russian-speaking world.
77. *Novaya Gazeta*, "Vozvrashcheniye Styda," February 2, 2004.
78. Alexandra Sopova, "Simvolom Rossii mozhet stat' Lomonosov, narisovannyy neft'yu," *Izvestia*, Deccember 24, 2012.
79. Alexandra Sopova, "Natsional'nuyu ideyu Rossii predlozhili vyrazit' v navoznoy kuche," *Izvestia*, January 17, 2013.
80. Pomerantsev, *Nothing Is True*, 66.
81. Irina Prokhorova, "Kakiye tsennosti nas ob'Yedinyat?," interview by Larina Ksenya and Shargunov Sergey, *2013*, Radio Echo Moskvy, December 27, 2013, https://echo.msk.ru/programs/year2013/1225381-echo/.
82. "Poyedinok. Efir Ot 27.02.2014," broadcast on February 27, 2014, on Rossiya1. http://russia.tv/anons/show/episode_id/970423/brand_id/3963/.
83. Followers of the Stepan Bendera, the leader of the Ukrainian independence movement who cooperated with the Nazis during the Second World War; a derogatory term used by Russians when referring to Ukrainians as Nazi collaborators and sympathizers.
84. Stephen Hutchings and Szostek Joanna, "Dominant Narratives in Russian Political and Media Discourse during the Ukraine Crisis," *E-International Relations*, April 28, 2015, http://www.e-ir.info/2015/04/28/dominant-narratives-in-russian-political-and-media-discourse-during-the-crisis/.
85. Ekman, "Political Participation," 29.
86. Wikileaks, "Medvedev's Address and Tendem Politics," accessed February 13, 2017, https://www.wikileaks.org/plusd/cables/08MOSCOW3343_a.html.
87. Putin opposed labeling Russia's actions in Crimea as an intervention. See Kremlin (website), "Address by the President of the Russian Federation," last modified March 18, 2014, http://en.kremlin.ru/events/president/news/20603.
88. "Poyedinok. Efir Ot 04.04.2014," broadcast on April 4, 2014, on Rossiya1. http://beta.russia.tv/anons/show/episode_id/978957/brand_id/3963/.
89. Tolz and Teper, "Broadcasting Agitainment," 14.
90. Leonid Gozman noted that from his personal experience on *Poyedinok*, with all the caveats, antigovernment speakers were still able to express themselves. Meanwhile, in the new formats with multiple speakers onstage, it was far harder to express antigovernment ideas. The speakers in these shows, many of whom were progovernment, assisted the host or hosts to quell the ability of antigovernment participants to speak. Gozman, pers. comm.
91. *Novaya Gazeta*, "My—Kollektivnyy Putin," April 8, 2001.
92. Margareta Bertilsson, "The Theory of Structuration: Prospects and Problems," in *Anthony Giddens: Critical Assessments*, ed. Christopher Bryant and David Jary (London: Routledge, 1997), 54.
93. Al-Jazeera, "Zygmunt Bauman."
94. Laruelle, *Russian Nationalism*, 7.

95. Andrey Mozzhukhin, "Epoha stabil'nosti v Rossii zakonchilas," Lenta.ru, September 29, 2015, https://lenta.ru/articles/2015/09/29/stabilnost/.

96. Although *Poyedinok* was suspended for over a year, Solov'yëv had a talk show in another format, as well as a radio show. *Poyedinok* returned to broadcast in 2015, alongside his other talk show. Moreover, in 2017 he was granted an exclusive series of interviews with Putin.

97. Levada-Center, "Odobrenie deytel'nosti V. Putina," accessed February 13, 2017. https://www.levada.ru/indikatory/odobrenie-organov-vlasti/.

98. Gudkov, "Epoha stabil'nosti."

99. Denis Volkov, pers. comm., 2017.

100. Fairclough, *Critical Discourse Analysis*, 150.

101. Fairclough, *Critical Discourse Analysis*, 151.

102. Adam Curtis, "Hypernormalisation," BBC, October 16, 2016, video, 2:46, https://www.bbc.co.uk/programmes/p04b183c.

5. From the Soviet Calendar to Russian Calendars

1. Eviatar Zerubavel, "Calendars and History: A Comparative Study of the Social Organisation of Time," in *States of Memory: Continuities, Conflicts, and Transformations in National Retrospection*, ed. Jeffrey K. Olick (Durham, NC: Duke University Press, 2003), 319.

2. Reinhart Koselleck, *Futures Past: On the Semantics of Historical Time* (New York: Colombia University Press), 2.

3. Emile Durkheim, *The Elementary Forms of the Religious Life*, trans. Joseph Ward Swain, (Mineola, NY: Dover, 2008), 10.

4. Unpublished archive materials from the Levada-Center.

5. Koselleck, *Futures Past*, 9.

6. Koselleck's analysis of modernity is similar to Bauman's analysis of late modernity. His emphasis was that the lack of concrete prophecy and focus on progress created disorientation, as noted by Tocqueville: "As the past has ceased to throw its light on the future, the mind of man wanders in obscurity." See Koselleck, *Futures Past*, 31. Bauman noted that in classic modernity "the major occupation of the modern mind was not so much about the technology of melting . . . as the design of the moulds into which metal was to be poured and the technology of keeping them there." Classical modernity had a fixed "finish line" (bright future), which liquid modernity lacks. Bauman, *Liquid Modernity*, x.

7. Anthony Giddens, *The Constitution of Society: Introduction of the Theory of Structuration* (Berkeley: University of California Press, 1984), 3, 14.

8. Amitai Etzioni, "Holiday Rituals: Neglected Hotbeds of Virtue," in *We Are What We Celebrate: Understanding Holidays and Rituals*, ed. Amitai Etzioni and Jared Bloom (New York: Nork University Press, 2004), 10.

9. For more on the production of Soviet normality through performances and ritualized acts, see Yurchak, *Everything Was Forever*, 1–29.

10. Law of the USSR No. 2-VIII "Ob utverzhdenii Osnovnogo zakonodatel'stva Soyuza SSR i soyuznykh respublik o trude," Presidium of the Supreme Soviet of the USSR, July 15, 1970.

11. Romanus Akintev, "7 Noyabrya 1982," September 22, 2012, YouTube video, 3:21, https://www.youtube.com/watch?v=FWuRxkzGoBA.
12. Also referred to as "developed socialism" (*razvitoy sotsializm*).
13. Yurchak, *Everything Was Forever*, 15.
14. Yurchak, 25; Olga D. Popova, "Kulinarnyy kod kul'tury prazdnika v Sovetskom obshchestve," *Modern History of Russia*, no. 2 (2016): 256, http://modernhistory.ru/d/1607380/d/popova.pdf.
15. Alexei Yurchak, "Post-Post-Communist Sincerity: Pioneers, Cosmonauts, and Other Soviet Heroes Born Today," in *What Is Soviet Now? Identities, Legacies, Memories*, ed. Thomas Lahusen and Peter Solomon (Berlin: LIT Verlag Munster, 2008), 270.
16. Alexievich, *Secondhand Time*, 25.
17. Evgenii Trostin, "Pervyy den' novoy ere," *Istorik*, April 16, 2016.
18. Reina Pennington, "'Do Not Speak of the Services You Rendered': Women Veterans of Aviation in the Soviet Union," in *A Soldier and a Woman: Sexual Integration in the Military*, ed. Gerard J. De Groot and Corina M. Peniston-Bird (London: Pearson Education, 2000), 157–58.
19. Choi Chatterjeee, *Celebrating Women: Gender, Festival Culture, and Bolshevik Ideology, 1910–1939*, (Pittsburgh: University of Pittsburgh Press, 2002), 4.
20. Chatterjeee, *Celebrating Women*, 3.
21. Gail Warshofsky Lapidus, *Women in Soviet Society: Equality, Development and Social Change* (Berkeley: University of California Press, 1978), 96, 114.
22. Lapidus, *Women in Soviet Society*.
23. I. K. Sivolap, ed., *Kniga o vkusnoy i zdorovoy pishche* (Moscow: Pischepromizdat, 1952), 17. On the formation of the Soviet food industry, see Edward Geist, "Cooking Bolshevik: Anastas Mikoian and the Making of the Book about Delicious and Healthy Food," *Russian Review* 71, no. 2 (2012): 300–5, http://dx.doi.org/10.1111/j.1467-9434.2012.00654.x.
24. Pennington, "Do Not Speak."
25. Lapidus, *Women in Soviet Society*, 246.
26. Nataliya N. Kozlova, "Mezhdunarodnyy zhenskiy den' 8 Marta kak instrument formirovaniya Sovetskoy politicheskoy kul'tury," *Zhenshchina v rossiyskom obshchestve*, no. 1 (2011): 37.
27. Kozlova, "Mezhdunarodnyy zhenskiy den'," 44.
28. Yurchak, *Everything Was Forever*, 131–32.
29. Fireworks took place in Hero Cities, which withstood hardships during the war. See Tumarkin, "Great Patriotic War," 605.
30. Daria Pashenko, "Prazdnik so slezami na glazakh," *Delitant*, May 9, 2017, http://diletant.media/articles/35551897/.
31. Tumarkin, "Great Patriotic War," 610; Illya Varlamov, "Progulka Po Moskve 1986 Goda," comment on *Make Russia Warm Again* (blog), December 20, 2015, https://varlamov.ru/1268819.html.
32. Hobsbawm and Ranger, *Invention of Tradition*.
33. Elizabeth A. Wood, "Performing Memory: Vladimir Putin and the Celebration of World War II in Russia," *Soviet and Post-Soviet Review* 38, no. 2 (2011): 182, http://dx.doi.org/10.1163/187633211x591175; Tumarkin, "Great Patriotic War," 612.

34. Valentina Efremova, "Gosudarstvennyy prazdniki kak instrumenty simvolicheskoy politiki v sovremennoy Rossii" (PhD diss., Institute of Philosophy, Russian Academy of Sciences, 2014).

35. The fir tree was a controversial tradition in tsarist Russia too, because it was imported from the West. During the First World War some critics of the tradition called to ban the fir tree celebrations in Russia. It was, however, finally banned by the Bolsheviks. See Elena Dushechkina, *Russkaya yëlka: Istoriya, mifologiya, literatura* (St. Petersburg: European University in St. Petersburg Press, 2014), 150, 167; Karen Petrone, *Life Has Become More Joyous, Comrades: Celebrations in the Time of Stalin* (Bloomington: Indiana University Press, 2000), 86.

36. Natalya Radchenko and Natiana Kuzmina, "Prazdnik novogo goda V Rossii v kontekste natsional'nykh traditsiy (Primer issledovaniya Respubliki Sakha—Yakutiya)," *Teoriya i praktika obshhestvennogo razvitiya*, no. 3 (2015): 130, http://teoria-practica.ru/rus/files/arhiv_zhurnala/2015/3/history/radchenko-kuzmina.pdf.

37. Petrone, *Life Has Become*, 17.

38. For instance, in 1939 *The Book of Tasty and Healthy Food* was first published as the first and main Soviet cookbook. Olga Jahno, "Poleznyye knigi o vkusnoy pishche: traditsiya XIX V. I sovetskiy etalon pitaniya," *Vestnik RUDN*, no. 3 (2007): 49–50.

39. Petrone, *Life Has Become*, 88.

40. Popova, "Kulinarnyy kod kul'tury prazdnika," 245.

41. Sivolap, *Kniga o vkusnoy*, 29.

42. Jahno, "Useful Books."

43. Sivolap, *Kniga o vkusnoy*, 47.

44. Christine E. Evans, *Between Truth and Time: A History of Soviet Central Television* (New Haven, CT: Yale University Press, 2016), 88.

45. Evans, *Between Truth and Time*, 88–89.

46. Evans, 88–89.

47. Evans, 86.

48. Alyssa DeBlasio, "The New-Year Film as a Genre of Post-War Russian Cinema," *Studies in Russian and Soviet Cinema* 2, no. 1 (2008): 43, http://dx.doi.org/10.1386/srsc.2.1.43_1.

49. Federal Law of the Russian Federation No. 35431, "On Amendments and Additions to the Code of Laws of Labour in the RSFSR," the Supreme Soviet, 1992. Pascha was not designated in the decree, as it is celebrated on last Sunday of Lent. In 1994 the Kremlin introduced a new holiday—Constitution Day (December 12), to mark the adoption of the 1993 constitution.

50. Svetlana Sorokina, Irina Khakamada, and Arina Holin, "O peratsiya po podchineniyu budushhih pokoleniy: zachem nuzhny Junarmiya, igrushechnyy Reihstag i otdyh sem'yami v okopah," broadcast on March 18, 2017, on Dozd TV.

51. Nurit Schleifman, "Introduction," in *Russia at a Crossroads: History, Memory and Political Practice*, ed. Nurit Schleifman (New York: Routledge, 2013), 3.

52. Nina Tumarkin, "The Religion of Victory," *Moscow Times*, May 11, 1995.

53. Oleg Moroz, comment on *Den' za dnem* (blog), Yeltsin Center (website), last modified in 2012, http://www.yeltsincenter.ru/author_comment/release/den-pobedy-v-1992-godu-bez-trezvona-i-lzhi#bottom.

54. Kathleen E. Smith, *Mythmaking in the New Russia: Politics and Memory During the Yeltsin Era* (Ithaca, NY: Cornell University Press, 2002).

55. Quoted in Moroz.
56. Quoted in Moroz.
57. K. Smith, *Mythmaking*, 86.
58. K. Smith, 86.
59. K. Smith, 86.
60. This decoration was used in tsarist Russia and reintroduced during the war. The colors of the decoration—orange and black—were used without making a direct connection to the Orthodox saint himself, and the emphasis was on continuity between the tsarist, Soviet, and post-Soviet phases of Russian history. At this point, the pattern only appeared on official decorations and was not worn by individuals in the form of a ribbon.
61. R. W. Davies, *Soviet History in the Yeltsin Era* (London: Palgrave Macmillan, 1997).
75. See footage from the parade on RedSamurai84, "Russian Army Parade, Victory Day 1995 Parad Pobedy (Victory Parade)," May 14, 2016, YouTube video, 56:49, https://www.youtube.com/watch?v=EQpLO4CWj18.
62. K. Smith, *Mythmaking*, 83.
63. Until 2000 VTSIOM and the Levada-Center were the same institute, hence their data for the 1990s are the same, but some of it, like the popularity of November 7, is available on the VTSIOM website and not on the Levada-Center website. See VTSIOM (website), "Kakiye iz sleduyushchikh prazdnikov dlya vas samyye vazhny?," accessed April 1, 2017, https://bd.wciom.ru/zh/print_q.php?s_id=393&q_id=32024&date=15.03.1998.
64. Illya Varlamov, "Piter glazami Putina v smutnoye vremya (1990–1991 gody)," comment on *Make Russia Warm Again* (blog), December 20, 2015, https://varlamov.ru/1268819.html.
65. Illya Varlamov, "Progulka po Moskve 1991 god," comment on *Make Russia Warm Again* (blog), December 20, 2014, https://varlamov.ru/1222852.html.
66. K. Smith, *Mythmaking*, 81.
67. Varlamov, "Progulka po Moskve 1991 goda."
68. Varlamov.
69. K. Smith, *Mythmaking*, 81. Varlamov, "Progulka po Moskve 1991 goda."
70. K. Smith, *Mythmaking*, 82.
71. Decree of the President of the Russian Federation No. 1537 "Odne soglasiya i primireniya," Presidential Administration, November 7, 1996.
72. K. Smith, *Mythmaking*, 84.
73. Unpublished archive materials from the Levada-Center.
74. Varlamov, "Progulka po Moskve 1991 god."
75. Giddens, *Modernity and Self-Identity*, 1.
76. *Izvestia*, "Ubyvayushchaya nostal'giya," December 24, 2001.
77. Yulia Larina, "Krasno-belo-goluboy ogonek," *Kommersant*, December 26, 2005.
78. Larina, "Krasno-belo-goluboy ogonek."
79. Efremova, "Gosudarstvennyy prazdniki."
80. Radchenko and Kuzmira, "Prazdnik novogo goda," 131.
81. Radchenko and Kuzmina, 132.
82. Zygmunt Bauman, "Consuming Life," *Journal of Consumer Culture* 1, no. 1 (2001): 9.
83. *Vogue Rossiia*, "Luchshiye podarki k 8 Marta," March 1999.

84. Mikhail Alekseev, "Novyye prazdniki postsovetskoy Rossii," Postnauka (website), January 13, 2016, video, 15:31, https://postnauka.ru/video/57319; for photos of Zheleznogorsk City Day in 1993, see Ilya Varlamov, "Rozhdeniye Imperii," comment on *Make Russia Warm Again* (blog), December 20, 2016, http://varlamov.ru/1596036.html.

85. Varlamov, "Rozhdeniye Imperii."

86. Ilya Varlamov, "Ty pomnish', kak vse nachinalos'? Kak Moskva otmechala 850," comment on *Make Russia Warm Again* (blog), September 6, 2015, http://varlamov.ru/1451877.html.

87. Schleifman, "Introduction," 7.

88. Bauman, "Consuming Life," 15. Giddens also asserted the importance of "the notion of lifestyle" as "increasingly important in the constitution of self identity." See Giddens, *Modernity and Self-Identity*, 5.

89. Bauman, *Liquid Times*, 82.

90. Bauman, 84.

91. Levada-Center, *Obshchestvennoye Mneniye—2011. Yezhegodnik* (Moscow: Levada-Center, 2012).

92. Stephen White, Ian McAllister, and Olga Kryshtanovskaya, "Religion and Politics in Postcommunist Russia," *Religion, State and Society* 22, no. 1 (1994): 82, http://dx.doi.org/10.1080/09637499408431625; Dubin, "Massovaya religioznaya kul'tura," 40.

93. Dubin, 40.

94. Aleksandr Verkhovsky, "The Role of the Russian Orthodox Church in Nationalist, Xenophobic and Antiwestern Tendencies in Russia Today: Not Nationalism, but Fundamentalism," *Religion, State and Society* 30, no. 4 (2002): 336, http://dx.doi.org/10.1080/0963749022000022879; Zoe Knox, *Russian Society and the Orthodox Church: Religion in Russia after Communism* (New York: Routledge, 2005), 134.

95. Knox, *Russian Society*, 137, 42.

96. Muslims constituted the largest religious minority, but in the 1990s only a small proportion identified as believers in Islam. In 1991, 1 percent identified as Muslim; in 1992, 2 percent; by 2000, it was 4 percent. See Levada-Center. "Religioznaya vera v Rossii," last modified September 26, 2011, https://www.levada.ru/2011/09/26/religioznaya-vera-v-rossii/.

97. Etzioni, "Holiday Rituals," 5.

98. Etzioni, 5.

99. Olga Atroshenko, Yulia Krivoshhapoa, and Ksenija Osipova, *Russkiy Narodnyy Kalendar'. Etnolingvisticheskiy Slovar'* (Moscow: AST, 2015), 304.

100. Atroshenko, Krivoshhapoa, and Osipova, *Russkiy Narodnyy Kalendar'*, 250.

101. Alexei Grazhdankin, head of research at the Levada-Center, noted that questions about religious holidays were not the focus of the center's research agenda in the 1990s and results are somewhat irregular. Alexei Grazhdankin, pers. comm., March 2017.

102. Unpublished archive materials from the Levada-Center.

103. Unpublished archive materials from the Levada-Center.

104. Unpublished archive materials from the Levada-Center.

105. Sivolap, *Kniga o vkusnoy*, 287–88.

106. Unpublished archive materials from the Levada-Center.

107. Levada-Center, "Rossiyane o religii," last modified December 24, 2013, http://www.levada.ru/2013/12/24/rossiyane-o-religii/.
108. White, McAllister, and Kryshtanovskaya, "Religion and Politics," 148–49.
109. Yurchak, *Everything Was Forever*, 22–23.

6. Putin's National Calendar

1. Svetlana Boym, *The Future of Nostalgia* (New York: Basic Books, 2001), 59.
2. Efremova, "Gosudarstvennyy prazdniki."
3. Valerie Sperling, "Making the Public Patriotic: Militarism and Anti-Militarism in Russia," in *Russian Nationalism and the National Reassertion of Russia*, ed. Marlene Laruelle (Oxford: Routledge, 2009), 245.
4. Efremova, "Gosudarstvennyy prazdniki."
5. RFE/RL, "Duma Approves New List of Military Celebrations," November 19, 2003, https://www.rferl.org/a/1143044.html.
6. The Time of Troubles (1598–1613) was a period between the end of the Rurik dynasty and the establishment of the Romanov dynasty in 1613, which ruled Russia until the 1917 Revolution. During this period, Russia lacked a legitimate ruler. In 1610, the Poles, amid internal political turmoil, invaded Russia and took over Moscow. In 1611–1612, a united effort between the Russian estates (Cossacks, town dwellers, and local nobility), led by Prince Dmitry Mikhailovich Pozharsky and the merchant Kuzma Minin, expelled the Poles from Moscow. A year later Michael Romanov was elected tsar, starting a dynasty that ruled Russia for hundreds of years and established the Russian Empire. In tsarist times, the date was commemorated with the Orthodox holiday—the Feast of our Lady of Kazan (which took place on November 5). In post-Soviet Russia, it acquired a military character—marking the successful campaign to eject a foreign invader from Moscow. See Efremova, "Gosudarstvennyy prazdniki"; Sperling, "Making the Public Patriotic," 257.
7. Ukaz Prezidenta Rossiyskoy Federatsii No. 549, "Ob ustanovlenii prof essional'nykh prazdnikov i pamyatnykh dney v Vooruzhennykh Silakh Rossiyskoy Federatsii ot 31.05.2006," Presidential Administration, 2006.
8. RedSamurai84, "HD Russian Army Parade, Victory Day 2005," May 13, 2010, YouTube video, 1:37:10, https://www.youtube.com/watch?v=L87HUIDcyL4.
9. RedSamurai84, "HD Russian Army Parade."
10. RedSamurai84.
11. In 2001–2004, veterans watched the parade from the audience.
12. RedSamurai84, "HD Russian Army Parade."
13. RIA Novosti, "Terakt V Kaspiyske na prazdnovanii Dnya Pobedy v 2002 godu," May 9, 2012, https://ria.ru/20120509/642029750.html.
14. Elena Ivanova, "V gorode Kaspiyske sovershen terakt—postradali okolo 20 chelovek, yest' pogibshiye," RIA Novosti, May 9, 2002, https://ria.ru/20020509/139364.html.
15. Moshe Gammer, "Nationalism and History: Rewriting the Chechen National Past," in *Secession, History and the Social Sciences*, ed. Bruno Coppieters and Michel Huysseune (Brussels: VUB Brussels University Press, 2002), 130.
16. Gammer, "Nationalism and History," 130.

17. RIA Novosti, "Den Pobedy," accessed June 20, 2015, http://www.9may.ru.

18. Anatoly Korolev and Dmitry Kosyrev, "National Symbolism in Russia: The Old and the New," *Sputnik News*, June 11, 2007.

19. Gennadiy Ivanov, "Slyamzili! Nekrasivaya Istoriya S Bessmertnym Polkom," comment on *Gennadiy Ivanov* (blog), Otkrytaya Rossiya (website), May 17, 2015, https://openrussia.org/post/view/7259/.

20. Ivanov, "Slyamzili!"

21. TASS, "V aktsii 'Bessmertnyy Polk' v Tomske 9 Maya mogut prinyat' uchastiye do 60 tys. Chelovek," May 5, 2016, https://tass.ru/sibir-news/3260160.

22. Mikhail Gabowitsch, "Are Copycats Subversive? Strategy-31, the Russian Runs, the Immortal Regiment, and the Transformative Potential of Non-Hierarchical Movements," *Problems of Post-Communism* 5, no. 5 (2018): 306, http://dx.doi.org/10.1080/10758216.2016.1250604.

23. Putin started to wear the Georgian ribbon on Victory Day from the time of the 2007 parade. See RedSamurai84, "Russian Army Parade, Victory Day 2007 Parad Pobedy (Victory Parade)," May 14, 2016, YouTube video, 53:44, https://www.youtube.com/watch?v=zoF6juLCGas.

24. Wood, "Performing Memory," 193.

25. Goscilo and Strukov, *Celebrity and Glamour*, 1; Peter Finn, "Designer to the Russian Military, Dressing to Kill," *Washington Post*, May 22, 2008.

26. Wood, "Performing Memory," 192.

27. Levada-Center, *Obshchestvennoye Mneniye—2015. Yezhegodnik* (Moscow: Levada-Center, 2016).

28. Obshchestvennoye grazhdansko-patrioticheskoye dvizheniya Bessmertnyy polk Rossii, "Istoriya Bessmertnogo Polka Rossii," accessed December 20, 2017, https://polkrf.ru/about/.

29. RFE/RL, "Ukraine Bans Russian St. George Ribbon," June 12, 2017, https://www.rferl.org/a/ukraine-bans-russian-st-george-ribbon/28542973.html.

30. The RIA Novosti news agency ran a competition for best Instagram photos of the Georgian ribbon. See RIA Novosti, "Luchshiye potografii konkursa 'Georgiyevskaya Lentochka' v Instagram," May 12, 2014, https://ria.ru/20140512/1007474075.html.

31. For examples, see the Instagram account for Doni.Blackstar, https://www.instagram.com/doni.blackstar/.

32. There are several studies that underline that Russian public and political practices are often neither progovernment nor antigovernment but that people cooperate with government-endorsed initiatives for a variety of reasons. See Julia Hemment, *Youth Politics in Putin's Russia: Producing Patriots and Entrepreneurs* (Bloomington: Indiana University Press, 2015); Mikhail Gabowitsch, "Pamyatnik I Prazdnik: Etnografiya Dnya Pobedy," *Neprikosnovennyy Zapas* 101, no. 3 (2015), http://www.nlobooks.ru/node/6370.

33. Daniil Dondurey, Karina Pipia, and Valery Fyodorov, "Kakikh Vsenarodnyh Prazdnikov Ne Hvataet Strane?," interview by Yuri Kobaladze and Svetlana Sorokina, *Vkruge Sveta*, Radio Echo Moskvy, November 18, 2016, http://echo.msk.ru/programs/sorokina/1869714-echo/.

34. Sorokina, Khakamada, and Holin, "Operatsiya po podchineniyu."

35. For more on the New Generation Wars, see Valeri Gerasimov, "Tsennost' nauki v predvidenii: novyye vyzovy trebuyut pereosmyslit' formy i sposoby vedeniya boyevykh deystviy," *Voyeno-promeshlineyi Kurier*, February 26, 2013, https://www.vpk-news.ru/articles/1463; Sergey G. Chekinov and Sergey A. Bogdanov, "The Nature and Content of a New-Generation War," *Military Thought*, no. 4 (2013): 12.

36. my3rd3y3, "Weapons of Mass Deception," March 6, 2012, YouTube video, 1:38:07, https://www.youtube.com/watch?v=wkkAXkhKg98.

37. my3rd3y3, "Weapons of Mass Deception."

38. In the 2000s, the holiday had 9–12 percent popularity. Information from unpublished archive materials from the Levada-Center.

39. Kremlin (website), "Vladimir Putin v Den' Zashchitnika Otechestva posetil voyennyy klinicheskiy gospital' Imeni Burdenko," last modified February 23, 2003, http://kremlin.ru/events/president/news/28215.

40. Sperling, "Making the Public Patriotic," 226; deti.mail.ru, "23 Fevralya: Zachem Nam Vospitaniye Patriotizma?," last modified 2016, accessed March 25, 2018, https://deti.mail.ru/teenager/23-fevralya-zachem-nam-vospitanie-patriotizma/.

41. The second war in Chechnya was viewed more favorably, but the shadow of controversy over human rights abuses and terrorist attacks in Russia was inescapable.

42. V. Lukin, "Chto dlya grazhdanina pravo, to dlya chinovnika dolg," *Rossiiskaya Gazeta*, January 31, 2005.

43. Daria Kultareva, "Chto podarit' muzhchine 23 fevralya," *GQ Russia*, February 18, 2018.

44. Gammer, "Nationalism and History," 130; Karina Gadzhieva, "In Chechnya, Authorities Equal Memory of Deportation Day to Dissent," Caucasian Knot (website), February 23, 2016, http://www.eng.kavkaz-uzel.eu/articles/34687/.

45. Liz Fuller, "Chechens Seek Ways to Circumvent Ban on Commemorating 1944 Deportation," RFE/RL, March 2, 2018, https://www.rferl.org/a/chechens-seek-ways-to-circumvent-deportation-commemoration-ban/29073203.html.

46. Demokraticheskiy soyuz (website), "Manifestatsiya Protiv Voyny V Chechne 23 Fevralya 2005 g," accessed January 9, 2018, http://ds.ru/antiv5.htm.

47. Fuller, "Chechens Seek Ways."

48. Fuller.

49. Ukaz Prezidenta Rossiyskoy Federatsii No. 549.

50. RIA Novosti, "Desantniki otmechayut svoy professional'nyy prazdnik," August 2, 2006, https://ria.ru/20140802/1018517032.html.

51. Regnum, "'Inzhir Ne Nuzhen!': Byvshiye desantniki izbili smuglykh torgovtsev na tsentral'nom rynke Novosibirska," August 2, 2006, https://regnum.ru/news/683181.html; Grigory Krasovski, "V den' VDV desantniki ustroili draku v tsentre Irkutska (Foto)," *Gazeta Irkutsk*, August 4, 2014, http://www.gazetairkutsk.ru/2010/08/04/id20456/.

52. "'Voyska dyadi Vasi' budut i dal'she gulyat' b parke Gor'kogo," editorial, RIA Novosti, August 2, 2016, https://ria.ru/defense_safety/20160802/1473414227.html.

53. Natalie Zemon Davis, *Society and Culture in Early Modern France: Eight Essays* (London: Duckworth, 1975), 97.

54. Unpublished archive materials from the Levada-Center.

55. Denis Zuev, "The Russian March: Investigating the Symbolic Dimension of Political Performance in Modern Russia," *Europe-Asia Studies* 65, no. 1 (2013): 102, http://dx.doi.org/10.1080/09668136.2012.738800.

56. Brian Whitmore and Maksim Yaroshevsky, "Antifa Takes on Nationalists in Russian Youth's Civil War," RFE/RL, November 20, 2009, https://www.rferl.org/a/Antifa_Takes_On_Nationalists_In_Russian_Youths_Civil_War/1883674.html.

57. Zuev, "Russian March," 110.

58. Moscow Patriarchate (website), "Prezident Rossii V. V. Putin posetil svayteyshego patriarha Aleksiya v ego rezidencii v peredelkine," accessed May 9, 2017, https://mospat.ru/archive/2003/05/nr305101/.

59. Marlene Laruelle, *Beyond Anti-Westernism: The Kremlin's Narrative about Russia's European Identity and Mission* (PONARS Eurasia, policy memo 326, Washington, DC, August 2014).

60. During Soviet rule, the Russian Orthodox Church split into two—the Moscow Patriarchate and the Russian Orthodox Church abroad, which was followed by immigrant communities and did not recognize the hierarchies of Moscow. In 2007, the two churches united their hierarchies. See Moscow Patriarchate (website), "Prezident Rossii vstretilsya so svyateyshim Patriarhom Moskovskim i vseja Rusi Aleksiem II i pervoierarhom Russkoy zarubezhnoi Cerkvi Mitropolitom Lavrom," accessed May 9, 2017, https://mospat.ru/archive/2004/05/7013-1/; Natalya Kongina, "Vremja Sobirat Tserkvi," *Rossisskaya Gezeta*, May 18, 2007.

61. Kremlin (website), "Vladimir Putin prisutstvoval na Rozhdestvenskom bogosluzhenii v Novoiyerusalimskom monastyre," last modified January 7, 2007, http://kremlin.ru/events/president/news/36993.

62. Zoe Knox, "Russian Orthodoxy, Russian Nationalism, and Patriarch Aleksii II," *Nationalities Papers* 33, no. 4 (2005): 540, http://dx.doi.org/10.1080/00905990500354004.

63. Elena Stepanova, "'The Spiritual and Moral Foundation of Civilization in Every Nation for Thousands of Years': The Traditional Values Discourse in Russia," *Politics, Religion and Ideology* 16, no. 2–3 (2015): 219, http://dx.doi.org/10.1080/21567689.2015.1068167.

64. Laruelle, *Russian Eurasianism*, 24.

65. Traditional religions in Russia include Chritianity, Islam, Buddhism, and Judaism, as was articulated in Federal Law of the Russian Federation No. 125-F3, "On Freedom of Conscience and Religious Associations," Federal Council of the Russian Federation, September 26, 1997.

66. RIA Novosti, "Putin: prazdniki v Rossii mozhno otmechat' kruglyy god," September 20, 2017, https://ria.ru/20170920/1505178633.html.

67. Cnaan Lipshiz, "Why Putin Embraces Russia's Jews, but Not Its Gays," *Times of Israel*, September 15, 2015.

68. Katja Sarajea, "'You Know What Kind of Place This Is, Don't You?' An Exploration of Lesbian Spaces in Moscow," in *Cultural Diversity in Russian Cities: The Urban Landscape in the Post-Soviet Era*, ed. Gordula Gdaniec (New York: Berghahn Books, 2013), 140.

69. Alexander Mihailovic, "Wings of Desire: The Changing Meaning of Same-Sex Desire in Putin's and Medvedev's Russia," in *The Meaning of Sexual Identity in the Twenty-First Century*, ed. Judith S. Kaufman and David A. Powell (Newcastle upon Tyne, UK: Cambridge Scholars, 2014), 118.

70. VTSIOM (website), "Press-Vypusk #2320 Zakon O Propagande Gomoseksualizma: Za I Protiv," accessed June 6, 2017, https://wciom.ru/index.php?id=236&uid=114190.

71. According to the Levada-Center, Valentine's Day became popular in Russia, and by 2006, 37 percent of respondents said that they celebrated the holiday, while almost 90 percent recognized it. Polling results from unpublished archive materials from the Levada-Center.

72. Interfax, "Svetlana Medvedeva Schitaet Vazhnym Vozrozhdenie Traditzii Prazdnovaniya Dnya Svyatyh Petra I Fevronii," July 9, 2008, https://pravoslavie.ru/27112.html.

73. Levada-Center, "Rossiyane o religii."

74. Levada-Center, *Levada Public Opinion 2012 Yearbook* (Moscow: Levada Centre, 2012), 164.

75. "Religioznaya vera v Rossii."

76. Levada-Center, *Obshchestvennoye Mneniye 2015* (Moscow: Levada-Center, 2012).

77. Unpublished archive materials from the Levada-Center.

78. Unpublished archive materials from the Levada-Center.

79. Unpublished archive materials from the Levada-Center.

80. In Dondurey, Pipia, and Fyodorov, "Kakikh Vsenarodnyh Prazdnikov."

81. Levada-Centee, *Obshchestvennoye Mneniye—2015*.

82. Larisa Butyl'skaya, "Sotsiokul'turnye aspekty izucheniya Russkoy novogodney otkrytki," *Gumanitarnyy Vektor 36*, no. 4 (2013): 146, https://cyberleninka.ru/article/n/sotsiokulturnye-aspekty-izucheniya-russkoy-novogodney-otkrytki.

83. Butyl'skaya, "Sotsiokul'turnye aspekty," 147.

84. Nika Belotserkovskaya, *V so Pod Yëlku. Moi Lyubimyye Retsepty K Prazdnichnomu Stolu* (Moscow: Eskimo, 2016), 44, 56, 62, 122.

85. Belotserkovskaya, *V so Pod Yëlku*, 50, 76, 88, 78, 90.

86. Novy god Israeli (website), "Novy god Israeli," accessed March 20, 2018. http://www.novygodisraeli.com/.

87. Anna Liesowska, "The Siberian Phenomenon of 'Monstrating,'" *Siberian Times*, May 1, 2013, http://siberiantimes.com/other/others/news/the-siberian-phenomenon-of-monstrating/.

88. *Ward No. 6* is an Anton Chekhov play about a mental institution.

89. Liesowska, "Siberian Phenomenon of 'Monstrating.'"

90. Lenta.ru, "V Novosibirske studenty vstretili 1 Maya prizyvami Ktulhu," May 1, 2009, https://lenta.ru/news/2009/05/01/novosib. (Cthulhu is a character from the science-fiction book *The Call of the Cthulhu*.)

91. Ben Judah referred to the rise of the non-Soviet generation in Russia—young people who are no longer molded by the Soviet experience. See in Ben Judah, *Fragile Empire: How Russia Fell in and out of Love with Vladimir Putin* (New Haven, CT: Yale University Press, 2013).

92. Timothy Snyder, *The Road to Unfreedom: Russia, Europe, America* (New York: Penguin Random House, 2018).

93. Gosindex.ru, *V glavnoy roli, Putin v sovremennoi culture* (Moscow: Gosindex.ru, 2016).

94. Wood, "Performing Memory," 175.

95. In 2002 the girl band Poyushchiye Vmeste released a song "Takovo, kak Putin" (Like Putin), describing him as a new idol of masculinity and admiration. In 2008 the Russian pop singer Natali performed this song on Russian federal television, popularizing it further. KARLOSPETROS, "Natali: Takogo, Kak Putin," March 22, 2009, YouTube video, 2:48, https://www.youtube.com/watch?v=hUh9pThGdm4.

96. Stephen Hutchings and Vera Tolz, *Nation, Ethnicity and Race on Russian Television: Mediating Post-Soviet Difference* (London: Routledge, 2015), 5.

Epilogue

1. Pelevin, *Babylon*, 173.

2. Michael Khodarkovsky, "Russia's Age-Old Question: Who Are We?," *New York Times*, May 18, 2017.

3. Lillia Shevtsova, "Humiliation as a Tool of Blackmail," *American National Interest*, June 2, 2015,

4. Brubaker, *Nationalism Reframed*, 1.

5. *The Economist*, "A Bigger World: A Special Report on Globalisation," September 20, 2008.

6. Gideon Rachman, "Nationalism Is Back," *The Economist*, November 5, 2014.

7. Paul Mason, *Postcapitalism: A Guide to Our Future* (London: Penguin Books, 2016), x.

8. Curtis, "Hypernormalisation"; Peter Pomerantsev, "How Putin Became the Che Guevara of the Right," Politico, March 11, 2016, https://www.politico.eu/article/how-vladimir-putin-russia-became-che-guevara-of-right-wing/; Owen Matthews, "Alexander Dugin and Steve Bannon's Ideological Ties to Vladimir Putin's Russia," *Newsweek*, April 17, 2017.

9. Giddens, *Modernity and Self-Identity*.

10. Bauman, *Liquid Modernity*.

11. Themes of imitation have been widely cited by researchers of Russia, such as Andrew Wilson, Arkady Ostrovsky, and Peter Pomerantsev. Arkady Ostrovsky, "Inside the Bear," *The Economist*, October 22, 2016; Wilson, *Virtual Politics*; Pomerantsev, *Nothing Is True*.

12. Tolz and Hutchings warned against the breaking apart of Russian society and the creation of two. See Hutchings and Tolz, *Nation, Ethnicity and Race*, 1.

13. Howard Amos, "Corps Couture: The Rise of Russia's Patriotic Fashion Industry," *Moscow Times*, August 15, 2016.

14. Peter Pomerantsev, "The Hidden Author of Putinism," *The Atlantic*, November 7, 2014.

15. *Moscow Times*, "Russia 'Not Ready' for Law Uniting Nation's Ethnic Groups, Says Expert," March 7, 2017.

16. Mason, *Postcapitalism*, ix.

Bibliography

Abrahamian, Atossa Araxia. *The Cosmopolites: The Coming of the Global Citizen.* New York: Columbia Global Reports, 2015.
Afidjamov, Rustam. "Midl i natsional'naya ideya." *Izvestia*, August 15, 1998.
Akintev, Romanus. "7 Noyabrya 1982." September 22, 2012, YouTube video, 3:21. https://www.youtube.com/watch?v=FWuRxkzGoBA.
Al-Jazeera. "Zygmunt Bauman: Behind the World's Crisis of Humanity." July 3, 2016. https://www.aljazeera.com/program/talk-to-al-jazeera/2016/7/23/zygmunt-bauman-behind-the-worlds-crisis-of-humanity.
Alekseev, Mikhail. "Novyye prazdniki postsovetskoy Rossii." Postnauka (website), January 13, 2016, video, 15:31. https://postnauka.ru/video/57319.
Alexievich, Svetlana. *Secondhand Time: The Last of the Soviets.* London: Fitzcarraldo Editions, 2016.
Ambrosetti Tafuro Eleonora. "Russia's Great Disease: The Demographic Decline." Italian Institute for International Political Studies (ISPI), November 4, 2019. https://www.ispionline.it/en/pubblicazione/russias-great-disease-demographic-decline-24313.
Amos, Howard. "Corps Couture: The Rise of Russia's Patriotic Fashion Industry." *Moscow Times*, August 15, 2016.
Anderson, Benedict. *Imagined Communities: Reflections on the Origin and Spread of Nationalism.* London: Verso, 2006.
Andreev, Nikolai, and Victor Litovkin. "Ne day Bog uvidet'sya cherez liniyu fronta." *Izvestia*, April 14, 1992.
antik.ws. "Boris Nadezhdin i Vl. Zhirinovskiy K Bar'yeru!" September 18, 2011, YouTube video, 1:01:38. https://www.youtube.com/watch?v=b3fXeuIn7e8&t=1608s.
Antonenko, Oksana. "Frozen Uncertainty: Russia and the Conflict over Abkhazia." In *Statehood and Security: Georgia after the Rose Revolution,* edited by Bruno Coppieters and Robert Legvold, 205–69. Cambridge: MIT Press, 2005.
Antushenina, Svetlana. "Grazhdanstvo po sobesedovaniyu." Lenta.ru, April 21, 2014. https://lenta.ru/articles/2014/04/21/grajdanstvo/.
Applebaum, Anne. "Russia's Ongoing Identity Crisis." *Telegraph*, September 22, 2002.
Aslund, Anders. *Russia's Capitalist Revolution: Why Market Reform Succeeded and Democracy Failed.* Washington, DC: Peterson Institute for International Economics, 2007.

Atroshenko, Olga, Yulia Krivoshhapoa, and Kseniya Osipova. *Russkiy narodnyy kalendar'. Etnolingvisticheskiy slovar'*. Moscow: AST, 2015.
Bablumian, Sergey. "Kto Khochet Otmenit' Den' Pobedy." *Izvestia*, January 3, 1991.
Baburin, Sergey. *Mir imperii. Territoriya, gosudarstva i mirovoii poryadok*. Moscow: Yuridichiskiy Tsentre, 2005.
Bacon, Edwin, Bettina Renz, and Julian Cooper. *Securitising Russia: The Domestic Politics of Vladimir Putin*. Manchester: Manchester University Press, 2006.
Barkey, Karen, and Mark von Hagen, eds. *After Empire: Multiethnic Societies and Nation-Building: The Soviet Union and the Russian, Ottoman, and Habsburg Empires*. Boulder, CO: Westview, 1997.
Bauböck, Rainer. "Studying Citizenship Constellations." *Journal of Ethnic and Migration Studies* 36, no. 5 (2010): 847–59. http://dx.doi.org/10.1080/13691831003764375.
Bauman, Zygmunt. "Consuming Life." *Journal of Consumer Culture* 1, no. 1 (2001): 9–29. https://doi.org/10.1177/146954050100100102.
———. "Identity in the Globalizing World." *Social Anthropology* 9, no. 2 (2001): 121–29. http://dx.doi.org/doi:10.1111/j.1469-8676.2001.tb00141.x.
———. *Liquid Modernity*. Cambridge: Polity, 2012.
———. *Liquid Times: Living in an Age of Uncertainty*. Cambridge: Polity, 2007.
———. "Wars of the Globalization Era." *European Journal of Social Theory* 4, no. 1 (2001): 11–28. http://dx.doi.org/10.1177/13684310122224966.
Bauman, Zygmunt, and Benedetto Vecchi. *Identity: Conversations with Benedetto Vecchi*. Cambridge: Polity, 2004.
BBC. "How Is the Migrant Crisis Dividing EU Countries?" September 19, 2015. https://www.bbc.co.uk/news/world-europe-34278886.
———. "Putin Blamed for TV Shutdown." January 22, 2002. http://news.bbc.co.uk/1/hi/world/europe/1775302.stm.
———. "Putin Deplores Collapse of USSR." April 25, 2005. http://news.bbc.co.uk/2/hi/4480745.stm.
———. "Russian Anti-US Feeling Grows." April 24, 1999. http://news.bbc.co.uk/1/hi/world/europe/327202.stm.
———. "Yeltsin Attacks Putin over Anthem." December 7, 2000. http://news.bbc.co.uk/1/hi/world/europe/1059784.stm.
Beck, Ulrich. *Risk Society: Towards a New Modernity*. London: Sage, 1992.
Becker, Charles M., Erbolat N. Musabek, Ai-Gul S. Seitenova, and Dina S. Urzhumova. "The Migration Response to Economic Shock: Lessons from Kazakhstan." *Journal of Comparative Economics* 33, no. 1 (2005): 107–32. http://dx.doi.org/10.1016/j.jce.2004.12.003.
Belotserkovskaya, Nika. *Vso Pod Yëlku. Moi Lyubimyye Retsepty K Prazdnichnomu Stolu*. Moscow: Eskimo, 2016.
Bertilsson, Margareta. "The Theory of Structuration: Prospects and Problems." In *Anthony Giddens: Critical Assessments*, edited by Christopher Bryant and David Jary, 44–61. London: Routledge, 1997.
Billig, Michael. *Banal Nationalism*. London: Sage, 1995.
Blackstar Wear (website). "Futbolka Luchshiy Drug." Accessed December 20, 2017. https://blackstarwear.ru/product/10790-219/.

Bocharova, Svetlana, and Farida Rustamova. "Vstupil v silu zakon o vtorom grazhdanstve." *RBC*, August 4, 2014. https://www.rbc.ru/politics/09/02/2021/6022a17e9a7947810ec2cfa8.
Borodin, Vladimir. "Vadim Gustov: ot pravitel'stva nam ne nado ni odnogo lishnego rublya." *Izvestia*, May 13, 1998.
Boym, Svetlana. *The Future of Nostalgia*. New York: Basic Books, 2001.
Breeze, Ruth. "Critical Discourse Analysis and Its Critics." *Pragmatics*, no. 214 (2011): 493–525. https://doi.org/0.1075/prag.21.4.01bre.
Breslauer, George W. *Gorbachev and Yeltsin as Leaders*. Cambridge: Cambridge University Press, 2002.
Brown, Archie. *The Gorbachev Factor*. Oxford: Oxford University Press, 1996.
Brubaker, Rogers. *Citizenship and Nationhood in France and Germany*. Cambridge, MA: Harvard University Press, 1992.
———. "Citizenship Struggles in the Soviet Successor States." *International Migration Review* 26, no. 2 (1992): 269–91.
———. *Nationalism Reframed: Nationhood and the National Question in the New Europe*. Cambridge: Cambridge University Press, 2009.
Brudny, Yitzhak M. *Reinventing Russia: Russian Nationalism and the Soviet State, 1953–1991*. Cambridge, MA: Harvard University Press, 1998.
Bunimovich, Yevgeniy. "Voyny ne zakanchivayutsya. Oni prosto stanut pamyat'yu." *Novaya Gazeta*, June 23, 1997.
Butyl'skaya, Larisa. "Sotsiokul'turnye aspekty izucheniya Russkoy novogodney otkrytki." *Gumanitarnyy Vektor* 36, no. 4 (2013): 141–48. https://cyberleninka.ru/article/n/sotsiokulturnye-aspekty-izucheniya-russkoy-novogodney-otkrytki.
Chatterjeee, Choi. *Celebrating Women: Gender, Festival Culture, and Bolshevik Ideology, 1910–1939*. Pittsburgh: University of Pittsburgh Press, 2002.
Chazan, Guy. "Putin Favours Restoring Soviet National Anthem." *Telegraph*, October 15, 2000.
Chekinov, Sergey G., and Sergey A. Bogdanov. "The Nature and Content of a New-Generation War." *Military Thought*, no. 4 (2013): 12–23.
Chernov, Andrei. "Yel'tsin pokhoronil perestroyku, Putin reanimiroval perelitsovku." *Novaya Gazeta*, October 23, 2000.
Chernyavsky, V. C. *Instruktsiya ot 22.08.2000 o dokumentirovanii vidami na zhitel'stvo*. Moscow: Ministry of the Interior, August 8, 2000, no. 1/15651.
Chouliaraki, Lilie, and Norman Fairclough. *Discourse in Late Modernity: Rethinking Critical Discourse Analysis*. Edinburgh: Edinburgh University Press, 1999.
CNN. "Yeltsin Warns of Possible World War over Kosovo." April 9, 1999. http://edition.cnn.com/WORLD/europe/9904/09/kosovo.diplomacy.02/.
Cohen, Roger. "Russia's Weimar Syndrome." *New York Times*, May 1, 2014.
csc302. "Discussion on Globalization." October 30, 2006, YouTube video, 10:58. https://www.youtube.com/watch?v=AHJPSLgHemM.
Curtis, Adam. "Hypernormalisation." BBC, October 16, 2016, video, 2:46. https://www.bbc.co.uk/programmes/p04b183c.
Daughtry, J. Martin. "Russia's New Anthem and the Negotiation of National Identity." *Ethnomusicology* 47, no. 1 (2003): 42–67. http://dx.doi.org/10.2307/852511.

Davies, R. W. *Soviet History in the Yeltsin Era*. London: Palgrave Macmillan, 1997.
Davies, William, and Aditya Chakrabortty. *The Limits of Neoliberalism: Authority, Sovereignty and the Logic of Competition*. Los Angeles: Sage, 2017.
Davis, Natalie Zemon. *Society and Culture in Early Modern France: Eight Essays*. London: Duckworth, 1975.
Dawisha, Karen. *Putin's Kleptocracy: Who Owns Russia?* New York: Simon & Schuster, 2014.
Dawisha, Karen, and Bruce Parrott. *Russia and the New States of Eurasia: The Politics of Upheaval*. Cambridge: Cambridge University Press, 1994.
De Waal, Thomas. "'Yeltsin Doctrine' Planned in Ex-USSR." *Moscow Times*, August 11, 1994.
——. "Zhirinovsky Sets Signature to Anti-Semitic Statement." *Moscow Times*, December 10, 1994.
DeBlasio, Alyssa. "The New-Year Film as a Genre of Post-War Russian Cinema." *Studies in Russian and Soviet Cinema* 2, no. 1 (2008): 43–61. http://dx.doi.org/10.1386/srsc.2.1.43_1.
Decree of the President of the Russian Federation No. 549. "Ob ustanovlenii professional'nykh prazdnikov i pamyatnykh dney v Vooruzhennykh Silakh Rossiyskoy Federatsii." Presidential Administration, May 31, 2006.
Decree of the President of the Russian Federation No. 637. "O merakh po okazaniyu sodeystviya dobrovol'nomu pereseleniyu v Rossiyskuyu Federatsiyu sootechestvennikov, prozhivayushchikh za rubezhom (vmeste s 'Gosudarstvennoy programmoy po okazaniyu sodeystviya dobrovol'nomu pereseleniyu v Rossiyskuyu Federatsiyu sootechestvennikov, prozhivayushchikh za rubezhom')." Presidential Administration, June 22, 2006.
Decree of the President of the Russian Federation No. 1537 "Odne soglasiya i primireniya." Presidential Administration, November 7, 1996.
Demokraticheskiy soyuz (website). "Manifestatsiya Protiv Voyny V Chechne 23 Fevralya 2005." Last modified 2005, accessed January 9, 2018. http://ds.ru/antiv5.htm.
Dergachev, Vladimir, Eugeni Safronov, and Dimitri Evstifeev. "V Rossiyu s lyubov'yu." Gazeta.ru, April 1, 2014. https://www.gazeta.ru/politics/2014/04/01_a_5972817.shtml.
Deti.mail.ru. "23 Fevralya: Zachem Nam Vospitaniye Patriotizma?" Last modified 2016, accessed March 25, 2018. https://deti.mail.ru/teenager/23-fevralya-zachem-nam-vospitanie-patriotizma/.
Dmitrieva, Galina K., and Igor I. Lukashuk. "The Russian Federation Law on Citizenship." *Review of Central and East European Law* 19, no. 3 (1993): 267–92.
Dondurey, Daniil, Karina Pipia, and Valery Fyodorov. "Kakikh Vsenarodnyh Prazdnikov Ne Hvataet Strane?" Interview by Yuri Kobaladze and Svetlana Sorokina, *V kruge Sveta*, Radio Echo Moskvy, November 18, 2016. http://echo.msk.ru/programs/sorokina/1869714-echo/.
Doni. "Doni feat. Natali—Ty takoy (Prem'yera klipa, 2015)." October 29, 2015, YouTube video, 3:37. https://www.youtube.com/watch?v=5Fix7P6aGXQ.
Draft federal law of the State Duma of the Federal Assembly of the Russian Federation No. 461-2 "O Vnesenii Izmeneniy I Dopolneniy V Preambulu I

Stat'i 2, 12, 13 I 18 Zakona Rossiyskoy Federatsii O Grazhdanstve Rossiyskoy Federatsii." State Duma of the Federal Assembly of the Russian Federation, June 13, 1996.

Dubin, Boris. "Massovaya religioznaya kul'tura v rossii (Tendentsii v gody 1990-Kh Godov)." *Vestnik obshchestvennogo mneniya*, no. 3 (2004): 35–44. https://cyberleninka.ru/article/n/massovaya-religioznaya-kultura-v-rossii-tendentsii-i-itogi-1990-h-godov.

Durkheim, Emile. *The Elementary Forms of the Religious Life*. Translated by Joseph Ward Swain. Mineola, NY: Dover, 2008.

Dushechkina, Elena. *Russkaya yëlka: Istoriya, mifologiya, literatura*. St. Petersburg: European University in St. Petersburg Press, 2014.

The Economist. "A Bigger World: A Special Report on Globalisation." September 20, 2008.

Efremova, Valentina. "Gosudarstvennyy prazdniki kak instrumenty simvolicheskoy politiki v sovremennoy Rossii." PhD diss., Institute of Philosophy, Russian Academy of Sciences, 2014.

Ekman, Joakim. "Political Participation and Regime Stability: A Framework for Analyzing Hybrid Regimes." *International Political Science Review* 30, no. 1 (2009): 7–31. http://dx.doi.org/doi:10.1177/0192512108097054.

Enterprise Estonia. "Citizenship." Estonia.eu, last modified 2014, accessed April 11, 2014. http://estonia.eu/about-estonia/society/citizenship.html.

Etzioni, Amitai. "Holiday Rituals: Neglected Hotbeds of Virtue." In *We Are What We Celebrate: Understanding Holidays and Rituals*, edited by Amitai Etzioni and Jared Bloom, 3-40. New York: New York University Press, 2004.

EurActiv.com. "France Tries to Attract Higher Qualified Immigration." May 4, 2006. http://www.euractiv.com/innovation/france-tries-attract-higher-qualified-immigration/article-154938.

Evans, Christine E. *Between Truth and Time: A History of Soviet Central Television*. New Haven, CT: Yale University Press, 2016.

Fairclough, Norman. *Critical Discourse Analysis: The Critical Study of Language*. London: Routledge, 2010.

Federal Council of the Russian Federation. Stenogramma zasedaniy Soveta Federatsii, , May 15, 2002.

Federal Law of the Russian Federation No. 71-f3."O vnesenii izmeneniy v Federal'nyy zakon 'O grazhdanstve Rossiyskoy Federatsii' i otdel'nyye zakonodatel'nyye akty Rossiyskoy Federatsii." Federal Council of the Russian Federation, April 20, 2014.

Federal Law of the Russian Federation No.99-F3. "O gosudarstvennoy politike Rossiyskoy Federatsii v otnoshenii sootechestvennikov za rubezhom. Federal Council of the Russian Federation, May 24, 1999.

Federal Law of the RSFSR No. 1948-1. "Ograzhdanstve RSFSR," Congress of People's Deputies of the RSFSR, November 28, 1991.

Federal Law of the Russian Federation No. 5206-1. "O vnesenii izmeneniy i dopolneniy v zakon RSFSR "o grazhdanstve RSFSR," The Supreme Soviet, 1993.

Federal Law of the Russian Federation No. 13-3f. "O vnesenii izmeneniy v federal'nyy zakon o grazhdanstve Rossiykoy Federatsii." Federal Council of the Russian Federation, February 6, 1995.

Federal Law of the Russian Federation No. 125-F3. "On Freedom of Conscience and Religious Associations." Federal Council of the Russian Federation, September 26, 1997.

Federal Law of the Russian Federation No. 35431. "On Amendments and Additions to the Code of Laws of Labour in the RSFSR." The Supreme Soviet, 1992.

Federal Law of the Russian Federation N.5242-1. "On the Right of Citizens of the Russian Federation to the Freedom of Movement, the Choice of a Place of Stay and Residence within the Russian Federation." The Supreme Soviet, 1993.

Federal Law of the Russian Federation. No.202-FZ. "On Introducing the Amendments and Addenda to the Law of the Russian Federation on the Forced Migrants." Federal Council of the Russian Federation, December 20, 1995.

Federal Law of the Russian Federation No. 53-FZ. "About the State Language of the Russian Federation." Federal Council of the Russian Federation, 2005.

Federal Law of the Russian Federation No. 115-FZ. "Concerning the Legal Status of Foreign Citizens in the Russian Federation of July 25, 2002." Federal Council of the Russian Federation, 2002.

Federal Law of the Russian Federation No. 62-FZ. "On Citizenship of the Russian Federation." Federal Council of the Russian Federation, May 31, 2002.

Federal Law of the Russian Federation. "On Citizenship of the Russian Federation." As amended by Federal Laws No. 151-FZ as of November 11, 2003; No. 127-FZ as of November 2, 2004; No. 5-FZ as of January 3, 2006; No. 121-FZ as of July 18, 2006; No. 296-FZ as of December 1, 2007; No. 328-FZ as of December 4, 2007; No. 163-FZ as of October 1, 2008; No. 301-FZ as of December 30, 2008; No. 127-FZ as of June 28, 2009. Federal Council of the Russian Federation, June 28, 2009.

Federal Migration Services. "Gosudarstvennaya programma po okazaniyu sodeystviya dobrovol'nomu pereseleniyu v Rossiyskuyu Federatsiyu sootechestvennikov, prozhivayushchikh za rubezhom. Administrativnyye Protsedury." Moscow, 2009.

Federal Migration Services. "Gosudarstvennaya programma po okazaniyu sodeystviya dobrovol'nomu pereseleniyu v Rossiyskuyu Federatsiyu sootechestvennikov, prozhivayushchikh za rubezhom." Moscow, 2012.

Ferguson, Niall. "Look Back at Weimar—and Start to Worry about Russia." *Telegraph*, January 1, 2005.

Finn, Peter. "Designer to the Russian Military, Dressing to Kill." *Washington Post*, May 22, 2008.

Flynn, Moya. *Migrant Resettlement in the Russian Federation*. London: Anthem, 2004.

Fuller, Liz. "Chechens Seek Ways to Circumvent Ban on Commemorating 1944 Deportation." RFE/RL, March 2, 2018. https://www.rferl.org/a/chechens-seek-ways-to-circumvent-deportation-commemoration-ban/29073203.html.

Fyodorov, Valery. "Russian Identity and the Challenges of the Time." Valdai Discussion Club, August 19, 2013. http://valdaiclub.com/culture/61340.html.

Gabowitsch, Mikhail. "Are Copycats Subversive? Strategy-31, the Russian Runs, the Immortal Regiment, and the Transformative Potential of Non-Hierarchical

Movements." *Problems of Post-Communism* 65, no. 5 (2018): 297–314. http://dx.doi.org/10.1080/10758216.2016.1250604.
———. "Pamyatnik I Prazdnik: Etnografiya Dnya Pobedy." *Neprikosnovennyy Zapas* 101, no. 3 (2015). http://www.nlobooks.ru/node/6370.
Gadzhieva, Karina. "In Chechnya, Authorities Equal Memory of Deportation Day to Dissent." Caucasian Knot (website), February 23, 2016. http://www.eng.kavkaz-uzel.eu/articles/34687/.
Gammer, Moshe. "Nationalism and History: Rewriting the Chechen National Past." In *Secession, History and the Social Sciences*, edited by Bruno Coppieters and Michel Huysseune, 117–149. Brussels: VUB Brussels University Press, 2002.
Ganushkina, Svetlana. "Detey bezhentsev vse chashche otkazyvayutsya brat' v Rossiyskiye shkoly." Interview by Olga Zhuravleva and Ilya Rozhdestvensky, *Dnevnoy Razvorot*, Radio Echo Moskvy, July 28, 2015. https://echo.msk.ru/programs/razvorot/1592682-echo/.
Gat, Azar, and Alexander Yakobson. *Nations: The Long History and Deep Roots of Political Ethnicity and Nationalism*. Cambridge: Cambridge University Press, 2012.
Geist, Edward. "Cooking Bolshevik: Anastas Mikoian and the Making of the Book about Delicious and Healthy Food." *Russian Review* 71, no. 2 (2012): 295–313. http://dx.doi.org/10.1111/j.1467-9434.2012.00654.x.
Gellner, Ernest. *Nations and Nationalism*. Malden, MA: Blackwell, 2006.
Gerasimov, Valeri. "Tsennost' nauki v predvidenii: novyye vyzovy trebuyut pereosmyslit' formy i sposoby vedeniya boyevykh deystviy." *Voyeno-promeshlineyi Kurier*, February 26, 2013. https://www.vpk-news.ru/articles/14632.
Gessen, Masha. *The Man without a Face: The Unlikely Rise of Vladimir Putin*. New York: Riverhead Books, 2012.
Giddens, Anthony. *The Constitution of Society: Introduction of the Theory of Structuration*. Berkeley: University of California Press, 1984.
———. *A Contemporary Critique of Historical Materialism*. London: Macmillan, 1981.
———. *Modernity and Self-Identity: Self and Society in the Late Modern Age*. Cambridge: Polity, 1991.
Ginsburgs, George. *From Soviet to Russian International Law: Studies in Continuity and Change*. The Hague: Martinus Nijhoff, 1998.
———. "From the 1990 Law on the Citizenship of the USSR to the Citizenship Laws of the Successor Republics (Part I)." *Review of Central and East European Law* 18, no. 1 (1992): 1–55.
———. "From the 1990 Law on the Citizenship of the USSR to the Citizenship Laws of the Successor Republics (Part II)." *Review of Central and East European Law* 19, no. 3 (1993): 233–66.
globoball. "Itogi s Evgeniem Kiselevym—ekstrenny vypusk ot 03 Aprelya 2001 goda." July 18, 2015, YouTube video, 2:15:52, https://www.youtube.com/watch?v=fD9hU8fkwBo.
Goscilo, Helena, and Vlad Strukov. *Celebrity and Glamour in Contemporary Russia: Shocking Chic*. London: Routledge, 2012.
Gosindex.ru. *V Glavnoy Roli, Putin V Sovremennoi Kulture*. Moscow: Gosindex.ru, 2016.

Grafova, Lidiia. "Nado Legalizovat' Migrantovv!" *Novaya Gazeta*, November 13, 2008.
Greene, Samuel A., and Graeme B. Robertson. *Putin v. the People: The Perilous Politics of a Divided Russia*. New Haven, CT: Yale University Press, 2019.
Greenfeld, Liah. "The Formation of the Russian National Identity: The Role of Status Insecurity and Ressentiment." *Comparative Studies in Society and History* 32, no. 3 (1990): 549–91. https://doi.org/10.1017/S0010417500016625.
Guseynov, Hasan. "The Shock of Irrevocability." In *1990: Russians Remember a Turning Point*, edited by Irina Prokhorova, 148–64. London: MacLehose, 2013.
Hartog, Eva. "Want to Become a Russian in Crimea? Join the Queue." *Moscow Times*, July 9, 2015.
Hemment, Julie. *Youth Politics in Putin's Russia: Producing Patriots and Entrepreneurs*. Bloomington: Indiana University Press, 2015.
Hobsbawm, Eric J., and Terence O. Ranger. *The Invention of Tradition*. Cambridge: Cambridge University Press, 2012.
Hollifield, James F. *Immigrants, Markets, and States: The Political Economy of Postwar Europe*. Cambridge, MA: Harvard University Press, 1992.
Hosking, Geoffrey. "Slavophiles and Westernizers in Russia." Valdai Discussion Club, March 21, 2012. http://valdaiclub.com/a/highlights/slavophiles_and_westernizers_in_russia/.
Hutchings, Stephen C., and Natalia Rulyova. *Television and Culture in Putin's Russia: Remote Control*. London: Routledge, 2009.
Hutchings, Stephen, and Joanna Szostek. "Dominant Narratives in Russian Political and Media Discourse during the Ukraine Crisis." *E-International Relations*, April 28, 2015. http://www.e-ir.info/2015/04/28/dominant-narratives-in-russian-political-and-media-discourse-during-the-crisis/.
Hutchings, Stephen, and Vera Tolz. "Fault Lines in Russia's Discourse of Nation: Television Coverage of the December 2010 Moscow Riots." *Slavic Review* 71, no. 4 (2012): 873–99. http://dx.doi.org/10.5612/slavicreview.71.4.0873.
———. *Nation, Ethnicity and Race on Russian Television: Mediating Post-Soviet Difference*. London: Routledge, 2015.
Hutchings, Stephen, Vera Tolz, and Elisabeth Schimpfoessl. "Race and Ethnicity in the Russian Media: Rights, Responsibilities and Representation; Public Debate, the Frontline Club, London, Thursday 18 October 2012." *Russian Journal of Communication* 5, no. 3 (2013): 301–3. http://dx.doi.org/10.1080/19409419.2013.819462.
Huysmans, Jef. "The European Union and the Securitization of Migration." *Journal of Common Market Studies* 38, no. 5 (2000): 751–77. http://dx.doi.org/10.1111/1468-5965.00263.
Ilina, Irina. "Ne problema, a konkurentnoye preimushchestvo." Cogita!ru, October 25, 2012. http://www.cogita.ru/grazhdanskaya-aktivnost/migranty/5-i-konkurs-esse-migraciya-i-integraciya-migrantov-v-evrope-i-rossii/irina-ilina.
Interfax. "Svetlana Medvedeva schitaet vazhnym vozrozhdenie traditzii prazdnovaniya dnya Svyatyh Petra i Fevronii." July 9, 2008. https://pravoslavie.ru/27112.html.
Ivanova, Elena. "V gorode Kaspiyske sovershen terakt—postradali okolo 20 chelovek, yest' pogibshiye." RIA Novosti, May 9, 2002. https://ria.ru/20020509/139364.html.

Izvestia. "Ideologiya suverennoy demokratii." April 21, 2006.
———. "Kakoy Shchet?" February 4, 2002.
———. "Krakh Chetvertogo Internatsionala." August 26, 1993.
———. "Ocherednaya gosudarstvennaya ideologiya Rosii ne nuzhna." July 17, 1996.
———. "Ubyvayushchaya nostal'giya." December 24, 2001.
———. "Vladimir Putin prinyal finalistov konkursa studencheskikh sochineniy." June 26, 2003.
———. "Vladimir Putin: Rossiya ne dolzhna byt' i ne budet politseyskim gosudarstvom." July 14, 2000.
Jahno, Olga.. "Poleznyye knigi o vkusnoy pishche: traditsiya XIX V. I sovetskiy etalon pitaniya." *Vestnik RUDN*, no. 3 (2007): 48–54.
Judah, Ben. *Fragile Empire: How Russia Fell in and out of Love with Vladimir Putin*. New Haven, CT: Yale University Press, 2013.
Kailitz, Steffen, and Andreas Umland. "Why the Fascists Won't Take Over the Kremlin (for Now): A Comparison of Democracy's Breakdown and Fascism's Rise in Weimar Germany and Post-Soviet Russia." Higher School of Economics (Moscow), Working Paper No. 14, 2010. http://dx.doi.org/10.2139/ssrn.1659929.
KARLOSPETROS. "Natali: Takogo, Kak Putin." March 22, 2009, YoutTube video, 2:48. https://www.youtube.com/watch?v=hUh9pThGdm4.
Khamraev, Victor, and Gleb Cherkasov. "Dmitriy Rogozin obyavil ul'timatum prezidentu Kazakhstana a stranam SNG posovetoval dogovorit'sya o yedinom grazhdanstve." *Segodnya*, February 18, 1994.
Khodarkovsky, Michael. "Russia's Age-Old Question: Who Are We?" *New York Times*, May 18, 2017.
Kichin, Valeri. "Nikita Mikhalkov: Tak Konchayutsya Smutnyye Vremenaa." *Izvestia*, July 1, 1998.
Kirch, Marika, and Aksel Kirch. "Ethnic Relations: Estonians and Non-Estonians." *Nationalities Papers* 23, no. 1 (1995): 43–59. http://dx.doi.org/10.1080/00905999508408348.
Kiselev, Stepan. "Grigoriy Satarov: Natsional'naya Ideya—Eto Nevol'no." *Izvestia*, July 19, 1996.
Knox, Zoe. "Russian Orthodoxy, Russian Nationalism, and Patriarch Aleksii II." *Nationalities Papers* 33, no. 4 (2005): 533–45. http://dx.doi.org/10.1080/00905990500354004.
———. *Russian Society and the Orthodox Church: Religion in Russia after Communism*. New York: Routledge, 2005.
Kobrin, Kirill. *Postsovetskiy Mavzoley Proshlogo*. Moscow: Novoye literaturnoye obozreniye, 2017.
Kolesnikov, Andrey. "Okna rosta." *Novaya Gazeta*, April 25, 2000.
———. "Posledneye pribezhishche." *Izvestia*, April 10, 1999.
Kolsto, Pal, and Helge Blakkisrud, eds. *The New Russian Nationalism: Imperialism, Ethnicity and Authoritarianism 2000–2015*. Edinburgh: Edinburgh University Press, 2016.
Koltsova, Olessia. *News Media and Power in Russia*. London: Routledge, 2006.
Kommersant. "Mnogopasportiynaya sistema." February 7, 2020.

Kongina, Natalya. "Vremja Sobirat Tserkvi." *Rossisskaya Gezeta*, May 18, 2007.
Korolev, Anatoly, and Dmitry Kosyrev. "National Symbolism in Russia: The Old and the New." *Sputnik News*, June 11, 2007.
Koselleck, Reinhart. *Futures Past: On the Semantics of Historical Time*. New York: Columbia University Press, 2004.
Kozlova, Nataliya N. "Mezhdunarodnyy zhenskiy den' 8 Marta kak instrument formirovaniya Sovetskoy politicheskoy kul'tury." *Zhenshchina v rossiyskom obshchestve*, no. 1 (2011): 36–44.
Krasovski, Grigory. "V den' VDV desantniki ustroili draku v tsentre Irkutska (Foto)." *Gazeta Irkutsk*, August 4, 2014. http://www.gazetairkutsk.ru/2010/08/04/id20456/.
Kremlin (website). "Address by the President of the Russian Federation." Last modified March 18, 2014. http://en.kremlin.ru/events/president/news/20603.
———. "Agreement on the accession of the Republic of Crimea to the Russian Federation signed." Last modified March 18, 2014. http://en.kremlin.ru/events/president/news/20604.
———. "Annual Address to the Federal Assembly of the Russian Federation." Last modified April 1, 2001. http://en.kremlin.ru/events/president/transcripts/21216.
———. "Direct Line with Vladimir Putin." Last modified April 17, 2014. http://eng.kremlin.ru/news/7034.
———. "Excerpts from an Interview Granted to the Media in the Krasnodar Region." Last modified September 17, 2002. http://en.kremlin.ru/events/president/transcripts/21722.
———. "Meeting of the Valdai International Discussion Club." Last modified October 18, 2018. http://en.kremlin.ru/events/president/news/58848.
———. "President of Russia Address to the Federal Assembly." Last modified May 16, 2003. http://en.kremlin.ru/events/president/transcripts/21998.
———. "President Vladimir Putin Held a Meeting with the Cabinet." Last modified June 3, 2002. http://en.kremlin.ru/events/president/news/27124.
———. "President Vladimir Putin Signed a Law on Introducing Amendments and Additions to the Law." Last modified November 13, 2003. http://www.en.kremlin.ru/events/president/news/29736.
———. "State of the Nation Address." Last modified April 25, 2005. http://en.kremlin.ru/events/president/transcripts/22931.
———. "Ukaz o priyome v grazhdanstvo Rossiyskoy Federatsii." Last modified January 3, 2013. http://kremlin.ru/events/president/news/17275.
———. "Vladimir Putin prisutstvoval na Rozhdestvenskom bogosluzhenii v Novoiyerusalimskom monastyre." Last modified January 7, 2007. http://kremlin.ru/events/president/news/36993.
———. "Vladimir Putin v Den' Zashchitnika Otechestva posetil voyennyy klinicheskiy gospital' Imeni Burdenko." Last modified February 23, 2003. http://kremlin.ru/events/president/news/28215.
Krume, Kristine. "Checks and Balances in Latvian Nationality Policies: National Agendas and International Frameworks." In *Citizenship Policies in the New*

Europe, edited by Rainer Bauböck, Bernhard Perchinig, and Wiebke Sievers, 63–88. Amsterdam: Amsterdam University Press, 2007.
Kultareva, Daria. "Chto podarit' muzhchine 23 fevralya." *GQ Russia*, February 18, 2018.
Kuzio, Taras. "Russian Passports as Moscow's Geopolitical Tool." *Eurasia Daily Monitor* 5, no. 176 (2008). https://jamestown.org/program/russian-passports-as-moscows-geopolitical-tool/.
Lalpychak, Chrystyna. "Over 90% Vote Yes in Referendum; Kravchuk Elected President of Ukraine." *Ukranian Weekly*, December 8, 1991.
Lapidus, Gail Warshofsky. *Women in Soviet Society: Equality, Development and Social Change*. Berkeley: University of California Press, 1978.
Larina, Yulia. "Krasno-belo-goluboy ogonek." *Kommersant*, December 26, 2005.
Laruelle, Marlene. *Beyond Anti-Westernism: The Kremlin's Narrative about Russia's European Identity and Mission*. PONARS Eurasia, policy memo 326, Washington, DC, August 2014.
———. *Russian Eurasianism: An Ideology of Empire*. Baltimore: Johns Hopkins University Press, 2012.
———. *Russian Nationalism and the National Reassertion of Russia*. London: Routledge, 2009.
Law of the Republic of Latvia No. 10 "On the Status of Those Former USSR Citizens Who Do Not Have the Citizenship of Latvia or That of Any Other State," Latvian Saeima, April 25, 1995.
Law of the USSR No. 2-VIII "Ob utverzhdenii Osnovnogo zakonodatel'stva Soyuza SSR i soyuznykh respublik o trude." Presidium of the Supreme Soviet of the USSR, July 15, 1970.
Law of the USSR No. 1518-1 "O Grazhdanstve SSSR." Presidium of the Supreme Soviet of the USSR, May 23, 1990.
Lazareva, Olga. "Russian Migrants to Russia: Choice of Location and Labor Market Outcomes." Paper presented at the 11th IZA European Summer School in Labor Economics, Lake Ammersee, Germany, May 12–18, 2008.
Lenta.ru. "Baburin, Sergei." October 19, 2014. https://lenta.ru/lib/14159613/.
———. "Putin v gostyakh u Izvestia: govorili pro Sankt-Peterburg, SSHA, TV-6 i smert-nuyu kazn." March 13, 2002. https://lenta.ru/news/2002/03/13/izvestia/.
———. "V Novosibirske studenty vstretili 1 Maya prizyvami Ktulhu." May 1, 2009. https://lenta.ru/news/2009/05/01/novosib.
———. "Vladimir Soloviev pereydet na kanal Rossiya 1." August 12, 2010. https://lenta.ru/news/2010/08/12/vsoloviev/.
Levada-Center. *Levada Public Opinion 2012 Yearbook*. Moscow: Levada-Center, 2012.
———. *Obshchestvennoye Mneniye—2011. Yezhegodnik*. Moscow: Levada-Center, 2012.
———. *Obshchestvennoye Mneniye—2015. Yezhegodnik*. Moscow: Levada-Center, 2016.
———. *Obshchestvennoye Mneniye—2019. Yezhegodnik*. Moscow: Levada-Center, 2020.
———. "Odobrenie deytel'nosti V. Putina." Accessed February 13, 2017. https://www.levada.ru/indikatory/odobrenie-organov-vlasti/.
———. "Prazdniki." Unpublished manuscript, 2017.
———. "Religioznaya vera v Rossii." Last modified September 26, 2011. https://www.levada.ru/2011/09/26/religioznaya-vera-v-rossii/.

———. "Rossiyane o religii." Last modified December 24, 2013. http://www.levada.ru/2013/12/24/rossiyane-o-religii/.
Lhene, Stephan. "The Tempting Trap of Fortress Europe." Carnegie Europe, April 22, 2016. http://carnegieeurope.eu/2016/04/21/tempting-trap-of-fortress-europe-pub-63400.
Liesowska, Anna. "The Siberian Phenomenon of 'Monstrating.'" *Siberian Times*, May 1, 2013. http://siberiantimes.com/other/others/news/the-siberian-phenomenon-of-monstrating/.
Lieven, Anatol. "The Weakness of Russian Nationalism." *Survival* 41, no. 2 (1999): 53–70. https://doi.org/10.1093/survival/41.2.53.
Lieven, Dominic. "The Russian Empire and the Soviet Union as Imperial Polities." *Journal of Contemporary History* 30, no. 4 (1995): 607–36. http://www.jstor.org/stable/261085.
Lipshiz, Cnaan. "Why Putin Embraces Russia's Jews, but Not Its Gays." *Times of Israel*, September 15, 2015.
Lukin, V. "Chto dlya grazhdanina pravo, to dlya chinovnika dolg." *Rossiiskaya Gazeta*, January 31, 2005.
Lesko, M. "Pechat' Ministra Lesina." *Kar'era*, June 2, 2003.
Mason, Paul. *Postcapitalism: A Guide to Our Future*. London: Penguin Books, 2016.
materik.ru. "Dokumental'naja khronika bor'by protiv ugolovno-politicheskih Ppesledovaniy Russkogo pravozashhitnika B.F. Suprunjuka Kazahstanskimi Vlastyami." Accessed October 12, 2017. http://observer.materik.ru/observer/N18_94/18_21.htm.
Matthews, Owen. "Alexander Dugin and Steve Bannon's Ideological Ties to Vladimir Putin's Russia." *Newsweek*, April 17, 2017.
Medvedev, Yuri. "Konflikty—nashe bogatstvo." *Izvestia*, July 26, 2000.
Migration Policy Institute. "Migration Policy Institute Homepage." Accessed February 12, 2018. https://www.migrationpolicy.org.
Mihailovic, Alexander. "Wings of Desire: The Changing Meaning of Same-Sex Desire in Putin's and Medvedev's Russia." In *The Meaning of Sexual Identity in the Twenty-First Century*, edited by Judith S. Kaufman and David A. Powell, 117–35. Newcastle upon Tyne, UK: Cambridge Scholars, 2014.
Miller, Alexei. "Istoriya ponyatiya "natsiya" v Rossii." *Otechestvennyye zapiski* 46, no.1 (2012): 162-186. https://strana-oz.ru/2012/1/istoriya-ponyatiya-naciya-v-rossi., 2012.
Moskovskie novosti. "Posledniy privet Gruzii ot SSSR." January 19, 1992.
Moscow Patriarchate (website). "Prezident Rossii V. V. Putin posetil svayteyshego patriarha Aleksiya v ego rezidencii v peredelkine." Accessed May 9, 2017. https://mospat.ru/archive/2003/05/nr305101/.
———. "Prezident Rossii vstretilsya so svyateyshim Patriarhom Moskovskim i vseja Rusi Aleksiem II i pervoierarhom Russkoy zarubezhnoi Cerkvi Mitropolitom Lavrom." Accessed May 9, 2017. https://mospat.ru/archive/2004/05/7013-1/.
Moscow Times. "Russia 'Not Ready' for Law Uniting Nation's Ethnic Groups, Says Expert." March 7, 2017.
Morozov, Rodion. "Leonid Shebarshin: Ya znayu, chto inostrannyye razvedki narashchivayut deyatel'nost' protiv Rossii." *Nezavisimaya Gazeta*, August 18, 1993.

Mozzhukhin, Andrey. "Epoha stabil'nosti v Rossii zakonchilas." Lenta.ru, September 29, 2015. https://lenta.ru/articles/2015/09/29/stabilnost/.
Morson, Gary Saul. *Bakhtin: Essays and Dialogues on His Work*. Chicago: University of Chicago Press, 1986.
my3rd3y3. "Weapons of Mass Deception." March 6, 2012. YouTube video, 1:38:07. https://www.youtube.com/watch?v=wkkAXkhKg98.
Nedicom.ru Advocates. "Kak poluchit' Rossiyskiy pasport bez propiski v Krymu I Sevastopole?" Accessed June 29, 2015. http://www.nedicom.ru/fakt-prozhivaniya-v-krymu.
Nezavisimaya Gazeta. "Natsional'nyy sostav pravitel'stva podvergnut ekspertize: budem nadeitsya chto prezident poshutil." July 4, 1992.
Nikiforova, Maria. "Prezident proshelsya po Ryurikovskim mestam." *Nezavisimaya Gazeta*, July 18, 2003.
Novaya Gazeta. "My—Kollektivnyy Putin." April 8, 2001.
———. "Novyye Russkiye prazdniki." November 11, 2004.
———. "Vozvrashcheniye Styda." February 2, 2004.
Novy god Israeli (website). "Novy God Israeli." Accessed March 20, 2018. http://www.novygodisraeli.com/.
Obshchestvennoye grazhdansko-patrioticheskoye dvizheniya Bessmertnyy polk Rossii. "Istoriya Bessmertnogo Polka Rossii." Accessed December 20, 2017. https://polkrf.ru/about/.
Ocak, Ozden. "Immigration and French National Identity under Neoliberalism: Sarkozy's Selective Immigration Politics as a Performance of Sovereignty." *Patterns of Prejudice* 50, no. 1 (2016): 82–95. http://dx.doi.org/10.1080/0031322X.2015.1127642.
Osipov, Alexander. "The Background of the Soviet Union's Involvement in the Establishment of the European Minority Rights Regime in the Late 1980s." *Journal on Ethnopolitics and Minority Issues in Europe* 15, no. 2 (2016): 59–77.
———. "Chto v Rossii oznachaet ponyatiy' regulirovanie migratsi'?" In *Migratzia I Natsionalnoe Gosudarstvso*, edited by Tatyana Baraulina and Oksana Karpenko, 15–45. St. Petersburg: Center for Independent Social Research, 2004. http://www.ecmi.de/fileadmin/downloads/publications/JEMIE/2016/Osipov2.pdf.
Ostrovsky, Arkady. "Inside the Bear." *The Economist*, October 22, 2016.
Oushakine, Serguei. *The Patriotism of Despair: Nation, War, and Loss in Russia*. Ithaca, NY: Cornell University Press, 2009.
Pain, Emil. "Events in Moscow 11th December 2010: Political Crisis." *Russian Analytical Digest*, no. 93 (2011). https://www.files.ethz.ch/isn/127703/Russian_Analytical_Digest_93.pdf.
Parfitt, Tom. "Gerard Depardieu Pleased at Russian Citizenship." *Telegraph*, January 3, 2013.
Pashenko, Daria. "Prazdnik so slezami na glazakh." *Delitant*, May 9, 2017. http://diletant.media/articles/35551897/.
Pelevin, Victor. *Babylon*. Translated by Andrew Bromfield. London: Faber, 2000.
Pennington, Reina. "'Do Not Speak of the Services You Rendered': Women Veterans of Aviation in the Soviet Union." In *A Soldier and a Woman: Sexual*

Integration in the Military, edited by Gerard J. De Groot and Corina M. Peniston-Bird, 152–174. London: Pearson Education, 2000.

Petrone, Karen. *Life Has Become More Joyous, Comrades: Celebrations in the Time of Stalin*. Bloomington: Indiana University Press, 2000.

Peyrouse, Sebastien. "Nationhood and the Minority Question in Central Asia. The Russians in Kazakhstan." *Europe-Asia Studies* 59, no. 3 (2007): 481–501. http://dx.doi.org/10.1080/09668130701239930.

———. *The Russian Minority in Central Asia: Migration, Politics and Language*. Kennan Institute, occasional paper 297, Washington, DC, 2008.

Pomerantsev, Peter. "The Hidden Author of Putinism," *The Atlantic*, November 7, 2014.

———. "How Putin Became the Che Guevara of the Right." Politico, March 11, 2016. https://www.politico.eu/article/how-vladimir-putin-russia-became-che-guevara-of-right-wing/.

———. *Nothing Is True and Everything Is Possible: Adventures in Modern Russia*. New York: Public Affairs, 2014.

Ponarin, Eduard. *Security Implications of the Russian Identity Crisis*. PONARS Eurasia, policy memo 64, Washington, DC, June 1999.

Popova, Olga D. "Kulinarnyy kod kul'tury prazdnika v Sovetskom obshchestve." *Modern History of Russia* 2 (2016): 252–67. http://modernhistory.ru/d/1607380/d/popova.pdf.

"Poyedinok. Efir Ot 04.04.2014." Broadcast on April 4, 2014, on Rossiya1. http://beta.russia.tv/anons/show/episode_id/978957/brand_id/3963/.

"Poyedinok. Efir Ot 20.01.2011." Broadcast on January 20, 2011, on Rossiya1. https://russia.tv/video/show/brand_id/3963/episode_id/91907/video_id/91907/viewtype/picture/.

"Poyedinok. Efir Ot 23.12.2010." Broadcast on December 23, 2010, on Rossiya1. https://russia.tv/video/show/brand_id/3963/episode_id/91904/.

"Poyedinok. Efir Ot 25.11.2010." Broadcast on November 25, 2010, on Rossiya1. https://russia.tv/video/show/brand_id/3963/episode_id/91696/video_id/91696/viewtype/picture/.

"Poyedinok. Efir Ot 27.02.2014." Broadcast on February 27, 2014, on Rossiya1. http://russia.tv/anons/show/episode_id/970423/brand_id/3963/.

Prokhorova, Irina, ed. *1990: Russians Remember a Turning Point*. London: MacLehose, 2013.

———. "Kakiye tsennosti nas ob'yedinyat?" Interview by Larina Ksenya and Shargunov Sergey, *2013*, Radio Echo Moskvy, December 27, 2013. https://echo.msk.ru/programs/year2013/1225381-echo/.

Putin, Vladimir V. "Vladimir Putin. Rossiya: Natsional'nyy vopros." *Nezavisimaya gazeta*, January 23, 2012.

Rachman, Gideon. "Nationalism Is Back." *The Economist*, November 5, 2014.

Radchenko, Natalya, and Natiana Kuzmina. "Prazdnik novogo goda V Rossii v kontekste natsional'nykh traditsiy (Primer issledovaniya Respubliki Sakha—Yakutiya)." *Teoriya i praktika obshhestvennogo razvitiya* 3 (2015): 130–34. http://teoria-practica.ru/rus/files/arhiv_zhurnala/2015/3/history/radchenko-kuzmina.pdf.

Raeff, Marc. *Origins of the Russian Intelligentsia: The Eighteenth-Century Nobility*. New York: Harcourt, Brace & World, 1966.
Ramirez, Anthony. "International Report: Pepsi Will Be Bartered for Ships and Vodka in Deal with Soviets." *New York Times*, April 9, 1990.
RedSamurai84. "HD Russian Army Parade, Victory Day 2005." May 13, 2010, YouTube video, 1:37:10. https://www.youtube.com/watch?v=L87HUIDcyL4.
———. "Russian Army Parade, Victory Day 1995 Parad Pobedy (Victory Parade)." May 14, 2016, YouTube video, 56:49. https://www.youtube.com/watch?v=EQpLO4CWj18.
———. "Russian Army Parade, Victory Day 2007 Parad Pobedy (Victory Parade)." May 14, 2016, YouTube video, 53:44. https://www.youtube.com/watch?v=zoF6juLCGas.
Regnum. "'Inzhir Ne Nuzhen!': Byvshiye Desantniki Izbili Smuglykh Torgovtsev Na Tsentral'nom Rynke Novosibirska." August 2, 2006. https://regnum.ru/news/683181.html.
Resolution of the State Duma of the Federal Assembly of the Russian Federation On the draft federal law No. 3931-3. "O vnesenii izmeneniy i dopolneniy v preambulu i stat'i 2, 12, 13 i 18 Zakona Rossiyskoy Federatsii o grazhdanstve Rossiyskoy Federatsii." Federal Council of the Russian Federation, 2003.
Resolution of the Constitutional Court of the Russian Federation No. 12-P. "Po delu o proverke konstitutsionnosti punkta 'g' stat'i 18 zakona Rossiyskoy Federatsii 'o grazhdanstve Rossiyskoy Federatsii' v svyazi s zhaloboy A. B. Smirnova." Constitutional Court of the Russian Federation, May 16, 1996.
RFE/RL. "Duma Approves New List of Military Celebrations." November 19, 2003. https://www.rferl.org/a/1143044.html.
———. "Legko li byt' natsionalistom?" January 25, 2016, YouTube video, 54:56. https://www.youtube.com/watch?v=NEiMDO2Cwec.
———. "Ukraine Bans Russian St. George Ribbon." June 12, 2017. https://www.rferl.org/a/ukraine-bans-russian-st-george-ribbon/28542973.html.
RIA Novosti. "Den Pobedy." Accessed June 20, 2015, http://www.9may.ru.
———. "Desantniki otmechayut svoy professional'nyy prazdnik." August 2, 2006. https://ria.ru/20140802/1018517032.htm.
———. "Luchshiye potografii konkursa 'Georgiyevskaya Lentochka' v Instagram." May 12, 2014. https://ria.ru/20140512/1007474075.html.
———. "Putin: prazdniki v Rossii mozhno otmechat' kruglyy god." September 20, 2017. https://ria.ru/20170920/1505178633.html.
———. "Terakt V Kaspiyske na prazdnovanii Dnya Pobedy v 2002 godu." May 9, 2012. https://ria.ru/20120509/642029750.html.
———. "Ubijstvo futbol'nogo bolel'shhika Egora Sviridova: hronika sobytiy." December 6, 2013. https://ria.ru/20131206/981951049.html.
———. "Voyska dyadi Vasi budut i dal'she gulyat' v parke Gor'kogo." August 2, 2016. https://ria.ru/defense_safety/20160802/1473414227.html.
Romanovskiy, Roman. "Khotyat Li Russkiye Domoy?" Cogita!Ru, November 1, 2012. http://www.cogita.ru/grazhdanskaya-aktivnost/migranty/5-i-konkurs

-esse-migraciya-i-integraciya-migrantov-v-evrope-i-rossii/hotyat-li-russkie-domoi.
Rosbalt. "Glavny slivy Shaltaya-Boltaya." January 31, 2017. https://www.rosbalt.ru/russia/2017/01/31/1587547.html.
Roslycky, Lada L. "Russia's Smart Power in Crimea: Sowing the Seeds of Trust." *Southeast European and Black Sea Studies* 11, no. 3 (2011): 299–316. http://dx.doi.org/10.1080/14683857.2011.590313.
Ross, Cameron. *Federalism and Democratisation in Russia*. Manchester: Manchester University Press, 2002.
Rostova, Natalya. "Gazetu sest' nel'zya." *Novaya Gazeta*, December 16, 2007.
Russkikh, Fedor V. "Grazhdanstvo Rossii ne podtverzhdayetsya . . . Priklyucheniya 'inostrantsa' v Rossii—1 Oktyabrya 2002 G." Pravda.ru, October 1, 2002. https://www.pravda.ru/politics/837513-grazhdanstvo_rossii_ne_podtverzhdaetsja_prikljuchenija/.
Sadchikov, Alexander. "Sergey Kiriyenko: kto ne protiv nas, tot s nami/byvshiy prem'yer pobyval v redaktsii Izvestia predlozhil svoyu obshchestvennogo dogovors." *Izvestia*, December 22, 1998.
Sakwa, Richard. *Putin: Russia's Choice*. London: Routledge, 2008.
——. "Regime Change from Yeltsin and Putin: Normality, Normalcy or Narmalisation?" In *Russian Politics under Putin*, edited by Cameron Ross, 17–38. Manchester: Manchester University Press, 2004.
Samoilova, Elena. "Vkladysh Do Vostrebovaniya." *Kommersant*, February 10, 2003.
Sarajeva, Katja. "'You Know What Kind of Place This Is, Don't You?' An Exploration of Lesbian Spaces in Moscow." In *Cultural Diversity in Russian Cities: The Urban Landscape in the Post-Soviet Era*, edited by Gordula Gdaniec, 138–64. New York: Berghahn Books, 2013.
Schenk, Caress. *Why Control Immigration? Strategic Uses of Migration Management in Russia*. Toronto: University of Toronto Press, 2018.
Schleifman, Nurit. "Introduction." In *Russia at a Crossroads: History, Memory and Political Practice*, edited by Nurit Schleifman, 1–7. New York: Routledge, 2013.
Service of State Statistics. "Mezhdunarodnaya migratsiya." Accessed May 19, 2014. http://www.gks.ru/wps/wcm/connect/rosstat_main/rosstat/ru/statistics/population/demography/#.
——. "Obshchiye itogi migratsii naseleniya Rossiyskoy Federatsii." Accessed May 19, 2014. http://www.gks.ru/wps/wcm/connect/rosstat_main/rosstat/ru/statistics/population/demography/#.
Seton-Weston, Hugh. "Russian Nationalism in Historical Perspective." In *The Last Empire: Nationality and the Soviet Future*, edited by Robert Conquest, 14–24. Stanford, CA: Hoover Institution Press, 1986.
Shachar, Ayelet. *The Birthright Lottery: Citizenship and Global Inequality*. Cambridge, MA: Harvard University Press, 2009.
Sharafutdinova, Gulnaz. *The Red Mirror: Putin's Leadership and Russia's Insecure Identity*. Oxford: Oxford University Press, 2020.
Shevel, Oxana. "The Politics of Citizenship Policy in Post-Soviet Russia." *Post-Soviet Affairs* 28, no. 1 (2012): 111–47. http://dx.doi.org/10.2747/1060-586X.28.1.111.

———. "Russian Nation-Building from Yel'tsin to Medvedev: Ethnic, Civic or Purposefully Ambiguous?" *Europe-Asia Studies* 63, no. 2 (2011): 179–202. http://dx.doi.org/10.1080/09668136.2011.547693.
Shevtsova, Lillia. "Humiliation as a Tool of Blackmail." *American National Interest*, June 2, 2015.
Sivolap, I. K., ed. *Kniga o vkusnoy i zdorovoy pishche*. Moscow: Pischepromizdat, 1952.
Slezkine, Yuri. "Commentary: Imperialism as the Highest Stage of Socialism." *Russian Review* 59, no. 2 (2000): 227–34. https://doi.org/10.1111/0036-0341.00118.
———. "The USSR as a Communal Apartment." *Slavic Review* 53, no. 2 (1994): 414–52. https://doi.org/10.2307/2501300.
Smith, Anthony D. *Myths and Memories of the Nation*. Oxford: Oxford University Press, 1999.
Smith, Kathleen E. *Mythmaking in the New Russia: Politics and Memory during the Yeltsin Era*. Ithaca, NY: Cornell University Press, 2002.
Snyder, Timothy. *The Road to Unfreedom: Russia, Europe, America*. New York: Penguin Random House, 2018.
Soloviev, Vladimir. *My—Russkiye! S Nami Bog!* Moscow: Eskimo, 2009.
Sopova, Alexandra. "Natsional'nuyu ideyu Rossii predlozhili vyrazit' v vavoznoy kuche." *Izvestia*, January 17, 2013.
———. "Simvolom Rossii mozhet stat' Lomonosov, narisovannyy neft'yu." *Izvestia*, December 24, 2012.
Sorokina, Svetlana, Irina Khakamada, and Arina Holin. "Operatsiya po podchineniyu budushhih pokoleniy: zachem nuzhny Junarmiya, igrushechnyy Reihstag i otdyh sem'yami v okopah." Broadcast on March 18, 2017, on Dozd TV.
Soysal, Yasemin Nuhoglu. *Limits of Citizenship: Migrants and Postnational Membership in Europe*. Chicago: University of Chicago Press, 1994.
Sperling, Valerie. "Making the Public Patriotic: Militarism and Anti-Militarism in Russia." In *Russian Nationalism and the National Reassertion of Russia*, edited by Marlene Laruelle, 218–71. Oxford: Routledge, 2009.
Steele, Jonathan. *Eternal Russia: Yeltsin, Gorbachev and the Mirage of Democracy*. London: Faber, 1994.
State Duma of the Russian Federation. Stenogramma zasedaniy, February 18, 1998.
Stepanova, Elena. "'The Spiritual and Moral Foundation of Civilization in Every Nation for Thousands of Years': The Traditional Values Discourse in Russia." *Politics, Religion and Ideology* 16, no. 2–3 (2015): 119–36. http://dx.doi.org/10.1080/21567689.2015.1068167.
Starostina, Yuliya. "Pochemu Rossii mozhet grozit' sokrashcheniye naseleniya vpervyye za 10 let," *RBK*, July 12, 2018. https://www.rbc.ru/economics/12/07/2018/5b477cdc9a794726717db27c.
Suny, Ronald Grigor. "The Empire Strikes Out: Imperial Russia, 'National' Identity, and Theories of Empire." In *A State of Nations: Empire and Nation-Making in the Age of Lenin and Stalin*, edited by Ronald Grigor Suny and Terry Martin, 23–67. Oxford: Oxford University Press, 2001.
Surkov, Vladislav. "Surkov: In His Own Words." *Wall Street Journal*, December 18, 2006.

TASS. "Putin: administratsiya SSHA vinit vo vsekh neudachakh na vneshniye faktory." December 23, 2016, YouTube video, 6:08. https://www.youtube.com/watch?v=ZjV6jjIchFU.

———. "V aktsii 'Bessmertnyy Polk' v Tomske 9 Maya mogut prinyat' uchastiye do 60 tys. chelovek." May 5, 2016. https://tass.ru/sibir-news/3260160.

Terent'yev, Igor and Olesya Volkova. "Skrytaya ugroza: Rossiya okazalas' na poroge 'demograficheskoy yamy'." *RBC*, February 3, 2016. https://www.rbc.ru/society/03/02/2016/56b1c3b69a7947bf91c297ce.

Teper, Yuri. "Official Russian Identity Discourse in Light of the Annexation of Crimea: National or Imperial?" *Post-Soviet Affairs* 32, no. 4 (2016): 378–96. http://dx.doi.org/10.1080/1060586X.2015.1076959.

Tidey, Alice. "Depardieu Throws House Party for New Belgium Neighbors." CNBC, August 26, 2013. https://www.cnbc.com/id/100987661.

Timofeev, Lev. "Naivnaya formula pobedy." *Izvestia*, August 9, 1996.

Tishkov, Valeri. "The Russian People and National Identity." *Russia in Global Affairs*, no. 3 (2008). https://eng.globalaffairs.ru/articles/the-russian-people-and-national-identity.

Tishkov, Valeri, Zhanna Zayinchkovskaya, and Galina Vitkovskaya. *Migration in the Countries of the Former Soviet Union*. Global Commission on International Migration, Geneva, September 2005.

Tolz, Vera. "Conflicting 'Homeland Myths' and Nation-State Building in Postcommunist Russia." *Slavic Review* 58, no. 2 (1998): 267–94.

———. *Russia*. London: Arnold, 2001.

Tolz, Vera, and Yuri Teper. "Broadcasting Agitainment: A New Media Strategy of Putin's Third Presidency." *Post-Soviet Affairs* 34, no. 4 (2018): 1–15. http://dx.doi.org/10.1080/1060586X.2018.1459023.

Trostin, Evgenii. "Pervy den' novoy ere." *Istorik*, April 16, 2016.

Tumarkin, Nina. "The Great Patriotic War as Myth and Memory." *European Review* 11, no. 4 (2003): 595–611. http://dx.doi.org/10.1017/s1062798703000504.

———. "The Religion of Victory." *Moscow Times*, May 11, 1995.

US Department of the Treasury. "Treasury Sanctions Russian Officials, Members of the Russian Leadership's Inner Circle, and an Entity for Involvement in the Situation in Ukraine." Press release, Washington, DC, March 20, 2014. https://www.treasury.gov/press-center/press-releases/Pages/jl23331.aspx.

The Venice Commission. *Consequences of State Succession for Nationality*. Strasbourg: Council of Europe, 1998.

Verkhovsky, Aleksandr. "The Role of the Russian Orthodox Church in Nationalist, Xenophobic and Antiwestern Tendencies in Russia Today: Not Nationalism, but Fundamentalism." *Religion, State and Society* 30, no. 4 (2002): 333–45. http://dx.doi.org/10.1080/0963749022000022879.

Vityazeva, Anastasia. "Hiding Dual Citizenship Now a Criminal Offense in Russia." Russia Beyond the Headlines, August 12, 2014. https://www.rbth.com/society/2014/08/12/hiding_dual_citizenship_now_a_criminal_offense_in_russia_38929.html.

Vogue Rossiia. "Luchshiye podarki k 8 Marta." March 1999.

VTSIOM (website). "Kakiye iz sleduyushchikh prazdnikov dlya vas samyye vazhnyy?" Accessed April 1, 2017. https://bd.wciom.ru/zh/print_q.php?s_id=393&q_id=32024&date=15.03.1998.
———. "Press-Vypusk #2320 Zakon O Propagande Gomoseksualizma: Za I Protiv." Accessed June 6, 2017. https://wciom.ru/index.php?id=236&uid=114190.
Vzyhutovich, Valeriy. "Mezhdu Terekom I Potomakom (between the Terek and the Potomok)." *Izvestia*, November 6, 1999.
Walicki, Andrzej, and Hilda Andrews-Rusiecka. *A History of Russian Thought from the Enlightenment to Marxism*. Oxford: Clarendon, 1980.
Weil, Patrick. "Access to Citizenship: A Comparison of Twenty-Five Nationality Laws." In *Citizenship Today: Global Perspectives and Practices*, edited by Thomas Alexander Aleinikoff and Douglas B. Klusmeyer, 17–36. Washington, DC: Carnegie Endowment for International Peace, 2001.
White, Stephen, Ian McAllister, and Olga Kryshtanovskaya. "Religion and Politics in Postcommunist Russia." *Religion, State and Society* 22, no. 1 (1994): 73–88. http://dx.doi.org/10.1080/09637499408431625.
Whitmore, Brian, and Maksim Yaroshevsky. "Antifa Takes on Nationalists in Russian Youth's Civil War." RFE/RL, November 20, 2009.
Wikileaks. "Medvedev's Address and Tendem Politics." Accessed February 13, 2017. https://www.wikileaks.org/plusd/cables/08MOSCOW3343_a.html.
Willsher, Kim. "Gerard Depardieu's Tax Move to Belgium Divides France." *The Observer*, December 22, 2012.
Wilson, Andrew. *Virtual Politics: Faking Democracy in the Post-Soviet World*. New Haven, CT: Yale University Press, 2005.
Wood, Elizabeth A. "Performing Memory: Vladimir Putin and the Celebration of World War II in Russia." *Soviet and Post-Soviet Review* 38, no. 2 (2011): 172–200. http://dx.doi.org/10.1163/187633211x591175.
Yablokava, Oksana. "Levada Leaves VTSIOM for VTSIOM-A." *Moscow Times*, September 10, 2003.
Yurchak, Alexei. *Everything Was Forever, until It Was No More: The Last Soviet Generation*. Princeton, NJ: Princeton University Press, 2006.
———. "Post-Post-Communist Sincerity: Pioneers, Cosmonauts, and Other Soviet Heroes Born Today." In *What Is Soviet Now? Identities, Legacies, Memories*, edited by Thomas Lahusen and Peter Solomon, 257–77. Berlin: LIT Verlag Munster, 2008.
Zasurski, Ivan. *Media and Power in Post-Soviet Russia*. Armonk, NY: M. E. Sharpe, 2004.
Zerubavel, Eviatar. "Calendars and History: A Comparative Study of the Social Organisation of Time." In *States of Memory: Continuities, Conflicts, and Transformations in National Retrospection*, edited by Jeffrey K. Olick, 315–39. Durham, NC: Duke University Press, 2003.
———. *Time Maps: Collective Memory and the Social Shape of the Past*. Chicago: University of Chicago Press, 2003.
Zeveleva, Olga. "Political Aspects of Repatriation: Germany, Russia, Kazakhstan. A Comparative Analysis." *Nationalities Papers* 42, no. 5 (2014): 808–27. http://dx.doi.org/10.1080/00905992.2014.916663.

Zhirinovsky, Vladimir W. "Migratsiya." Interview by Yuri Kobaladze and Svetlana Sorokina. *V Kruge Sveta*, Radio Echo Moskvy, August 27, 2013. https://echo.msk.ru/programs/sorokina/1143798-echo/.

Zhuravsky, Alexander, and Olga Vykhovanets. "Compatriots: Back to the Homeland." Russian International Affairs Council, May 31, 2013. https://russiancouncil.ru/en/analytics-and-comments/analytics/compatriots-back-to-the-homeland/.

Zubarevich, Natalia. "Gastarbaytery v rossiyskoy ekonomike: plyusy i minusy." Interview by Marina Koroleva, *Bolshoi Dozor*, Radio Echo Moskvy, February 12, 2014. https://echo.msk.ru/programs/dozor/1256500-echo/.

Zuev, Denis. "The Russian March: Investigating the Symbolic Dimension of Political Performance in Modern Russia." *Europe-Asia Studies* 65, no. 1 (2013): 102–26. http://dx.doi.org/10.1080/09668136.2012.738800.

INDEX

Note: Page references in *italic type* refer to illustrations.

Abkhazia, 26, 35, 70, 71, 197n113. *See also* Georgia
Abrahamian, Atossa Araxia, 60
admission into citizenship. *See* citizenship; naturalization
Afanasiev, Yuri, 96
Afidjamov, Rustam, 80–81, 82
After Empire (Barkey and Von Haggen), 2
Alexievich, Svetlana, 15, 131
Anderson, Benedict, 7
Anniversary of the October Revolution (November 7), 97, 130–131, 136–137, 138, 140–142, 155, 164–165
anthem, national, 6, 92–95
Applebaum, Anne, 2
Armenia, 70
Azerbaijan, 36, 70

Baburin, Sergei, 33–34, 197n102
Babylon (Pelevin), 1, 177
Baikal-Amur Mainline (BAM) railway, 23
Bakhtin, Mikhail, 68
Baltai, Shaltai, 207n43
Baltic states, 17, 24, 192n6. *See also names of specific nations*
Barkey, Karen, 2
Bashkirs, 6
Bauböck, Rainer, 30, 37
Bauman, Zygmunt: on identity and globalization, 4, 8, 121, 147, 182–183; on migration, 62; on modernity, 7–8, 64, 210n6
Belavezha Accords (1991), 20, 34
Belorussia, 5, 6, 24, 74
Belotserkovskaya, Nika, 171
Bendera, Stepan, 209n83
Benderovtsy, 116, 209n83
Berberova, Irina, 73
Berezovsky, Boris, 95

Billig, Michael, 9, 69, 85
birth citizenship, 18, *20*, 33
Bishkek Treaty (1992), 23
Blackstar, 58, 203n98
Blakkisrud, Helge, 3
Bolotnaya Square protests (2011–12), 115
Bolsheviks, 4, 130. *See also* Anniversary of the October Revolution (November 7)
The Book of Tasty and Healthy Food (cookbook), 132, 134, 136, 150, 172, 212n38
Bourdieu, Pierre, 129, 130
Boym, Svetlana, 154
Brezhnev administration, 23, 133, 138, 140, 156–157, 160
Brubaker, Rogers, 3, 6
Brudny, Itzhak, 2
Bunimowich, Yevgeny, 82

calendar, 11, 127–129, 180; military, 132, 139, 155–165; personal-local, 143–147, 170; political, 137–143; religious, 147–151, 165–170; Russian national, 154–155, 174–176; Soviet, 129, 130–136. *See also* holidays; *names of specific holidays*
celebrations. *See* holidays
Chechnya, 88–89, 111, 120, 155, 157, 162, 217n41
Chomsky, Noam, 198n141
Christmas holidays: Rozhdestvo, *128*, 136, 148–150, 152, 166, 168, *169*, 181; Western traditions, *128*, 144–145, 148, 172
Chubais, Anatoly, 5, 9
citizenship, 10–11, 15–16, *20*, 61–64, 180; in 1989–91 Soviet Union, 17–18; by birth, 18, *20*, 33; Citizenship Law (1990), 17; Citizenship Law (1991), 16, 18–23; Citizenship Law (2002), 6, 42–49; Compatriots Law (1999), 34–35, 38; of Crimeans, 31, 55–56, 202n89; dual, 21,

242 INDEX

citizenship *(continued)*
  28–30, 57–58; globalization and, 61–64; institutional erosion of, 29–32; migration and, 36–39; national in-group, as term, 10, 16, 61, 110; naturalization method, 19–20, 26; purchase of, 59–61; registration method (propiska), 19, *20*, 21, 22–23, 24–25, 30–31, 194n36; Smirnov case on, 32–33; Turkmenistan and, 28, 195n69; in Ukraine, 26, 29, 31; zero option of, 18, *20*, 25, 193n18. *See also* identity; legal gray zone of citizenship; migration; national in-group, as term
Citizenship Law (Latvia; 1996), 196n94
Citizenship Law (Russia; 1991), 16, 18–23
Citizenship Law (Russia; 2002), 6, 42–49
Citizenship Law (Soviet; 1990), 17
City Day (Den' goroda), 143, 146–147, 173
Civil Assistance Committee, 52, 55
civil wars, 26–27, 84–85, 130, 155
common senses, 81–82
Communist Party, 77, 84, 131, 135, 141
Compatriots Law (1999), 34–35, 38
Compatriots' Resettlement Program, 41, 49–54, 62, 202n72
"Conflicts are our fortune" (Stepanov), 111–112
Constitution Day (December 12), 212n49
Constitution Day (October 7), *128*, 130
cookbooks: *The Book of Tasty and Healthy Food*, 132, 134, 136, 150, 172, 212n38; *Everything for under the Fir Tree*, 171
Cosmonautics Day (April 12), 130, 131
The Cosmopolites (Abrahamian), 60
Crimea: annexation of, 2, 56–57, 159, 202n89; citizenship in, 31, 55–56, 202n89; media coverage and discourse on, 115, 117–118, 161; population in, 16; Russian homelands and, 6. *See also* Ukraine
critical discourse analysis (CDA), defined, 68
Curtis, Adam, 123

Day of Accord and Conciliation (November 7), 97, 141, 164
Day of Airborne Forces (Den' VDV, August 2), 156, 163
Day of Declaration of State Sovereignty of the Russian Federation. *See* Independence Day (June 12)
Day of Our Lady of Kazan (November 4), 191n41, 207n34, 215n6
Day of Peter and Fevronia (July 8), 167

Day of the Defender of the Fatherland (February 23), *128*, 155, 161–164, 175, 217n38
democracy, as term and identity, 102–103, 140–141, 181–187. *See also* neoliberal economics
Den' Pobedy. *See* Victory Day (May 9)
"Den' Pobedy" (song), 133–134, 160
Den' VDV (August 2), 156, 163
Depardieu, Gerard, 59–60, 61
dislocations and identity, 4–12. *See also* identity
Dondurey, Daniil, 170
Dovlatov, Sergey, 73
dual citizenship, 21, 28–30, 57–58. *See also* citizenship
Dubin, Boris, 148
Dugin, Alexander, 5
Durkheim, Emil, 127, 129, 138, 148
Dzhamshut (fictional character), 58, 203n99

Easter holiday (Pascha), *128*, 148–150, 152, 166, 168–169, 175, 181, 212n49
East Ukraine, 16, 56. *See also* Ukraine
economic conditions, 90–91, 141. *See also* neoliberal economics
economic migration, 36, 58–61. *See also* migration
effective, as concept, 91
Eid El-Adha, *128*, 168–169
Estonia, 17, 21–22, 25–26, 31–32, 43, 193n10, 196n94
ethnic minority groups, 16
Etzioni, Amitai, 129, 148
Eurasianism, 5
Eurasian Union, 5
European Union, 8, 63, 179
Everything for under the Fir Tree (cookbook), 171

Fairclough, Norman, 123
Father Frost (Ded' Moroz), 134, 145
Federal Migration Service (FMS), 50, 109
Ferguson, Niall, 3
fir tree celebration, 134, 171, 212n35
fluid citizenship. *See* citizenship
fluid identity. *See* identity
fluid Russianness, overview, 1–4, 10, 12, 39–40, 177–187. *See also* citizenship; identity
Flynn, Moya, 22, 39
football, 105, 106
forced migrants, 28, 36, 195n72. *See also* migration

INDEX

France, 37, 59–60, 63
free-market economy. *See* neoliberal economics
"friendship of the people," as concept, 104, 208n54
Fyodorov, Valery, 2

Gabowitsch, Mischa, 158
Gagarin, Yuri, 131–132, 177
Gaidar, Yegor, 5, 9
Gamsakhurdia, Zviad, 71–72
Gat, Azar, 7
Gaynetdin, Rawil, 166
Gazprom, 96, 100
Gellner, Ernest, 7
Generation P, 1
George (saint), 156, 213n60
Georgia, 35, 36, 70–72, 159
Georgian ribbon, 158, 159–160, 175, 182, 184, 213n60, 216n23, 216n30. *See also* Victory Day (May 9)
Germany, 37, 52
Giddens, Anthony, 7–8, 9, 121, 129, 138, 143
Ginsburgs, George, 16, 28, 36
Glinka, Mikhail, 92
globalization: identity and, 3–4, 147, 182–183, 214n88; liberal democracy and, 181–187; migration and, 39; modernity and, 7–10; Russian citizenship and, 61–64. *See also* modernity; neoliberal economics
Goluboii Ogonek (television show), 135, 136, 144
Gorbachev, Mikhail, 17–18, 140
Governmental Commission on the Affairs of Compatriots, 29
government discourse, 95–99, 120–123. *See also* media discourse; *names of specific political leaders*
Gozman, Leonid, 107–109, 122, 207n47, 209n90
Grebennikov, Valerii, 44
Gudkov, Gennady, 116–117, 122
Gudkov, Lev, 6–7
Gusman, Yuli, 103–104
Gustov, Vadim, 79–80

Herzen, Alexander, 4–5
high modernity, 7–8. *See also* modernity
Hobsbawm, Eric, 7, 133
holidays: Anniversary of the October Revolution (November 7), 97, 130–131, 136–137, 138, 140–142, 155, 164–165; City Day (Den' goroda), 143, 146–147; Constitution Day (December 12), 212n49; Constitution Day (October 7), *128*, 130; Cosmonautics Day (April 12), 130, 131; Day of Accord and Conciliation (November 7), 97, 141, 164; Day of Airborne Forces (August 2), 156, 163; Day of Our Lady of Kazan (November 4), 191n41, 207n34, 215n6; Day of Peter and Fevronia (July 8), 167; Defender of the Fatherland Day (February 23), *128*, 155, 161–164, 175, 217n38; fir tree, 134, 171, 212n35; Independence Day (June 12), 127, *128*, 136, 138, 140, 142; International Labor Day (May 1), *128*, 130, 136; International Women's Day (March 8), *128*, 130, 132–133, 136, 143–145, 147, 152, 162; Kurban-Bayram (Eid El-Adha), *128*, 168–169; Monstratsiya (May 1), 173–174, 183; Novy God (December 31), 113, *128*, 130, 134–136, 138, 143–145, 147, 152, 170–173; Pascha, 128, 148–150, 152, 166, 168–169, 175, 181, 212n49; Red Army Day (February 23), 130, 132, 155, 162; Rozhdestvo, *128*, 136, 148–150, 152, 166, 168, *169*, 181; Teacher's Day, 130; Unity Day (November 4), 6, 97, 155, 156, 164–165, 175; Valentine's Day, 167, 219n71; Victory Day (May 9), 70–71, *128*, 132–133, 136, 138–142, 147, 156–161, 175, 181; Western Christmas, 144–145, 148, 172. *See also* calendar
homophobia, 166–167, 170
Homo sovieticus, 15, 16, 19, 39
Hungary, 63
Hutchings, Stephen, 176
Hypernormalisation, 123

identification, as term, 10
identity, 67–68, 119–123; discursive techniques and, 95–99, 105–115; fluid Russianness, overview, 1–4, 10, 12, 39–40, 177–187; globalization and, 3–4, 147, 182–183, 214n88; history of dislocations and, 4–12; holidays and, 129, 131, 151–153; as *midl*, 80–81, 82; national calendar and, 136; of non-Soviet youth, 174, 184; as *normal'ny chelovek*, 82; patriotism and, 2, 83–84, 88–89, 174–176; *Poyedinok* episodes on, 103–105, 107–109, 154; Putin on, 1–2, 6–7, 154; social polylogue on, 68–74, 78–81, 121–123; Western embodied notions of, 4–5, 9. *See also* citizenship; holidays; media discourse

Ilina, Irina, 52
Immortal Regiment procession, 158, 159, 160, 175, 182
Independence Day (June 12), 127, *128*, 136, 138, 140, 142
internally displaced persons (IDPs), 36. *See also* migration
International Labor Day (May 1), *128*, 130, 136
International Monetary Fund (IMF), 8
International Women's Day (March 8), *128*, 130, 132–133, 136, 143, 145–146, 147, 152, 162
International Worker's Solidarity Day to Spring and Labor Day. *See* May Day (May 1)
Ironiya sud'by, ili S logkim paroml (film), 135, 144, 172
Islam, 83, *128*, 168

Just Cause. *See* Union of Rightist Forces (formerly Just Cause) political party

Kadyrov, Akhmet, 157
Kadyrov, Ramzan, 162
Kaliningradskaya Oblast, 50, 53
Kamchatski Krai, 50
Karnaukhov, Sergey, 77
Kazakhstan: citizenship in, 26, 52; in Eurasian Union, 5; migration from, 23, 36; work force of, 194n48. *See also* North Kazakhstan
K Bar'eru. *See Poyedinok* (talk show)
KGB, 75, 93, 94, 141
Khodarkovsky, Michael, 178
Khrushchev, Nikita, 194n48
Kirienko, Sergey, 80
Kiselev, Dmitry, 116–117
Kiselev, Yevgeny, 96
Klishas, Andrei, 57
Kobrin, Kirill, 3, 105, 166
Kolsto, Pal, 3
Komsomol, 131
Koselleck, Reinhart, 127, *128*, 210n6
Kozyrev, Andrei, 5, 28
kulich cake rituals, 149, 150
Kurban-Bayram (Eid al-Adha), *128*, 168–169
Kuzio, Taras, 31
Kuzmina, Tatiana, 145
Kuznetsov, Alexandra and Nina, 59
Kyrgyzstan, 5, 23, 26

labor migration, 38, 44–45
Lad (political party), 26
language. *See* Russian language

Laruelle, Marlene, 2, 165
Latvia, 17, 21–22, 25–26, 31–32, 43, 196n94
Law on Citizenship of the USSR (1990), 17
Law on Russian State Policy towards Compatriots Abroad (1999), 34–35, 38
Law on the Rights of Citizens to Freedom of Movement (1993), 22–23
Lebed, Alexander, 27, 195n67
legal gray zone of citizenship: case examples of, 32–33, 46–47; defined, 24–25, 29, 47, 181, 182; fluid Russianness and, 35–36, 39–40; illegal migrant status in, 52, 61; Osipov on, 24, 45, 48; poverty and, 59; registration process and, 30–31, 42; Ukrainian refugees in, 57. *See also* citizenship
Leontyev, Mikhail, 103–104
Lesin, Mikhail, 67
LGBTQ community, 166–167, 170, 175
liberal democracy. *See* democracy, as term and identity; neoliberal economics
Liberal Democratic Party of Russia (LDPR), 84
Lieven, Anatol, 3
lifestyle, 214n88
liquid modernity, 4, 7–8, 210n6. *See also* modernity
liquids, properties of, 8
Lithuania, 52, 193n10
Lithuanian occupation of Moscow. *See* Polish-Lithuanian occupation of Moscow
localism, 173–174. *See also* City Day (Den' goroda)
loss in media discourse, 74–78
Lugovoi, Andrei, 57, 60
Luzhkov, Yuri, 38, 146

Maidan Square protests (2013–14), 115–117
Manezh Square riots (2010), 105–107
Margelov, Vasily, 163
Mason, Paul, 186
May Day (May 1), *128*, 130, 136, 174
MC Doni (Doni Islamov), 58–59, 60, 160
media discourse, 67–68, 86; of 1990s, 68–69; governmental use of, 87, 95–99, 120–123, 209n90; Lesin on, 67; on loss, 74–78; on national holidays, 135; national ideology in, 70–74, 78–81; television, 99–105, 123; on war in Yugoslavia, 84–85. *See also* identity
Medvedev, Dmitry, 105, 158
Medvedeva, Svetlana, 167
Meskhetian Turks, 26, 38

midl, 80–81, 82. *See also* identity
migration: after 1991 transition, 5, 20–21, 24–25; Bauman on, 62; citizenship and, 36–39; economics and, 38, 58–61; forced migrants, 28, 36, 195n72; globalization and, 39, 61–64; movement of people vs. capital, 198n141; during Soviet era, 23–24. *See also* citizenship; refugees
Mikhalkov, Nikita, 82–84, 92
Mikhalkov, Sergey, 6, 92–95
military calendar, 132, 139, 155–165. *See also* calendar
modernity, 7–10, 62–64, 210n6. *See also* globalization
Moldova, 24, 26–27, 35, 36, 70, 197n113
Monstratsiya (May 1), 173–174, 183
music, 58, 113, 209n76, 220n95; national anthem, 6, 92–95
Muslim holidays, *128*, 168
Muslim population, 83, 214n96

Nadezhdin, Boris, 101–103
Nagorno-Karabakh, 26
Nashi movement, 165
Natali (singer), 58, 220n95
nation, as term and concept, 7, 10, 192n65
Nation, Ethnicity and Race on Russian Television (Hutchings and Tolz), 176
national anthem, 6, 92–95
national calendar. *See* calendar; holidays
national holidays. *See* calendar; holidays
national identity. *See* identity
national in-group, as term, 10, 16, 61, 110. *See also* citizenship
National Salvation Front, 77
naturalization, 19–20, 26. *See also* citizenship
Nazarbayev, Nursultan, 26
Nazism, 70, 116, 160, 209n83
Neo-Eurasianism, 5
neoliberal economics, 8, 11, 36–38, 44–45, 141. *See also* democracy, as term and identity; economic migration; globalization; labor migration
newspapers. *See* media discourse
New Year's celebrations, 136, 144. *See also* Novy God (December 31)
1990: Russians Remember a Turning Point (Prokhorova), 77
Nizhny Novgorod, 162
normal'ny chelovek, 82. *See also* identity
North Kazakhstan, 6, 16. *See also* Kazakhstan

Nothing is True and Everything is Possible (Pomerantsev), 91
Novgorodskaya Oblast, 50
Novy God (December 31), 113, *128*, 130, 134–136, 138, 143–145, 147, 152, 170–173
NTV, 87, 96, 99–100, 102, 144, 206n27

October Revolution anniversary. *See* Anniversary of the October Revolution (November 7)
one-time allowance, 50–51, 195n72, 201n56. *See also* citizenship
Orban, Victor, 63
Order of Documentation of Residence Permits (2000), 42
originality and citizenship, 34–35. *See also* citizenship
Orthodox Christianity, 83, 97, 147–151, 165–170, 218n60
Orthodox Christmas. *See* Rozhdestvo (Orthodox Christmas)
Orthodox Easter. *See* Pascha (Orthodox Easter)
Osipov, Alexander: on 2002 citizenship law, 41; on failure of state programs, 54; on legal gray zone, 24, 45, 48; on nationalism, 69
Ossetia, 26
Oushakine, Serguei, 3
Outline of a Theory of Practice (Bourdieu), 129

painting eggs ritual, 149, 150
Pascha (Orthodox Easter), *128*, 148–150, 152, 166, 168–169, 175, 181, 212n49. *See also* Velikiy Post (Lent)
"Patriotic Song" (anthem by Glinka), 92
patriotism, 2, 83–84, 88–89, 174–176. *See also* identity
Pelevin, Victor, 1, 177
perelitsovka, 93–94, 96, 98, 206n15
perfidy. *See verolomsvo*
permanent vs. temporary registration, 20, 21, 22–23, 194n36. *See also* citizenship
personal-local calendar, 143–147, 170. *See also* calendar
Peskov, Dmitri, 60
Peter the Great, 4, 98
Polish-Lithuanian occupation of Moscow, 97, 155, 191n41, 207n34, 215n6. *See also* Unity Day (November 4)
political calendar, 137–143. *See also* calendar

polylogue on national identity, 68–74, 78–81, 121–122. *See also* identity
Pomerantsev, Peter, 91, 100, 114
population statistics, 198n120; of Crimea, 56, 202n89; of ethnic minority groups, 16; of migration, 36; of Muslims in Russia, 214n96; of resettled compatriots, 49, 51; in Ukraine, 26
Poyedinok (talk show): broadcast history of, 210n96; episode on Crimea, 115, 117–118; episode on Maidan Square protests, 115–117; episode on Manezh riots, 105–107; episode on Russian and Western values, 118–119; episodes on identity, 103–105, 107–109; government discourse of, 121–122; Gozman on, 209n90
Poyushchiye Vmeste (band), 220n95
Pozharsky, Dmitry Mikhailovich, 215n6
Prokhanov, Alexander, 5, 105–107, 118–119
Prokhorova, Irina, 77
propiska, 19, 22–23, 24–25, 30–31. *See also* citizenship
Pugacheva, Alla Borisovna, 113, 209n76
Putin, Vladimir: citizenship laws and program by, 41–49; on collapse of Soviet Union, 104, 208n55; on Crimea, 118, 209n87; KGB service by, 93, 94; power and discursive techniques by, 88–92, 120, 121, 179–181; as prime minister, 87; on Russian identity, 1–2, 6–7, 154, 178–179; Russian music about, 220n95; "Russia: The National Question," 110. *See also* calendar

Rachman, Gideon, 179
Radchenko, Natalya, 145
railway, 23
Ranger, Terence, 133
Ravshan (fictional character), 58, 203n99
recognition. *See* citizenship
Red Army Day (February 23), 130, 132, 155, 162
refugees, 28, 195n72. *See also* migration
registration. *See* citizenship
religion, 83, 214n96, 218n60, 218n65
religious calendar, 147–151, 165–170. *See also* calendar
religious holidays. *See* holidays
Republic of Sakha-Yakutia, 145
residency permits, 42, 43
RIA Novosti, 158
Ribbentrop-Molotov Pact, 192n6
ribbons. *See* Georgian ribbon
riots, 105–107

Rogozin, Dmitry, 27, 28–29
Romanovsky, Roman, 53, 202n72
Rossiyane, 10, 108, 109, 118. *See also* identity
Rozhdestvo (Orthodox Christmas), *128*, 136, 148–150, 152, 166, 168, *169*, 181
Rozovsky, Mark, 105–107
Runet, 122
"Russia is an Independent Subject of History" (Surkov), 98
Russian Constitution Day. *See under* Constitution Day
Russian identity. *See* identity
Russian Independence Day. *See* Independence Day (June 12)
Russian language, 50, 55–56
Russian national calendar, 154–155, 174–176. *See also* calendar
Russianness. *See* fluid Russianness, overview
Russian Soviet Federative Socialist Republic (RSFSR): citizenship laws of, 16, 18–23; as territory, 2, 5–6; Yeltsin on sovereignty of, 127
Russian Union of Foreign Workers in Construction, 62
"Russia: The National Question" (Putin), 110
Russkaya Obshchina, 26
Russkikh, Fedor, 46–47
Russkiy (ethnic Russians), 10, 73, 101, 104–108, 110, 112, 118. *See also* identity
Russkiy March (November 4), 165
Russkiy narod, 76

Samoilenko, Vladimir, 166–167
Sarkozy, Nicolas, 63
Satarov, Gregoriy, 78
Schleifman, Nurit, 137–138, 146
self-identity. *See* identity
Sevastopol, 2, 31, 56. *See also* Crimea
Shachar, Ayelat, 45, 198n141
shadow economy, 37–38
Sharafutdinova, Gulnaz, 3
Shebarshin, Leonid, 75–76
Shevel, Oxana, 16, 41, 52
Shevtsova, Lillia, 96, 178
Slavophilism, 5
Smirnov, A. V., 32–33
Smith, Anthony, 7
Snyder, Timothy, 175
Soares de Morais, Welliton, 106, 208n62
Solovyov, Vladimir, 52, 87–88, 102, 111, 118, 119, 210n96. *See also Poyedinok* (talk show)

INDEX 247

South Ossetia, 26, 35, 70, 71, 72, 197n113. *See also* Georgia
sovereignty, 98–99
Soviet Army, 71, 75, 132, 159–160
Soviet calendar, 129, 130–136. *See also* calendar
Soviet identity. *See* identity
Soysal, Yasmin, 37
Soyuz pravykh sil. *See* Union of Rightist Forces (formerly Just Cause) political party
space race, 131
sports, 106, 208n62
Stalin, Joseph, 133, 157, 162
state holidays. *See* calendar; holidays
State Program for Assistance of Voluntary Resettlement to the Russian Federation of Compatriots Residing Abroad. *See* Compatriots' Resettlement Program
Steele, Jonathan, 26
Stepanov, Eugenie, 111–112
Strana OZ (film), 172
structuration theory, 129, 138, 143
Surkov, Vladislav, 97–99, 103, 114, 123, 185
Suslov, Mihail, 131
Sviridov, Egor, 105

Tajikistan, 26, 36, 59, 70, 166
talk shows. *See* television
Tatars, 6, 83
Tatarstan, 145, 146, 166–167
taxation, 59–60
Teacher's Day, 130
television, 99–105, 123. *See also* media discourse; *Poyedinok* (talk show)
temniki, 100
temporary residency permit, 42, 43
temporary *vs.* permanent registration, *20*, 21, 194n36. *See also* citizenship
This Evening with Vladimir Solovyov (television show), 118, 119
Tikhonov, Georgy, 34
Timati (Timur Yanusov), 58
Timchenko, Gennady, 60
Time of Troubles (1598–1613), 98, 175, 191n41, 207n34, 215n6
Tishkov, Valery, 19, 44, 48, 186
Tocqueville, Alexis de, 210n6
Tolz, Vera, 2, 176
Transdniestria, 26–27, 35, 70, 197n113
Trotsky, Leon, 132
Trump, Donald, 123, 179, 186–187
Turkmenistan, 28, 195n69

Udmurtia, 46
Ukraine: 1991 referendum on independence of, 194n36; citizenship in, 26, 29, 31; migration from, 36, 56; Nazism and, 116, 209n83. *See also* Crimea; East Ukraine
Umland, Andreas, 3
"Unbreakable Union" (anthem by Mikhalkov), 92
uniformity, 135–136
Union of Rightist Forces (formerly Just Cause) political party, 101–103, 208n51, 208n67
United Kingdom, 37, 63, 123, 179
United States, 37, 123, 179
Unity Day (November 4), 6, 97, 155, 156, 164–165, 175
Universal Declaration of Human Rights, 33
Uvarov, Sergey, 95
Uzbekistan, 26, 29; migration from, 36

Valentine's Day, 167, 219n71
Varlamov, Ilya, 142, 146
Velikiy Post (Lent), 148, 150, 169. *See also* Pascha (Orthodox Easter)
verolomsvo, 96, 101–103, 115, 117, 121, 184
Victory Day (May 9), 70–71, *128*, 132–133, 136, 138–142, 147, 156–161, 175, 181. *See also* Georgian ribbon
violent conflicts: Manezh Square (2010), 105–107; migration and, 36; in post-Soviet era, 26–27, 70; in Yugoslavia, 84–85
Virgin Lands Campaign (1954), 23, 53, 194n48
Von Haggen, Mark, 2
Vykhovanets, Olga, 50, 52

Weimar Russia scenario, 3
Western holiday, *128*, 144–145, 148, 172
Western principles: discursive techniques used in, 122–123; embodied notions of identity, 4–5, 9; migration and, 37; on modernity and globalization, 18; nationalism and, 69; *Poyedinok* episode on, 118–119. *See also* neoliberal economics
women. *See* International Women's Day (March 8)

Yarmarka Masterov, 171
Yarosh, Pyotr, 56, 202n89
Yeltsin, Boris: calls for resignation of, 141; on citizenship, 17, 18, 21; on national anthem, 6; national holidays and, 127, 139; neoliberal reforms by, 1, 5, 75, 137; on Putin as prime minister, 87
youth movements, 160, 165

Yudasgkin, Valentin, 158
Yugoslavia, 84–85, 155
Yungvardiya movement, 160
Yurchak, Alexei, 82, 131, 133

Zemon-Davis, Natalie, 164
zero option, as term, 18, *20*, 25, 193n18.
    See also citizenship

Zevelva, Olga, 52
Zhirinovsky, Vladimir, 6, 38, 61–62, 77, 101, 107–109
Zhukov, Marshal, 139–140
Zhuravsky, Alexander, 50, 52
Zlobin, Nikolai, 118, 119
Zuev, Denis, 165
Zyuganov, Gennady, 6, 77, 141

www.ingramcontent.com/pod-product-compliance
Lightning Source LLC
Chambersburg PA
CBHW030536230426
43665CB00010B/909